A COMMUNION OF THE SPIRITS

A COMMUNION OF THE SPIRITS

African-American Quilters, Preservers, and Their Stories

ROLAND L. FREEMAN

RUTLEDGE HILL PRESS

Nashville, Tennessee

Published by Rutledge Hill Press
211 Seventh Avenue North, Nashville, Tennessee 37219

Distributed in Canada by H.B. Fenn & Company, Ltd., 34 Nixon Road, Bolton, Ontario L7E 1W2. Distributed in Australia by Millennium Books, 33 Maddox Street, Alexandria NSW 2015. Distributed in New Zealand by Tandem Press, 2 Rugby Road, Birkenhead, Auckland 10. Distributed in the United Kingdom by Verulam Publishing, Ltd., 152a Park Street Lane, Park Street, St. Albans, Hertfordshire AL2 2AU.

Cover and book design by Gore Studios
Photography by Roland L. Freeman
Typography by E.T. Lowe Publishing Co.

Library of Congress Cataloging-in-Publication Data
Freeman, Roland L., 1936–
    A communion of the spirits : African-American quilters, preservers, and their stories / Roland L. Freeman.
        p.   cm.
    Includes bibliographical references and index.
    ISBN 1-55853-425-3 (hardcover)
    1. Quilting—United States—History.   2. Afro-American quiltmakers.   3. Afro-American quiltmakers—Interviews.
4. Afro-American quilts.   I. Title.
TT835.F744   1996
746.46'08996073—dc20   96-26202
                                                      CIP
Printed in the United States of America

1 2 3 4 5 6 7 8 9 — 01 00 99 98 97 96

CONTENTS

**IT IS WITH PRIDE AND HUMILITY
THAT I DEDICATE THIS BOOK TO**

*my mother, Dorothy Vaughan Freeman, who first tucked me in
under a quilt and told me that its warmth and spirits would protect me;*

———————

*my great-grandmother Mae Arbia Rounds Janey and my grandmother Goldie Janey Addison,
who preserved and passed on our family's healing quilt and its power;*

———————

*my country grandmother, Elizabeth Briscoe Miles,
who taught me to remember and honor our ancestors; and*

———————

*my country cousin, Jeannetta Chase, who helped me make sense of it all
through our culture and history.*

FOREWORD

For the long-awaited book by Roland L. Freeman, *A Communion of the Spirits: African American Quilters, Preservers, and Their Stories*, great expectations were held. It was believed because of Freeman's coupled urban and rural childhood background, his attainment of premier status as an international photojournalist, his extensive collaborative documentation of African-American folklife, his pioneer role as a major collector of African-American quilts, no one other than he could have written this book. Would not the sequence of events that led to Freeman's absorbing interest in African-American quilts affect profoundly both the methodologies employed and the substance of his text? These questions are answered, and the great expectations held are met in Roland Freeman's landmark volume.

In the early 1970s, while engaged on a Mississippi Heartland folklife project for the Smithsonian Institution, Freeman contacted numerous African-American women in the region. It was only after he had established friendly relationships with these southern black women that he become fascinated with the quilts that many of the women made. Thus his quilt collecting course was set, one that he has maintained throughout subsequent years. Priority was given first to a study of the quiltmakers, their heritage, their beliefs, their experiences, their associations, their environments. Later, upon consideration of the quilts, he always placed the covers in the context of their creators' lives.

Cuesta Benberry, quilt historian and author.
ST. LOUIS, MISSOURI, JANUARY 1993 (2-66466/11, 2¼ CN)

As Freeman continued to build his African-American quilt collection, he also entered into numerous quilt-related, collaborative projects with folklorists, anthropologists, historians, artists, other academics, as well as with lay people involved in quilting. His associations with these collaborators made him privy to their different ideological interpretations, analytic theories, and perspectives relative to African-American quilters and quiltmaking. Some of the insights he gained from these practitioners from multiple disciplines were frequently incorporated into his studies. Yet subsequently, when Freeman conducted his own African-American quilt documentation program, his work was not merely a pastiche of his earlier collaborators' concepts. Instead he developed a new, distinctive, and independent documentation project, unlike any other heretofore produced. Who other than Freeman, a cultural documentarian of the first order, has treated his African-American quilter subjects with such humanness or valued the individual quilter equally with the quiltwork produced or offered proof of the enormous creativity and diversity within the black quilt community on such a large scale?

All of Freeman's dedication and stamina was needed when he embarked on the months-and-months long, exhausting journey that resulted in the publication of this book. He traveled thousands of miles as he crisscrossed the United States from the East coast to the West coast, to the North, to the South, and all through the Midwest to visit, to interview, and to photograph African-American quilters and their quiltworks. His objective was to present a never-before-attempted comprehensive picture of the breadth and scope of the contemporary African-American quiltmaking community.

A Communion of the Spirits: African-American Quilters, Preservers, and Their Stories represents the successful culmination of Roland Freeman's lengthy career. His monograph, singularly absent of the conjecture and cant occasionally found in other reports of African-American quiltworks, invites the reader to visit with some of today's most captivating quiltmakers. The stories the quilters tell are as diverse as are they— sometimes provocative, other times amusing, frequently affecting, and always compelling. Through the lens in the hands of a masterful photographer, the readers will see an array of images of African-American quilters, nationwide, and the exceptional works they have fabricated. Implicit in this unique compendium of African-American quilts is a firm promise to the readers of countless pleasurable visits with the quilters.

Cuesta Benberry

PREFACE

Roland L. Freeman's *A Communion of the Spirits: African American Quilters, Preservers, and Their Stories* synthesizes more than twenty years of ongoing documentation. Several important characteristics together differentiate it from other related work:

> First, the scope of Freeman's work is both national and inclusive. It traces quiltmaking by African Americans from its southern roots, over time and space as practitioners and preservers have migrated north and west throughout America. All the material is drawn from Freeman's own fieldwork and includes the full variety of quilts made by African Americans, whether traditional or improvisational, whether produced primarily to be slept under or as textile art.

> Second, the project focuses on people—on those who make or preserve the quilts. It provides them a first opportunity to tell their own stories, documented through interviews and photographs, at home and in their communities, surrounded by quilts that are intertwined with their lives.

> Third, and most important, the project relates quiltmaking to the social contexts of the quilters and preservers, as interpreted by them. They have been directly involved in the project research, sharing their and their families' histories, their art and its evolution, and their perspectives on the roles quilts and quiltmakers have played in the broader continuity of African-American traditions and struggles.

A Communion of the Spirits builds on roots in Freeman's childhood experiences with quilts, quiltmaking, and related folk culture. Conscious project development began in the mid-1970s when, as director of the Mississippi Folklife Project, he began documenting traditional crafts and practitioners for the Smithsonian Institution's Center for Folklife Programs and Cultural Studies. In 1979, he published *Something to Keep You Warm* (now out of print), the first book about quilts made by African Americans, and also curated the related national touring exhibit, the first of its kind. Over the years, as he continued his fieldwork, documentation, and research, he has involved, and benefited from the assistance of many scholars, folklorists, community tradition bearers, and other recognized contributors to our knowledge of quilts made by African Americans.

As Freeman's understanding of the world of African-American quiltmaking grew, the project evolved and expanded. As the vitality and power of its traditional roles became clearer, the quilt, often seen as "just something to keep you warm," became much "more than just something to keep you warm"; and, as Freeman viewed the impact of the quilts as they passed from generation to generation, *A Communion of the Spirits: African-American Quilters, Preservers, and Their Stories* took shape.

Roland L. Freeman with nine of the quilts in his collection.
, D.C., 1994 (2¼ CT)

Fieldwork both reflected and shaped this evolution:

- Quilters who had been documented in the South early in the project moved to other parts of the country, and, when contacted in their new homes, often provided access to additional quilters and networks;
- Younger generations of quiltmaking families were sought out and documented, and when they had preserved family quilts, Freeman added historical photographs of the deceased quiltmakers to his documentation;
- Often, during interviews, quilters would identify others for Freeman to document, sometimes located nearby, and other times across the country;
- Over time, Freeman realized that these individual stories were each part of an important collective, and he bagan systematically to link them, ultimately covering the country region by region, revisiting areas to fill in gaps and follow new leads.

The book covers fieldwork through early 1996, including individual quilters in thirty-eight states and Washington, D.C.; in seventeen of these locations (noted on the following list with asterisks) he identified formal quilting clubs to which they belonged. There is documentation from Alabama*, Arizona*, Arkansas*, California*, Colorado*, Connecticut, Florida, Georgia*, Illinois*, Indiana*, Kansas, Kentucky, Louisiana*, Maryland*, Massachusetts, Michigan*, Mississippi*, Missouri, Nebraska, Nevada, New Hampshire, New Jersey, New Mexico, New York*, North Carolina, Ohio, Oklahoma, Oregon, Pennsylvania*, South Carolina, South Dakota, Tennessee, Texas*, Utah, Vermont, Virginia*, Washington, West Virginia, and Washington, D.C.*

In addition to its landmark scope, the photodocumentation has yielded some truly special results, including documentation of some families that spans more than twenty years and four or more generations of quilters. It includes others that, though dispersed geographically, have reaffirmed their cultural and spiritual connections through the sharing of family quilts and the histories they represent. It also includes Freeman's collection and presentation to the State Historical and Smith Robertson Museums in Jackson of thirty Mississippi quilts to assure their preservation and accessibility.

The book is organized chronologically, though in later chapters containing documentation from repeated visits to a single state over a limited time period, the chronology is presented by state to strengthen continuity. The book's more than 300 photographs are, with few exceptions, sequenced with the text, and where a photograph is separated from its related text, cross-references are provided. Following each photograph's caption is a coded identification of the negative from which it was reproduced, as in the following examples:

(5-82316/4)   Black/white negative series number with
                         frame number of image

(35 MM CT)	35 mm. color transparency (no frame number)
(FRAME 4, 2¼ CT)	2¼" x 2 ¼" color transparency with frame number of image
(9-66200/7, 2¼CN)	2¼" x 2 ¼" color negative with negative series number and frame number of image
(FRAME 5, 35 MM CN)	35 mm. color negative with frame number of image
(FA-6)	Family archives photograph, Freeman's or indicated source

Those people documented in the book have provided Freeman with the bulk of what you'll read about themselves, the quilts, and their histories. In general, this has been accomplished through taped field interviews, supplemented with information from post-interview questionnaires; some are his best recollections if there was no taped source.

In addition to names, places, and organizations encountered in the text, the index contains entries for the major topics addressed. It incorporates sub-listings by state of the quilters and preservers, any local quilting organizations, and the specific in-state locales where documentation was done.

The project's results are being made available through this book and through a similarly titled national touring exhibition. The exhibit, produced by The Group for Cultural Documentation (TGCD) of Washington, D.C., contains a selection of the photographs and surveyed quilts, interpretive panels, and other artwork related to the quilters (see pp. 382–86 for some examples). Educational materials, outreach for schoolchildren, quilt workshops, and public forums will accompany the exhibition. It will open in January, 1997, at the Mississippi Museum of Art in Jackson, with a planned tour of three or more years to sites throughout the country where African-American quiltmakers have made major contributions to their tradition.

TGCD is proud of its contribution to bringing *A Communion of the Spirits: African-American Quilters, Preservers, and Their Stories* to fruition and is confident that you will share our excitement and pleasure as you embark on Freeman's journey.

David B. Levine
Board of Directors
The Group for Cultural Documentation

ACKNOWLEDGMENTS

In the mid-1970s, when Worth Long and I started to document traditional African-American folklife practices, little did I realize that my fascination with quilts and how they reflect their creators' lives would become an ongoing quest, so remarkably rewarding and powerful that twenty years would pass before I would pause long enough to share it! Now that I have, I want to acknowledge the many people whose contributions have been vital to the richness and success of these years. I beg forgiveness of any others whom I may have inadvertently omitted.

First of all, I all too rarely express how much my wife Marcia has contributed to whatever success I've had throughout my career. She has put up with my peculiar madness and work habits, remaining a true partner through thick and thin. She has been supportive throughout my long absences for the fieldwork and, despite the demands of her own career, has always found the time and strength necessary to be there for me when I needed her.

The work would have been impossible without the support of many colleagues over the years. Foremost among these is Worth Long, initially my mentor and for more than two decades a most trusted and faithful companion, who has traveled these roads with me. Carolyn Mazloomi, Coordinator of the Women of Color Quilters' Network, provided invaluable help in identifying quilters nationally and in assuring gracious receptions to my intrusions on many people's lives. She has said to me, "Roland, you just call us and have us doing everything for you. I want you to know you owe us big time and I mean really big time"—and she is right. Then there are those at the Smithsonian's Center for Folklife Programs and Cultural Studies, specifically the late Ralph Rinzler, Peter Seitel, Richard Kurin, Phyllis May Machunda, and Diane Parker. In addition, folklorists Charles Camp, Gerald Davis, Cassandra Gunkel, Glenn Hinson, Catherine Jacobs, and Jerrilyn McGregory provided important support in both research and fieldwork.

Valuable assistance, guidance, and hospitality were provided to me virtually wherever I went. In addition to those mentioned earlier, the following made the fieldwork possible: in Alabama, Kelly Reynolds, Sandral Hullett, Mabel Means, Estelle Witherspoon, and Dorothy Davies; in Arizona, Vera Peeler and Odiemae Elliott; in Arkansas, Janice Rosenberg; in California, Gerald Weintraub; in Connecticut, EdJohnetta Miller; in Georgia, Darlyne Dandridge, Tamara Jeffries, Stephanie Hughley, Beverly Guy-Sheftall, Ja Jahannes, Tracy Alexander, Fred C. Fussell, and Florene Dawkins; in Illinois, Reginald and Edna Patterson-Petty; in Indiana, William Wiggins and Steve and Pam Connelly; in Kentucky, Victoria Faoro; in Louisiana, Joyce Jackson, Valerie Jackson-Jones, and Tom Dent; in Maryland, Barbara Pietila; in Michigan, Darryl and Malaika Mitchell, Marguerite Berry-Jackson, and Joseph and Lucille

Rolston; in Mississippi, Alfredteen Harrison, Dave and Patty Crosby, Mary Lohrenz, Alice Lewis, John Horhn, Hank Ingebretsen, Barbara Phillips, Bill Ferris, and Thelma Williams; in Missouri, Cuesta Benberry and Kyra Hicks; in Nevada, Nancy and Owen Justice; in New Mexico, Maria Varela; in New York, Philip Freeman and Ruth Howard; in Ohio, Catherine Willis and Sandy Mason; in South Carolina, Emory Campbell, Vanessa Greene, and Laurel Horton; in Tennessee, Judy Peiser, Sonia Walker, Eddie and Yvonne Jones, and Bets Ramsey; in Texas, Anita Knox and Della Collins; in Vermont, Eleanor Ott and Jane C. Beck; in Virginia, Vanessa Thaxton; in Washington, D.C., Viola Canady and Sandy Hassan; and, in West Virginia, Delton Allen.

Each of the following read early manuscript drafts and provided important, critical, and fruitful feedback: Shlomo Bachrach, Allison Blakely, Dave Crosby, Gerald Davis, Beverly Guy-Sheftall, Glenn Hinson, Eleanor Ott, Bets Ramsey, Bernice Johnson Reagon, Peter Seitel, Betty Carol Sellen, and Sam Smith. Cuesta Benberry, who has encouraged me over the years, generously agreed to provide the foreword.

Over the years, I received extensive financial support for the project. For this, I am grateful to my family and friends, the National Endowment for the Arts, the National Endowment for the Humanities, the Maryland State Arts Council, the Mississippi Arts Commission, the Smithsonian Institution's Center for Folklife Programs and Cultural Studies, the Women's Center at Spelman College, and the many quilt clubs and churches that took up collections.

Since its establishment in 1991, The Group for Cultural Documentation has played a central role in the effort, both through institutional support and guidance and, more importantly, through the many hours of pro bono personal and professional contributions provided by board members Judith H. Katz and David B. Levine. David has been involved from the start, providing a supportive and critical strategic voice at every step of the way and spending countless hours helping me shape the final manuscript and incorporating the suggestions of the other readers.

Finally, I am humbled by the graciousness of all the families and friends who put me up—and put up with me—and fed me along the way; to all of those who gave me encouragement to carry on when I doubted I could; to those whose lives are the story; and to all the ancestral spirits who held my hand while I ran this race.

INTRODUCTION

Over the past twenty years, there has been an explosion of interest in traditional and contemporary quilting, and for more than a decade that interest has included quilting by African Americans. Their quilts have received extensive attention in the academic, craft, art, and museum worlds. Art historians are intrigued by the possible continuities between quilts made by African Americans and West African textiles; designers are impressed by the dynamic traditional and contemporary designs in these quilts; artists are exploring new directions in textile art by learning and adapting quilt patterns and techniques; growing numbers of quilt collectors aggressively assure an active market; and, in general, quilting now receives recognition as a creative medium.

These changes in our appreciation of quilting have been reflected in the books already published. So why another one? The simplest answer is that I believe the primary focus of both the text and photographs of this book differs enough from those already available to provide an important and complementary contribution. One aspect of this difference is its focus on the world of African-American quilting; that is, the lives of the quilters provide the context within which their artistry is presented. A second difference is personal, namely, how my life has intertwined with this world for almost sixty years—as an African-American male; as a child who was deeply influenced by the cultural traditions and magical powers of quilts; and, for more than three decades, as a photographer and folklorist documenting the continuity of African-American expressive culture from its African roots, across generations, and throughout the diaspora.

These elements provide the source of the "communion of the spirits" so central to the book. That "communion" is multifaceted. It refers to the power of quilts to create a virtual web of connections—individual, generational, professional, physical, spiritual, cultural, and historical. It refers to my deeply personal experience of those connections and their profound influence on my life. It also refers to my entry, as a professional, into the world of African-American quilting, and the remarkable access to their lives that quilters and preservers provided me, sharing their graciousness and their vulnerability. And, it refers to the linkages—at times acknowledged, more often unconscious—among these "cultural tradition-bearers" across time and space.

Over the years, while I've shared the excitement of the remarkable growth in attention to quilts and the overdue recognition of its wonderful artists, I've also felt somewhat uneasy about the insufficient attention to who these quilters were, what quilting meant in their lives, and what it represented more generally for cultural understanding and continuity. This book addresses these gaps, while significantly expanding the available documentation of African-American quilters and preservers. My challenge was to recount personal journeys objectively, making the communions understandable, crystallizing the literal and implied meanings of what I learned, and putting it all in the broader contexts of quilting and cultural continuity.

The more I explored the world of quilting by African Americans, the more I appreciated its power and intimacy and the heavier weighed my responsibility to get the stories right. At times I felt virtually terrorized by what I came to see as a sacred trust extended to me by many of those you'll meet in the book. At the same time, the rewards of sharing and understanding their experiences and triumphs were extraordinary.

The Power of Quilts

As an adult, although I was aware of the power of my childhood experiences, I had no idea that so much of my life's work would ultimately become focused on the world of quilting by African Americans. It was relatively early in my career that I defined the continuity of black expressive culture across place and time as the broad framework for my ongoing work, but only significantly later that I realized how important a role quilting was to play in my personal and professional journeys.

Studying the world of African-American quilting provided me a unique opportunity to bring together important currents running through my life. First, quilting has an almost universal presence among African Americans. As there is virtually no community without quilters and family quilts—even when no other traditional crafts can be found— and as my assignments usually related to cultural continuity and evolution, the sheer quantity of my documentation grew over the years. There was a richness and complexity to the world of quilting that further justified this attention, evidenced through quilting's remarkable range of cultural roles, its incredible variety of techniques and styles, and the ways in which its study defies simple conclusions and generalizations.

When I was a child, quilts were special, even magical to me. They could heal and they could curse; they could capture history and affect the future; they could transform pain to celebration. As an adult, I began to recognize that I had a special understanding of and connection to quilts, and that this was a providential gift that provided me an access I dared not ignore. Added to this was an irresistible fascination I have always felt with being among groups of African-American women. I sensed that there were powerful differences in substance, energy, and style from predominantly male or mixed-gender groups, and I wanted to understand those differences and share in the power that women manifested.

The evolution of this study also helped free me from some of the pressures that might have altered my understanding of quilting by African Americans. First, as a folklife documenter, my point of departure was my own personal and cultural exposure. I was able to draw on rich and substantive experiences with both urban and rural traditions. The general goal of my early assignments was to present, fully and accurately, the images I found in the field, and my previous life experience predisposed me to seek out aggressively the many crafts and craftspeople that I knew were out there. As a result, I often succeeded in finding a more extensive range of traditional expressive culture than the assignments had anticipated, and sometimes my work yielded a range of information and images that assisted other researchers in broadening the inclusiveness of their own efforts.

When I began concentrating on the world of quilting by African Americans, I maintained this holistic approach, and I was usually able to present my images with enough of a context to communicate at least some of the broader cultural frame. Consistent with the nature of my early assignments, I saw neither the quilts I was photographing nor the quilters to whom I was talking as just quilts or quilters. I was looking at them as elements within an overall framework of expressive culture throughout the diaspora, and quilting was just one piece of a larger fabric.

More often than not, I was able to document a creative range far broader than that suggested by what was usually accessible through educational and cultural institutions. The patterns and techniques used in the quilts that were shared with me—whether they were newly made or long preserved—defied much of the categorization I saw being used by others. What I learned from the stories of the quilts' origins and uses was also different, and it became clear to me that to understand these quilts, one had to understand the vital roles they played in the community, as one among many art forms and skills that provided vibrant cultural expressions.

Although I quickly realized—and was somewhat concerned—that what I was finding at times ran counter to the hypotheses and emphases of the emerging scholarly research, I kept at it, steering as clear as I could of the ongoing controversies about what "African-American quilting" was and wasn't. I came to believe that many of the misdirections in our understanding of quilting by African Americans arose from attempts to impose pre-existing ideas about cultural transmission and "Africanness" on a limited and nonrepresentative body of work that excluded much that was accessible and became understandable if approached through the broader cultural context of the quilters and preservers.

The book combines my childhood recollections of quilts and quilting with documentation of fieldwork that has extended across twenty-five years. It relies heavily on the words of the quilters and preservers, captured by me through extensive field interviews and follow-up. At first I focused on African-American quilters in Mississippi. I then expanded the work, first to include other southern states and eventually to a national scope, exploring the world of quilting within a broad range of African-American communities. All in all, I estimate that I've driven more than 20,000 miles, crisscrossing the country several times.

The range of quilts I've been able to document runs the gamut— traditional and improvisational, strip and string, representational and abstract, throw-together and copied—some excellently crafted, some poorly made. I've included people who create quilts as works of art, with no intention for them to be slept under, as well as those who adapt quilting techniques to other textile art. I've included individuals whose understanding of quilting came other than from childhood exposure: African-American quilters who learned from white practitioners or formal study or books and magazines or as members of quilting clubs. Perhaps you'll be surprised at the degree and variety of involvement of African-American men in the world of quilting, and how that relates to what we often think of as a woman's world.

In the pages of this book, you'll discover the incredible variety and richness of the roles that quilting plays in African-American life. Many quilts are made as "just something to keep you warm," and many are intended for far more. Some are used directly as instruments of cultural transmission: they, along with the stories of their origins and histories, are part of the family legacy, at times explicitly recording significant events from individual, familial, or cultural life—sometimes memorializing great pain, and other times, great triumphs. Other quilts are created with specific powers: to heal, protect, woo, resolve, or acquire. Still others are made as gifts, usually across generations, and honor significant rites of passage or are a key part of a dowry. For some, quilts are made to be sold for economic survival, while for a few, they become the road to real economic empowerment.

Perhaps more importantly, you'll join me in bearing witness to the life stories of these quilters, many of whom represent the ever smaller numbers of a generation that links the years following the end of slavery with our more recent past. I hope you'll share my pleasure in helping provide these people their appropriate places in history. For the most part, they're the everyday cultural strength we draw on—their voices must be heard and their stories told.

You'll also be able to struggle with what it means that so many African Americans, across so large an area, are involved with quilting. What is it about quilting that is so important to our culture? It is certainly more than just the aesthetics. There's a reason why so many of us quilt—no matter how well we may do it—or preserve and treasure the quilts we've obtained from others. There's something about the experience of quilting that draws us to it—it keeps us warm, it soothes our pain and relieves our burdens, it commemorates important occasions, it preserves family history, it demonstrates skill, it encourages social interaction, and it supports intimate communication. It's all these things and more.

I hope that my approach to quilting as a window to far broader aspects of cultural, social, and personal lives and histories, contributes to the continuing growth of interest and that the book will draw a readership that may have not yet recognized the richness that is there. I also believe the book will prove valuable to those with particular interests in quilting, textile art, or photography, as well as to those with related interests in such fields as African-American studies, women's studies, folklore, history, and sociology.

Thank you for joining me on this exciting journey. Together, let us celebrate the remarkable achievements of those we'll visit, and the strangeness of much that we'll learn. It has been a profound experience for me, and I am eager to share it with you.

A COMMUNION OF THE SPIRITS

Something to Keep You Warm, 1976, 95" × 81"
Strip quilt, designed and fabric selected by Roland L. Freeman.
Hand-quilted by Annie Dennis of Wilkinson County, Mississippi.

PART ONE

SOMETHING TO KEEP YOU WARM

Origins,
the Southern Survey,
and Its Initial Expansions
(1940–92)

CHAPTER 1
Growing Up with Quilts (1940–73)

BALTIMORE, MARYLAND, 1940–48

Clear memories of quilts in my life start in 1940 when I was three years old. One of the earliest is of a cold and snowy Thanksgiving eve in the living room of our large second-floor apartment on the corner of McMechen and Pennsylvania Avenues in Baltimore. Centered against one wall was a Victrola on which my father played the blues and my mother played gospel music. Furniture was arranged in a semicircle around the stove. Evenings at home were storytelling time,

My mother, Dorothy Vaughan Freeman (1918–78) in her twenties. BALTIMORE, MARYLAND, EARLY 1940s (FA-1)

and there was often a lot of talk about ghosts, spirits, and "haints."

On this particular evening, my mother was seated in a rocking chair nursing my baby brother Albert. Across from her sat my father in his favorite big spruce-green chair next to a small table with a flickering oil lamp. Between them was what seemed then a huge, dark brown sofa, on which my older sister, Delores, and I were snuggled under a quilt. We were very excited about the snowfall and our visit to our grandmother Goldie's for Thanksgiving.

My father, Albert, had just finished reading us the story of Thanksgiving, and I kept thinking about the killing of the turkeys. Earlier that day my father's sister, Aunt Margie, had taken us to nearby Lafayette Market, which covered four city blocks. It was a forerunner of today's supermarket, except that you could buy poultry freshly killed. We had seen lots of live turkeys in crates. Also, the market's holiday decorations included pictures of Pilgrims with hatchets, chasing turkeys. I had been frightened by the noise the turkeys made, and my sister had teasingly said that their heads would be chopped off and the blood would get all over me.

I think it was the first time I realized that someone had to kill the meat I ate. As I often had heard my father and Aunt Margie speak of the presence of their mother Lena's spirit (she had died the year before I was born), I thought the slaughtered turkeys would also have spirits and they would come and get me if I ate the turkey. Although Delores, who was two years my senior, reassured me that I could eat as much turkey as I wanted without turkey spirits bothering me, her words were of little comfort. As a bedtime story, my mother would often read James Whitcomb

Riley's poem "Little Orphan Annie," which includes the lines:

An' the Gobble-uns 'at gits you
Ef You
Don't
Watch
Out!

To my ears, that always sounded like the "gobblers" were going to get you, and I understood gobblers to be turkeys.

Grandma Lena had made all the quilts we had in our house at that time. My father's parents, Phillip (1872–1919) and Lena (1886–1935) Freeman, had migrated to Baltimore from the Tidewater area of Virginia in the early 1900s, my grandfather from Carroll and Hanover Counties, and my grandmother from Richmond County. I remember Aunt Margie (1911–78) saying, "There were two things Mama would always do: church on Sunday and her club meeting on Wednesday evening." One of the social club's biggest activities was quilting bees. Lena had made quilts for all her children and grandchildren before she passed. For the most part, these were not fancy quilts, but they were heavy and warm, made for use in houses without central heat.

On that Thanksgiving, lying under Grandma Lena's quilt, I got scared and started shaking. I imagined its red pattern was the blood of the dead turkeys and that their spirits were about to get me. At first, this amused my father and sister, but Mother realized how frightened I was and came over to calm me down. I was still frightened at bedtime, and Mother tried to comfort me further by warming our bedsheets, something she knew I loved. She got one of the old flat irons that she had heating on the kitchen stove, pulled back the covers on our bed, and ran the hot iron over the sheets. But that wasn't enough to calm me this evening, and I still was worried when she tucked in my sister and me under another of Grandma Lena's quilts.

I was preoccupied with the idea that the red on her quilts was turkey blood and that my grandmother's spirit was also in the quilt. Mother, in her wise and gentle voice, stopped Delores from teasing me and explained that my Grandma

My grandmother Goldie Addison (1899–1983) being interviewed by Oprah Winfrey.
BALTIMORE, MARYLAND, AUGUST 1981 (1-27680/33A)

Lena had been a very kind person and had made these quilts for her family with a lot of love. I should not think of the red patterns as blood but rather as warmth, like the fire in the stove and the sun in the sky. Mother went on to explain that Grandma Lena's spirit was in the quilts but that it was a friendly spirit that would comfort us, keep us warm, and protect us from bad spirits.

The next morning, Thanksgiving Day, we arrived at 1312 Mosher Street in Baltimore's Sandtown, a seven-room, two-story, marble-stepped rowhouse where my maternal grandmother Goldie Addison (1899–1983) lived with her mother, Arbia Janey (1874–1963); my mother's two younger sisters, Marie (1922–85)

and Hortense (b. 1921); and my stepgrandfather, Freddie (1911–74), whom I really liked. He was from Cheraw, South Carolina, and was one of the best storytellers I had ever heard. When we arrived that day, I didn't see him, so I kept calling his name. My sister was busy telling everyone how afraid I was of the turkey spirit, but my grandmother, who always took me seriously, stopped everyone from teasing me and then told me to go upstairs because Freddie was sick in bed.

Just to the left at the top of the dark stairway was my grandmother's bedroom. This was the one room in the house that was never dark, because there were always candles burning and their flickering light cast dancing shadows across the ceiling and walls. I would come to think of this as the room where friendly spirits dwelled. Along the wall on the right was a vanity table. It had a central mirror that was lower and taller than the two side mirrors; the top of the vanity was covered with jewelry and an assortment of grooming and make-up supplies. My grandmother always had a votive candle burning in front of each of the side mirrors. In the center of the south wall between two windows stood a chest of drawers. It was about five feet tall and had an altar on top that always had at least four lit candles. There was an easy chair (which we called a comfort chair) in each of the southern corners, near the windows. On the eastern wall my grandmother had a big four-poster bed. Just above the headboard, a wooden cross draped with palm leaves was mounted on the wall. To the left of the bed in the corner was a closet.

When I entered the room, the first thing I noticed was that Freddie was lying under a big dark quilt made of old woolen coats and men's pants. I didn't see any red in it, but I still wondered whether there were good or bad spirits in that quilt. When Freddie saw me, he started talking, but all I wanted to know was who had made the quilt. He said his mother, Julia Brown Grace (1872–1945), had made it and he had brought it with him from South Carolina. Was his mother's spirit in that quilt?

At that moment my grandmother walked in with a bowl of soup for him and said jokingly, "You don't look like you're getting any better. Maybe it's time I get down my healing quilt," to which Freddie replied, "Why you holding back with all your good stuff? Don't you want me fit enough to eat your turkey and all that good stuffing you're putting in it? Honey, you know how much I love your stuffing!" She reached over and gave him one of her warm, therapeutic hugs, the kind that thrills you to your soul. A few moments later and in a much more serious tone, she wanted to know what this spirit quilt was we'd been talking about. Before I could answer, my sister came in to get me to go help her build a snowman.

In March 1945, when I was eight years old and in the hospital with pneumonia, my grandmother Goldie and my great-grandmother Arbia came to visit and brought the healing quilt. After covering me with the quilt, my great-grandmother lit a candle and started reading from the Bible. My grandmother took out a thermos of tea and was helping me sip it. A young nurse came into the room, and with a curious look on her face inquired about the strange smell. My grandmother ignored her, so the nurse left and soon returned with a doctor and another nurse. The doctor angrily demanded to know what they were feeding me. My grandmother answered, "I know what I'm doing. I've been taking care of people for years."

The doctor then asked Goldie and Arbia to step outside the room, and I could hear them arguing. Then the doctor said he didn't want any of that "hoodoo mess" in this hospital and asked her to please leave quietly. When they came back into the room, he took the quilt off me and gave it to my grandmother, telling her to take this "stinking thing" away. She was so mad I thought she was about to cast a spell on them, but all she said was, "If anything happens to my grandson, I'll get all of you." She and Arbia then kissed me and left. It could have been my imagination, but it seemed that just having that quilt on me made me feel better.

A kid named Roy, a Catholic, was in the bed across from me. His priest came to see him every day; occasionally nuns who taught him came to bring his lessons; and on Sundays the priest brought communion. I was really curious about their prayers, especially the part that dealt with the Holy Ghost, and so I paid close attention. I didn't understand why it was okay for the priest, the nuns, and his family to work this Catholic stuff on him, while my grandmother wasn't allowed to help me.

I knew a little about the Holy Ghost from the Holiness Church my mother used to take me to, where folks would say they were "sanctified, saved, and full of the Holy Ghost"; some people would start shouting, falling out, and speaking in tongues. I didn't see any of this happening with Roy, so I wanted to know which Holy Ghost this was. I asked him one day if he felt the Holy Ghost. He said he didn't understand what I was talking about! The next day while my mother was visiting, the priest came and Roy must have told him about my questions, because he asked my mother if it was all right for him to talk with me. She consented, so he and the nuns stopped to see me every time they came to see Roy. After leaving the hospital, I started going to St. Peter Claver Church for catechism lessons, and a year later was baptized in the Catholic Church—all because of my curiosity about spirits and ghosts and thinking that this Holy Ghost must have been the main ghost. I thought if I got tight with him, I wouldn't have to worry about any bad spirits bothering me.

I must admit that my grandmother Goldie wasn't exactly thrilled about all this, but she didn't interfere. She told me that one day I'd find out the Catholic Church wasn't all it was cracked up to be, and added, "Those priests and nuns aren't all that holy. They sin just like everybody else." For years I had heard the neighborhood women in my grandmother's kitchen talk about all kinds of shenanigans going on in other churches, whom the preachers and deacons were going with, and all sorts of petty jealousies. Even though Goldie was a deeply spiritual person, she almost never went to anyone's church. Her attitude was that the preachers needed to come and seek *her* counsel!

During those long sessions that the neighborhood women spent talking in my grandmother's kitchen, several women would almost always be piecing quilt blocks. To those who gathered there, Goldie's kitchen was in many ways a place of special sharing, full of love, happiness, and sorrow, a place where certain things could be talked about that weren't

discussed anywhere else. This was the women's club of the neighborhood, where a lot of problems were solved; and when I saw them piecing quilt blocks, I thought that was all part of the magic they were using.

During those gatherings, I would often hide under the back steps and try to listen to what the women were saying, because I thought they were discussing the secrets of women and how to work "roots" on people. When my grandmother realized I was there, she'd interrupt the conversation and say loud enough for me to hear: "Wait a minute. I don't hear that dog barking out in the yard. That means my grandson Roland is up under those steps trying to listen to us. If you don't come out from under there and go about your business, you're going to hear something that'll make you deaf and see something to make your eyes pop out of your head." And all the ladies would break out laughing and say, "Yeah, Miss Goldie, and we know you could put that on him, too." Someone might say, "That stuff you gave me sure humbled my man," and someone else, "Mine has stopped messing around since I did what you told me."

One of the most frequent visitors was a neighbor named Miss Rosie. One day she and a few of the other regulars had gathered in Goldie's kitchen to talk about the quilt blocks they were making for a "love quilt." Miss Rosie was trying to capture a man's heart, but it sounded as though he was seeing two or three women at the same time. The ladies were putting something in the quilt blocks that was supposed to make him love only her. I could hear someone say, "Child, you need to put some of this in that block. That's what I got my man with." Another lady said, "I'm putting red and black crosses in this block. When the quilt is finished, just be sure he sleeps under the side with this block on it. This'll drive the devil out of him and make him talk in his sleep. And you can bet it'll make him stop messing around." And my grandmother Goldie added, "Just for a little extra insurance, put some of this in his coffee, and put a little in yours too. I guarantee your power over him will be so strong, he'll never go anywhere."

By this time in my life, I'd heard a lot of talk about people having power over others, and my

My great-grandmother Mae Arbia Rounds Janey (1874–1963).
BALTIMORE, MARYLAND, 1955 (FA-3)

curiosity was overwhelming. The men in the stableyard talked about it, people talked about which ministers and entertainers had drawing power, and some people said you could get power by belonging to secret organizations. However, it was plain to me that the women sewing those quilt blocks in my grandmother's kitchen weren't just talking about it—they really had the power to humble men. So I asked my grandfather Freddie about all of this. With a serious look on his face, he stared me straight in the eye and said, "I've been watching you go in that basement. You're trying to hear what those witches are saying, aren't you?" "Witches?" I said. Freddie burst out laughing. "That's what they're doing in there, working witchcraft on everybody. Men don't stand a chance when women get their heads

together. Just look at me. Goldie's got me under her spell and won't cut me loose."

I really liked women. Not only was I curious to know what they were talking about, I just liked to sit and look at them. There was something magical about just hugging them, and for many years, I would almost rather hug a woman than kiss her. I would imagine my arms were like a big nurturing love quilt that I'd wrap around her, protecting her and keeping her warm. I remember my mother asking me, "Roland, you just sitting there staring at me. Is something wrong?" I just liked looking at her. Then I would go over and hug and kiss her. I remember one day before we moved in with my grandmother, my father and mother had had an argument and my mother was sitting in his big comfort chair wrapped up in Grandma Lena's quilt, half-singing and half-humming to herself, "In the great getting up morning, fare you well, fare you well." She sang it real slow, and on this particular day there seemed to be a distant look in her eyes as she sang it. I slowly approached her, climbed up in her lap, and gave her a big hug as she pulled the quilt over me. I lay there feeling the warmth and power of her body, every breath, every heartbeat, and just hummed with her. I've cherished that special moment ever since.

By the time my parents divorced in 1942, and my mother, sister (Delores), brothers (Albert and Jerome), and I went to live with my grandmother, I had come to understand more about how powerful my grandmother was in the community. Goldie was a traditional healer, a midwife, and a source of community information related to history and tradition; she was very much into the business of "putting stuff on" and "taking stuff off" people—a person who worked "roots."

During the winter of 1946 I got sick again. My mother wanted to take me to the hospital, but my grandmother insisted that she would take care of me. I remember my great-grandmother Arbia telling her that she was going to put the healing quilt on me. This quilt had big bold patterns, all red and black. The two of them sprinkled stuff from several bottles onto the quilt and lit three candles. My grandmother brought me hot, bitter tea, and my great-grandmother read to me from the Bible. They worked on me for three days, bathing and feeding me, and praying, until they broke my fever.

I remember clearly asking about the big red and black quilt and what healing powers it had. At first, they told me it was "just a quilt" made by Arbia's mother, my great-great-grandmother, Laura Virginia Rounds (1850–88) from Worcester County on the Eastern Shore of Maryland. But over the years I had seen this healing quilt brought out on special occasions, and not always when someone was sick. Although my great-grandmother Arbia wouldn't say anything else about it, finally my grandmother told me about the spirits of the "old ones" (ancestors) and said that some of the material in this quilt was from the clothing of Laura Virginia Rounds's mother, Eliza Harmon (1830–60), who was born and died a slave. Arbia had always said her grandmother, who was part Indian, was gifted with the power of healing and had doctored both black and white people; she therefore had been revered throughout the lower counties of Maryland's Eastern Shore in spite of her being a slave.

I had trouble putting into perspective a great-great-great-grandmother, but I did know my grandmother kept this quilt by itself on the top shelf of her bedroom closet! None of us ever played in my grandmother's room, but I would often go in and sit quietly and stare for hours at that closet, waiting for the spirits to say something to me—but they never did. It would still be many years before I felt I could communicate with the spirits. For the time being I took solace in imagining myself dancing with them.

My grandmother Goldie watched and encouraged my meditating. She was also greatly interested in my telling her about my dreams. She always knew if I was embellishing or exaggerating them and would ask, "What did you really dream?" She labeled some of them good dreams and others bad dreams, and would even play the daily numbers (lottery) based on my dreams.

Often, when there was a birth in the family, the baby was brought to my grandmother's house and put on the healing quilt to take a nap. In this way, the baby was supposed to get in touch with the old ones and receive their blessing and protection. My clearest memory of this was in

March 1944, when my sister Marie Arbia, the first of my mother's six children from her 1943 marriage to John Tyler Grace, was born. When Marie was placed on the healing quilt, she screamed as though she were in great pain, and the longer they let her lie there, the louder she hollered. Finally, my great-grandmother Arbia picked Marie up and handed her to my mother. She then took the quilt off the bed, turned it over, and sat in a chair with the quilt in her lap. Wrapping Marie in the reverse side of the quilt, Arbia sat there humming and rocking her to sleep. When Marie finally fell asleep, the women turned the quilt back over and placed her on it, and she continued to sleep. Arbia then said Marie had hollered because the spirits had frightened her. My mother asked her what this meant, and Arbia said, "It means she's going to travel a rocky road. There will be much confusion in her life, because she'll have trouble trusting people."

In January 1946 my sister Goldie Ruth, the second child from my mother's remarriage, was born. A few days after our mother returned home from the hospital, my great-grandmother said it was time for Goldie Ruth to meet the old ones. Unlike Marie, when Goldie Ruth was placed on the healing quilt, she didn't make a sound. Arbia said that Goldie Ruth would have a gentle personality and a good ability to cope with difficulties. Later that day I asked my grandmother Goldie if I had ever been put on this quilt. She said, "Yes, and you cried when we took you off it. You really kicked up a fuss, so much that Momma [Arbia] told us to put you back on it. Maybe that's why you're always asking questions about that quilt."

Only some of the babies in our family had been put on the quilt, about twenty of Arbia's more than thirty grandchildren and great-grandchildren. I believe that to a person, their sense of connectedness to the family remains stronger than that of any of those who were not put on the quilt. As an adult, I came to understand that a lot of what Goldie and her mother did was not respected and appreciated by all family members. Some referred to it as "real ooga, booga, voodoo stuff." And for years, these beliefs were the source of much family controversy.

Another experience with the healing quilt involved my mother. She was very saddened when she and my father separated. One day I saw my mother sitting in a chair all wrapped up in the healing quilt, even though it was midsummer and as hot as the dickens. A few days later her whole attitude had changed, and she wasn't sad anymore.

Not all of my early experiences with quilts were in the company of women. From the ages of seven to twelve, I used to hang around a stable my Uncle Handy owned. The stable boss was a man called "Doc." Because of Doc's wisdom and healing powers, many people, both black and white, came to seek his counsel. No white people ever came to see my grandmother, which prompted me to ask her about Doc. She told me that he was a "hougan" (voodoo priest) and that I was never to trifle with him. Doc, whose real name I never knew, healed people and horses and every other kind of animal in the stableyard. My grandmother would send people she couldn't help to Doc. Doc had a couple of old quilts he would lay across horses when they got sick. The closest I ever came to understanding anything about Doc's quilts was when an eccentric old junkman I worked with (everyone called him "Swayback") got one.

Swayback was what we used to call a "saltwater Geechie," meaning the Gullah people from the Carolina and Georgia coastal Low Country. Although his family had been poor farmers just outside Charleston, South Carolina, they had managed to send him to college. He had tried his hand at teaching, had worked on the railroad, and as a merchant seaman had been to Africa. Through a strange set of circumstances he had wound up in Baltimore working as a junkman. He intrigued me and, over time, I learned a lot from him.

On my initial visit to Swayback's three-room apartment, one of the first things I noticed was a black cat lying on a quilt made of small red and white squares. It looked like a checkerboard thrown across one end of a sofa. Hanging over the back of a rocking chair was another quilt made of larger, multicolored squares of varying sizes. Swayback noticed me examining the quilt on the rocking chair. It was well worn, and cotton

was coming through in places. I didn't remember ever seeing exactly what was inside a quilt before. He looked at me and laughed, saying, "That there is my rheumatism quilt, and I'm going to have to fix it before I lose all the good stuff in it." Of course I wanted to know what this "good stuff" was. "This cotton here is the real stuff right from down home. I put it in there myself." I then asked, "You mean your mother didn't make this for you?" He replied, "No, I pieced and quilted this one myself. This isn't as heavy as the ones Mama made. She makes 'em pretty and warm."

Then I asked if she had made the red and white quilt. Swayback said, "No, my auntie made that for me for Christmas, but it gives me the willies just like she does." I said, "Well, the cat seems to like it," to which he replied, "Yeah, old Black Jack took to it right away. You want to see one of Mama's quilts, look in there on the bed." When I walked in his bedroom, I said, "Wow!" This quilt had nine big blocks in the center, each about eighteen inches square. In the middle one, on a red background was a black rooster that seemed to have been made out of a velvet-like material. In the four blocks, one at each corner of the center square, was a red rooster on a black background. The top center square had an appliquéd man who looked like a blacksmith; he held a hammer and was hitting something on an anvil. The two center squares, on each side of the black rooster, had what looked like two swords or machetes, and the bottom center square had some appliquéd trees. Around these nine center squares were three strips of fabric, one yellow, one red, and one black, each about six inches wide, and the outside border was made of red, green, and black triangles.

I had never seen a quilt like this one. I asked Swayback, "What is this quilt for?" He looked at me quizzically and said, "Well, I'll have you know that this quilt is real special. When that hawk [wind] blows in from the northwest, it keeps me very warm." "Why did your mother put roosters on it?" I asked. "Well, you see, when I was a little boy I had these pet roosters, and I made one of my friends mad when I got the best of him in a fight, so he got back at me by killing my roosters. Everybody knew how much I loved those roosters—my godmother told me that I was

Ogun's child—so Mama made this quilt for me so these roosters would always be with me." I was already familiar with this spirit, Ogun; Doc had taught me he was mighty powerful, a spirit of iron who kept order. I asked if the rooster spirit was in the quilts, and Swayback said, "Oh yeah. Not only are rooster spirits in there, Ogun's and Mama's spirits are in there too. There's a lot of fond memories in that quilt. That's why it's so warm. You can sleep real good under that one."

Sometimes Swayback played records that reminded me of the African or Caribbean drumming I'd heard in the movies. Although I had listened to drum solos before, it was Swayback who first made me understand how important the rhythm of drums was in our music. He explained to me that he didn't trust any churches that didn't use drums in their service. He said that the old spirits traveled through the rhythm of the drums, and that when people got happy and possessed was when those spirits moved them. He was the first person to tell me about our African heritage and Marcus Garvey's "back to Africa" movement. There were a lot of things he would try to explain to me that I didn't understand then, but I would just sit there fascinated and listen to him. Later in life I'd often remember those things.

Doc had given Swayback linaments for his arthritis and a quilt to put over his lap while driving his horse and wagon. This quilt had the weirdest odor, and when I asked what it was, Swayback said it was some of those "herbs and stuff" Doc had put in it. I would laugh and say that if the odor didn't cure you, it was strong enough to kill you. He would come back at me saying, "Speaking of killing somebody, that's what your grandmother is going to do to you when she finds out you've been hooking school."

Swayback was right. I had become an unmanageable kid of the streets. I had already spent three months in a reformatory for petty theft and gang fighting, and my mother and grandmother were quite concerned about me. Without my knowledge, they had arranged through a Catholic organization for me to go live with a family in southern Maryland.

For a couple of weeks before I was to leave for the country, I had noticed that my mother was more quiet than usual. Again I found her in my grandmother's room wrapped up in the healing quilt. As I approached her, she stood up and opened her quilt-draped arms and drew me close to her. "You know, Roland, I really love you," she said. I repeated, "Yes, I love you too, Mama." For the next few moments an ocean of tears gushed forth. We stood there in the middle of August with this quilt wrapped around both of us, sweating and crying and my mother saying over and over, "You know I love you but I got to get you away from this city. We are not giving you away but we have to get you out of this city, else you will wind up in jail for a long time." She took my head in both of her hands, staring me in the eyes, and with tears streaming down her face she said, "You know I am doing this for your own good." I tried to reassure her that I understood why this was necessary. As hot as it was standing there, I didn't want to let her go. Suddenly I felt someone behind me, hugging me and my mother. It was my grandmother Goldie. After a few minutes she just simply took the quilt from around us and said, "You are going to be all right now. Everything's going to be all right."

WHITE PLAINS, MARYLAND, 1948–54

It was late August in 1948, a few weeks after my twelfth birthday, when my Uncle Handy and his new black Ford arrived at my grandmother's house. Most kids in my community went to visit their grandparents in the summer, generally to North or South Carolina, Georgia, or Virginia. I had never been "down South," and I was eager to go, despite some of the stories I'd heard. Billie Holiday's song "Strange Fruit," about black bodies hanging from poplar trees, particularly frightened me. But my grandmother Goldie would always say, "I'll have you know, when it comes to dealing with white folks, life for black people in Baltimore isn't any different from any of those states down South."

I was all eyes and ears as we drove out of the city and headed down Route 301. For the next few hours, I looked at fields of corn and tobacco. As we passed a house with several quilts hanging on a line, I reached over and touched my grandmother to draw her attention to them. She just looked at me, smiled, and said, "Yes, Roland, I see them. They're pretty, aren't they?" I was waiting for her to say more, but she didn't.

We arrived at the Miles's farm in White Plains, Maryland, about noon. As the car made its way down an old gravel road, we were flanked on one side by a cornfield and on the other by tobacco. Just behind their house were clotheslines where four brightly colored quilts were airing out.

It was a white, two-story, seven-room, shingled house, which faced south, with a screened-in porch that ran across the front and around the right corner to the kitchen door. The house had a large yard on three sides, enclosed by a white picket fence, and in the southwest corner a huge oak shade tree made the front porch a nice, cool place to sit. It looked to me like something out of a movie or magazine—a place I had always imagined I wanted to visit. As we approached the gate, we were welcomed by two dogs and by Elizabeth Briscoe Miles and her husband, Thomas. I liked the Mileses immediately; both of them had soft, gentle voices that made you feel right at home.

For a while, we sat on the porch talking about the fact that school was going to start in two weeks and that I had been failing miserably. This and my having been something of a juvenile delinquent didn't seem to disturb the Mileses. Nor did the information they had from the Catholic organization that had placed me with them, that the year before I had run away with the circus. It actually wasn't a real circus, but more like a small traveling carnival, and I didn't consider what I had done running away from home. I had been visiting Big Jim Diamond's Circus every evening it was in town and happened to be around the day they were preparing to leave. One of the young guys asked if I wanted to go with them, and I simply got on the truck and left. It never dawned on me that someone would think I was running away. Things had gone well for about six weeks. I didn't get homesick, I just got tired of traveling with them and went home.

My mind kept drifting to the quilts out back. The midday sun made them appear even brighter than they were, and I began to wonder if they were special and what spirits might be in them.

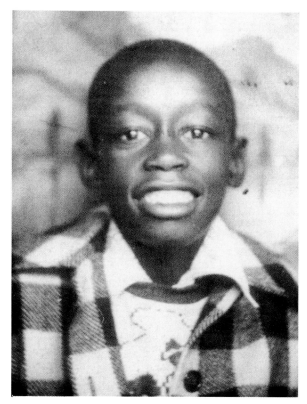

Roland L. Freeman, age twelve.
CHARLES COUNTY, MARYLAND, 1948 (FA-2)

Most people I knew who had special quilts had brought them to the city from somewhere down South, and now I had come to the land where these quilts were made. Beyond the clotheslines, I could see the trees, and I wondered if this was the forest where the spirits lived. Swayback had once told me of men gathering in the woods to play drums and talk to the spirits, and I desperately wanted that experience.

After dinner, while my mother sat and talked to Mrs. Miles, my grandmother and I went for a short walk. She reaffirmed that she thought these were nice people. When I hugged my grandmother, she whispered in my ear, "I put a 'Big John the Conqueror' root [a "mojo," to ward off bad spirits] and a couple of candles in your bag. If you get lonesome, light one and think of home and everyone who loves you." Uncle Handy said, "Stay out of trouble, little man, and

Elizabeth Briscoe Miles, age seventy-seven.
CHARLES COUNTY, MARYLAND, 1950 (FA-4)

if you want to come for the holidays, I'll come get you. Keep an eye out for a couple good roosters for Doc, because you know he's always looking for some fine roosters." My mother seemed sad and we hugged for a long time. As the car started to pull out, Mrs. Miles put her arm around me and told them, "Don't you all worry about him none. We'll take good care of him." It was in this pleasant, serene setting that I, a twelve-year-old streetwise city kid, experienced six of the most fruitful years of my life.

Mrs. Miles took me up to the second floor. At the top of the stairs was a very large bedroom. The first thing I noticed was the beautiful quilt covering an old brass bed. I later learned that the pattern was called a Double Wedding Ring. In the center of a table next to their bed was a statue of Mary, with two votive candles flickering in front of it, forming the first of two altars in the room. Next to this altar was a window, and just beyond it in the corner was a white oak cabinet. This cabinet and the things on it intrigued me more than anything else in the house. The top was adorned with photographs, a series of unfamiliar

woodcarvings, herbs, bottles, shells, and about eight votive candles. The room made me feel very comfortable because it reminded me of my grandmother Goldie's room.

The second bedroom belonged to Mrs. Miles's daughter, Theresa, and her husband, Lloyd Jackson, who were living at the house. Their bed was covered with a quilt in a Log Cabin pattern, made of earth colors. At the end of the hallway was my room. It contained a bureau and a wardrobe with a quilt made of dark woolen squares inside it, a washstand, and a wrought-iron bed covered with a pretty quilt that looked like a good-luck charm. It really lit up the room. It had four large squares, each with a green four-leaf clover appliquéd on an off-white background, with a darker green border around each square and around the entire quilt. In the four corners of each square were appliquéd pink flowers, and in the four corners of the border of the quilt were pink squares.

As I picked up a corner of the quilt to examine it, I brought it up to my nose to smell it. Mrs. Miles had by now noticed my fascination with the quilts in each room and was curious to know my reason for smelling this quilt. I just said, "I don't know." Although I wanted to find out if she had put something special on or in it like my grandmother's healing quilt, I had decided for the time being to follow my grandmother's advice. Knowing how much I liked to talk, she had advised me to keep my mouth shut, listen, and learn.

After supper, I remember Theresa asking her mother, "Mama, is it time?" She answered, "Yes," and everyone got up and went to Mrs. Miles's room. Here the whole family knelt down for evening prayers. Theresa opened the cabinet in the corner and brought out the family Bible. Mrs. Miles told me to kneel down next to her. We said the rosary, which, with its more than sixty prayers, seemed to me quite a bit of praying. But they didn't stop there. I soon learned that the second altar in the corner, full of old pictures and other things, was an ancestral altar. Each evening the family prayed for the souls of their ancestors and asked the ancestors in heaven to pray for them. In this way memory of the family genealogy was kept alive.

That night I got a case of the "lonelies." As hot as it was, I went and got the old quilt out of the wardrobe and wrapped it around me and just sat in the bed and began to rock and hum my mother's favorite song, "In that great getting up morning, fare you well." The next morning Mrs. Miles's gentle hands touching my forehead woke me up. She was looking at me rather oddly, asking if I was cold. I guess she asked because I had fallen asleep wrapped up in this quilt. I told her I wasn't cold; I just liked this quilt because it reminded me of one my grandmother had.

After a few months, I was informed that I was one of the family and was to start calling Mrs. Miles "grandmother." Everyone else became aunts, uncles, and cousins. This acceptance also applied to the ancestors, and so from then on I spoke to and about them in prayer every night. The Miles family thought it quite important to pray regularly for the ancestors.

The Miles family was indeed into the spirit world, and even though I never got a sense that they had a healing quilt, they did have an ancestral quilt. It was a Log Cabin pattern. On each block was embroidered the name and birth and death dates of a family member. Usually both the quilt and the Bible were brought out each evening during prayers.

The Miles were a very conservative family that had been on the same land since the middle 1800s. Except for two nearby families, all the other immediate neighbors were white. Mrs. Miles was totally different from my grandmother Goldie, but both were highly respected in their communities. She was a midwife to both black and white people; she taught catechism, sewing, and etiquette to white children in the community; and her family used to "lay people out" (prepare their bodies for burial).

Once or twice a month during the winter, black and white women would gather in our dining room for a quilting bee while the men sat in the kitchen playing cards. It seemed no one ever used the living room in this house; most activities took place in the kitchen and the dining room, where the suspended quilting frame hung. When not in use, it could be pulled up to the ceiling out of the way by ropes attached on all four corners.

Theresa and Lloyd Jackson.
CHARLES COUNTY, MARYLAND, 1949 (FA-6)

Mrs. Miles would go to great lengths preparing food the evening before one of her quilting bees. Everyone would bring something, so there would be almost as much food as at a church picnic. They would sit around sewing, eating, and joking, as if there wasn't any difference in their skin colors. Most of the tops quilted in these bees were fancy designs and were made to be given to someone for a special occasion. I would find myself the only male in the room, trying to be inconspicuous as I listened and watched.

These women were pleasant and seemed to be enjoying each other's company, but it was a far cry from the cut-loose, get-down, soul-searching sessions in my grandmother Goldie's kitchen. Here they certainly weren't talking about the private lives of the preachers and the deacons (for one thing all of them belonged to the same Catholic church, and the whole time I lived in the

The Miles family. *Back row (left to right):* Lucy Miles (mother-in-law of Elizabeth Miles), Elizabeth Briscoe Miles, Louise Taylor, Harriet Briscoe Taylor, Mary Catherine Briscoe Taylor, Mrs. Proctor (neighbor), Nellie Marshall (cousin), Jim Lovis, and Edward Chase (Mary Catherine's husband). *Front row (left to right):* Josephine Miles, Henrietta Taylor, Jeannetta Chase, Marjorie Miles, Orville Taylor, Cecilia Chase, and Edward Chase Jr.

CHARLES COUNTY, MARYLAND, CIRCA 1910 (FA-7)

country, the worst I heard about the priest was that he sometimes drank a little too much), nor did they discuss whether their husbands were messing around.

The quilting bees would generally start in midmorning and last four to six hours. Most of the women were from farming families and needed to be home in time for evening chores. One of these women, Shirley Robie, was an English teacher, a white woman whom Mrs. Miles had asked to help me with my lessons. Quilting seemed to be a larger part of Miss Robie's life than it was for any of the other women. She had quilt books, magazines, and patterns all the time. After noticing my interest in quilting, she started giving me things to read. The first was a book entitled *The Romance of the Patchwork Quilt in America*, which was all about patterns. Another was Marie D. Webster's book, *Quilts, Their Story, and How to Make Them*. She also showed me the quilting column in the *Ladies Home Journal*, and

patterns printed in the county newspaper. I enjoyed these materials, but none of them dealt with my primary interests, healing quilts and the spirits in quilts.

Over time, I began to notice lots of details that didn't fit for me. While Grandmother Miles was well respected by all, virtually no white people called her "Mrs. Miles"; they all referred to her as "Aunt Liza." Because I had heard so many stories about race mixing in the South, I thought the white people who called her "Aunt" were actually related to her, because there were some white-looking people in the family. So I asked Lloyd one day how they got all these white relatives. It took him a minute to realize what I was talking about, and he seemed to find my question a bit amusing and wanted to know how I had come to that conclusion. I told him that when men, women, and children came to the house, they always affectionately greeted Mr. and Mrs. Miles as "Aunt" and "Uncle," and I was curious if they were relatives. He began to explain at length, pointing out to me his sense of the practice of manners, courtesy, and etiquette by Southern white people toward blacks at that time. He told me how they teach their children manners so that they seem courteous and respectful to older black people, but that their etiquette is really based on a contemptible racist system. He told me that while white people may warmly greet a black person by saying "aunt" or "uncle," showing good manners according to their system, they won't accept the black person on an equal status as they would another white person.

I also asked Lloyd about the people I heard called "we sorts." He explained, "We are all a mixture of Indians, blacks, and whites, and these are people who emphasize their Indian blood."* I recalled that back in Baltimore, I'd frequently met colored people who ran the gamut from light to dark, and some who said they were part Indian. My grandmother Goldie would say, "Some colored people always talk about being something else, about how much Indian or white blood they got in them. What you don't hear enough of is how much African they got in them, and that's what we are. We are African people, and don't you ever forget it. And the white man thinks the same of all of us—to him, we are all niggers."

The quilting in Mrs. Miles's home of course took place in a social context in which, once you left the farm, everything was segregated: movies, beer parlors, schools. Although we all went to the same church, African Americans sat in the balcony and in the back. There were separate church picnics every year, and blacks and whites competed in raising the most money for the church. There were even separate county fairs, so quilts done by this integrated group of women would win prizes at both fairs, with the judges ignoring their mixed manufacture. There was always so much work to be done on the farm that Grandmother Miles usually made only two quilts of her own each year. She always made one for

---

* I believe that "we sorts" was a term peculiar to southern Maryland. Some of the "we sorts" with whom I grew up became active in the Native American movement and see those roots as their primary cultural identification.

Left to right: Sisters Harriet Ann Briscoe (1871–1916), Elizabeth Briscoe (1873–1954), and Mary Catherine Briscoe (1868–1916). CHARLES COUNTY, MARYLAND, 1890s (FA-5)

exhibition at the county fair; and each year she won a blue ribbon for first place. She never sold these quilts but gave each to a family member. Her second quilt was raffled off at the annual church picnic.

Grandmother Miles had a niece known as "Cousin Jeannetta." Her house sat to the right of ours, across the cow pasture. Jeannetta, who had been a teacher all her life, worked at Bowie State College and came home on the weekends. Among her most prized possessions were a dozen or so quilts. I had a particular interest in the patterns on three of them that had something to do with the Underground Railroad, which Jeannetta had explained to me. (It wasn't until many years later that I learned the actual significance of their particular patterns and how they were used.) Jeannetta also had a quilt on which she embroidered the names and birth and death dates of famous black people, as well as a family quilt similar to the ancestral quilt I saw each night at prayer. Sometimes, in a solemn voice and with moist eyes, she told me of the "free spirits," to whom this quilt was related, the eleven members of the Briscoe family who had run away and were never heard of again.

Jeannetta was the only person in the country I could talk with about my grandmother Goldie's healing quilt. She wrote the story down and told me it was a very important part of my family history. Jeannetta would always make a big deal out of which quilt she was going to sleep under. Some had been given to her by different families whose children she had taught; others were from her own family. Her most treasured quilt was a Log Cabin pattern, and it was the last quilt her mother, Mary Chase (1869–1916), had made. Jeannetta told me it had been made from strips of their old dresses.

I wanted to know if she felt anything different from particular quilts. She explained that she always slept under her mother's quilt to cheer herself up. I would laugh and say, "That's those friendly spirits I was telling you about." She had one quilt that was made just of three huge pieces of material, with no real design. This had been given to her by an older woman who didn't have much schooling and whom Jeannetta had spent many evenings teaching to read.

Jeannetta and I would sit for hours talking about art, poetry, local history, and the patterns on her quilts. She also had some old copies of the *North Star,* the newspaper edited by the great abolitionist Frederick Douglass, a runaway slave from Talbot County, Maryland, who educated himself and became one of the country's most outstanding statesmen. Jeannetta always assumed that I would go to college. She told me, "Roland, you're going to make a fine history professor." She encouraged my interest in the history of black people and put the spirit world in perspective for me. She told me about Katherine Dunham, the famous anthropologist and choreographer, and Zora Neale Hurston, the author, folklorist, and anthropologist. She knew personally the great educators Carter G. Woodson, Mary McLeod Bethune, and W. E. B. Du Bois; her father also knew Matthew Henson, the black explorer who helped discover the North Pole. I didn't learn about any of these people in school, and Miss Robie certainly never mentioned them.

I felt very comfortable asking Jeannetta to clarify things that confused me. Quite often I'd heard different neighbors and members of the Miles family refer to certain things I mentioned as "hoodoo" or "voodoo mess." Jeannetta explained that while many people carried some sort of "mojo," and some even had a little bag of roots or powder (also known as "scooby dust" or "dust"), most didn't talk about this very easily, and if you asked them about it, they'd usually make a wisecrack or laugh it off. As closely as I remember, here's what Jeannetta told me:

But Roland, when you refer to these things, and you do a lot, it's very clear that you're serious. And that frightens these folks who profess to be good Catholics. From what you've told me about your grandmother, Doc, and Swayback, you've been fortunate to witness things others haven't. I think it might be best if you stopped telling people around here that you're Damballah's child, because they don't understand that. You've got to realize that these people are often conflicted in their own practice of the old ways, and most of them are trying to forget they're Africans, even though much of what they do daily is very African. It is clear to me that Doc took you through an initiation or rite of passage ceremony, and that's when you became Damballah's son. What you might not know is that Damballah had a high position in the pantheon of African gods.

Roland, what you have to understand is that as a people we've always had a strong spirituality, and that before we were forcibly removed from the motherland, our spirituality was deeply rooted in a complex religious system that had sustained us for centuries. But in the New World, the Church and the slave-owners viewed Africans as pagans with no belief systems, just a bunch of bizarre, unrelated rituals and superstitions. So the Church outlawed all of these activities and saw it as its moral duty to give Africans a true faith and to convert them to Christianity.

However, the old African faiths never died; they simply went underground. The slaves recognized in Catholicism, especially in the stories and images of the saints—who were pictured with swords, shields, snakes, and other animals—some of the same features they had worshiped in their own

Jeannetta Chase (1900–76).
CHARLES COUNTY, MARYLAND, JANUARY 1975 (1-11014/8)

deities. Because many of these saints were not in the Bible, but were learned about largely through visual images and oral tradition, slaves easily grafted onto their own beliefs what they saw and heard about them. And so the logic and spirit of African faiths came together with the imagery and narratives of Catholicism. The underlying understanding that emerged remained African, but with a Catholic overlay. The Africans' understanding of spirits and of the role of ancestors in everyday life did not change.

And to make clearer to me what she had said, Jeannetta took out a group of Holy Cards of Patron Saints. I had seen similar cards for years, but had never thought of them in this way. She also gave me a book about voodoo by Zora Neale Hurston called *Tell My Horse*.

In the summer of 1950, when I turned fourteen, Jeannetta gave me four books that left an indelible impression on me: another book of Zora Neale Hurston's, *Of Mules and Men*; Margaret Walker's *For My People*; Richard Wright's novel *Native Son*; and, the one that stimulated the most conversation, Carter G. Woodson's *The Miseducation of the Negro*. For the next four years,

we talked about this book and what it meant. Jeannetta always explained it in the context of the segregated society in which we lived and the psychological damage it caused. Jeannetta put Woodson's name on her own family quilt, saying that even though he wasn't a blood relative, she considered him a part of her extended family and that I should pray for him just as I did for our other ancestors. She felt strongly that every black man, woman, and child should read *The Miseducation of the Negro*, because it provided a counterweight to the European-centered education black people received, when they received any at all.

I remain deeply indebted to Jeannetta for her impact not only on my education, but also on my attitude toward books and education. One of the reasons I had avoided school in Baltimore was that I was dyslexic and had severe reading problems. Teachers either didn't understand the problem or did nothing to deal with it. Classmates and adults called me a dummy, and I responded by acting out and frequently cutting school during my elementary years. Miss Robie, an English teacher, had already tried to help me with reading and spelling, but she became frustrated with my lack of progress and continually told me I wasn't trying hard enough. Luckily for me, she discussed this with Jeannetta, who then took a totally different approach to helping me.

For whatever reasons, perhaps her prior experience in teaching in one-room schoolhouses with students with spotty education and foundations, Jeannetta seemed to understand my learning problems. She realized how well I could remember things I heard, and so she would first read stories to me. We'd discuss them, and then she would have me re-read them, looking for certain things that she wanted to discuss. She underlined the experiences of people like Frederick Douglass, who had taught himself to read, even though it was against the law to teach slaves to read and write, and she encouraged me to keep struggling. I did, but even with all of her help and the resulting improvement, my dyslexia continued to be a serious problem for me across the years.

Jeannetta and I were a mutual admiration society. I really loved this short, plump, jolly lady with her many strange hats, always pleasant smile, and warm hugs. The years I spent under her tutelage added to and clarified what I had learned from Doc, Swayback, and my grandmother Goldie, and provided a solid foundation for much of what lay ahead.

In July 1951, Jeannetta's father died. His body was put on view in their house. At some point during the wake I noticed that Jeannetta's ancestral quilt had been placed on a little stand in the room with the casket. During the final viewing of the body, I noticed that a small block from the Log Cabin quilt made by Jeannetta's mother had been placed in the casket, along with a little picture of her and his medals from the Spanish-American War. I asked Jeannetta why she had put the quilt block there, and she said that she hadn't, but that Grandmother Miles had.

Almost a year later, Grandmother Miles's husband, Thomas, died. Grandmother Miles again placed a quilt block in his casket. A few weeks later, while helping her pack up his things, I noticed that a corner was missing from a quilt Thomas had had on his bed, and I learned this was a quilt his mother had given them for their wedding.

On March 3, 1954, Grandmother Miles died. When her body was brought to the house, the ancestral quilt was again brought out. Instead of being placed on a stand, however, it was draped over the coffin. At the final viewing in the church, I noticed there was no quilt piece in her casket, but there was a wooden figure from the ancestral altar. Everyone in the car was very quiet as we headed home from the funeral, and I felt empty inside, as if my heart had been taken out of me. My extended family had become as real and as important to me as my biological family, and I had grown to love Grandmother Miles as much as I loved Grandmother Goldie. Uncle Handy had brought Goldie, my mother, and three aunts to the funeral, and that was a real comfort to me.

I didn't want to go inside with all the people, so I went for a long walk around the fields where Grandmother Miles and I had talked about putting this year's garden, along the hillsides where we had picked blackberries, through the woods where we had gathered roots and herbs that she used for cooking and in healing, and by the creek where the best blueberries grew, past the swimming holes and the fishing holes where we had caught eel, catfish, and turtles, and I felt her presence. I saw her face, but she didn't speak to me, only smiled, and I felt that everything would be all right.

I realized how much I had learned here: how if you took care of the land, it would take care of you; how never to put off until tomorrow what you can do today; how going to school could be just as enjoyable as running the streets had been. Things seemed to be falling into place. I suddenly realized that the security I had found with these people in this setting was liberating, and that my earlier city knowledge had been greatly enhanced by my rural experiences.

I also thought of my still unresolved ambiguity about the Catholic Church. First, my being Catholic had helped me to be placed with this wonderful family. For that I was truly grateful, and I believed it to be the best thing that could have happened to me at that time in my life. At the same time, I couldn't understand how this mighty Catholic Church, the leader of the Christian world, could permit its churches and schools to remain segregated. Jeannetta had told me that the Jesuits at one time had had hundreds of slaves on their plantations right there in southern Maryland. I found that as amazing as the fact that the priest was still standing in front of our segregated congregation every week and never told people that this was wrong.

My mother, who had remarried and journeyed to the funeral from Farrell, Pennsylvania, wanted to know what I was going to do now that both Mr. and Mrs. Miles were dead. I didn't know, but I did know that I wasn't going to Farrell. I had gone there for the funeral of my younger brother Jerome (1939–52) and had developed an instant dislike for its smoke and stench from steel mills. I was angry at my stepfather for taking my mother there, and I blamed him for Jerome's death. I told Goldie that I would probably come and spend some time with her after getting in this year's crop.

That night I couldn't sleep. I got up and went into Grandmother Miles's room, took out the ancestral quilt, and found the block with the name Elizabeth Briscoe Miles, 1873; with needle

Dorothy Vaughan Freeman and her son Roland L. Freeman. WASHINGTON, D.C., AUGUST 1968 (PHOTOGRAPH BY MORT BROFFMAN, 4-5463/10)

and thread I added 1954. And then for the first time, I looked closely at the black square in the center of this quilt. Written in its upper right corner were the words: "They are gone but not forgottten." In it were the names of eight men and three women, all born between 1810 and 1840, but without death dates for any of them. I suddenly realized they were the "free spirits" about whom Jeannetta had spoken.

For a moment I tried to imagine what it must have been like for runaway slaves. It certainly took a lot of courage to venture into the unknown darkness, especially knowing that you would be hunted and, if captured, face the lash, or dismemberment, or be sold "down the river of no return" to the Deep South. In addition, you knew your loved ones would remain behind and would grieve for you, left with only their memories and prayers. I went back to my room, lit one of the candles Grandmother Goldie had given me, and then for the first time slept under the ancestral quilt. I lay there a while listening to the house as it stood fast against the howling northwest wind. Slowly I felt the warm, soothing spirits of the ancestors fill the emptiness I felt inside. As though she were still alive and in the

flesh, Grandmother Miles appeared sitting on the side of my bed and, as she had done when waking me on my first morning in her home, brushed my forehead with her gentle touch, told me not to worry but to be strong, and said that she and the others would always be with me. That night was the fulfillment of a childhood dream. For the first time, I was really talking to the spirits, and for many years to come in my hours of greatest need, they would be there to guide me.

That summer I turned eighteen, and in the fall after the harvest, I left the farm, though I continue to return to this area of southern Maryland as a source of rejuvenation. I had no way of knowing then how much this dual urban and rural upbringing would mean to the path I would choose in my life's work. I had been both a street kid and a farm boy, and now I was a young man who wanted to see the world.

YOUNG ADULTHOOD, 1955–73

Rather than continue my formal education, I chose to go into the United States Air Force, which took me around the world. I experienced a remarkable cultural and personal awakening during my four-year stay (1955–59) in Paris, France, where I was exposed to the "Negritude" movement, the African and Algerian liberation struggles, and existentialism. Among the many expatriates I met were the writers James Baldwin, Richard Wright, Henry Miller, Lawrence Durrell, and Ernest Hemingway; and the musicians Bud Powell, Sydney Bechet, Kenny Clark, Oscar Pettiford, Quincy Jones, and Memphis Slim. In 1956, a Nigerian woman I was dating took me to the First International Congress of Negro Writers and Artists. I learned about Africa and Africans, and I began to come to grips with the realities of black life in America.

The cumulative effect of these experiences, occurring in a society that seemed to treat African people with dignity and respect, was to give me a new perspective on my own responsibilities. Encouraged by some of my friends who were involved in the African liberation movement, in 1959 I left my leisurely and stimulating Paris life and returned to the United States to become a part of our liberation struggle for civil rights. I was pained to see how little race relations had changed in America, and after a difficult initial reacclamation, I settled in Washington, D.C.

Throughout the 1960s, I was deeply involved in the Civil Rights movement and eager to find a way to make a special contribution to it. Although I had taken some pictures both while I lived with the Mileses and when I was in the Air Force, I had certainly never considered becoming a photographer. However, shortly after the March on Washington in August 1963, I saw a photography exhibit that seemed to capture and communicate what this struggle was all about. While standing in front of those pictures, I decided to become a photographer and to focus on documenting black culture.

I worked hard to add knowledge of photographic history, its past masters, and technical skills to the natural gifts with which I seemed to have been blessed. Friends supported my efforts, and I was hired as the staff photographer for the *Capitol East Gazette* (later called the *D.C. Gazette*). The work of two African-American photographers, Roy DeCarava and Gordon Parks, had a tremendous impact on my work. I also met photographer Burk Uzzle of Magnum Photos, Inc., who opened many doors for me and, along with Gordon, became a primary photographic mentor. Also during this time, Eleanor Ott, then a doctoral student in folklore at the University of Pennsylvania, and still a close friend and colleague, gave me a book called *Visual Anthropology*, which heavily influenced my photography and my sense of direction.

In 1968, I married Marcia Felton, who has shared my life since, and by the end of that year, I felt confident enough in my skills and experience to become a full-time, freelance photographer. Over the subsequent years, I established a successful, mainly commercial, practice, with an emphasis on photojournalism.

CHAPTER 2

Early Photodocumentation (1974–84)

Initial Work in Mississippi, 1974–77

In 1972, I started doing assignments as a field research photographer in folklore for the Smithsonian Institution's Center for Folklife Programs and Cultural Studies. In the spring of 1974 they sent me to Mississippi, the state which was to be featured in that year's Festival of American Folklife. I was teamed up with Worth Long, one of the best fieldworkers in African-American folklife. Our assignment was to survey the state's black folk culture to help the Mississippi State Historical Museum and the Mississippi Department of Archives and History identify and document the people who would represent the state at the Festival in Washington, D.C. We explored many areas of traditional black music and material culture, and my photo-documentation became part of a festival exhibit called *Mississippi: Tradition and Change.*

Meeting Worth Long was the best thing that could have happened to me. While photographing African-American life over the previous ten years, I had been desperately looking for an African-American folklorist who had the same passion for fieldwork that I had. In Mississippi, I realized I had found that person in Worth. We had just left a basketmaker named Lee Willie Nabors who lived near Okolona in the northeast part of the state, in circumstances that confirmed the stereotypical image of the neglect in which folk artists live and die. This experience added to the chagrin we had felt earlier that week in Lexington, when we learned that the blacksmith we'd come to photograph had passed away.

"When the elderly craftspeople pass on," I said to Worth, "it could be the end of these traditions, because very few young black people are interested in learning them. And since we are keenly aware of this and understand their importance, we have a moral obligation to do something about it." Worth jokingly said to me, "Big, hotshot photographer like you? You mean you want to stop working for those big magazines and move to Mississippi just to photograph craftspeople?" I told him that I had become a photographer to document black life. Yes, I was no different from most photographers in wanting to know if I could compete in the major leagues. But now, having proved to myself that I could, I was ready to get back to what I had become a photographer to do. And what could be more important than to document some of the last vestiges of our traditional folk culture? As it turned out, Worth and I were so inspired by our experiences and initial research that we returned to the state a year later to direct an independent study we called "The Mississippi Folklife Project." Thus started a partnership that exists to this day.

At the same time, Dr. Bernice Johnson Reagon and Dr. Gerald Davis were completing their initial development of the African Diaspora Research Project at the Smithsonian Institution. Through her civil rights and singing activities, I had already known Bernice for years and always experienced her as committed, effective, hard-working, steadfast, and clear thinking. Our relationship has continued across the subsequent two decades, and she is one of very few individuals on whom I have regularly relied for valuable advice, encouragement, and support. Her own work—as a cultural and political leader, as a scholar and writer, as founding director of the Program in African-American Culture at the

Smithsonian's National Museum of American History, and with the vocal group "Sweet Honey in the Rock"—has been nationally recognized in her designation as a MacArthur Foundation Fellow and in her receipt of a 1995 Charles Frankel Prize in the Humanities from the National Endowment for the Humanities. Bernice is currently Distinguished Professor of History at American University, Washington, D.C., and Curator Emeritus at the Smithsonian. She is also a quilter and is one of those presented later in this book (see pp. 340ff.).

I had not known Gerald Davis before his work at the Smithsonian, and in fact, he was the first African-American male folklorist I came to know. After leaving the Smithsonian, Gerald became a faculty member in the Department of Africana Studies at Rutgers University in New Jersey and recently moved to the University of New Mexico's Department of American Studies. Our relationship has continued over the years, with Gerald remaining a valuable advisor and supporter.

Having established contacts with Bernice, Gerald, and others, Worth and I felt that our commitment joined us to those African Americans doing similar work. We saw ourselves as a new phenomenon in the folklife world— where most of those involved were white— following a path pioneered by Zora Neale Hurston in the 1920s and 1930s. It was an exciting period: many young African Americans who had had their consciousness raised in the Civil Rights movement were now moving out of the national campaigns and the front lines of marches and were taking their skills and awareness into government, educational, cultural, and financial institutions. Many of us had held hands with and shared the dream of Dr. Martin Luther King Jr. and had sung "We Shall Overcome." Through those experiences we gained collective courage, and believed we had arrived at a point from which we would never turn back. I was inspired by the challenge Bernice had put before a group of African Americans gathered at the Smithsonian Institution. She said there was a lot of misinformation out there about black people, and that it would take a lifetime and more to change it; that we were now

moving onto a new front in our quest for equality and, like those before us who led the way, we could not rest.

It was in the spirit of this commitment that Worth and I returned to Mississippi in the spring of 1975, not to lead a civil rights march or a voter registration drive, but to capture some of the last vestiges of our traditional folklife before the present generation of practitioners passed on. Equipped with a small folk arts grant from the National Endowment for the Arts, some money Worth had received from the Ford Foundation, and my old 1965 Dodge Dart, we embarked on a research project incorporating photodocumentation, interpretation, exhibition, and publication. We decided to focus on the old Natchez district in the southwest corner of the state where colonization and slavery had begun. Our hypothesis was that in this area, known as the Mississippi "Heartland," we should be able to find African-American folklife practices that were continuations of African traditions.

Worth has an amazing sixth sense when it comes to understanding Southern culture. He knew that I was constantly afraid in Mississippi and tried to help me overcome it. He also understood that it was healthy for me to be afraid and that if I weren't careful, my quick temper could get me killed. Thus he took great pains in describing to me the history of the civil rights struggle in the areas in which we were working.

On an early trip we were driving south on Interstate 55 from Brookhaven toward McComb. Worth warned me to watch my speed because he had spotted two state troopers. Even when we were laughing and joking, his eyes never stopped scanning the horizon. I was not going over the speed limit, but we were stopped anyway. One car pulled in front of us and the other stopped behind. Worth cautioned me, "Whatever you do, stay calm." After the troopers examined my license and registration, they asked us to open the trunk and asked where we were going and why. I let Worth do all the talking, and I don't even remember what he said. All I could think of was a young teacher I had met in Marks, Mississippi, in 1968 after Dr. King's assassination, who told me she'd been kicked in the face by a state trooper. They didn't give us a ticket,

Roland L. Freeman and Worth Long during the Mississippi Folklife Project.

HINDS COUNTY, MISSISSIPPI, 1976 (9-14644/33)

but warned us we'd better be careful because folks were watching us.

We proceeded cautiously to McComb, where we stopped to have lunch. Worth then told me the story of how some Student Nonviolent Coordinating Committee (SNCC) workers had been beaten so badly in McComb that SNCC had had to retreat up to the Delta. We left McComb and headed toward Centreville on Highway 48, which passes through a small town called Liberty. As we approached the town,

Worth told me to be especially careful and to drive slowly as we went through it. I liked the way Liberty looked and suggested we explore this area for a while, but Worth then told me about a black man named Herbert Lee who had been working in voter registration and was shot to death in front of the Liberty courthouse in broad daylight by a state legislator named E. R. Hurst. Hurst alleged that Mr. Lee had come at him with a tire iron and that he had shot him in self-defense, but this story was denied by the blacks who witnessed the killing.

Suddenly I lost interest in staying there. Worth started laughing. "If stories like these are going to scare you away from working in a certain area, then you can't work in Mississippi, because there are no areas in the state where similar things have not happened. That's the legacy of our struggle. And if we're going to do this project right, you'll soon find it's a lot more than just photographing quaint old folks making things. These quilters, blacksmiths, basketmakers, and woodcarvers have been making these things in communities where black people were being raped, beaten, and murdered, and over time you will come to understand this the way I do."

It had already become clear to me as we moved throughout the region that even if we couldn't find other craftspeople in a community, there were always quilters. As virtually every home had quilts, made by either a family member or a neighbor, I wouldn't ask people if they quilted; I would simply ask to see their quilts. And it was while looking at them that I would be told who made them—as well as how, when, and why.

In the winter of 1975, I became well acquainted with Julius Mason, a blacksmith in Roxie, Mississippi. Mr. Mason had a clearer understanding of the significance of our project than most people I met, and he constantly asked how he could help us. One day while having lunch with Julius and his wife Viola, I asked them about the quilters in the community. They then arranged for me to meet several women, all of whom did traditional patterns. It was only later that I met Julius' sister-in-law, Annie Mason (see p. 43), who everyone said was the best fancy quilter in the area.

A short time later, while taking a break in his blacksmith shop, Julius was telling me stories about how things used to be and, since many black folk didn't have much money, how his services were often paid for by bartering. When I asked what kinds of things were exchanged, he said, "Here's something I just got from Aunt Betty [Betty Tolbert Taylor (1897–1978), known as Mrs. Tolbert] for those dog irons I made for her fireplace." He pulled a quilt out of a bag, and it just about knocked my eyes out. It was different from most of the quilts I had seen, and it didn't appear to be a variation on a traditional pattern. It was what local people called a "scrap" quilt, made in earth tones, and with more of a design than others of this type I had seen. I wanted to meet this woman, and Mr. Mason pointed out her house, just around the corner. As I approached her front gate, I could barely see a woman sitting on the screened-in porch.

As I attempted to open the gate, she said, "Just hold it right there." I quickly started to introduce myself, but she interrupted, "That's far enough. I know just who you are. You're the one going around taking pictures and asking about all this old-time stuff. Well, I don't feel like talking today, and doubt if I'll feel like it tomorrow." I said I just wanted to ask her about the quilt she had given Mr. Mason, but right then a car with two elderly women, one white and one black, pulled up. The two women got out and came toward the gate, and Mrs. Tolbert opened the screen door and told me she had some business to take care of and to come back another day.

For the next eight months, I returned periodically to Mrs. Tolbert's home, but never got past her front gate. I even asked Mr. Mason to accompany me there, and he told me that, even though she was revered in the community, Aunt Betty was a little on the strange side and wasn't anyone to trifle with. He said, "I know people come from far and near to see her, and she turns most of them away. She isn't about money, she's about doing good." At that moment, I realized Mrs. Tolbert might "work roots," be a healer, or what some people called a "seer." This really increased my curiosity.

Mr. Mason continued, "I've never heard of her putting any bad stuff on anyone. I always try to

Betty Tolbert (1897–1978).
FRANKLIN COUNTY, MISSISSIPPI, 1975 (35 MM CT)

stay on the right side of her, but I doubt if I'm ever going to sleep under this quilt. Since you like it so much, why don't you take it?" I did, and I slept under it that very night, following a practice I had developed of sleeping under all the quilts I collected. That night the faces of Mrs. Tolbert and an older woman I didn't recognize appeared in my dream. They just stared at me, saying nothing. I awoke to a bright and brisk fall morning, with Mrs. Tolbert still on my mind. I drove straight to her house, and, lo and behold, there she was in the front yard washing clothes with a tub and washboard. I got out and said, "How are you today, Aunt Betty? I ran across some pecans and thought you could use a few of them." "That's mighty nice of you, young man. Just put them there on the porch."

I was shocked at her openness. She was talking to me as if she hadn't been putting me off for nearly nine months. As I put the bag of pecans down, I spotted through the doorway a bold red, blue, black, and white quilt on a bed. Returning to the yard, I said, "Couldn't help from noticing that pretty red quilt. Does it have a name?" Without looking up, she said, "Sure does. Would you help me with this tub?" She had finished her washing, and together we poured out the water and rested the tub and washboard up against her house. I mentioned to her that I knew a man who carved washboards out of white oak and she said,

"Yes, I've seen them. My grandmother had one." I was sniffing because the change in the weather had given me a slight cold. Mrs. Tolbert then invited me in, saying, "Let me give you something for that before it gets worse." I was even more surprised and overjoyed, because I had been dying to go inside her house.

She led me through her bedroom right past that quilt into a most unusual room, a combination of kitchen, pantry, living room, and den, all in one and only about fifteen-by-fifteen-feet square. On the north wall was a fireplace, and she asked me to add some wood and stoke the fire.

Trees at Sunset, Fall, 1971, 76" × 62"
Strip quilt by Betty Tolbert.
   (35 mm ct)

There were two windows in the east wall that looked out on a garden. Against the south wall was a white enamel woodburning stove. A big table sat in the middle of the room, covered with all sorts of jars, some holding dried herbs and others containing freshly canned fruits and vegetables. Just below the ceiling, crisscrossing the room, stretched several ropes from which hung many bunches of different herbs. There were piles of clothes, papers, and books everywhere, but it was an orderly mess, the kind of room you didn't want to straighten up because then you wouldn't be able to find things.

Mrs. Tolbert gave me a cup of tea, which I sipped slowly while she sat down by the fireplace, lighting a pipe. I noticed that the tea had a soothing and calming effect on me. Then from out of nowhere, she said, "That's not only good for your cold, it will also help with your blood pressure, so I'll give you some to take with you." I didn't say anything, but I wondered how she knew about my blood pressure problems. While I was still trying to figure that out, she said, "That's a good sleeping quilt of mine you got, isn't it?" I began to feel a little eerie. She went on to say, "That quilt's called *Trees at*

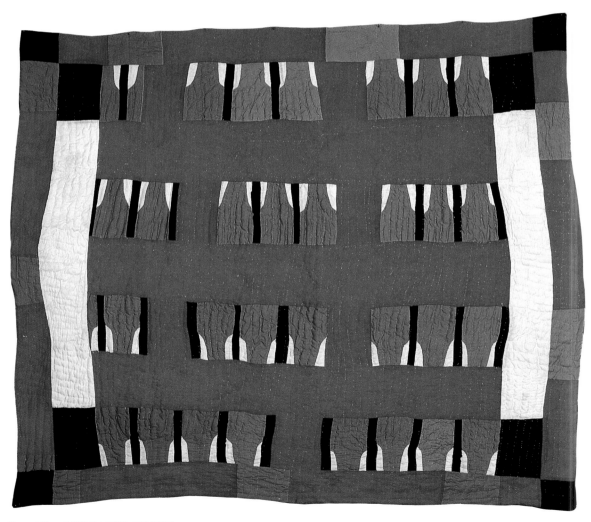

Trees at Sunset, Winter, 1972, 78" × 63"
Strip quilt by Betty Tolbert.
(35 MM CT)

Sunset, Fall, and the red one in there on the bed you asked about earlier is *Trees at Sunset, Winter"* (see pp. 25–26). I asked her to explain the names. "Well, the one you just slept under was done in the fall when all the leaves were turning. That's why I put those colors in it." Then she got up and led me to the front porch, saying, "I'm going to show you something."

The sun was setting. "See that red sun behind those trees? That's where I got the idea for the quilt. I saw my grandmother's spirit." I asked what she meant. "Well, the last thing I remember doing with my grandmother was picking some pecans, and on our way home a red winter sun was going down, and she told me, 'That's the last sunset I'm going to see, and I'm going to have to pass the gift on to you.' She then said she wished there was more time to teach me more." Then Mrs. Tolbert took me back into the bedroom where she carefully explained, "The way I do these quilts is when the spirits talk to me." I repeated, "The spirits talk to you." "Yes, you know what I mean. They talk to you, too. That's why you're here." She saw me looking at her in a puzzled way and went on. "Isn't that why you came here today, because my grandmother's spirit

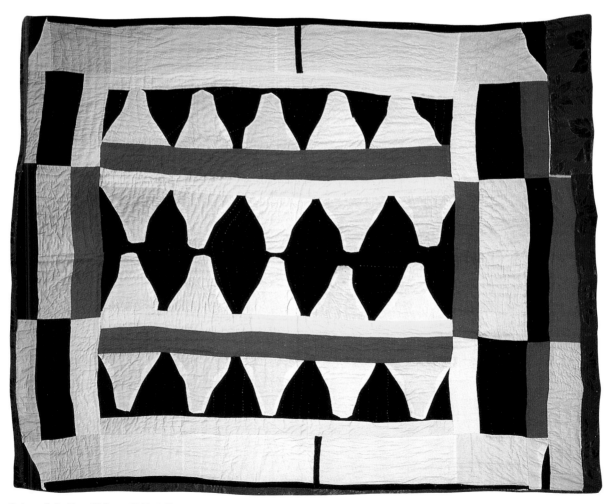

Strip quilt by Betty Tolbert, 1960, 75" × 64".
(35 mm ct)

told you to bring me some pecans and to get this other quilt? You see, the one you slept under was *Trees at Sunset, Fall,* and this one is *Trees at Sunset, Winter.* It was made in the winter without any leaves on the trees, just like now."

She then continued explaining how she makes some of her quilts. Following her inspiration, she would cut out her pieces and arrange them in a pattern on her bed. In this way she could be sure she got it the way she wanted before sewing it together. She said this was the same way her grandmother designed her quilts. I asked how she quilted them, and she first said, "Well my aunt had a quilting frame that hung from the ceiling, and me and my sisters would help her. But Grandmama never used no quilting frame. After she pieced the top, she'd either sit here by the bed and just quilt it plain, or do it on her lap. She never did use a frame, and that's how I quilt now." She then said that for a while she had made the traditional patterns, using a quilting frame like her aunt, and she showed me a few she had made years ago (see p. 27). However, I was far more excited by her quilts inspired by dreams and spirits.

She never did tell me how she knew that Mr. Mason had given me her quilt and that I had seen her and her grandmother in my dream. I didn't feel a need to press the question, and I was grateful and pleased that she was finally extending me an intimacy beyond my expectations. The steady flow of tea was soothing, and I was beginning to feel hungry. As if reading my mind, she asked, "Feel like something to eat?" "Yes," I replied, "I could use a little something." She said, "Won't be no trouble. Everything's ready anyway, just got to heat it up." We had smothered catfish, cornbread, greens, and more tea. We didn't sit at the table, but ate from plates in our laps right there by the fireplace. Mrs. Tolbert gave me a fork, but she ate with her hands. This was about the third time I'd noticed old folks in Mississippi eating with their hands, so I decided to try it too. She noticed and smiled.

She asked where I was staying, and I told her about Abraham Hunter, a farmer in Wilkinson County. She said, "No sense in your driving all the way back there tonight. You might as well stay

Worth Long and Beulah Smith.
PIKE COUNTY, MISSISSIPPI, NOVEMBER 1975 (3-13285/9)

here." I was very tired and accepted her invitation. With that settled, she began telling me about her life on the railroad. She had been married to a man who was part of a railroad gang that traveled around doing track maintenance. She traveled with them, working as a cook. She explained that the crews lived in railroad cars, one of which had a kitchen and dining room. She went into great detail about how blacks and whites ate in separate areas in the dining car, how the sleeping quarters were arranged, how the men sang and gambled and played around at night, and how she doctored them, both black and white, when they got sick or busted up in a fight.

Being the only woman in this group created problems for both her and her husband:

> We were making good money, we had good times, and all the fellas respected me, except the white boss man. Soon as the fellas was out working, he'd be coming after me, and I'd have to fight him off every day. This fool made me every offer you could think of, and when it got so bad I didn't think I could handle it anymore, I thought I'd leave before he raped me, and my husband found

out about it. See, you got to remember how things were.

My husband was a rough brawler, a big, strong, strapping guy, and in a fight he could handle two or three men. And if he'd found out that cracker was bothering me, he would've broken his neck. And then, of course, the white folks would've killed my man. So I played like I was sick and had to go home, and left. But I'll have you know, that crazy white man didn't have no shame. He wanted me so bad, he came all the way here looking for me. I got word of it and had to leave, and went over and spent some time with my sister in Vidalia, Louisiana. When my husband came to see about me and found out what happened, he never went back to his good railroad job. And that's a true story.

And on that note, she took me into her second bedroom, showed me where to wash up, and said good night.

I stood for a long time at the foot of the bed, staring in utter amazement at the quilt on it, wondering what could have possibly inspired this design (see p. 27). In the center were double vertical rows of big white and black conical shapes, flanked on each side by yellow and red stripes, and then a single row of the conical shapes outside them. The wide border had different-sized blocks of white, black, and tan fabric, and the quilt was backed with a heavy maroon material used for draperies.

I was very tired and drifted off into a deep sleep. I dreamed about Swayback, my old childhood mentor, the first African American I knew who had been to Africa. Swayback had never come to me in a dream before, but this night here he was as plain as day, saying, "You used to be so curious about down South, well you're deep in the thick of it now, boy! But don't be afraid. Trust these people, you are in good hands. Listen carefully and you will learn. Hold your camera steady so you can see past the eyes." Then a sudden noise woke me up.

I caught the scent of sausage cooking and heard Mrs. Tolbert moving about in the kitchen. I got up, dressed, and joined her. She asked with a

Janie Nichols (18??–1976).
JEFFERSON COUNTY, MISSISSIPPI, 1975 (20-13262/33)

smile, "How did you sleep?" I sensed she already knew and merely said, "That's some quilt I slept under." She acknowledged with a long "Uh-huh," and I asked what inspired the pattern. She said, "Don't feel like talking about that right now. Expecting someone here in about an hour who might need some serious help." I thanked her for the wonderful hospitality and said my good-byes.

A very congenial ninety-five-year-old white man, a veritable walking encyclopedia, had told Worth and me about Beulah Smith, who made animal figurines from clay. We finally located her in the middle of the afternoon, just in time to rescue a quilt. As we arrived, she was preparing to use what she called a "summer" quilt as batting for another quilt she was making. Later in this project, I realized this was a common practice and that inside some of the heavier quilts are some wonderful old ones. She explained to us that she really didn't have any more use for this lightweight quilt, and as she didn't have money to buy new batting, she was going to use it as the filler for her new quilt. I immediately offered to go buy her some batting if she would sell me this quilt. And that's how we saved a unique folk quilt.

Mrs. Smith told us that someone passing through had bought all of her figures a while back and she no longer made them. She directed us to other quilters in Tobeytown, and that same day we met Lillian Baker, who didn't want to be photographed. However, she proudly showed us some of her decorative quilts, which were nicely sewn traditional patterns. Then I asked if she had any scrap quilts, and she replied, "I do have a few old things I throw together from time to time." Even though she didn't think much of these and couldn't imagine what our interest was in them, Worth really liked a strip quilt she had made in 1968, and we bought it.

One cool November day in 1975, as we were leaving Fayette on Route 33, Worth was trying to show me how to follow my sixth sense. "Sometimes you see things that dictate you should investigate further." Down an embankment just to the right of the road sat a little white shotgun house, so-called because the rooms and the doors to those rooms usually fall into a straight line, and a bullet would go straight through them all. He suggested that he wait in the car while I went inside.

I was greeted by Annie Turner, a soft-spoken woman in her seventies who invited me in and listened attentively as I explained our project. I found out that she was a quilter, but at the time didn't have any of her own quilts. However, she still had two that were made by her mother and showed them to me. I asked when they were made, and Annie said, "Oh, they've been around just about as long as I have." I then asked when her mother had passed, and she chuckled, "Mama's still with us. She's in bed right in the next room." When I inquired about her age, I got the shock of my life. She said her mother, Janie Nichols, was 108. I had never met anyone over

95, and I'm sure my excitement was showing. When I asked to speak to Miss Nichols, she warned me that her mother's mind often drifted. However, I was able to get a few questions answered. She had been born on the Whitney plantation where she lived for about 102 years.

When I returned to the car, Worth could see the excitement on my face. I blurted out, "I've just met Janie Nichols, who was born right after the Civil War. She has two old quilts, and I don't know how old they are, but I'm more interested in all that good history she's got. Her daughter has asked me to come back in a few days, and I want you to do the interview because you're better at asking questions."

When Worth and I returned, Annie's brother Warren had come to have his picture made with his mother as well. It was very pleasing to see the pride with which this brother and sister prepared their mother to be photographed; I first shot them all together, and later Miss Nichols by herself. I asked if we could put one of her quilts on her lap for a picture, and Miss Nichols responded, "Oh, this is just one of those Friendship quilts I made during the depression" (see p. 29).

She had seemed very excited, but as Worth attempted to interview her again she became more and more frustrated because she couldn't stay focused. She finally said to him, "I'm sorry, young man. I have trouble remembering things these days." Because I had been making such a fuss over the old friendship quilt, Annie said, "If you like it that much, why don't you take it?" Her brother, however, was hard-pressed to understand why I would even want it. It's true the quilt was tattered and very fragile, but I explained that at some point I would probably put it on exhibit as something made by the oldest person I'd met on this project. He said, "Well, I hope you clean it first." Annie added, "If he tries to wash that quilt, it'll fall completely apart."

This was one of the first quilts I collected, and I brought it back to the Smithsonian Institution in Washington, D.C., to be archivally cleaned. I then slept under it for the first time. Maybe my expectations were too high, but nothing happened: no dreams, no visitations from the spirits. I jokingly told myself that having it

Fancy Pants, 1970, 70" × 60"
Strip quilt by Betty Tolbert.
(35 mm ct)

cleaned that way had destroyed its soul, and I have never done that again.

The Whitney plantation where Miss Nichols had been born became known later as Whitney Hill. Her father, Willis Nichols, had bought some land there and built two houses. This land stayed in the family until her brother Charles got into some trouble with the law and was jailed. Having very little cash, most of the brothers and sisters decided to put up the land as collateral for his bail. Somehow, in the legal process, the land was lost.

Miss Nichols had very little formal education and had never traveled more than fifty miles from her birthplace. She had had five children by two different common-law husbands. At one point, she remembered the names of all her midwives. The church she now attended was started in a brush arbor, an outdoor shelter made of poles and roofed with branches and brush to ward off the sun. Logs were used for seats. She had outlived everyone on Whitney Hill where she had been born. She'd never been to a hospital and started seeing a regular doctor only after leaving her homeplace at 102 to come and live with her daughter.

In the winter of 1976, Miss Nichols had a stroke that paralyzed her throat and made it

Fancy Horseshoe, 1975, 76" × 75"
Strip quilt by Betty Tolbert.
(35 mm ct)

difficult for her to eat and communicate. On March 14, 1976, Miss Nichols passed away in her sleep. There was standing room only at her funeral. I photographed the funeral procession as it entered the church, but didn't feel comfortable taking pictures during the service.

There were different estimations of Miss Nichols's age; some people thought she was 113, some 108. Even some members of her family said that it seemed she had stayed 85 for a number of years, which contributed to the uncertainty about her age. The uncertainty led me to the census records at the Mississippi Department of Archives and History. Assisted by the chief archivist, Ann

Lipscomb, I found Willis Nichols in the 1880 U.S. Census, age 57, married to Julia Nichols, age 38, with seven children: Charley, 18; Emily, 16; Penny, 14; Jane, 10; Heywood, 7; Rosa A., 3; and Howard, 1. The 1890 census for most of the United States had been destroyed, so we then checked 1900.

Willis Nichols does not appear in 1900, and Julia Ann Nichols is listed as head of household, now 68 and having had fourteen children, with nine still living. Janie's age is listed, not as 30 as we would expect, but as 21. She also now has three children, all with the last name of Hudson: Henry, 8; Nathan, 6; and Willie, 4. In the 1920 census Janie Nichols is listed as a head of household, age 48, (rather than either 41 or 50) along with her two youngest children, Annie Turner, 13, and Warren Turner, 10.*

Miss Nichols's official obituary read:

> It was the will of the Great and Almighty God that Sister Janie Nichols departed this life on Sunday, March 14, 1976 at 9:20 A.M. at Jefferson County Hospital in Fayette, Mississippi. She was born May 10, 1867 in Jefferson County, Mississippi. She united with the Hollywood Baptist Church in 1880. Her membership there encompassed 95 years of faithful service. She enjoyed life and lived it to the fullest. This was quite evident in her recollections of her past 108 years. Sister Nichols loved her pastor and deacons. She often asked about and spoke highly of them. She also loved her church. There was no generation gap between "Big Mama," as she was fondly called, and her grandchildren, great-grandchildren and great-great-grandchildren. She leaves to mourn her passing a daughter, Annie Turner of Fayette, Mississippi; a son, Warren Turner of Fayette, Mississippi; 23 grandchildren; 100 great-grandchildren; 57 great-great-grandchildren; and a multitude of nieces, nephews, relatives, and friends.

Victoria Bennett (1885–1989).
WILKINSON COUNTY, MISSISSIPPI, 1976 (11-13733/19)

Mrs. Tolbert had been on my mind a lot, and by the time I returned to Mississippi in late January 1976, I'd had several dreams about her and her quilts. Worth was heading to Warren County to explore several leads, and as quite often happened, we split up and I went south to Roxie. I arrived at Mrs. Tolbert's just before lunch. She was in, but had company, and said she'd be done soon and to wait around town because she wanted to talk with me.

When I returned, she said, "Have I got something to show you!" She took me back to the

*These kinds of descrepancies are not uncommon in African-American genealogical research. The records are only as good as the accuracy of the information provided and how that information has been interpreted and documented by the census taker.

bedroom where I had slept. Spread across the bed was a red and white quilt. "My God, Mrs. Tolbert, what's this about?" She explained that years ago her husband had gotten a horseshoe from Mr. Mason and then nailed it just above the screen door inside the front porch for good luck. After dreaming about him for several nights, she'd found herself sitting on the front porch staring at his good-luck horseshoe over the door. She decided then and there to make this quilt, called *Fancy Horseshoe*. She then showed me another quilt that she called *Fancy Pants* (see p. 31), which was inspired by her husband's dressing up when they were going out on Saturdays.

While I was still trying to absorb all of this, something shocking happened. She took my hand and looked right in my eyes, saying, "I've been thinking a lot about what you're doing,

Mary Handy *(right)* with her two daughters in front of her house.
AMITE COUNTY, MISSISSIPPI, 1976 (35 MM CT)

taking these pictures and all, and I've been talking with Julius [Mason], and I want you to have these two quilts. A lot of white folks been through here trying to get them, but I want you to have them. Julius says you're going to show them in a museum up there in Jackson. You write down just what I told you about them."

After a few days in Roxie, I headed south again. As Highway 33 South leaves Franklin County it crosses the Homochitto River. Driving this road before, I had frequently seen an old lady walking. Now I spotted her once again, heading up a gravel road toward a small frame house. She stopped on her front porch and waited for me as I drove up the road. Her name was Victoria Bennett, and she was affectionately called "Aunt Vic." She invited me in. She said she had seen me at a church taking pictures, and that's why she wasn't afraid of me. Without my asking, she started to pull out some of her quilts. I jokingly asked her why, and she answered, "Word gets around. You are the one interested in quilts, aren't you? I don't make no fancy quilts, but I do make them warm" (see p. 33).

Mrs. Bennett was one of six children born to Leannie Shine Jones and Cy Jones in Alabama, near the town of Snow Hill in Wilcox County. Her mother, Leannie, was a prolific quilter and a good seamstress, and she made all of her children's clothes. Victoria never had any children of her own. However, she was given a baby girl named Rosie, whom she raised for five years. When Victoria's curiosity and adventurous spirit took her to Chicago for a brief spell, she left Rosie with her own mother. Victoria came back south as a cook in logging camps, where she met her husband, John Bennett. For a number of years Victoria and John sharecropped around lower Mississippi, until her hot temper caused her to hit the white boss in the head with a hoe for cheating them out of their share. As she told it, "I just got sick and tired of working for nothing and being in the hole. We was making good crops and not running up any extra bills; plus I was always making extra money by sewing for people and making quilts, but the white folk always had a way of figuring out things so we still owed them. I don't know what came over me. I just said I wanted some money and I wanted it now, and I went after him. Didn't do no time [in jail]; just had to move on."

Over the years I would always stop and see Victoria. She spent her last few years in Birmingham, Alabama, with Rosie Jones Oliver, now 79, the woman who had been given to her as a baby. Victoria Bennett died on September 5, 1989, during her 104th year, and is buried at the

Elmwood Cemetery in Birmingham. With eyesight failing, she made her last quilt in 1988 as a gift for Rosie's granddaughter.

Highway 33 South from Fayette to Centreville had become one of my favorite routes. It passes through Gloster, in Amite County. In late March 1976, I picked up a man named Mr. Thompson who had run out of gas. He told me about several basketmakers and quilters who lived in the area. Following his lead, I ventured out the old Berwick Gloster Road looking for Mrs. Katie Handy. About three miles outside Gloster, I found her.

After I introduced myself, she informed me that she didn't quilt anymore and wasn't really interested in getting out any of her old ones, but she did direct me to her daughter-in-law, Mrs. Mary Handy. I hit it off with Mary right away. She told me that it was about time I got around to her. Six months earlier while she had been shopping in town, an agricultural extension worker had pointed me out to her and told her what I was doing. She said to me, "I know exactly what you're up to." Mrs. Handy was a widow with twelve children, and lived in an old wood-frame house. She explained that she had

Rainbow Block, 1975, 96" × 85"
Strip quilt by Mary Handy.
(35 MM CT)

been sewing on something as long as she could remember. She laughingly said, "With as many chaps as I have running around here, I have to make a lot of quilts to keep them warm." Her quilts ran the gamut from fancy and decorative on the one hand to scrap and throw-together on the other. She made a king-size quilt that she called a "feel good" quilt for my queen-size bed, which I gave to my wife that Christmas. It's blue and beige, and I've slept under it more than any other quilt I own. I've had many pleasant dreams under this quilt, and it is truly something that keeps me warm, in more ways than I know how to describe.

One of my fondest memories of this family concerns two of her sons who had graduated from college and were having difficulty finding jobs in Mississippi. While doing a photo-journalism assignment on offshore drilling for *Black Enterprise* magazine, I met a black oilman from Lafayette, Louisiana, who was desperately looking for some young black men with college degrees to work for him. I called Mrs. Handy from Lafayette and asked her two sons to come down. They did and were hired immediately. As a

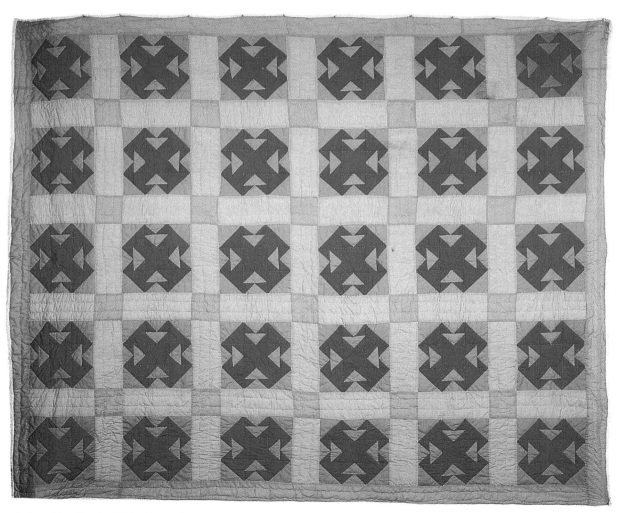

Quilt by Mary Handy, 1976, 90" × 105"
(35 mm ct)

result of this employment, the entire family began to construct a six-bedroom brick house on what Mrs. Handy called her "pay-as-you-build plan." Each payday her two sons would buy all the building materials they could afford, and then all her children and a few neighbors would work together. Using this plan, by the time the house was completed in 1979, it was paid for. On my last visit, Mrs. Handy told me, "Praise the Lord, I finally got space enough to hang a quilting frame I can leave up."

Doloroso is a small community in Wilkinson County on Highway 61 just south of the Homochitto River. There a black man named Wyatt Barnes owned a grocery store that I frequented. One April day an old man named Mr. Robinson saw me there and asked me for a ride. He lived about two miles west of Highway 61 on a gravel road known as the Univesta Baptist Church Road. Funny how word gets around. He knew just what I was interested in, and before I could start my customary line of questioning, he started telling me about some basketmakers and a quilter named Annie Dennis. He'd been sick that winter, and Mrs. Dennis had made him a quilt. After I'd driven about a mile and a half, he told me to pull over on the left side of the road and park. He told me to come on and meet Mrs. Dennis. We found her sitting on the front porch of her house piecing a quilt top. After being introduced, she gladly showed me her beautiful quilts, most of which were what she called fancy quilts. She said she had learned as a little girl from her mother, who was now ninety-two and was still piecing quilts daily. She said if I'd like to meet her, she'd take me over there (see p. 38).

We headed back out to Highway 61, drove south for about two miles, and then turned left at Sanders Fork. We went down Cold Spring Road, a gravel road, about two more miles until we reached the land owned by her family in the Piney Creek area. We found her mother, Phoeba Johnson, and Mrs. Johnson's young great-grandson, whom they called "Pete" (his real name was Arthur Johnson), standing in the yard waiting for us. I didn't know many people in their nineties, but Mrs. Johnson didn't look a day over

Annie Dennis.
WILKINSON COUNTY, MISSISSIPPI, 1977 (35 MM CT)

seventy to me. For the next three hours, we did nothing but look at and talk about quilts. Mrs. Johnson was sharp, had a keen memory, and loved to talk about her experiences.

One day in May 1976, as I was thinking about how completely overwhelmed I was by the joy of knowing this family, the telephone rang. It was my wife calling to tell me that Jeannetta Chase had died of a heart attack. As crazy as it sounds, my first reaction was disbelief. Gone was the person who had first made me aware of the importance of our history and culture.

On the plane back to Washington, my mind kept replaying those wonderful days under her inspired tutelage. Aside from my grandmother Goldie, Jeannetta was the only family member I had ever seriously talked with about quilting and

Annie Dennis, with three quilts hanging outside her home.
WILKINSON COUNTY, MISSISSIPPI, 1977 (35 MM CT)

my dreams. Arriving at the old home place in Maryland was like stepping back in time. In many ways this was like a sacred place to me. Jeannetta was loved by many, and they were all present; those not in the flesh were there in spirit. Following the family tradition, her body was placed in the living room and people attended the wake throughout the night. I sat up all night in the room with her body. In one corner of the room, a quilt had been placed on a small table. When I examined it closely, I discovered that it wasn't the ancestral quilt Grandmother Miles had used at evening prayers, but rather the Log Cabin quilt on which Jeannetta had embroidered the names of African-American leaders.

In the midst of all this, something truly strange and wonderful happened—a communion of our spirits. Jeannetta's body was still lying in the room, and I was sitting near her, but our spirits were in another space. The experience was different from what had happened the night after we buried Grandmother Miles, and I didn't feel as strange about it. I proceeded to tell Jeannetta all about my Mississippi project and the wonderful quilters I was meeting, and she just smiled and said, "I told you one day you'd be a fine historian. I just didn't know you'd do it through photography." Then our spirits drifted apart and I

found myself still sitting and looking at her body. It was now morning.

I didn't know that this would be the last time I would see Jeannetta's black-history quilt. All of her quilts were put in storage in the attic of her house but disappeared while the house was rented out. Mrs. Miles's ancestral quilt was also lost when in the early 1980s the family home burned down. And as so often happens, no one, including me, had ever thought to photograph these quilts.

Returning to Mississippi proved to be good medicine. Worth and I rented an apartment in Jackson, and worked from there. Early on, I met Mrs. Martin, a quilter who lived right across the street from us.

I visited Phoeba Johnson often, and if I didn't stop to see her at least once a week, she was on the telephone to Washington to see if something had happened to me; and if I visited Annie but not her, she'd have a fit. Mrs. Johnson had severe arthritis in her hands, which kept her from quilting, but it didn't stop her from piecing quilt tops daily on her sewing machine. Of her three daughters, only two quilted: Annie and her sister Emma Russell, who lived in Louisiana.

Annie and Phoeba talked so much about me that Emma sent word for me to come and visit her and her husband; but I soon learned that there was going to be a big family gathering for Mrs. Johnson's ninety-third birthday on August 27, 1976. I tried to think of something special to give Mrs. Johnson. I remembered that she had once taught school on old Lake Mary plantation, near where the Homochitto River joins the Mississippi, and then, over a twenty-five-year period, had also taught at four other schools in Wilkinson County. I decided to use some connections I had been developing to get Mrs. Johnson some special recognition. By now, word of our project had spread, and I was able to arrange for Governor Cliff Finch to send her an official letter of appreciation for her contributions to the state as an educator and craftswoman. This letter was read at her birthday party and it really shocked the family. Nothing like this had ever happened in this area to a black person. After that, folks who had been reluctant to talk began stopping me everywhere I went.

I was fascinated with Mrs. Johnson's first name, Phoeba, and wanted to know how she had gotten it. She had been named after her great-

Mrs. Martin showing quilt to neighborhood kids at her home on the corner of Central and Hughes Streets.
HINDS COUNTY, MISSISSIPPI, 1976 (17-15274/12)

Emma Russell, quilter, and her husband Will Henry Russell (1905–90).
BIENVILLE PARISH, LOUISIANA, 1976 (15-15690/23)

grandmother Phoeba Mae (b. ca. 1814), who had been a slave on the Eastern Shore of Maryland and was later sold to a family in Virginia. Phoeba Mae had a daughter named Tomasie (known as "Thomsy"), born in 1830, who was sold at the age of fourteen to the Phipps family in Mississippi, where she became the plantation seamstress. Mrs. Johnson said Thomsy had learned to sew from her mother, Phoeba Mae, who made dresses for white people and also made fancy quilts for and with them.

As Mrs. Johnson told it, the white plantation owner, John Phipps, had two sons by Thomsy: Isaac (b. 1850), who became Phoeba's father, and George (b. 1859). Both sons were raised in their father's house and taught to read and write. Then Phoeba began to talk about her mother, Virginia, who was also the product of a mixed union.

Virginia Dawson was the daughter of one of the Dawson brothers from a neighboring plantation and a black cook who had died shortly after giving

Virginia Dawson (1856–1944), mother of Phoeba Johnson. Photo courtesy of Annie Dennis.

WILKINSON COUNTY, MISSISSIPPI (14-15274/3)

Isaac Phipps (1850–1924), father of Phoeba Johnson. Photo courtesy of Annie Dennis.

WILKINSON COUNTY, MISSISSIPPI (14-15274/2)

Phoeba Johnson (1883–1984).

WILKINSON COUNTY, MISSISSIPPI, 1976 (3-15595/34)

birth to Virginia in June 1856. It is reported that Virginia's father was so upset by the death of her mother that he decided to leave Mississippi, and he asked his brother to raise Virginia. It is also reported that though he left money with his brother to have her educated, the brother never did.

Mrs. Johnson made it very clear that her father, Isaac, had fared much better than her mother, because he and his brother were acknowledged by their white father and while growing up were afforded privileges enjoyed by few other blacks in their community. Isaac and Virginia grew up in the same church and fell in love in their early teens. As Mrs. Johnson related, "When Isaac turned seventeen, he went to the Dawson place and stole Virginia away one evening, and they eloped. The Dawsons did not like it, but were afraid to come up against the Phippses." Virginia and Isaac, who later became a minister, were the parents of seven children: Cornelia (b. 1876); Lewis; Elisabeth (b. 1880); Phoeba; Henry (b. 1885); Joseph (b. 1889); and John (b. 1895). Phoeba said her father had also learned to sew from his mother, and that when she was young he would often join them at the quilting frame. He also made some of his own

clothes. Isaac died on May 10, 1924, and Virginia died twenty years later. Both are buried in the Phipps cemetery, which is located on the land where Isaac was born and raised.

In a later interview, I asked Phoeba about some of her quilt patterns. One of her quilts looked like links of chain. She explained that this reminded her of a family heirloom quilt that had a similar pattern of brown and black links on a white background, with just a little color in the border. She added that the family affectionately called this heirloom the "Slave Chain" quilt, and that her great-grandmother Phoeba had given it to her daughter when she was sold down South. When I asked to see this quilt, Mrs. Johnson suddenly became very sad and told me that this old quilt had worn out and that the last piece of it had been put in her brother's casket when he died. She went on to say that when she started making the new quilt, she had meant to use dark material, but it depressed her too much. And even though she knew it resembled an oblong Double Wedding Ring pattern, she thought of it as the Slave Chain.

At Mrs. Johnson's birthday party, I finally met her daughter Emma. She again invited me to visit her

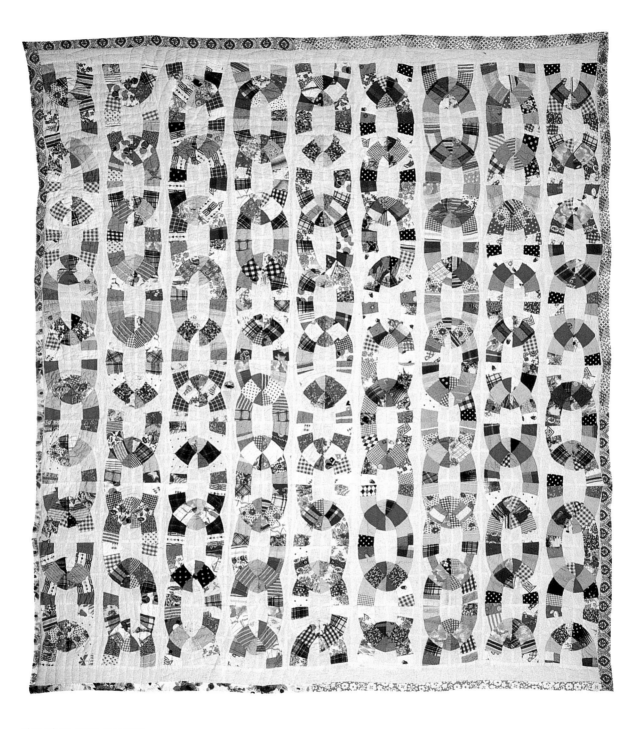

Slave Chain, 1969, 81" × 67"
Quilt by Phoeba Johnson.
   (35 MM CT)

Annie Mason (1896–1984).
FRANKLIN COUNTY, MISSISSIPPI, 1976 (35 MM CT)

and her husband in Louisiana, and early that fall I did (see pp. 39 and 91). Several memorable things happened during this visit. First, I learned that her husband helped her quilt. Second, Emma told me wonderful stories about her life growing up on a farm in Mississippi, and she had started piecing a quilt top that reflected some of those memories. One section of the quilt had a squirrel on a tree stump. Emma explained, "Oh, that's the pet squirrel that the kids at school used to feed." Next to it was a person falling off a horse that she said no one could ride. In the middle of the quilt I noticed two figures holding a quilt pattern. When I asked about them, she burst out laughing, "That's me and Mattilee."

Mattilee Knight was a neighbor of Phoeba Johnson's who had grown up almost like a sister to Annie and Emma. Emma said that she and Mattilee enjoyed piecing quilts so much that they would hook school and go sit in a cave in the woods and piece all day. When I returned to Mississippi, I wanted to ask Mrs. Knight about this story, but she was hesitant to talk with me. Her husband didn't

Annie Mason (1896–1984) sitting on her porch with quilts on the clothesline.
FRANKLIN COUNTY, MISSISSIPPI, 1976 (35 MM CT)

understand the project and had forbade Mattilee to let me photograph or talk to her.

One day, while exploring the Utica area, I noticed some quilt tops hanging on a clothes line outside the home of Ms. Edna Mae Jones. I introduced myself to Ms. Jones and over time got to know her and her family.

In August 1976, Spring Hill Baptist Church near Roxie was preparing for its annual baptism, and I was photographing some of the people who had gathered for the baptismal procession. I spotted a woman dressed in white and stooped down to get a head shot of her without any other people in the background. As I went to take the picture, I noticed that the cross on the church was framed just above her head. Normally I would not have considered this a good photograph, but it felt right, so I took it. When I approached the lady to get her name, she said, "You know me, you've been asking about me for about a year. You know Julius, the

blacksmith? Well, I'm his sister-in-law, Annie Mason. I know you're anxious to see my quilts, so you can come by later today, but I have a family reunion to go to right after church." So I went to the reunion with her, made a group picture, and afterward took her home. She lived in a double-barrel shotgun house just south of Roxie.

I returned a couple of weeks later, and found Mrs. Mason sitting on her front porch with her daughter-in-law, Rosie, and her great-grand-children who lived near her. She was all excited because her grandson Isaiah, who was living in San Bernardino, California, had told her that he wanted to preserve her house just as it was and make it into a family museum. I had midday dinner and supper that evening with them, and we talked late into the night about local history and genealogy. She really did make some beautiful quilts, but I was more interested in the older patchwork ones she did not consider beautiful. She too no longer quilted, and she wanted to keep all she had for her family.

The Divinity family (these are nine grandchildren and one great-grandchild of quilter Edna Mae Jones). *Clockwise (left to right):* George, Arlene, Dexter, Sherlene, Leroy Jr., Edna Mae Jones (1919–88), Llewellyn (baby), Charlesetta, Edward, Linda, Dewitt, and Gregory.
HINDS COUNTY, MISSISSIPPI, 1976 (6-14664/17)

Charlotte Smith's quilt.
FRANKLIN COUNTY, MISSISSIPPI, AUGUST 1976 (12-15128/19)

Charlotte Smith.
FRANKLIN COUNTY, MISSISSIPPI, AUGUST 1976 (35 MM CT)

At about this same time, I photographed Charlotte Smith and her quilts.

Sometime in mid-August I was back in Doloroso looking for a basketmaker named Hal Barnes. After I spent most of the morning with him, his wife, Hettie, asked me to stay for lunch. Among her many strip quilts, she had one that was backed with old fertilizer sacks. Quilters often backed their quilts with either bleached or dyed flour and feed-sack material, but I thought this one was special because the fertilizer sacks showed an image of a black man playing a banjo and the words from a Stephen Foster song, "I Hear 'Em Callin' Old Black Joe" (see p. 46). I made such a fuss over this quilt that Mrs. Barnes said, "Anyone who likes this old thing that much

ought to have it," and she gave it to me. It was that evening that I photographed Hettie Barnes's granddaughter plaiting her grandmother's hair, a picture that was to become one of the most admired images from the Mississippi Folklife Project.

Early that fall Annie Dennis asked me to give her a ride to see Cleola McFarland, who lived about one mile away off Highway 61 South. Mrs. Dennis thought I would want to meet her and see her quilts, which she described as being different. Mrs. McFarland was a stout, medium-height woman in her late fifties, with long, straight, white hair. She told me her grandmother was an Indian who had married a black man. Mrs. McFarland said that Annie Dennis had gotten her into quilting. She added that even though her grandmother, mother, aunts, and sisters had all quilted, she didn't have much interest in it growing up. She had moved to St. Louis in her late teens and returned to Mississippi about ten years ago with her husband, who was a retired railroad worker. After being encouraged by Mrs. Dennis, she started quilting.

Mrs. McFarland's quilts didn't have the

ordered symmetry I saw in the work of most other women in this community (see pp. 47–48). As she said, "I just sew them whatever way I happen to feel at the time. I like them bright and heavy. My quilts won't only make you warm; if you aren't careful, you'll burn up under them." She smiled and continued, "When you start getting old, it takes a lot more fire to keep you warm. You ought to get one of these for you and your wife to sleep under, and you'll find out what I'm talking about."

Later that fall, while exploring the area around Hermanville in Claiborne County, I located Malissa Banks, a quilter in her early seventies (see p. 49). I could never get her to talk much about how she started quilting or why she made quilts the way she did. She said, "Mama quilted and I've been quilting as long as I can remember." The day I met her she had about eight tops she had just finished piecing together but had not yet quilted.

The first thing that came to my mind was that they looked like modern paintings (see pp. 50–52). They were all done in black and white or in dark, muted colors. When I questioned her about the colors and patterns, she said that a lady friend had brought her a big bag of scraps and these were from that bag. She went on to say, "I don't have any names for these patterns. I just arranged the materials so it would look good and this is what happened." I was fascinated by Mrs. Banks's style and visited her several times. She was always willing to let me photograph her, but she never had much to say about her life or what quilting meant to her. In an interview she did five years later with Patricia Morris, published in the magazine *I Ain't Lyin'*, Mrs. Banks explained something about cleaning tacked quilts that I'd never heard before. Unlike most others, a tacked quilt is not sewn through the top, batting, and back with many hundreds of tiny stitches. Instead, it is held together by a few knotted stitches that may be five inches or more from one another in any direction. Mrs. Banks expressed a preference for tacking her quilts, because it was faster than quilting and made them easier to clean. "And see, if you want [to] wash them, you can clip all of these a-loose, and then wash the materials and then tack them back. See, it be too

Hettie Barnes and her granddaughter.
WILKINSON COUNTY, MISSISSIPPI, AUGUST 1976 (5-15274/25A)

heavy to go in a machine. You go to the wash house and wash them and then dry them and come back and spread it on the bed and put that back on there and get to tacking."

In February 1977, I decided it was time to explore the area around Raymond. It was here that I met Suttie Nelson, a quilter in her mid-sixties. She had the usual array of what I called "common" quilts, meaning variations on traditional patterns. After knowing her for several months, however, she showed me a quilt she called *Rainbow Strips*. It was totally different from her others. When I asked her about it, she said it was inspired by a beautiful rainbow that had appeared after a summer storm.

Just then her husband brought in a sack of raw cotton and said, "Suttie asked me to put this aside, because the next time you came through she wanted to show you how they used to make batting." Suttie then spoke up, "Since you're interested in old-time stuff, let me show you how they used to whip cotton to make batting." She got out a big piece of cloth, took it out into the yard, and dumped the cotton on it. She then took several small, flexible branches her husband had taken off a tree and began to whip the cotton, explaining that this was the way her grandmother and mother used to do it. "You see, you just whip this cotton until it's nice and fluffy. Then you just spread it out and lay the top on it you're going to quilt. Then you hook it to your quilting frame, roll it up and then quilt it out. I did many a quilt this way. Nobody uses raw cotton for batting any more because it's a little rough on the hands. They buy that polyester stuff, because it's a lot lighter and easier to quilt" (see p. 53).

One Sunday afternoon in September 1977, I headed north from Jackson on Highway 49 which

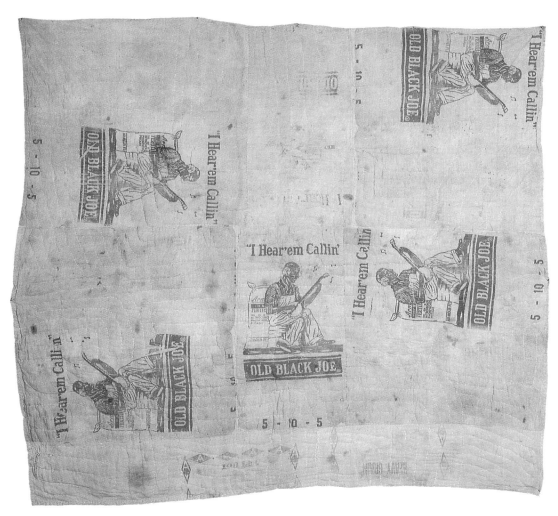

Quilt made by Hettie Barnes from 5-10-5 fertilizer sacks, 1930–35, 74" × 67". *I Hear 'Em Callin' Old Black Joe.* (35 MM CT)

Cleola McFarland in her backyard with quilt and washbasins.
WILKINSON COUNTY, MISSISSIPPI, 1976 (35 MM CT)

winds through Madison, Yazoo, and Holmes Counties. On a flat stretch somewhere between Keirn and Cruger, I spotted two quilts hanging on a line. I pulled over and went to investigate. It was the home of the Baker family, and these quilts were the work of Rosie Lee Baker. One quilt was made from men's worn-out pants and coveralls (see p. 54). "Times are hard, and poor people have to get all the use they can out of everything," she said. Mrs. Baker thought I was crazy to want to buy it, but she gladly sold it to me.

GROWING INTEREST IN QUILTS, 1976–81

As Worth and I started preparing for our first exhibition, I was excited about all the interest in what were called "strip" or "improvisational" quilts. The exhibit, *Folkroots: Images of Mississippi Black Folklife,* opened at the Mississippi State Historical Museum in September 1977 and then toured nationally for two years. As an adjunct to

the photographs, we displayed many of the artifacts we had collected, including quilts by Betty Tolbert, Suttie Nelson, Melissa Banks, and Lillian Baker.

Later that fall Patti Carr Black, director of the Mississippi State Historical Museum, asked me to do some collecting for the museum's textile department. I told her that I had already collected quite a few quilts. "Would you please exhibit them here before showing them anywhere else?" she asked. She added that as far as she knew, this would be the first-ever exhibition of African-American quilts. So in January 1978, an exhibit called *Something to Keep You Warm* displayed thirty-five quilts at the Mississippi State Historical Museum. The title came from an expression I first heard Annie Dennis use: "I don't make anything fancy, I just make something to keep you warm." This phrase also inspired me to design my first quilt, which Mrs. Dennis then quilted (see p. xx). It was especially moving to see all of those

Quilts on clothesline with woodpile, Cleola McFarland's backyard.
WILKINSON COUNTY, MISSISSIPPI, 1976 (21-15774/34)

wonderful quilts from the Mississippi Heartland hanging in the state's old Capitol. I invited the quilters and their families—most of whom had never been to a museum before—to the opening, and they were thrilled to see their work displayed in a museum. Soon this exhibit also began touring nationally.

Piney Woods School was founded in 1909 by Lawrence C. Jones to educate underprivileged black children. When Mr. Jones first came to this area of Mississippi, he stayed with Ms. Nellie Cox's family for a short period of time. In late 1978, when I was working with Dr. Alfredteen Harrison on a history of Piney Woods, we visited Nellie Cox and saw her marvelous quilt collection, and I photographed her and her daughter, Rosie Cox McLaurin (see p. 53).

In 1977, *Southern Exposure* magazine had published a special issue on folklife in the South. Of the

seven-page photo essay we contributed, two pages highlighted quilter Mrs. Phoeba Johnson, her daughters Annie and Emma, and their quilts. Then in November 1978, the third national conference of the Association of African and African-American Folklorists was held at the University of Maryland, College Park. One of the highlights of the conference was the opening of *Something to Keep You Warm*, which was then at Howard University. The November 1978 issue of *Essence* magazine did a six-page spread on these quilters and their quilts, and in February 1979, part of this exhibit hung in the new East Building of the National Gallery of Art in Washington, D.C., in a special showing arranged in the Study Center by the Folk Arts Program of the National Endowment for the Arts.

During the same period we were contacted by folklorist John Vlach, who was doing extensive research on African-American material culture for an exhibit called *The Afro-American Tradition in Decorative Arts*. He wanted to use some of the

Malissa Banks.
CLAIBORNE COUNTY, MISSISSIPPI, NOVEMBER 1976 (35 MM CT)

pieces we had located and was most fascinated with a Betty Tolbert strip quilt. We loaned the quilt to his exhibit, and it was reproduced in the exhibition catalog. Vlach wrote about strip quilting:

> Although black quilters have made all manner of pieced quilts, often using the same approaches as Euro-American quilt-makers, the strip technique is the method found most frequently in Afro-America. It has been observed in black communities in coastal South Carolina, southwestern Geor-gia, Alabama, Mississippi, Tennessee, southern Maryland, and in Washington, D.C., and Philadelphia. This wide distribu-tion makes the strip quilt the most com-monplace domestic example of black material culture in the United States. Why a single approach to the task of quilting should be so dominant among Afro-American quiltmakers may be traced to the retention of design concepts found in African textiles.

During this time I began corresponding with Cuesta Benberry in St. Louis whose research focused on the history of African-American quilts. I was excited to find another African-American scholar working with our quilting heritage, and as you'll see, Cuesta's contributions have been significant, and she has remained a valued colleague over the years.

As a result of renewed interest, the Mississippi State Historical Museum again exhibited my quilt collection in June 1981, this time with a catalog, supported through a National Endowment for the Arts grant. The catalog contained material by Patti Carr Black, Gladys-Marie Fry, Maude Wahlman, and me. Maude used the opportunity for an initial statement of her theories about strip quilting

Strip quilt, variation on a Log Cabin pattern, 1973, 86" × 72"
Quilt by Malissa Banks.
    (35 MM CT)

and the kente cloth connection (see pp. 116ff.). I believe this catalog to have been the first publication that dealt exclusively with African-American quilting. The exhibit toured intermittently through the mid-1980s, and requests for the long out-of-print catalog continue to this day.

AFRICA TRIPS, TEXTILES, AND EXHIBITS, 1981–83

In the summer of 1981, I was busy planning my first trip to sub-Saharan Africa. The quilt project was just one part of my ongoing study of black life. As far back as 1974, after seeing Robert Farris Thompson's exhibit, *African Art in Motion*, Worth and I had discussed the necessity of going to Mother Africa. I arrived in Nigeria to work as a photographer documenting a World Bank–funded, agriculture improvement project. This afforded me a great opportunity to observe traditional folklife practices in rural African settings, which in many cases were the root sources of African-American traditions I had been studying (see p. 55).

I was most fascinated with the beautiful and exciting patterns in the fabric used for clothing—and amazed that most of the popular trade fabrics

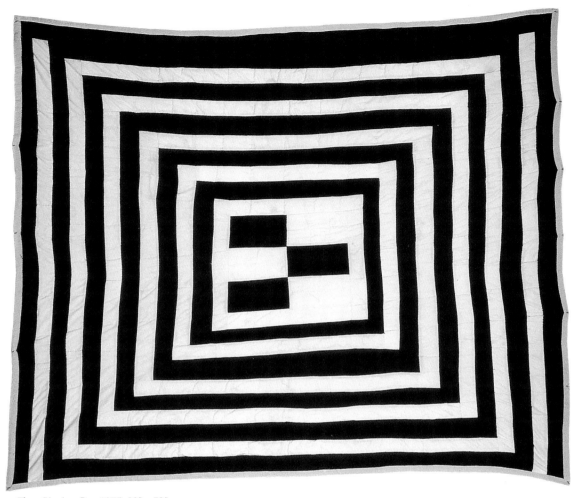

Three Pigs in a Pen, 1975, 82" × 73"
Quilt by Malissa Banks.
(35 mm ct)

then distributed worldwide were made not in Africa but in European factories. At the same time, many traditional fabrics are made and used throughout Africa for everyday and ceremonial wear. Examples include the raffia cloth panels from Zaire, woven by men and embroidered by women; from Ghana, the very recognizable Asante and Ewe cloths popularly termed "kente," which while originally made of silk for royal families, today are widely used in African-American fashions and home decor, and on special occasions may be worn the way a minister or holy man would wear a stole; from Nigeria, the intricate patterns in the indigo resist-dyed wraps; and, from Mali and neighboring

countries in West Africa, the popular "mud cloth" which is widely used in African-American fashions by both men and women.

The father of my Nigerian assistant, Akim Shere, was a traditional Yoruba strip weaver, whose cloth was used to make women's wraps. I was particularly interested in Mr. Shere because he was passing on this tradition to his young apprentices. Also, in the north of Nigeria, in the states of Bauchi, Kano, and Borno, I met Muslim women who did broadloom weaving.

While riding through a fertile agricultural region in Bauchi state, we came upon large burlap sacks piled in the shape of pyramids two to three

Variation on a Log Cabin pattern, #2, 1975, 80" × 65"
Quilt by Malissa Banks.
    (35 MM CT)

stories high. Upon examination, we discovered that these sacks were filled with cotton. When I climbed up on one of the piles to get a better view, in the distance I spotted a field of people, mostly women and young girls, picking cotton. My assistant, Akim, wanted to know why I kept saying, "This is unbelievable." For the rest of that day and night, I tried to find the appropriate words to explain to him the dramatic role that cotton played in the historical struggle of enslaved Africans in the American South. Knowing that most African Americans romanticize Africa, I also tried to convey that few of us could ever imagine returning to the

motherland and actually seeing people picking cotton, especially as 99 percent of the cotton picked in the United States today is done by machine.

The image of these Nigerians picking cotton haunted me for days as I thought about the role cotton has played in the lives of people throughout the world: how it is generally the poor masses who provide the labor to grow, harvest, and export it; and, how some of the fabric and clothing that is then produced is imported by those same countries that had grown the cotton, and even sold to those who had picked it, for them to wear back to the same fields to grow a new crop—with most of the profit from the value added to the original cotton never reaching them or their country-people.

My own naiveté was further exposed as I learned more about African history and its impact on many of those not exported as slaves, including aspects of both tribal warfare and European colonization that remain unfamiliar to many diaspora blacks. I was particularly struck at how, during the colonial era, large-scale plantation agriculture was introduced into many African countries, emphasizing commercial, export-oriented production of such crops as cotton and cacao. The production systems most often relied on underpaid, or even forced,

African labor and often required resettlement, the splintering of families, and living conditions that included corporal punishment for violations of rules and of production expectations. Understanding this history brought home to me in a dramatic way some of the residual and devastating effects of colonialism. It also added a dimension to my awareness of some of the terrible aspects of the heritage shared by many people of African descent.

I searched in vain for people using old clothes or scraps of material to make something that resembled an American quilt. Later, in Liberia, I went looking for descendants of African Americans who had migrated to Liberia and who

Suttie Nelson whipping raw cotton to use as batting in a quilt.
HINDS COUNTY, MISSISSIPPI, OCTOBER 1978 (6-20765/26)

Rosie Cox McLaurin and her mother, Nellie Flowers Cox (1884–1979).
RANKIN COUNTY, MISSISSIPPI, OCTOBER 1978 (11-20779/12A)

Rosie Lee Baker.
HOLMES COUNTY, MISSISSIPPI, SEPTEMBER 1977 (6-17766/18)

quilted. I wasn't very successful in these efforts because of the brevity of my stay, and, in the aftermath of the then recent bloody coup, many of the Liberian descendants of these African Americans were reluctant to talk with me. It was several years later that I finally saw examples of the wonderful quilts they had made.

In 1983, at the request of Bets Ramsey, director of the Southern Quilt Symposium, I curated a section of her exhibit *Quilt Close-Up: Five Southern Views* for the Hunter Museum of Art in Chattanooga, Tennessee. My section, "Quilts from the Mississippi Heartland," featured the work of five quilters from Wilkinson County.

As was my practice, I sent copies of the catalog to Phoeba Johnson and the other Mississippi quilters represented. In response, Mrs. Johnson and her daughter Annie teased me about making them famous. They jokingly said, "We hope this

new catalog doesn't result in a whole new bunch of people calling to worry us." Mrs. Johnson had said many times over the years that she would live to be at least 100, and by then would be tired of piecing on these old quilts and would retire and go home. In the summer of 1983, while I was on a United States Information Agency (USIA) tour in West Africa, Phoeba Johnson died, only fourteen days after her 100th birthday. By the time I learned of this and got a call through to her family, they had laid her to rest. For the next three days, I couldn't get her off my mind. I talked to her in my dreams and as I lay awake at night.

As I lectured during the day in connection with my photo exhibition *Southern Roads/City Pavements*, which included photographs of Mrs. Johnson and had just opened at the National Museum in Lagos, Nigeria, I told the heart-wrenching story of her Slave Chain quilt (see pp. 38–41). As people listened and looked at her

Mr. Shere teaching traditional strip weaving to his apprentice.
OYO CITY, OYO STATE, NIGERIA, WEST AFRICA, 1981
(35 MM CT)

Sacks of cotton piled in a pyramid shape.
BAUCHI STATE, NIGERIA, WEST AFRICA, 1982
(35 MM CT)

Young women picking cotton.
BAUCHI STATE, NIGERIA, WEST AFRICA, 1982 (35 MM CT)

Muslim woman doing traditional broadloom weaving.
BAUCHI STATE, NIGERIA, WEST AFRICA, 1981
(35 MM CT)

Left to right: Annie Dennis, Mattilee Knight, and Cleola McFarland.
WILKINSON COUNTY, MISSISSIPPI, 1983 (3-31978/14A)

image, they cried. They understood that this lost descendant, though long removed from this land, was one of Mother Africa's children, and they shared my sorrow.

In preparation for another tour in the winter of 1983, the USIA wanted to videotape my *Southern Roads/City Pavements* exhibit, have me do a voice-over similar to what I did for gallery talks, and then send this video to Europe and Africa in connection with my exhibit. I convinced them, however, that it would be far more meaningful and rewarding if they would let me take a video crew back to the actual settings where the photographs were made. They agreed and we traveled to Mississippi that spring.

The first person I called there was Annie Dennis of Wilkinson County. I wanted her to get together with her friends Mattilee Knight (who now had decided to participate despite her husband's objections) and Cleola McFarland so that we could shoot them quilting. The next quilter I contacted was Annie Mason of Franklin County, who simply said, "I'm home every day, so come on by when you're ready."

Her great-grandchildren were at home with her when I arrived, and I seized the opportunity to make a picture of four generations of women in her family. While I sat on the floor, she relaxed in her rocker with a quilt spread on her lap and, holding a Bible, explained her family genealogy. I was very much in awe of how comfortable and natural people seemed while being videotaped. They made our job easy, and a good thing about video is that you can immediately show people on a monitor what you've just taped. Even better, people would look at what had been shot and respond, "That's

Annie Jane Mason with four generations of women in her family. *Back row, left to right:* Aretha Mason, Wardell Sanders, Rosa Mason, Gwen Mason Stewart, and Angela Stewart. *Front row, left to right:* Passion Mason, Aleasea Stewart, and Annie Jane Mason.
FRANKLIN COUNTY, MISSISSIPPI, 1983 (35 MM CT)

nice, it looks just like me." Little did I realize that afternoon as I left Mrs. Mason's that she would never see the finished video. About a year later, she passed away. Her obituary included the following: "On July 30, 1984, another flower was plucked from the garden of life to be transplanted to the garden of eternal life. The flowers discharge their bright ministry of love, elaborate their seed and die, but not until their work is done."

In September 1983, I had to cut short my USIA tour of West Africa because when I reached Senegal my wife called to tell me that my grandmother Goldie, who was then eighty-three, was seriously ill and wasn't expected to live another ten days. As it turned out, my grandmother had been fighting a losing battle with cancer for quite a while but had just recently told the family.

I dropped everything and headed straight home. On the long flight back I began to reflect on how much my grandmother and my early family and community folklife had influenced what I was now doing. My first curiosity about quilts had come from my two grandmothers. I'd never met Lena Freeman, my paternal grandmother, but I had slept under her quilts as a kid. On the maternal side, there was my great-great-grandmother, Laura Virginia Rounds, whom I knew only through the mysterious quilt she had made that was sacred to my family, who believed it possessed healing powers.

From my early childhood, I remember my great-grandmother, Arbia Rounds Janey, telling us that her grandmother was half Indian and a medicine woman. Although I could not find any documented proof of my Native American ancestry during my extensive family genealogy research, this aspect of our family's heritage has been accepted as common knowledge by family members from Maryland's Eastern Shore and has persisted from generation to generation until today.*

Once I was home, I waited until I was alone with Goldie and her sister, my Aunt Ruth, and asked why she didn't have the healing quilt there. Aunt Ruth looked at me inquisitively, "You don't remember, it was Mama's [my great-grandmother Arbia's] request that when she died we wrap and bury her in it. And that's what we did, back in January 1963." Goldie then said, "Roland wasn't at her funeral, he was in Europe." Indeed, I had gone back to Paris at the end of 1962 for one month, and no one had

known how to contact me, and so I had missed Arbia's funeral.

I then went home and got one of Betty Tolbert's quilts. She was the only quilter I knew who was a traditional healer, and I thought that might help. I took her quilt to the hospital and put it over my grandmother, which really pleased her. For about three weeks, I thought it was working: it seemed to cheer her up and the family stopped the death watch, but by the fourth week, her condition began to deteriorate again. They moved her to intensive care and on November 4, 1983, she passed. At the church, just before they closed her casket, I slipped a little piece of Mrs. Tolbert's quilt into her hand and said good-bye.

---

* From my own research, the general situation regarding Eastern Shore Native Americans during the eighteenth and nineteenth centuries certainly adds plausibility to this story of our genealogy. There were many tribes on the Eastern Shore, including the Nanticokes and Wicomicos in the area closest to where my family lived. By the end of the seventeenth century, skirmishes between Maryland and Virginia colonists and Eastern Shore Native American tribes were occurring with increasing frequency as pressure on tribal settlement, hunting, and fishing lands increased with the expansion of the colonists' permanent farming and trading communities. By the mid-eighteenth century, major emigration of Eastern Shore tribes had begun, and by the end of the century, remaining local populations numbered only in the hundreds. Although perhaps smaller in total numbers, this forced resettlement was as drastic as, and no less painful than, that later experienced by other tribes on the Trail of Tears during the Great Plains marches. All during this period, to avoid resettlement while retaining some proximity to traditional lands, a small but significant number of Eastern Shore Native Americans, along with others up and down the eastern seaboard, intermarried or otherwise were assimilated into white, as well as African-American populations, both free and slave. Much of this information is from Clinton A. Weslager, *The Nanticoke Indians—Past and Present* (Cranbury, N.J.: Associated University Presses, 1983).

CHAPTER 3
Expanding the Project
(1985–90)

REDEFINING THE PROJECT

Several threads that came together in 1985 resulted in my redefining and broadening the scope of the quilt project. First, 1985 marked the tenth year I had been exploring the world of African-American quiltmakers, primarily in Mississippi. Throughout this time, Worth and other folklorists who knew the southern region had told me about quilters in other states and had urged me to include them in my work. Also, quilters in Mississippi often referred me directly to friends or relatives now living elsewhere.

THE WOMEN OF COLOR QUILTERS' NETWORK

In addition, there were some important institutional developments. Carolyn Mazloomi, a quilter in Cincinnati, Ohio, was building a network to facilitate communication among African-American quilters. Although few of these quilters were ever found at quilt functions, we knew that wherever African Americans lived, there were quilters, and in general they quilted either in small church or senior citizen groups, or by themselves. They had little interest in joining larger, predominantly white quilting groups. In addition, many couldn't afford the costs of attending big quilt shows or symposiums.

Understanding the situation, yet determined to find some like-minded souls, Carolyn placed an ad in the reader's request column in the August 1985 *Quilter's Newsletter* magazine. Ten African-American quilters responded, and to a person, they all expressed a profound sense of gratitude. One wrote, "Thank you, sister, for reaching out." The original respondents were Claire E. Carter of Gap Mills, West Virginia; Arma Carter of Dorchester, Massachusetts; Melodye

Boyd of Hanover, and Barbara Pietila of Baltimore, Maryland; Peggie Hartwell and Marie Wilson of New York City; Rosalyn Bond of Tallahassee, Florida; Della Collins of Houston, Texas; Dorothy Nelle Sanders of Wauwatosa, Wisconsin; and Judy Wellington of London, England. Together they formed the Women of Color Quilters' Network (WCQN).

Sandra K. German, a current WCQN member, wrote the following account for the 1993 issue of *Uncoverings*, a newsletter published by the American Quilt Study Group:

> With Carolyn at the hub, a whirlwind of activity began with such a groundswell of pent-up energy, love, gratitude, and down-right relief, that soon the fledgling group was swamped with the cumulative weight of it all. After an extended period of euphoria during which the individual respondents gloried triumphant in their newly discovered quilt soulmates, the eager crew settled down to find a way of interacting that wasn't so costly, time-consuming, and emotionally charged.
>
> Carolyn agreed to accumulate their writings and distribute them to everyone, along with notices of important events and activities. Then by mail and telephone, the group articulated and agreed upon common goals. Finally, they embarked upon adopting a philosophy of unconditional acceptance, affirmation, and validation for each and every African-American quilter.
>
> This caveat was born of the emphatic awareness that African-American quilters suffer from the same stereotypes, stigmas, and barriers that can delineate and constrict

almost every other aspect of their American social experience. "There is a tangible pressure to conform in the 'other' quilt world," Mazloomi offered. "It is not a healthy thing when you're the only black person in that kind of guild. The need to be accepted, to qualify, is often expressed by cloning what everybody else is doing. You can get lost. You can lose your soul." Perhaps in recognition of this, the Network's founding members all agreed that it was neither fitting nor proper for the Women of Color Quilters' Network to adopt the same oppressive, arbitrary standards that had for so long denied them the esteem and acknowledgment their work deserved. Carolyn credits Cuesta Benberry as the originator of this all-encompassing philosophy. Quilt styles and techniques will come and go, affirmed the group, but the value and worth of African-American quiltmakers would never again be undermined or denied—at least not within the network.

"We are creative, caring people," Carolyn expounded. "Much of our members' main body of work comes from a different aesthetic. We want to celebrate creative freedom, and we frequently break the rules of traditional quiltmaking. Consequently, much of what we do is not always well received by those who don't understand or who are incapable of tolerating differentness without passing judgment. At the same time, many of our members are masters of traditional quilt forms. They do exquisite needlework. Their work shows exceptional research and attention to detail."

The goals of the Women of Color Quilters' Network were delineated as follows:

1. To foster and preserve the art of quiltmaking among women of color.
2. To research quilt history and document quilts.
3. To offer expertise in quiltmaking techniques in order to enhance our skills.
4. To offer authentic handmade African-American quilts and fiber arts to museums and galleries for shows.
5. To help with writing grant proposals for those persons who may have such needs.
6. To aid quilters who wish to sell their work obtain the best price possible.
7. To give quilting workshops.
8. To facilitate knowledgeable services in quilt restoration and repair.

THE FIRST REDEFINITION

Also during 1985, the Institute for the Arts and the Humanities at Howard University, at which I was a research associate, was eliminated in a major budget cutback. I was crushed and knew I would miss the invaluable encouragement of my work that had been provided to me by my Institute colleagues and by the many black scholars I met there over seven wonderful years. Dr. Steven Henderson, the Institute's brilliant founder and director, impressed upon me in his quiet and gentle way the importance of what I was doing and how I had to find a way to stay the course, despite these difficulties and the lucrative attractions of commercial photography.

I knew that through our work in Mississippi, Worth and I had developed an approach to our fieldwork and documentation that was exciting and effective. We knew how to develop trust, and we were successful in gaining access to people's lives, histories, and dreams while they shared their quilts and stories with us. While our work had provided us with remarkable satisfaction, its results had been received by others as a great success. As I thought through what we had done so far, I realized that it was clearly time to expand the work beyond Mississippi. I began to see the project as documenting African-American quiltmakers throughout the South, their quilts, and their personal stories.

After talking over the implications of this decision with my wife, I began by reviewing my plans. I saw that on the one hand, I would be able to incorporate some additional attention to the project by "piggybacking" on plans for work already scheduled and could use this same strategy when planning additional work and travel. On the other hand, it was clear that I would not be able to focus my efforts either as systematically or as intensely as I'd have preferred. For at least the next year or so, the

Lillian Beattie (1879–1988).
HAMILTON COUNTY, TENNESSEE, OCTOBER 1985 (17-40435/13)

expansion would be based on seizing targets of opportunity.

The first of these came about in the early fall, during a two-month trip through the South during which I was able to accomplish some work specifically related to the quilting project. I first drove to Atlanta to spend a day or so with Worth, refining and clarifying my approach. While driving, I gave a lot of thought to Worth's advice over the ten years since we first had worked together in Mississippi and to his tremendous help in my making the decision to stay the documentary course.

After I arrived at Worth's home in mid-afternoon, we ate and talked into the night. One of my main concerns was how I would fund this work. Our shortage of money always seemed to bother me more than Worth, and when I brought it up, he simply said, "Forget the money, the work is needed." As Bernice Reagon would put it, "When something needs to be done and you're up against it, you can make a way out of no way." That evening Worth and I mapped out long-range plans and some specific ideas to build more quilt work into this trip, which would take me across Tennessee, down through Mississippi to New Orleans, back through Alabama, across Georgia, and then over to St. Helena's Island, South Carolina, where I would meet up with him.

TENNESSEE, 1985

My first stop was in Chattanooga, to see Bets Ramsey. I had known Bets since the late 1970s when she reviewed *Something to Keep You Warm*. A respected critic and quilt historian with long-term relationships with African-American quiltmakers of the area, she brought me up to date on current happenings in the quilt world.

She also identified some local quilters for inclusion in the project. Although we visited several of these women, I was able to photograph only one that day, Lillian Beattie. Mrs. Beattie is an innovative quilter who incorporates in her designs lively appliqué figures from comics and other publications and whose quilts have been shown in major museums across the country. Although Mrs. Beattie didn't look a day over 80, I found out she was 105 years old, having been born in Athens, Tennessee, in 1879.

Memphis is a special place for me. My first impressions of it came through music, starting in my youth with W. C. Handy, Jelly Roll Morton, and "Memphis Slim" (whom I had known when I lived in Paris), and later Al Green, Isaac Hayes, and Hoagy Carmichael. My first visit to Memphis was in April 1968, as a photographer for the Southern Christian Leadership Conference, right after the assassination of Dr. Martin Luther King Jr. In recent years, I'd been back several times, mainly in connection with the Center for Southern Folklore, which was located downtown on Peabody Street. This was the first regional folklife center in the country and was started by Judy Peiser (who was still the director) and William Ferris, who is now at the University of

Mississippi. In 1975 the Center had been the funding conduit through which Worth and I received initial support of the Mississippi Folklife Project. Over the years, I'd also been meeting with and encouraging a group of men and women who made up the Memphis Afro-American Photographers Forum. One of them, Robert Jones, now worked at the Center while attending the Memphis College of Art. I was curating an exhibit of his work called *Southern Rhythms*, which was scheduled to open at the State Historical Museum in Jackson, Mississippi, that October, and I had stopped in Memphis to review his photographs. At the end of the week, I then proceeded to Jackson.

The next morning I went to Jackson State University to see historian Dr. Alferdteen Harrison, director of the Margaret Walker Alexander Research Center there and an old friend. She had just taken over the Center and shared with me her plans to revitalize it; she also asked if I would be a board member and help her with strategies for some badly needed fundraising. I said I would, and then shared with her my overall plans for expanding the project. Before leaving, I told her I was on my way to AfricaTown and asked if she had any information on it. She said, "Oh, you're going to the place where the last slave ship was supposed to have come in. That should be exciting. I haven't been there in years." She reached into her files and gave me a copy of the 1983 AfricaTown Folk Festival program guide and a copy of the book *Historic Sketches of the South**by Emma Langdon Roche, and said, "This should give you some insight. Try to read these before you get there."

ALABAMA, 1985–86

AFRICATOWN

After a stop for other work in New Orleans, I headed into Alabama. On the east side of Mobile, where the Mobile River empties into the Gulf, are the towns of Prichard and Magazine, also known as AfricaTown. While at the office of Prichard's mayor, John H. Smith, I met Dorothy

*New York: Knickerbocker Press, 1914.

Viola Allen.
AFRICATOWN, MOBILE COUNTY, ALABAMA, NOVEMBER 1985 (35 MM CT)

Davies, who was from the area and had recently returned from a business trip to Nigeria. We exchanged Nigeria stories and she volunteered to show me around AfricaTown, which was reached by crossing a little bridge from Prichard. My initial reaction to AfricaTown was disappointment, mainly in myself for being naive enough to expect AfricaTown to look significantly different from other African-American communities.

My mood began to change, however, as I read the book and festival guide that Dr. Harrison had given me, including the story of the slave ship she'd mentioned. The guide said that although the U.S. government had officially outlawed importing enslaved Africans in 1808, for years the lucrative trade in human cargo was continued by smugglers. In 1859, a group of men entered a high-stakes wager as to whether, despite the efforts the government was finally making to suppress the slave trade, Captain Tim Meaher, a steamboat builder and riverman, could bring a cargo of slaves through the port of Mobile. Under the auspices of Meaher, his brother, and a

Captain Foster, their ship, the *Clotilde*, and its cargo of more than one hundred slaves returned just before the Civil War broke out. This proved to be the last cargo of slaves brought into the United States, and they were sold off in lots along the Alabama River in Clarke County, Wilcox County, and Dallas County, as far north as Selma. After war was declared, those Africans belonging to Foster and Meaher were taken to the Meaher settlement at Magazine Point, and over the years this area became known as AfricaTown. Most of those brought on the *Clotilde* remained enslaved for about five years. The last of them, Kazoola (Cudjo), died in Mobile in 1935.

After reading this I couldn't sleep. Whether it was true or not, the idea appalled me that a group of white men, undoubtedly professing to be Christians, made a bet, and for sport, adventure, or profit ruined the lives of hundreds of people they considered less than human.

The next morning Ms. Davies and I discussed all this at length. I was excited when

Eva Jones, the daughter of Polee Allen, who got off the slave ship *Clotilde* that arrived in Alabama in 1859.

AFRICATOWN, MOBILE COUNTY, ALABAMA, NOVEMBER 1985 (21-40501/7, 2¼)

The Clinton Community Club of the Retired Senior Volunteer Program meets to quilt together at the community center in Eutaw, Alabama. *Seated (left to right):* Edna Mae Rice, Addie M. Pelt, and Gertrude Eatman. *Standing (left to right):* Juliette Noland,

Mary Jones, Mary Crawford, Louella Craig, Mary Freeman, Martha Ann Busby, Ethel Mae Barnes, Margreat Rice, Fannie L. Edwards, and Annie Mobley.

GREENE COUNTY, ALABAMA, APRIL 1986 (35 MM CT)

she said, "Now let's go meet some of the first-
and second-generation descendants of the
Africans who got off the *Clotilde*." She
explained to me that her mother's maternal
grandfather, Polee Allen, was a young boy when
he arrived in Alabama on the *Clotilde*. He later
fathered two sets of children. First he married
Mary Allen and she had a daughter named
Viola Allen. His second wife, Lucy, had one
daughter, Eva Jones (1885–1992), whom we
were about to meet, and who was then ninety
years old (see p. 63). Lucy had taught her
daughter Eva to quilt and Eva taught her
daughter Mrs. Olivette Jones Howze, who now
lives in Pittsburgh, Pennsylvania.

My excitement increased as we delved deeper
into the community. When we reached the
house of Viola Allen (Miss Vi), she was cleaning
her backyard. Miss Vi was a quilter, and despite
her life in AfricaTown, her quilts were
essentially no different in style or craftsmanship
than hundreds of others I had seen across the
South. I thought Miss Vi had an incredible face,
and she agreed to let me photograph her,
provided she could fix herself up first (see
p. 62).

Late that afternoon we visited Mr. Henry
Williams, who is a walking history of AfricaTown.
He was in his office in an old building behind his
house. There he sat among piles of papers and
books and overflowing file cabinets. He
mentioned many people who had come through
AfricaTown, but the one that most interested me
was Zora Neale Hurston, who had once lived
there and dated a man there. I also learned that
through intermarriage with freed slaves from
North Carolina, some descendants of the
Clotilde's Africans live in other nearby parts of
Alabama, such as Gee's Bend.

After leaving AfricaTown, I next got back to
Alabama and the quilting project in the spring of
1986.

EUTAW

In late March 1986, I headed for the Black Belt
region of Alabama to photograph African-
American quilters who were to be featured in the
Smithsonian Institution's Festival of American

Minnie Kimbrough's dog trot house.
GREENE COUNTY, ALABAMA, APRIL 1986 (35 MM CT)

Folklife. The Smithsonian's Center for Folklife
Programs and Cultural Studies had teamed me up
with a young folklorist, Phyllis M. May, who had
connections with the area. Assisted by Etta B.
Edwards, a community scholar, we spent five
intensive days photographing quilters in a variety
of settings.

We met the Clinton Community Club
quilters (see p. 63) a group of older women who
met twice a week to have "big fun" as they shared
stories while quilting. Up until this time, most of
the quilters I had met usually worked alone or
with one other person. This was the first real
quilting bee I had seen since my youth.

We then met Mabel Means, a community
elder and quilter, who gladly helped us locate
others. We spent several hours with Minnie
Kimbrough, who lived in a "dog trot" house (a
house built around an open central space that
has a common roof but no front or back wall)
and loved listening to B. B. King. Next was Mary
Williams, who usually makes "Frog" pattern
quilts but didn't have one at the time. However,
my visit yielded a picture of Mrs. Williams
teaching her granddaughter to quilt. Mamie
McKinstry showed us how she stored her quilts. I

met George and Beatrice Gosa, who had been sweethearts since they were teenagers and were still together (see pp. 66–68).

We spent the better part of one day at Lucius and Mary Scarbrough's home. She had just made a king-size Double Wedding Ring quilt to celebrate their fiftieth wedding anniversary. Mary is an exquisite seamstress who quilts with her daughter Geraldine Atmore, and she has kept many quilts made by her mother, Charity Noland Shambley. In an interview conducted by Phyllis May, Mrs. Scarbrough said:

> I worked thirty-two years. I've been used to working all my life. They had a senior citizen's group that was quilting down at my church in the Masonic Hall Building, and after I was home for a while, I decided I would join them. I enjoy going down and quilting with the group since I retired. . . . I

Three generations of quilters. *Left to right:* Delois Ann Smith, her mother, Mary K. Williams, and her daughter LaChandria Smith. GREENE COUNTY, ALABAMA, APRIL 1986 (16-41830/14)

have some of mother's quilts quilted by the piece. Those were her spread quilts. She put those on top of the bed. They didn't sleep under those quilts. They called those their "nice quilts." On the weekends, when she'd have time to dress the house up, then she would put those nice quilts on the bed. And then when night'd come and it was time to get ready to go to bed, she'd take those nice quilts and fold them up and just use the common quilts on the bed.

Of the twenty-eight quilters we met and photographed that week, we selected three to represent the area at that year's Festival of American Folklife: Mamie McKinstry, Mary Scarbrough, and Eloise Dickerson. The Festival takes place on the Mall in Washington, D.C., and has an average attendance of more than one million. The women quilted around a quilting frame in their demonstration area, and this public setting didn't seem to bother them though they were used to quilting at home or in small community settings. We also arranged for folklorist Dr. Gladys-Marie Fry to present them once a day in a public forum.

As part of the Alabama program, the Smithsonian had prepared a mini-exhibit to introduce Festival visitors to the quilters' homes and communities. It hung in the demonstration tent and included nineteen of my photographs. While Phyllis and I had been completing our fieldwork in Eutaw, several community leaders had expressed interest in seeing the exhibit photographs. Pursuing an idea from Worth, I called Dr. Sandral Hullett, one of those who had expressed interest, and suggested a showing of the panels from the Festival in Washington during Eutaw's annual Folkroots Festival during the fall. Dr. Hullett, a staff physician at the Greene County Hospital and Nursing Home in Eutaw, helped coordinate everything. Eutaw became so excited about this exhibit that Dr. Hullett arranged for the town to keep it indefinitely, hanging in the waiting room of the Maddox Health Center, adjacent to the hospital. Later that year, the state folklorist, Joey Brackner, also arranged for it to hang in the gallery of the Alabama State Council on the Arts and

Humanities in Montgomery, after which it was returned to the permanent installation in the Maddox Health Center.

MICHIGAN, 1986

Phyllis May and I also teamed up for the field-work for the 1987 Festival, in which Michigan was to be the featured state. We started on our work in early October. Unlike in Alabama, where our focus was on quilting, in Michigan we focused on the whole spectrum of African-American folk culture.

Cuesta Benberry had told me about a group called the Wednesday Night Quilting Sisters, headed by Dr. Sarah Carolyn Reese, which met at the Hartford Memorial Baptist Church in Detroit. After I explained the purpose of our

interest to Dr. Reese, she agreed to let me photograph them.

In Lansing, Phyllis had met Marguerite Berry-Jackson, who told her of three family history quilts that are displayed at an annual reunion of several families who had settled near School Section Lake in Mecosta County in the late 1870s. She showed us a genealogy quilt that she was making but said we really needed to see the Todd family quilts. These were currently with a relative, Deonna Todd Green, who was away at the time, and it was only years later that I finally saw them (see pp. 253ff.). She then directed us to her sister, Marie Berry-Cross, who is also a quilter and lives in Mecosta County about two hours northwest of Lansing. Over the next two days, Phyllis and I got to know this family and their folk culture, which

Left to right: Mary L. Scarbrough, Catherlean Lavender, Mamie McKinstry, Eloise Dickerson, and Amanda S. Burton.

GREENE COUNTY, ALABAMA, APRIL 1986 (35 MM CT)

Mr. and Mrs. George Gosa and Beatrice Gosa resting on their couch under quilts.
GREENE COUNTY, ALABAMA, APRIL 1986 (1-41830/11A)

Mr. and Mrs. Lucius Scarbrough and Mary L. Scarbrough in bed with her king-size Double Wedding Ring quilt, which she made to celebrate their fiftieth wedding anniversary.
GREENE COUNTY, ALABAMA, APRIL 1986 (35 MM CT)

featured fiddle players, basketmakers, guitar makers, storytellers, and several quilters.

Among African Americans there is a saying that goes, "Light and bright, almost white," and this best describes how most of this family looked. While questioning the Todds about their genealogy, a fascinating story began to emerge involving a long association of the Todd and Berry families, dating back to when they had migrated to Michigan together in 1877.

When we stopped in Lansing to say good-bye to Mrs. Berry-Jackson, she invited us to lunch. As we ate, I inquired about some of the old photographs on her walls. I was particularly interested in one of an old white woman who she said was her grandmother Lucy Millard. Lucy was a Mormon who had married Mrs. Berry-Jackson's grandfather,

Isaac Berry. I asked if Isaac was a black man, and she said, "Yes, they met while he was a slave."

Dorothy Aldridge, one of the members of the Wednesday Night Quilting Sisters (see p. 69) who had volunteered to help me locate some other quilters in Detroit, asked me, "How would you like to photograph Mrs. Rosa Parks?" Over the years I had read a lot about Mrs. Parks, who is known as the "Mother of the Civil Rights Movement." On December 1, 1955, with quiet strength and determination, Rosa Parks (b. 1913), an administrator in the Alabama office of the National Association for the Advancement of Colored People (NAACP), was arrested and jailed for refusing to give up her seat to a white man on a Montgomery city bus. E. D. Nixon, president of the

Left to right: Geraldine Scarbrough Atmore and her mother, Mary Scarbrough quilting together at home.
GREENE COUNTY, ALABAMA, APRIL 1986 (35 MM CT)

Dr. Gladys-Marie Fry (*second from right*) presenting Eutaw, Alabama, quilters on the workshop stage at the 1985 Festival of American Folklife.
NATIONAL MALL, WASHINGTON, D.C., JULY 1985 (1-42570/25)

State NAACP and director of the regional chapter of the International Brotherhood of Sleeping Car Porters, organized a bus boycott. The Montgomery Improvement Association was formed with the Reverend Martin Luther King Jr. as its president, and for 381 days it supported the 50,000 black people who decided to walk, bringing public transportation in the city to a halt until buses were integrated. Parks's action became the stimulus for twelve years of mass nonviolent protests against segregation in cities throughout the South. King called Parks "the great fuse that led to the modern stride towards freedom."*

Needless to say, my immediate response to Mrs. Aldridge's offer to photograph Mrs. Parks was, "I'd love to." I added, "Does she quilt?" I knew she was a seamstress, but had never seen any mention of her quilting. Mrs. Aldridge said she had known Mrs. Parks (who then lived in Detroit and worked in U.S. Representative John Conyers's office) for quite a while but had only recently asked her if she quilted. She said Mrs. Parks's reply

* "Black Women, Achievements against the Odds, Calendar 1981–83," GMG Publishing, 25 W. 43 Street, New York, NY 10636. ©1978 Smithsonian Institution. December 1981 calendar page.

was an emphatic "Any good woman my age from Alabama definitely knows how to quilt." Dorothy then set up a breakfast meeting with Mrs. Parks, after which I would photograph her. As a member of the Washington press corps, I had met a lot of people through the lens of my camera, but I don't ever remember having a feeling as special as the morning I met Mrs. Parks. With warm hugs, she welcomed us into her modest apartment. She had only a few of her quilts and an unfinished top. Being very used to photographers, she suggested, "Why don't I just sit here and sew on this top while you make your photographs?" (See p. 70.) I stared at her through the lens and tried to imagine how this soft-spoken, petite, and gentle lady had found the courage to do what she had done. My mind drifted to that day when she challenged the entire legal and social system of racial discrimination, and I marveled.

Another feeler I put out led me to Cledie C. Taylor, a gallery owner and art supervisor for the Detroit Public Schools, who introduced me to her parents, the Reverend Theodore R. Matthews and Mrs. Osie G. C. Matthews, a quilter, who were both retirees from the Dodge Company. Being an artist, Cledie had a good sense of what situations

Wednesday Night Quilting Sisters of Detroit, who meet at the Hartford Memorial Baptist Church. *Clockwise from top center:* Patricia Johnson (leaning on table), Evangeline Ashley, Dr. Sarah Carolyn Reese (program designer/developer), Vernita Beverly, Raeschelle Jackson, Effie Hayes, Mattie Douglas, Shirley Gibson Bell, Pearl L. Ephrain, Irene Yancy-Maddox, Mary Turner, and Dorothy Dewberry Aldridge.

WAYNE COUNTY, MICHIGAN, OCTOBER 1986 (46-43344/35A)

might make good photographs, and because I was interested in black folklife in general, she suggested I might want to spend at least half a day with her mother. I arrived at the Matthews's home early one morning, and Mrs. Matthews invited me back to the kitchen.

While I was scanning the situation to find a vantage point from which to take pictures, my mind's ear suddenly flashed to blues singer Robert Johnson singing, "Come On in My Kitchen." Cledie started setting the table as her mother rolled out dough with a rolling pin and cut out biscuits with a tin can. All the while, the aroma of bacon and sausage frying and coffee brewing filled the room. Cledie grabbed a cup of coffee and left to go to work, and the Matthews and I sat down for an old-fashioned, down-home

breakfast. The Reverend Matthews, who was a Baptist minister, was the quietest preacher I'd ever met. Even his grace was short. After breakfast, Mrs. Matthews showed me her quilts. Many of them were scrap, or throw-together quilts, but she seemed to be most proud of her Star quilt. For the rest of the day, Mrs. Matthews and I sat in the kitchen and talked, as she pieced a top.

As she told it, she was born in 1907 in Brinkley, Arkansas, and learned to quilt from her mother, Annie Gaines (1872–1926). Mrs. Matthews migrated from Brinkley to Detroit in the fall of 1930 to keep from having her life snuffed out. At seventeen she had fallen in love with and married a country blues singer and cotton sharecropper, Dallas Collins, who was almost twice her age.

Mr. and Mrs. Theodore and Osie Matthews at breakfast.
WAYNE COUNTY, MICHIGAN, OCTOBER 1985 (8-43344/26)

He was a nice enough man, and he could really play that guitar, but when he wasn't performing in those juke joints or at somebody's party, he really didn't want to be around people that much. He wanted to live way back in the woods where he could hunt. That was fine for him, but I had three children in four years, and between chopping and picking cotton and caring for my children, and him always gone, my life was downright miserable. I loved him, and he provided good for us—we never went hungry—but that love was leading to my ruination. Some of my happiest moments were after I put the kids to bed and would sit alone piecing my quilt tops.

My mother had always told me, "I don't care how hard times are, always manage to put a little money aside your husband don't know you have." One afternoon when I hadn't seen Dallas in a few days, it came to me that if I didn't leave this place soon, I would go out of my mind. So to keep from going crazy, I took my quilts, bundled up my children, and packed what little I had and left. I didn't stop to say good-bye to nobody. Both of my parents had passed, but I had a sister, Lilly, about nine years older than me, who'd moved to Detroit. Even though I'd lost her address, I went there anyway, knowing the good Lord would help me find her. When we got here, it was really cold, and we sat in that bus station wrapped in the quilts. I didn't know what to do, but I'd been sitting there so long a white lady asked if I needed any help. I told her my situation, and she helped me find a place for a few days and I got a job at the Pioneer Laundry. And I'm proud to say neither me or my children have ever been on welfare.

After a few weeks God answered my prayers and I located my sister. We got a nice, big house together and when the war [World War II] broke out, I went to work in the Dodge plant. That's where I met Theodore. When he asked to keep company with me, I told him I didn't want no man who wasn't going to treat my children right. He agreed to do right by them and soon after we got married. He's old and

Rosa Parks, the "mother of the Civil Rights movement."
WAYNE COUNTY, MICHIGAN, OCTOBER 1986 (63-43344/11)

Left to right: Curtis and Osie Collins Hurst, and Osie's daughter Cledie C. Taylor.
WAYNE COUNTY, MICHIGAN, OCTOBER 1995 (75926/33)

sickly now, but we've been together for over forty years. We have a happy life and I don't think I could've done much better. He's been good to me and my children all these years.

I was curious about what happened to her first husband, Dallas, and she explained.

As soon as I got settled in Detroit, I sent word back to him that the kids and I were fine. I never harbored any bad feelings toward him and never kept our children away from him. From about the time they were six years old, they'd go back and spend summers with him. My oldest girl, Cledie, even went to school there one year. You see, he took up with another woman, Jane Anna, just as soon as I left, and had four children by her. So one year my children would go there, and the next year his children would come here. I treated them just like they was my own. After we got divorced, he remarried Jane Anna and I married Theodore, but I never had any more children.

I asked if she taught her daughters to quilt.

My oldest, Cledie, could read sixth-grade books when she was in first grade, and she never missed a day of school. She loves art, but all her artistic talent goes into the metal sculpture she makes today. Quilting is just too soft for her. It was only my youngest, Dorothy, who took to quilting, but she died in 1977. But I'm still yet quilting.

In 1992, Mrs. Matthews's daughter wrote to me saying that her stepfather had died, and in early 1993 I received another note telling me that her eighty-five-year-old mother had just married her third husband, Curtis Hurst, who was born in 1918 in Atlanta, Georgia, and was eleven years her junior. While a child, Mr. Hurst helped his mother, Anna Horn Hurst (1899–1989), quilt. His family migrated to Michigan in 1929. Today Mr. and Mrs. Hurst sew and quilt together.

Almost a year passed before I was again able to focus on the quilting project. However, during that time, I continued to receive inquiries about my 1980 book, *Something to Keep You Warm*. One, in July 1987, came in a letter from Barbara Pietila, who was from Baltimore and was then living in Moscow with her Finnish husband, who was the Moscow correspondent for the *Baltimore Sun*. She had been referred to me by someone in the Women of Color Quilters' Network. Barbara was teaching quilting to a group of women from fifteen different countries, including some Africans, and desperately wanted to share my book with them. Quoting from her letter, "As you may be aware, most of the quilt books published feature only white quilters and traditional patterns. I am developing a pattern based on the *Five Little Colored Girls* quilt from your book and will credit Ms. Dennis with the pattern, but I would like to show my class the book from which it came. I guess I should admit also that deep in my heart I want to show them that an African American has written a book about us, too." This letter started a long chain of communication that led to our trying to bring an exhibit of quilts to Moscow, including traditional quilts from my collection, some of my original designs, and innovative contemporary quilts. Unfortunately, because of

political complications, this exhibit never came to fruition. However, Barbara and I stayed in touch, and when she returned to Baltimore, she helped organize the African-American quilters there and also helped make *Mother Africa's Children*, one of the quilts I designed for the Columbus Quincentenary (see pp. 107ff.).

SOUTH CAROLINA, 1987

In October 1987, Worth and I were approached by Emory Campbell, director of the Penn Center on St. Helena Island in Frogmore, South Carolina, to assist in preparing and documenting their seventh annual Heritage Festival that November, which would coincide with the 125th anniversary of the Penn School's founding. We were both familiar with the Penn Center's historical and contemporary significance for black culture, and I had last been there in the late seventies to document a pre-service training program for health and nutrition workers being carried out by the Center under contract with the Peace Corps.

Left to right: Redell Rivers and her sister Josephine Perry, both quilters.
ST. HELENA ISLAND, BEAUFORT COUNTY, SOUTH CAROLINA, NOVEMBER 1987 (35 MM CT)

Janie Hunter, storyteller, gospel singer, and quilter, from Johns Island, South Carolina, who won a 1984 NEA Heritage Fellowship Award for storytelling and singing, at the Penn Center on St. Helena Island.

BEAUFORT COUNTY, SOUTH CAROLINA, NOVEMBER 1987 (35 MM CT)

Victoria Scott.

ST. HELENA ISLAND, BEAUFORT COUNTY, SOUTH CAROLINA, NOVEMBER 1987 (5-47287/17A)

St. Helena Island was one of the first communities in the Atlantic coastal "Low Country" to be liberated by the Union Army during the Civil War. In 1862, several Northern educators came to the island and established the Penn School, the first school for freed slaves. Over the years, the Penn School evolved into Penn Center (more formally, Penn Community Services, Inc.), still a focal point for programs and services addressing a wide range of community, cultural, and economic issues.

On my way to Penn Center, I stopped in Raleigh, North Carolina, to see my cousin Sonny Williams and his wife, Ella Perry, who is from St. Helena Island. She still has family living there and put me in touch with her mother, Josephine Perry, and her aunt, Redell Rivers, both quilters.

YORUBA VILLAGE

As I continued south, near Sheldon, South Carolina, I spotted a small sign that said "Yoruba Village." Though I had been unaware of its exact

location, I knew of this village through Oba Oseijeman, one of its chiefs, whom I'd met ten years earlier at the founding conference of the Association of African and African-American Folklorists at Howard University in Washington, D.C. He had invited me to visit, and I decided to take the opportunity to inquire after him. At the visitors center, I explained why I had stopped, and I paid my respects to the shrine of Elegba.* I was then escorted to the chief's compound, where although he was in Nigeria at the time, I was warmly greeted and fed by his family. I then toured the village, which I experienced as an idealized version of a Nigerian Yoruba village, with a library, a school, many shrines, a burial ground, and traditional African clothes worn by everyone I saw. Although invited to stay the night, as I was expected at Penn Center, I continued on my way.

* Also known as Legba, "the Keeper of the Road" or the "Old Man at the Gate."In Afrocentric religious ceremonies, one often has to go through Elegba to reach the other African deities.

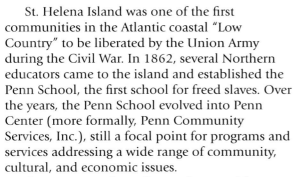

Helen Lawrence with her daughter Sharon Lawrence Brown. The quilt to the left was made by her mother, and the one to the right by her, as were all the quilt tops in front of her. BERKELEY COUNTY, SOUTH CAROLINA, NOVEMBER 1987 (FRAME 12, 2¼ CT)

ST. HELENA ISLAND

After checking in at the Center, I went looking for Josephine Perry, who lived about a mile away. When I pulled into her driveway, she was sitting on her front porch waiting for me. I don't know what Ella had told her, but she greeted me like a long lost relative, saying, "You look just like my daughter said you would, a big smile and a skinny body. My sister Redell is on her way over here to show you some of her quilts, and there's some of mine piled up in there on the bed."

I saw about ten of her quilts, which I'd describe as big squares sewn together out of whatever material she had, with no particular pattern. Some had been quilted, and others tacked, and they were all very colorful and heavy.

Her sister arrived with four or five similar quilts, and after a wonderful dinner, they took me on a tour of the island. I was particularly interested in the old churches, graveyards, and praise houses (small community buildings dedicated to singing the Lord's praises in informal services). We also stopped by Penn Center, and I left word for Worth that I'd be spending the night with family and would see him the next day.

The next morning was bright and overcast, my favorite light for making black-and-white pictures. Even though it was November, it was still very warm. I hung some of their quilts on the clothesline and posed them right in front (see p. 72).

Through Ms. Perry, I met Victoria Scott, a third-generation quilter (see p. 73). Ms. Scott was born in 1900 and learned to quilt from her mother, Julia Washington (1880–1948), and her maternal grandmother, Grace Jenkins (1855–1928), both of whom were born on St. Helena Island. Some of Mrs. Scott's fondest memories of her early childhood were going to praise houses to sing and

Ora Switzer, the oldest woman in Nicodemus.
NICODEMUS, KANSAS, JULY 1988 (35 MM CT)

pray, and women gathering at her house for quilting bees.

Among the bearers of traditional culture presented at Penn Center's Heritage Festival itself was Mrs. Janie Hunter of Johns Island. She is best known as a storyteller and singer, for which she was awarded a National Heritage Fellowship in 1984 by the National Endowment for the Arts Folk Arts Program. But this day she was displaying some of her quilts. Her tops were made of squares similar in size to those of the other local quilts, and the muted earth-tone colors of the fabric she used, embraced by the late afternoon sunlight, looked stunning (see p. 73).

There had been so much written about African retentions among the Gullah people in these Sea Islands that I expected their quilts to reflect this and to look quite different. However, neither here nor elsewhere in the area did I perceive these anticipated variations in design or materials.

Penn Center had recently hired a new curator for its museum, Vanessa Thaxton, a recent graduate from Hampton University in Virginia. Prior to coming to the Center, she had known little about the area, and as Worth and I planned some local fieldwork after the Festival, we invited Vanessa to accompany us, and we left St. Helena together. During that time, we photographed one quilter, Helen Lawrence. As we were driving on Highway 41 just south of Huger in Berkeley County, Worth spotted some quilts hanging on a line. We stopped to investigate and met Mrs. Lawrence. As a young woman, she had migrated to New York from South Carolina to work in the factories and she returned after she retired about a year before. She was now making quilts as Christmas gifts.

A Second Redefinition

We returned home for Thanksgiving, and over the holidays I began to get ready for what looked like a very busy 1988. As I reflected on the two years since my 1985 decision to expand the project's scope, I realized a couple of things. First, although I had somewhat succeeded in documenting non-Mississippi quilters, my progress and coverage were more limited than I'd hoped. Second, not all of the expansion had been to the South; some had been to northern states, such as Michigan. And, as I looked ahead, my immediate plans included another northern state, New Jersey, where I'd be curating an exhibition of quilts from my collection at the Bergen Museum of Art and Science in Paramus. I decided that I would continue to document African-American quilters wherever I could—North or South, East or West—while keeping my overall Southern focus, at least for now.

Missouri, Kansas, and Indiana, 1988

The summer of 1988 provided a significant opportunity for attention to the project. To celebrate our twentieth wedding anniversary, my wife and I were going to drive across the country. After stops in Cincinnati and East St. Louis, Illinois, we made our first quilt-related stop in St. Louis, Missouri.

Black Jack Scarecrow, 1988, 68" × 81"
Quilt by Emma Downs.
    (35 MM CT)

Lorraine A. Mahan.
DELAWARE COUNTY, PENNSYLVANIA, 1989 (35 MM CT)

St. Louis, Missouri

We stopped in St. Louis so that I could finally meet Cuesta Benberry, whom I knew only through our phone calls and correspondence over the previous decade. Cuesta is a teacher, writer, lecturer, and historian, but these vocations hardly describe the accomplishments of this notable woman. The 1983 recipient of the Quilter's Hall of Fame award, she was selected for her tireless contributions to two important aspects of the world of quilting: history research and pattern collecting. Her work has continued, highlighted by the publication of her book *Always There: The African-American Presence in American Quilts*. Her skill and dedication in documenting these key areas have provided encouragement and inspiration, as well as historical documents invaluable to anyone working in the world of quilting. After a wonderful meal in her home, we sat and talked for hours. She had just returned from England where she had

Chuck Stone, former columnist for the *Philadelphia Daily News,* and his wife Louise D. Stone. The quilts were made by her grandmother.
DELAWARE COUNTY, PENNSYLVANIA, 1989 (NG 398/6)

seen an exhibition of South African quilts and had met a quilting group known as the "Soweto Sisters." I photographed her with one of their small quilts and one that she had designed. Early the next morning, we headed west and after a quick stop in Topeka, Kansas, continued to an all-black town called Nicodemus.

Nicodemus, Kansas

After the Civil War, the oppression of racism and Jim Crow laws swept the country, which in turn gave rise to a black separatist movement. Although the majority of black separatists held the view that colonies of black citizens should be formed in lands outside the United States, others held that autonomous colonies or communities should be set up within the territorial boundaries of this country. The West beckoned as a "safety valve" for black frustrations; it provided the promise of economic opportunity as it did for other Americans.

One of the best-known promoters of the idea of separate colonies within the United States was

Elizabeth T. Scott and Joyce J. Scott.
BALTIMORE COUNTY, MARYLAND, JUNE 1982 (35 MM CT)

Monsters, Dragons, and Flies (close-up), 1982, 59" × 70"
Quilt by Elizabeth T. Scott and Joyce J. Scott.
(35 MM CT)

Monsters, Dragons, and Flies, 1982, 59" × 70"
Quilt by Elizabeth T. Scott and Joyce J. Scott.
(35 MM CT)

Benjamin "Pap" Singleton, a native of Tennessee who organized a successful movement of these black settlers, or "exodusters," to the state of Kansas in 1879; others moved into the Oklahoma Territory. Of the thirty or more black towns that sprang up throughout this region, only a few remain today—the best known of which are Langston and Boley in Oklahoma, and Nicodemus, Kansas. Although I'd seen a PBS documentary that reported that many of these towns, including Nicodemus, were now just shells of what they once had been, I was excited to be

visiting one of the few places in middle America that relate primarily to African-American history.

We reached Nicodemus about three that afternoon. On the edge of town, I stopped to talk with a middle-aged man, Mr. Donald Moore, who was working in his yard. I explained to him my interest in black culture and he called out to Pearlena, his wife, and they invited us into their home. Right there in the living room, staring me in the face, was a big quilting frame. Mrs. Moore said, "You'll have to excuse the house, but I've got this quilting frame up." I asked, "Many women

African Diaspora, 1987, 110" × 116"
Designed and fabric selected by Roland L. Freeman.
Pieced by Annie Dennis et al. (See text.)
  (4 × 5 CT)

Ann S. Dickerson.
WASHINGTON, D.C., APRIL 1982 (35 MM CT)

Julee Dickerson Thompson.
WASHINGTON, D.C., APRIL 1982 (35 MM CT)

quilt here?" She replied, "Not anymore. At one time just about everybody did. It gets awfully cold here in the winter." After telling us the history of Nicodemus, Pearlena took us on a tour. There appeared to be no more than one hundred residents, there were no businesses, and the old four-room schoolhouse was abandoned. There was a Baptist church, a new community center, and some small apartment units that the U.S. Department of Housing and Urban Development had recently built for senior citizens. In one of these lived the oldest woman in Nicodemus, quilter Ora Switzer (b. 1904). All of the quilts I found here had been recently made (see p. 75).

SOUTH BEND, INDIANA

The only other stop on this trip relating specifically to quilts was in Indiana, on our way back home. Gerald Davis had told me about an African-American friend, Erskine Peters, an English professor at Notre Dame University in South Bend, who had a collection of quilts Gerald thought worth documenting. Erskine invited us to spend the night at his home, giving us time to see the collection. Most had been

made by family members who lived in and around Augusta, Georgia. I was especially intrigued by the unique design of a quilt made by his aunt, Emma Downs, called *Black Jack*. Before we left, I made arrangements with Erskine for his aunt to make one for my collection. She agreed, and had it ready for me when I met and photographed her in 1990 (see pp. 76, 87, and 99).

STAND BY ME: THE PHILADELPHIA PROJECT, 1988–89

Starting in the fall of 1988, and continuing through the first half of 1989, I was intensely involved with a project documenting African-American expressive culture in Philadelphia, Pennsylvania. The project had tie-ins to, and was supported by, both the Smithsonian Institution's Center for Folklife Programs and Cultural Studies and the National Geographic Society. The project team included folklorists Glenn Hinson, with whom I'd worked in 1985 when Philadelphia was featured at the Festival of American Folklife, and Jerrilyn McGregory, an African-American. Both were doctoral candidates in folklore at the

University of Pennsylvania. The project culminated in an exhibition at the Afro-American Historical and Cultural Museum in Philadelphia that coincided with the 1989 Centennial Conference of the American Folklore Society, and was featured in the August 1990 *National Geographic* magazine.

One of the highlights of the project for me was when Jerrilyn took me to meet quilter Lorraine Mahan. Right off Mrs. Mahan said something that set me back on my heels. "Young man, if you're looking to photograph some folklore, you might be in the wrong place." I looked at Jerrilyn and then back at Mrs. Mahan, who seemed almost to be sulking. At first I wondered if it was something I'd said or done; sometimes in my overly zealous way, I'm a little insensitive. So I asked, "Please tell me why you're saying this," and she replied, "Well, I done made quilts for President Jimmy Carter and even our mayor, Wilson Goode, and when I heard they were putting a quilt show together down at the museum, I took some of mine by. They looked at me like I was crazy and said, 'We're sorry. We're not looking for anything like this, and these have nothing to do with black folk.'" Mrs. Mahan just looked at me as though she was about to cry, saying, "You know, that really hurt me. My ideas for quilts come from my background and the way I feel. You know, whatever I take a notion to make, I just make it. You know how we black folk are. When I'm troubled at mind, I read the Bible, and I got some nice ideas for quilts out of that Good Book."

I asked her which quilts the museum had rejected:

> Well, let me tell you. When you're reading the Bible, you learn about all God's children, and it's a lot of talk about Jewish people. Even Jesus Christ was born a Jew. Well,

African-American Women, 1982, 83" × 93"
Squares by Julee Dickerson Thompson and her mother, Ann Dickerson, of Washington, D.C.; design by Roland L. Freeman; pieced and quilted by Annie Dennis of Mississippi. (FRAME 5, 2¼ CI)

> one day I decided to make me a quilt about these Jews, and I put me a big Star of David in the middle and a lot of other information right out of the Bible. I put it all on the quilt. It really looked pretty, and I was real proud of it. That was one of the quilts I took. After the museum rejected it, I gave it to a friend, Mr. Newman, my insurance man, who was Jewish. I've known him since I was seventeen. He's been aware of my quiltmaking and had a particular fondness for my Jewish quilt. I asked his advice when I was making it, so I know I have everything correct. You see, I don't sell my quilts, I give 'em to people I want to have them, so I gave it to him. Mr. Newman told me his son

heal her. [Then Mrs. Mahan started to laugh.] I do believe she used up all the power this quilt had, because the sixth time she went to the hospital it just wouldn't help her no more, and she died.

Mrs. Mahan's Bible reading had inspired her to make the largest quilt I'd ever seen. It consisted of 176 squares, one for each verse of Psalm 119, the Bible's longest. The whole quilt measures about 150 square feet, and she had cut out each letter of each word and appliquéd it. I was truly impressed. I told Mrs. Mahan that I thought her work was absolutely wonderful and that I was going to make her famous (see p. 77).

I also photographed Chuck and Louise Stone, preservers of quilts made by Louise's grandmother (see p. 77).

We decided to call the exhibit *Stand by Me* after the gospel song by Charles A. Tindley (1851–1933), who was born a slave in Berlin, Maryland, which is in Worcester County on Maryland's Eastern Shore—the same county where my great-grandmother Arbia Rounds Janey was born. Mr. Tindley had migrated to Philadelphia in 1875, where his first eight gospel songs were published in

African-American Men, 1982, 74" × 94"
(See *African-American Women,* p. 82)
(FRAME 6, 2¼ CT)

1901. He later became a prolific gospel composer and minister, and today Tindley Temple, one of the city's largest churches, stands as a memorial to him.

> When the storms of life are raging,
> Stand by me, stand by me;
> When the world is tossing me
> Like a ship upon the sea,
> Thou who rulest wind and water,
> Stand by me, stand by me.

really liked it too, and it's going to be willed to him. So you see, that quilt's going to be in his family for a long time, and that really pleases me.

Also, while doing some genealogy research on the family, one of my cousins discovered that we were mixed with Choctaw Indians, so that inspired me to make an Indian quilt. You know, it's like a medicine wheel. This one is my healing quilt. Every time I'm feeling bad, I put it over me and it makes me feel better. My cousin-in-law, Dorothy Oshby, had all kinds of sickness. She was in the hospital five times and each time she'd ask me to bring the quilt. This medicine wheel quilt would

At the October 1989 opening of *Stand by Me,* the Smithsonian Institution presented special certificates of appreciation to a select group of Philadelphia culture-bearers for their contributions to America's folk culture. One of these went to Mrs. Mahan. With tears in her eyes,

Hystercine Rankin.
CLAIBORNE COUNTY, MISSISSIPPI, FEBRUARY 1993 (35 MM CT)

Denver Gray, father of Hystercine Rankin. Photo courtesy of Hystercine Rankin.
JEFFERSON COUNTY, MISSISSIPPI (5-77228/41)

Laula Gray, mother of Hystercine Rankin. Photo courtesy of Hystercine Rankin.
JEFFERSON COUNTY, MISSISSIPPI (5-77228/47)

Left to right, standing: Essie Mae Buck, quilter; Patricia Crosby, director of Mississippi Cultural Crossroads; and Worth Long, folklorist. *Sitting:* Mary Ann Norton, quilter, and Geraldine Nash, quilter.

NATIONAL MALL, WASHINGTON, D.C., JUNE 1996 (35 MM CT)

she thanked me, saying, "You said you were going to get me some recognition." As we hugged, I whispered in her ear, "The best is yet to come." Mrs. Mahan's quilts were highlighted in the *National Geographic* spread, and she became world famous.

BALTIMORE, MARYLAND

While consolidating material from my Baltimore Arabbers Project, I ran into artist Joyce Scott, who in 1977, along with her mother, Elizabeth Scott, (see p. 78) had been presented at the Festival of American Folklife as quiltmakers. Joyce was a popular and successful young black artist, who was creatively blending traditional methods of quilting learned from her mother with her own academic background in fine arts. Mother Scott, as Elizabeth was affectionately known, had also long since moved away from anything traditional in her quilting. Independently, each of these wonderfully creative women was producing truly innovative quilts, and I asked them to make a collaborative

On April 2, 1939 at 8 o'clock Farrel Humphrey kill my father Denver Gray age 33, on Highway 20 near Union Church, Mississippi as long as I live I will never forget that morning. He sent me to the spring to get a bucket of water, but he didn't wait to get the water, as I went to dip the water, I heard the 4 shots that killed my father. Wasn't nothing did about it they didn't even arrested him. As I come back to the house Farrel Humphrey's son was standing in front of the steps, he said Laula if you want Denver he is in the middle of the road. Mother said, lord have mercy, she didn't have any one to go and pick him up. He stayed there until a log truck came and picked him up and brought him to the house. Mother buried him the next day Blacks was afraid to come to the funeral

My Father Left 8 Children,

Earnestine Gray	12
Juanita Gray	11
Hystercine Gray	10
Garie Gray	8
Vera Gray	6
Walter Gray	4
Wilbert Gray	2
Lovie Gray	6 wks

Hystercine Rankin's quilt *Memories of My Father's Death* (detail).

CLAIBORNE COUNTY, MISSISSIPPI, 1989 (35 MM CT)

Hystercine Rankin's story quilt, 43" × 64", about her life on the farm.
JEFFERSON COUNTY, MISSISSIPPI, 1993 (FRAME 3, 2¼ CT)

Emma Downs.
COLUMBIA COUNTY, GEORGIA, NOVEMBER 1990 (35 mm c1)

Alice Brunsonn.
HOUSTON COUNTY, ALABAMA, NOVEMBER 1990 (6-90016/4)

quilt for me. A few months later, they presented me with an incredible quilt they called *Monsters, Dragons, and Flies* (see pp. 78–79), which for some reason scares the living daylights out of me. I'm still trying to find the courage to sleep under it! In general, both Joyce and Elizabeth make quilts that are meant not necessarily as bedcoverings but more as works of art to be displayed—a phenomenon that continues to spread throughout the quilt world today.

In July 1990, I curated *More Than Just Something to Keep You Warm*, an exhibition of thirty quilts from my collection, at the Apex Museum in Atlanta, Georgia, as part of the second biannual National Black Arts Festival. I was touched by the many letters I received from African-American collectors, quilters, and quilt lovers expressing their pride in seeing such a wide range of quilts that related specifically to them and their culture, and encouraging me to continue the work.

Designing Quilts, 1990

African Diaspora

Starting back in 1976, I had periodically designed quilts to represent what I was learning about the relationship of quilters' lives and the collective African-American experience to their individual creations. The phrase, "I don't make anything fancy, I just make something to keep you warm," was the inspiration for my first design. More recently, guided by what I heard in the voices of those I was meeting, I had begun to envision quilts depicting the historical legacy of our struggle. The concept for the *African Diaspora* quilt (see p. 80) that I designed at this time grew out of the story about her family Slave Chain quilt told to me by ninety-four-year-old Mississippi quilter Mrs. Phoeba Johnson (see p. 40). The idea had been taking shape for the better part of ten years and hadn't really come together until now, when I saw it more clearly as a quilt representing the scope of black slavery and the African diaspora. Once I had drawn the design, I bought the material, cut and tacked down the chain links and the eight African maps, and then sent them to Mrs. Johnson's daughter, Annie Dennis, who also lives in Mississippi. She, assisted by her sister Emma Russell, who lives in Louisiana, embroidered around the chain, the maps, the African masks, and all the words. I then took the pieces of the quilt top to David Jones, an African-Jamaican tailor living in Maryland, and Cleophas Nampoza, a Ugandan seamstress who was a student at the University of Maryland, who machine-pieced the big blocks together. With the

Left to right: Eltha and her great-grandfather James "Highpocket" Lee.
HOUSTON COUNTY, ALABAMA, NOVEMBER 1990 (35 MM CT)

Gladys Wicker *(left)* and her niece folklorist Joyce M. Jackson.
EAST BATON ROUGE PARISH, LOUISIANA, NOVEMBER 1990
(FRAME 8, 2¼ CT)

help of Sophie Degan, an American citizen of Polish birth and the executive director of the Capital Area Division of the United Nations Association of the U.S.A., I found the flags I needed for the border, present-day flags of most African countries and of those countries to which slaves were exported.

Next, a group of students, some hearing and some deaf, some white and some black, from the Model Secondary School for the Deaf at Gallaudet University in Washington, D.C., and two of their teachers, Margaret Reichard and Matt Goedecke, attached the flags. Julee Thompson, a Washington, D.C. artist, hand-embroidered the three children's faces across the top, and her mother, Ann Dickerson, hand-embroidered the lines around the border (see p. 81). The black, green, and red are emphasized as the traditional colors of African liberation. Then everything was sent back to Annie Dennis to be quilted.

AFRICAN-AMERICAN WOMEN AND AFRICAN-AMERICAN MEN

Throughout my studies, whenever I met creative fiber and soft-sculpture artists, I started thinking

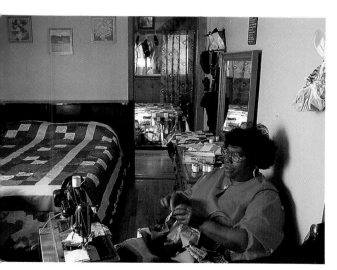

Hattie L. Childress.
SHELBY COUNTY, TENNESSEE, NOVEMBER 1990 (35 MM CT)

Myrtis W. Lord's bedroom with a quilting frame suspended from the ceiling.
BIENVILLE PARISH, LOUISIANA, NOVEMBER 1990 (35 MM CT)

of ways to blend their talents into quiltmaking. For years, I had been watching the wide range of things that Julee Thompson was doing; I was particularly fascinated with the dolls she made in collaboration with her mother. At about this time I based two other quilts on these women's work (see pp. 82–83). I first asked Julee if she could put variations of a doll pattern on different pieces of cloth. For each quilt, she agreed to do nine squares, each with a different doll. She designed and appliquéd the bodies and then embroidered the facial features and hair; then her mother designed and appliquéd the clothes and accessories. I worked each set of nine squares into a design and asked Annie Dennis to quilt it. Julee had never quilted, and her mother had made only traditional quilts, but after I showed them what Mrs. Dennis had done, they became so excited that they've both been making quilts ever since.

MISSISSIPPI CULTURAL CROSSROADS, PORT GIBSON, MISSISSIPPI, MARCH 1990

One of the hardest and most enjoyable jobs I do each year is to help with the Mississippi Cultural Crossroads (MCC) quilt competition and exhibition. MCC is a remarkable organization in Port Gibson, run by Patty Crosby. Patty's husband, Dave, teaches at nearby Alcorn State University, a black land-grant college, in Lorman, Mississippi. I've known the Crosbys for about twenty years now and am continually impressed with the rare combination of professionalism, skills, enthusiasm, commitment, and willingness to immerse themselves in the local culture that this white family has brought to their work in Mississippi. Dave, Patty, and their three young daughters came to Mississippi from Evanston, Illinois, in 1973 when Dave accepted a teaching position at Alcorn. Once I asked them why they had chosen Mississippi, and Patty simply had answered, "Well, it seemed like a nice idea at the time. We were eager to be in a place where the kids could run and play safely, and Dave wanted to teach in a college where he thought his teaching might make a difference." I had first met Dave in 1976, in connection with the Mississippi Folklife Project. We have been close friends and professional colleagues ever since.

The Crosbys' three kids helped integrate the Port Gibson public schools. Patty was working part-time for the U.S. Census Bureau doing

Talmadge and Myrtis W. Lord.
BIENVILLE PARISH, LOUISIANA, NOVEMBER 1990 (1-90013/12A)

monthly unemployment surveys—work that afforded her an opportunity to gain insight into the local community. She recalls being warmly received in a lot of black homes, which she attributes to her kids' attending the public schools and Dave's teaching at Alcorn.

Realizing that there were no art or other cultural enrichment activities in the community for black or white kids, Patty established MCC and obtained a series of grants that enabled her to employ local black quilters to teach quilting in the public schools. Another project that involved school kids interviewing and photographing community elders evolved into a very colorful magazine called *I Ain't Lyin'*. MCC initiated a summer arts project, which later expanded into both in-school and after-school programs, and also put together a theatrical troupe of high-school students called "Peanut Butter and Jelly Theater" that tours the state every summer.

In fifteen years of struggling to survive, Mississippi Cultural Crossroads has evolved into a nationally known culture, arts, and education organization. Building on its early efforts with just a few quilters, it has become well-known in the quilt world and many of its quilters are widely recognized, with their quilts being sold around the world. In 1988, MCC pioneered the first annual integrated quilting competition in the state's history. At this event, quilts are not judged according to one set of artistic standards, but instead are categorized based on style (genre) and on whether the quilter is novice or experienced, with an additional category for collaborations between adults and children. Since that first year, I have proudly served as a judge for the competition.

Both the breadth and reputation of MCC's programs have grown continuously, and the Smithsonian invited MCC's quilters to represent the South during the summer of 1996, first at the Festival of American Folklife in Washington, D.C., and then later as part of the cultural program associated with the Olympic Games in Atlanta (see p. 84).

A long-time supporter and major benefactor of MCC is Camille Cosby (Bill Cosby's wife), a quilter and quilt collector herself (see pp. 164ff.). Patty first met Camille in the mid-1980s when helping her locate some examples of rural housing to photograph for inclusion in research for her master's degree program. As Patty puts it, "I was very happy to help Camille, because she wasn't one of these people who takes from the community and doesn't give back. True to her word, a few weeks later, she sent pictures back to everyone whose home she had photographed." Camille was so impressed with Patty's work in the community and the quilters she met there that she has contributed toward the purchase of some badly needed new buildings, and she also buys several quilts annually for herself and as gifts for others.

MASTER QUILTER HYSTERCINE RANKIN

MCC's 1990 quilt competition was special, because it served as a time to recognize their senior quilter-in-residence, Hystercine Rankin, who had recently won the Mississippi Arts Commission's Susan B. Herron Fellowship. I felt very proud to have played even a minor role in helping her receive this $5,000 award. One evening at dinner, while chatting with her and her husband, Ezekiel Rankin, an incredible story of her family began to unfold (see p. 84). Both Hystercine and Ezekiel came from a long line of proud, independent, and

Memories, 1979, 80" × 71"
Quilt by Emma Russell.
      (35 mm ct)

Scripture, 1987, 77" × 84"
Quilt by Emma Russell and her sister Annie Dennis.
(35 mm CT)

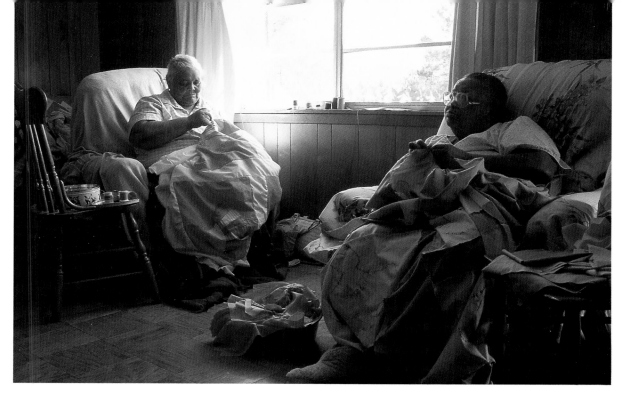

Left to right: Louida Davis and Bonnie Square.
EAST BATON ROUGE PARISH, LOUISIANA, NOVEMBER 1990 (35 MM CT)

strong-willed people in Jefferson County, Mississippi. Mrs. Rankin's great-great-grandmother was part Indian and partnered an African slave. This man and his eleven- and twelve-year-old sons were conscripted into the Confederate Army to dig trenches, carry water, and gather wood. All three of them were killed during the siege of Vicksburg (1863). Her great-grandfather, Joseph January, was the youngest child of that union, and although he barely remembered his father, he passed on this story his mother told him.

Joseph had two sisters, Ida and Seles. In her teens, Ida went to work as a cook on the nearby Segrest plantation, and even though slavery had ended, she was still taken advantage of by white men there and bore three children by them. It is not known what happened to those children, except for her son, who went to Chicago. Then Ida got tired of being abused and returned to the family place to live with her brother Joseph. There she took up with a middle-aged fiddler, Wesley Rankin, and around 1893 bore a daughter, Mary, who lived to be ninety-four. As a child, Hystercine quilted with Mary, her distant cousin, and learned this history. Her great-grandfather Joseph January, affectionately known as "Daddy Joe," married

Elvira Segrest in 1878, and they had one son and four daughters. A white man named Shelton, a neighboring farmer, was notorious for raping black women and bragging about it. One day when Daddy Joe was working in the field, Shelton raped Elvira, and she gave birth to his daughter, Olivia, who was her last child. Daddy Joe raised and cared for Olivia as he did his own five children. All five girls graduated from Alcorn College in Lorman, Mississippi. Olivia later married a Mr. Bailey from Red Lick, Mississippi, and they had a daughter, Idella. Idella married a Mr. Porter from Jackson, Mississippi, and they migrated to California, where Idella worked to put herself through college and raised her daughter Lillie Mae, who today is a successful businesswoman.

As the three of us sat in Mrs. Rankin's kitchen, I studied her face as she sorted through a bag of scrap material to add to the quilt top she was piecing. I didn't want to upset her, but I was very curious about Daddy Joe, so I asked whether anyone had ever done anything to the Shelton man for raping Elvira. Mrs. Rankin replied:

> Well, you gotta remember, I wasn't born yet and this was told to me, but white folks

could do anything they wanted to do in those days, and if one of our men said something, they'd just kill him. Daddy Joe was a fiercely independent man—he bought about one hundred acres of bottom land, most of it swamp, and cleared all of it himself. He didn't want his children to ever work for any whites, especially his daughters, because he knew how the men would be after them. Let me explain what happened.

Daddy Joe's daughter Alice, my grandmother, was working as a teacher down in Fayette, and this white man named Meeks raped her, and wasn't nothing for her to do but come home and tell her father. Daddy Joe sat in the hallway of the big house he'd built, with a shotgun on his lap, and just cried like a little baby. That thing hurt him so bad he didn't know what to do. He had his family to look after, and if he went for that white man, they would've killed Daddy Joe, probably burned his place and taken the land. That's just the way it was for us in those times. Alice had the baby, Laula, who was my mother, and Daddy Joe raised her. Mama had red hair and freckles, looked just like that white man, and he insisted that she be educated at a Catholic school in Natchez and he paid for it. And when she finished there, he sent her to Alcorn College. After graduation, she started teaching around Jefferson County. When she was assigned to the old Galbreath School on Highway 20 in Union Church, she boarded with Walter and Garie Gray's family.

The Grays had a son named Denver, who at sixteen had been sent away to live in St. Louis. You see, even as a young man he didn't take no stuff off white folk. One day, him and some of his cousins, boys and girls, were making molasses out at the cane mill, and there was this old white man winking and beckoning to one of the girls to come with him. When Denver saw what was happening, he grabbed a shotgun and fired at this white man. Even though he missed, his daddy knew there'd be trouble, so he hurry

up and sent him away to stay with some of his relatives in St. Louis. But Mr. Gray was worried about sending him there too, because his brother Allen, who was a musician, had been killed in the horrible race riots they had up there in 1917. The old folks talked about them riots for years, and lots of people who left here came back for a while.

I then asked Mrs. Rankin, "What relation is Denver Gray to you, and who told you all of this?"

Well, Denver Gray was my father, and it was Garie, his mother, who told me the story. You see, we'd be sitting around quilting, and she'd tell me everything. Denver came home for a visit, took one look at my mother, and didn't want to leave. They got married on Christmas Day 1925 in Daddy Joe's house. I got a letter right here where my great-auntie wrote to a cousin in St. Louis saying we had a big wedding last night, and Laula married Denver Gray. Mama kept on teaching and Daddy went to farming, and they had eight children. I'm the third girl, and I was born in 1929.

I wanted to know how her father got along after he came back.

He was still a man who didn't cow down to white folks, and people thought he was crazy because if he saw a white man bothering anybody colored, he'd stop him. They didn't like that. Mama got transferred to another school closer to Fayette, the old Highland School, a one-room school that went to the eighth grade, but Daddy rented a house near the school so she wouldn't have far to walk every morning. And that's where it all happened.

We were sitting on the front porch, and Daddy sent me down to the spring to get him some water. I must've went to playing or something, and when I came back he was gone. He just went down the road, I guess death was on him, because he didn't wait to get his water. I was ten years old, and I'll never forget it as long as I live. Just as I went to dip some water, I heard some shots, but I thought it was somebody hunting because it was back behind the house. When I got back to the house with the water, that young white Humphrey boy was standing there, and he said to my mama, "Laula, if you want Denver, he's down in the road."

We were about a quarter mile off the road, up on a hill. Mama cried out, "Lord have mercy." She didn't have no way to get my daddy from the road. And Denver laid there for three hours until a lumber truck came through. They picked my daddy up and brought him to the house, and we all gathered round him until my grandparents came. They stayed up with him all night. Grandmother Gray went and got a casket, they put him in it and put it on a wagon, and we all walked to the cemetery. The cemetery was right near the woods and black folks was scared to come because they thought those white people was gonna come and shoot them too and the rest of us. It was just us family put my daddy in the ground.

It was that Farrell Humphrey that did it. He's the one that shot my daddy down in that road. My daddy must have been trying to get to him because he shot him four times in the chest. We ain't never known how many was there when this happened, but we do know that Farrell Humphrey went around bragging he killed this uppity nigger. Granddaddy Gray, who was a real proud man, took his other four sons who had come here from Brookhaven and they drove down there to the old Cato store in Union Church. They tell me all these white folks were standing there like buzzards on a cow waiting to see what would happen. He went right up to that store and told his boys not to get out of the car, "I'm going in and let Paul Cato and all these other rednecks know they're not gonna scare me out of here." You see, these Catos already cheated his daddy out of a bunch of land. But didn't nothing happen.

After what happened, Mama was too scared to stay in that house, so after we buried Daddy, my grandparents came back to the house and got the beds and stove, and the little ones rode in the wagon and the rest of us walked about fifteen miles from Union Church to the Blue Hill community. Daddy Joe just put his arms around us and said, "This is y'alls home now." My mother didn't finish out the school year, she just stopped teaching for a while.

My grandmother Garie Gray came and got me and I stayed with my father's parents for about three years until Garie died. It was during this time I learned a lot of what I'm telling you now about the Gray side. All them Grays played music: Granddaddy played the drums and his brothers played horns. My great-uncle Ed Gray had a swing band up in Greenville and they traveled all over the country. He had a daughter named Jessie Lee McBride who taught school up there, and today right there in Greenville they got a school named after her.

In 1941, two years after my father died, Daddy Joe passed, and a year later when Grandma Garie died, I moved back to Daddy Joe's place. Right on that same hill, "Sister Alice," my mother's mother, had built a house, but it wasn't big as Daddy Joe's. And my great-uncle Lovie, who was a World War I veteran and had been to Paris—he stayed there, too. He was married but didn't have no children. You see, the whole family helped raise us. We all worked together, raising our corn, our cotton, and our animals. Only time you sit down was to quilt, and I learned most of my quilting from my grandma Sister Alice.

Sister Alice had taught for thirty years and was retired. We did a lot of quilting. We helped out needy people, we even made overalls for people with big families, like fourteen or fifteen kids, sewed for white and black folk. Wasn't no buying and selling quilts in those days. You just gave them away. Poor folk didn't have nothing. We weren't rich, but we had our land and a big garden so we didn't go hungry. Everybody was poor then.

Nora Lee Ezell, who was recognized in 1992 as a Master Traditional Artist by the National Endowment for the Arts Folk Arts Program and awarded a National Heritage Fellowship. GREENE COUNTY, ALABAMA, NOVEMBER 1992 (35 MM CT)

We quilted in the front room, in front of the fireplace. We did our cooking at that fireplace too. We'd have sweet potatoes in the ashes, a pot full of sweet peas, and make biscuits in a black iron pot. To this day, I don't know how them biscuits never burned. Sometimes we'd have a quilting bee with two or three neighbors, and the young girls standing around that frame. After we'd come from school and finish our homework, she'd have a lamp on the mantelpiece and we'd quilt into the night. We'd quilt on weekends and rainy days. I've been quilting on something ever since I was twelve.

I remarked to Mrs. Rankin, "I notice you call your grandmother 'Sister Alice,'" and she explained:

You see, young folks follow what old folks say. When Mama was growing up, she heard her aunts and uncles call her mother Sister Alice, so she never called her mother

"Mama," she just said "Sis Alice," and that's why we call her that.

All the while this was going on, Mama was back teaching, and she'd go up to Chicago to work in the summertime to get extra money for our clothes and stuff. Folks up there just sent us a lot of clothes. You see, people was trying to help the lady whose husband had been killed down South, and we got some real good stuff. In the same apartment house where Mama was staying, she met a Mr. Herman Wilson. They married around 1943 up in Chicago, and when they got off the train in Port Gibson, a mob of white men start to gather. They wanted to kill this nigger from up North who came down here with a white woman. Mr. Roy Lutson, an old German man, stepped in and stopped them. He said, "I know that lady, she's Joseph January's granddaughter. She's not white." And that's the only thing that stopped

Martin Luther King Jr., 1986, 90" × 82"
This quilt by Nora Ezell is now in the collection of the Robert Cargo Folk Art Gallery.

(35 MM CT)

Wini McQueen.
BIBB COUNTY, GEORGIA, DECEMBER 1990 (35 MM CT)

them. Mr. Herman rented a house and started sharecropping on the Brasfield plantation in the Blue Hill community. All the boys went with them and us girls stayed with Sister Alice. And him and Mama had one son.

I asked Mrs. Rankin if her mama ever quilted. "She did a little sewing and a little crocheting, but no quilting." I was also curious if Mrs. Rankin finished Alcorn College. "No, I went to the twelfth grade, but didn't finish." And finally, I wanted to know how she met her husband.

> I met Ezekiel at St. Marks Church in the Blue Hill community, and right off he started writing to me. He served four years in the Army and when he came out we got

married on March 9, 1946. I was sixteen years old. You see, Ezekiel is eleven years older than me, and by now I was helping Mama raise the children. Four years after I got married, Mama died of cancer. She was only forty-four, and left five boys behind, so me and Ezekiel raised my five brothers, and seven children of our own. I'm proud to say that all of my kids finished college at Alcorn, and Ezekiel has just retired from working there for many years.

I suggested to Mrs. Rankin that she consider making a story quilt of her father's death. She looked at me quizzically and said, "How would I do that?" I said she could appliqué the figures, and write the words and then embroider over them. She was a bit apprehensive and said she'd never done an appliquéd quilt. After a few weeks, I called and she said she'd started working on it. I asked her what it was like when she was alone, making this quilt.

> To me it was a joy, knowing after all these years, something I had kept inside of me, I mean just how that hurting feeling was, it was now coming out in the open. Wasn't nothing ever done about my daddy getting killed. No sheriff ever tried to arrest Farrell Humphrey. That white man robbed me of my daddy. The joy was doing that quilt. Daddy came to me in a dream and I said to him, now everybody will know how you got killed, and it seemed like after all those years a burden was being lifted off me and put into that quilt. Word got out that I was making this quilt, and I had people coming to the house, but I covered it up because some of them was white. I wasn't scared, I just didn't want them to see it before black people laid eyes on it.

I first exhibited this quilt (see p. 85) at the 1990 National Black Arts Festival as part of my exhibit, *More Than Just Something to Keep You Warm*. You could see tears in people's eyes as they stood in front of it. Faith Ringgold, a well-known New York artist who has designed several story quilts, came to see the exhibit and told me that Mrs. Rankin's quilt left her speechless. Over the years,

Mrs. Rankin continued to make story quilts of her life (see p. 86).

THE NATIONAL BLACK ARTS FESTIVAL, ATLANTA, GEORGIA, JULY–AUGUST 1990

The biannual National Black Arts Festival (NBAF) takes place in Atlanta, utilizing venues all over the city. The first Festival was in 1988, and I have found each of the three since then to be so meaningful and joyous as to set the NBAF apart from all other local, regional, and national festivals that I've experienced.

In 1988, I curated an exhibit of my photographs as part of the NBAF, and in 1990, I curated an exhibit at Atlanta's Apex Museum of quilts from my collection. Other quilting activities included demonstrations and exhibits by the local Reynoldstown Quilters.

While at the Festival, I had lunch with Beverly Guy-Sheftall, founding director of the Women's Research and Resource Center at Spelman College, whom I'd met only on the telephone. Although not a quilter, Beverly is a quilt collector. A respected feminist, she was one of several editors of an upcoming anthology called *Double Stitch: Black Women Write about Mothers and Daughters.**

GEORGIA, ALABAMA, MISSISSIPPI, TENNESSEE, AND LOUISIANA, NOVEMBER–DECEMBER 1990

Jerrilyn McGregory, one of the two folklorists I'd worked with on the Philadelphia project, was now teaching at the University of Georgia in Athens. She was engaged in a study of African-American folk culture in what is called the Wiregrass, the area where southwest Georgia, southeast Alabama, and northwest Florida meet. She had asked me to assist with photodocumentation of that area, and I was able to do that in early November 1990, combining it with a stop at Penn Center for its annual festival, and documenting quilters in Georgia, Alabama, Mississippi, and Louisiana.

Near Augusta, Georgia, I stopped and met Emma Downs, who had made the *Black Jack*

*Boston: Beacon, 1991.

Johnnie R. Jackson (1904–96).
BOX SPRINGS, GEORGIA, DECEMBER 1990 (35 MM CT)

Scarecrow quilt for me after I'd admired a similar one in her nephew, Erskin Peter's Indiana home back in 1988 (see pp. 76, 81, and 87). Then I set off to Dothan, Alabama, the center of the Wiregrass.

Southeast of Dothan, near the town of Ashford, I was joined by Kelly Reynolds, a friend who had recently migrated back to Alabama from Washington, D.C., and who had agreed to show me the Wiregrass. I met several traditional quilters there, two of whom especially excited me. One was Alice Brunsonn (see p. 87), who was in her nineties and for whom the street in front of her house had been named, and the other was James "Highpocket" Lee. Mr. Lee had preserved some family quilts, and his warm relationship with his young granddaughter was a pleasure to see (see p. 88).

I then went from the Alabama Wiregrass country to Mississippi and, with Dave Crosby accompanying me, continued my in-depth documentation of the quilters who work with Mississippi Cultural Crossroads.

I next stopped in Memphis, Tennessee, where I photographed quilter Hattie I. Childress (see p. 89). I also stopped in Bienville Parish, Louisiana to visit Emma Russell, one of Phoeba Johnson's daughters, whom I'd seen almost every year since first meeting her at Ms. Johnson's party in 1976. During this trip, I bought two quilts from her for my collection (see pp. 91–92). While I was there, Emma introduced me to Myrtis and Talmadge Lord. In their bedroom, for the first time, I saw a quilt suspended from the ceiling directly over their bed (see pp. 89 and 90).

From there, I continued to Baton Rouge, Louisiana, where folklorist Joyce Jackson was taking me to Zachary to photograph her aunt and several other quilters. Joyce is a very comfortable person to be with, and although we had met only a few times, I felt as if I'd known her a lifetime. I'll never forget the evening I first met her. She'd just come to Washington for a short visit with some friends who lived in LeDroit Park. Some of our mutual folklore friends, knowing we had similar interests, thought we should meet. When I arrived at the house, Joyce was in tears. She had neglected to unload her car when she first arrived, and someone had broken in and stolen her bags, one of which had the only typed copy of her dissertation. When I met with Joyce in Louisiana, she was teaching at Louisiana State University.

The town of Zachary is about twenty minutes north of Baton Rouge, and we spent the morning there with Joyce's aunt, Gladys Wicker. I went about making my photographs of them as Mrs. Wicker pieced a top and they reminisced about old times (see p. 88). After lunch at a neighbor's home, we met eighty-five-year-old quilter Louida Davis, her granddaughter Wanda D. Knighten, and another quilter, Mrs. Bonnie Square, who had recently come to live with them (see p. 93).

My next stop was in Eutaw, Alabama, first to say hello to the quilters I had brought to the Festival of American Folklife in 1986, and then to see Nora Ezell, a feisty but lovable quilter I'd first met in 1984 at a community empowerment conference in Epes, Alabama. At that time, Mrs. Ezell had been showing only her traditional quilts, but at the time of this visit she was becoming well-known for her story quilts (see pp. 96–97).

From Eutaw, I drove to Columbus, Georgia, to meet Fred Fussell, a fine folklorist, who was then curator at the Columbus Museum of Arts and Sciences. I had first met him through Worth Long at the 1982 World's Fair in Knoxville, Tennessee, and he had subsequently booked my *Southern Roads/City Pavements* exhibit. For years, he had been exploring the Chattahoochee Valley and had agreed to introduce me to some quilters, including Johnnie R. Jackson. When I asked Ms. Jackson with which of her quilts she would like to be photographed, she picked a scrap quilt made from old coveralls (see p. 99).

After stopping by the home of blues singer Precious Bryant and listening to some fine music, I thanked Fred and continued to Macon to meet quilter Wini McQueen. Wini was one of the first to put photographs on cloth in her storytelling quilts, and she also used a lot of African symbolism (see p. 98).

CHAPTER 4
Sickness and Healing
(1991–92)

THE SMITHSONIAN'S QUILT CONTROVERSY

The year 1991 marked one of the largest and most important controversies in the recent history of the American quilt community. It started when the Smithsonian's National Museum of American History granted a license for the replication of several of their important historic nineteenth-century quilts. Of the first four, three were representative Americana: the Bride's quilt, an 1851 wreaths-and-flowers work by a Carroll County, Maryland, bride-to-be; the Great Seal quilt, made in mid-nineteenth-century Frederick County, Maryland; and the Sunburst quilt, a calico design stitched around 1840 by a Funkstown, Maryland, woman. The fourth was an appliqué quilt depicting scenes from the Bible, made in 1886 by an ex-slave from Georgia named Harriett Powers.

There was nothing strange about this; it was business as usual for the Smithsonian. Indeed, for years American museums have been making modern reproductions of American crafts as a mainstay of most museum shops. So the museum was taken by surprise when its action upset many people within the quilt community, not realizing that to this community quilts were much more than mere artifacts. Many of the academics involved were also surprised by the depth of feeling that was expressed, especially as people have been copying and modifying quilt patterns for years.

As best as I can reconstruct it, here is what occurred. The controversy started in July 1991 when American Pacific Enterprise was granted the license for the reproductions and arranged to have them produced in China. The *Washington Post* ran an article on December 20, 1991, announcing that these historic quilts were being replicated and would soon be for sale at prices ranging from $200 to $500, which was at most one-third of what they would have cost if handmade in the United States. Shock and disbelief was the initial reaction of many, including quilter Hazel Carter, the founder and president of the Quilter's Hall of Fame (1979) and one of American quilting's strongest proponents. Word quickly spread and resulted in a grassroots groundswell of protest. Mrs. Carter was among those who spearheaded a letter-writing campaign to the U.S. Congress and the Smithsonian, with copies sent to the *Washington Post*.

After meeting with Mrs. Carter, the *Post* responded to these actions on March 19, 1992, with a second article titled, "The Quilts that Struck a Nerve." A sidebar to the article, called "A Bible of Black History," talked about Harriett Powers and her quilt and showed an 1897 picture of her. The day after the article appeared, the Smithsonian did the right thing and called to ask Mrs. Carter to select a group of quilters to come there for a meeting to discuss this matter further. Then on Saturday, March 21, which the National Quilting Association had designated as the first "National Quilting Day," many quilters converged on Washington and, wrapped in quilts, marched in protest at the National Museum of American History.

Among those attending the meeting at the Smithsonian, held on April 10, 1992, were Bonnie Leman from Denver, founder and editor of *Quilter's Newsletter* magazine and *Quiltmaker* magazine, and an outspoken critic of imported Chinese-made quilts; Karey Bresenhan from Houston, Texas, who is the organizer of the world's largest annual quilt market and who

Appliqué Bible Quilt, ca. 1886, 73¾" × 88½"
Harriett Powers.
(PHOTOGRAPH COURTESY OF THE NATIONAL MUSEUM OF AMERICAN HISTORY, SMITHSONIAN
INSTITUTION, WASHINGTON, D.C., 35 MM CT, SLIDE# 75-2984)

provided statistical data on how these imports would affect the American quilting industry; Lee Porter, from Washington, D.C., a board member of the American Quilt Study Group and a quilt artist, who spoke eloquently of her reverence for the Harriett Powers quilt; Jinny Beyer from Virginia, an international quilting teacher and lecturer; Fred Calland, a quilter from Virginia; Lorraine Carter, who worked on the Maryland state quilt survey; and Viola Canady, founder of the Daughters of Dorcas and Sons quilting group

in Washington, and the only African American in the delegation.

Each side presented its views and there was a heated, somewhat acrimonious, debate; nothing was resolved. Because of disappointment with the initial meeting, passions ran high and new action emerged on two different fronts. Feeling that writing letters and speaking with department store personnel had not been effective, a quilting group of five women in Knoxville, Tennessee—Merikay Waldvogel, Linda Claussen, Eva Earl

Kent, Rebecca Harriss, and Jean Lester—proposed to form the American Quilt Defense Fund (AQDF) to focus on the involved institutions, and in particular to get the attention of top management at the Smithsonian. The AQDF was funded by the money these women had accumulated from prizes, commissions, and donations. It took the position that by reproducing these quilts in China, the Smithsonian had cut itself off from the very people who cared the most about their quilt collection, and that under better circumstances, these same people could become allies in generating significant support.

Concurrently, Quilts, Inc., of Houston, Texas—the company headed by Karey Bresenhan and Nancy O'Bryant that runs the International Quilt Festival, as well as several domestic and overseas quilt markets—also launched a massive lobbying effort. Armed with 25,000 petitions of protest signed by quiltmakers from all fifty states, Quilts, Inc., joined forces with the AQDF and brought enough pressure to force another high-level meeting at the Smithsonian. This time, with a more enlightened Smithsonian and a more diplomatic approach by the quilters, a compromise was reached. Of the seven quilt selections remaining under the contract with American Pacific, only three would be made in China, and the remaining four would be made in the United States. The Smithsonian would offer the quilt community more access to their collection, a major show in 1997, and opportunities for seminars and research.

Two issues dominated the controversy: the first was the mass reproduction of the quilts; and the second was having the work done in China. However, the whole matter might have gone unnoticed if not for the inclusion of the Harriett Powers quilt, which seems to have been regarded as a kind of living treasure and therefore invested with a sacredness one doesn't normally associate with conventional art objects.

In the mid 1970s, Dr. Gladys-Marie Fry had brought widespread attention to the Harriett Powers quilt through her research for the exhibit *Missing Pieces: Georgia Folk Art 1770–1976*, and since that time any serious study of American quilts that does not include the Powers Bible quilt would be considered incomplete. This unique icon of Americana is so widely revered

Descendants of quilter Harriett Powers pose very proudly with her famous quilt, which they have just seen for the first time, the Museum of Fine Arts, Boston, Massachusetts, February 19, 1996. *Sitting (left to right):* Oscar Powers, Daisy Powers, and LaPheris Powers. *Standing (left to right):* Stephanie Brooks and Joan Halimah Brooks.

(2¼ CT)

that to many quilters it was unthinkable and downright sacrilegious to replicate it. Often when people see the Harriett Powers Bible quilt, even if they're neither versed in the Bible nor know African-American history, they still respond intuitively to her images and recognize that her quilt possesses incredible integrity and meaning. It is also powerful in its cross-cultural use of imagery with echoes of African culture. When you add the poignancy of her story, it's an almost overwhelming icon: Harriett Powers was a freed slave living in Athens, Georgia, who in 1890, four years after an art teacher first spotted her quilt, was forced to sell it for five dollars because of financial hardship. It's arguably everyone's favorite African-American quilt; overall probably more quilters have a better knowledge of it than of the one at Mt. Vernon made by America's first First Lady, Martha Washington.

Marilyn Green.
WASHINGTON, D.C., FEBRUARY 1991 (FRAME 12, 2¼ CT)

Barbara Pietila.
BALTIMORE COUNTY, MARYLAND, OCTOBER 1991 (35 MM CT)

It seems that, in essence, this event became the focal point for a range of emotionally charged issues, that though not individually resolved, led to some significant results. First, there was the Smithsonian Memorandum of Understanding mentioned above. Also, the AQDF underwrote the Smithsonian's 1995 symposium "What's American about American Quilts," and initiated a successful fundraising effort for a permanent quilt showcase, inaugurated on the third floor of the National Museum of American History early in 1996. Another result was to stimulate mobilization of the quilting community, which led to the establishment of the Alliance for American Quilts. The Alliance is a nonprofit entity that hopes to serve as the umbrella organization under which all elements of the quilt world may unite to establish and fund a proposed American Quilt History Center and International Quilt Index.

What began as a naive miscalculation by the Smithsonian has resulted in a far more shared understanding across a far more inclusive quilt world. A coalescing among quilt groups of all kinds occurred nationally—from such fields as publishing, commercial suppliers, historians,

collectors, and art museums—resulting in a much easier exchange among American quilt groups, and between them and other such groups being formed around the world. The ultimate irony is that a quilt made in 1886 by an ex-slave who out of financial desperation sold it for $5 was the major catalyst for all of this.

An interesting postscript to this story is that until quite recently the Powers family was unaware that their great-grandmother Harriett was the Harriett Powers who had created these wonderful quilts. I was excited to have had the opportunity to photograph the family at the Museum of Fine Arts in Boston in February 1996 at their first viewing of the Powers quilts on display there (see p. 103).

WASHINGTON AND BALTIMORE, 1991

I photographed local quilter Marilyn Green in February, and then, later that year, Barbara Pietila, now back in Baltimore from Moscow, introduced me to a group of quilters with whom she was working. I included her work and that of five others in the group (four of whom I photographed) in *Expressions of the Soul: Three*

Edna Robinson.
BALTIMORE COUNTY, MARYLAND, 1991 (35 MM CT)

Melody Gordon-Healy.
BALTIMORE COUNTY, MARYLAND, OCTOBER 1991 (35 MM CT)

Perspectives on Baltimore's African-American Folklife, which I curated at the end of the year.

Barbara G. Pietila was born in 1942 and remembers seeing a nine-patch quilt that her grandmother had on her bed. After seeing Georgia Bonesteel quilting on television, she made her first quilt fifteen years ago in Baltimore, and since then has made about 35. Though she makes most of her quilts as gifts for special events, she also accepts commissions, and sells and shows quilts locally and nationally. She belongs to the Heritage Quilters, the Baltimore City Quilters Guild, the National Quilters Association, and the American Quilter's Society.

Edna Robinson was born in 1939 and is a novice quilter whose first quilt (made in 1986) was in the exhibit. She can't remember ever seeing anyone quilt in her family, and says she became fascinated with quilting after seeing the Mississippi quilts exhibited when *Something to Keep You Warm* toured to Baltimore in 1978. She took classes from quilter Elizabeth T. Scott, whom she met at Baltimore's Walters Gallery.

Melody Gordon-Healy was born in 1939 and was five or six years old when she started piecing. Though her mother's sister, Violet Gordon Seaborn, quilted, Melody says no one really taught her—"I just picked it up." There was a strong tradition of needlework in her family that is maintained as she now quilts with her mother. The first quilt she made as an adult, in her late twenties, was fashioned out of her children's old clothes. Of the twenty-five quilts she has made, about half have been commissioned; the others were made as gifts for family and friends.

Bernadette Gayles (see p. 106) was born in 1946 in Baltimore, and is from a family with a strong tradition of needlework. Her aunts and grandmothers quilted, and she has been sewing as long as she can remember. She has made about fifteen quilts, and has been exhibited in group shows in Maryland and Kentucky. Her quilted

Shelley C. Moody.
(35 MM CI)

Bernadette Gayles.
HOWARD COUNTY, MARYLAND, DECEMBER 1991 (35 MM CI)

jackets have become popular and are sold across the country.

Shelley C. Moody was born in 1950 and started quilting in 1983, and since that time has made eight quilts. She learned to quilt from Barbara Pietila, and also has an aunt, Annie Taylor, who quilts.

SICKNESS AND COMMUNION

In 1991 my own life changed dramatically. After returning from my annual visit to Mississippi Cultural Crossroads for that year's very successful quilt exhibition, I didn't feel rejuvenated as I usually did after the exhibit. For quite a few years, I'd been spreading myself too thin with the constant pressure of trying to accomplish a lot in a short period of time, always underfunded, and as I started my annual check-up, I felt as if my body was finally rebelling against those many years of abuse. Sadly, I was correct; I was diagnosed with cancer.

I knew that my great-grandparents, grand-parents, parents, a sister, and two aunts had all died of cancer, and it looked as though it was now my turn. I rapidly fell into a deep depression. I

didn't want to talk to anyone—not family, friends, or neighbors; not even my wife, Marcia. I went through an operation and then started treatments.

One night, in a dream, my grandmother Goldie appeared, putting a quilt over me and saying, "You'll be all right now." But it wasn't the family healing quilt. It was Betty Tolbert's red, black, and white strip quilt. In the middle of the night I got Mrs. Tolbert's quilt out of storage and slept under it. Little by little I began to feel better. My meditation room became my sanctuary: I would light all the candles on the altar and begin to look inward, past the pain, past the mental anguish, going deeper and deeper into the inner sanctum of my soul to find my inner light, to find the necessary strength to live.

And while at the altar of my innermost core, there was a communion of the spirits. My mother, father, grandmother, all my grandparents and great-grandparents, family and extended family, people I had met in Africa, the Caribbean, and my many travels throughout the Americas, were all telling me to be strong and that I must overcome this to finish my life's work.

During this time people I hadn't heard from in years sent short notes telling me to hang on, that they were praying for me. Others sent crystals, herbs, books, potions, candles, talismans, and all sorts of ornaments that they believed to possess healing powers. All of these efforts seemed to generate one tremendous force of energy to make me well. My creative juices started to flow, and things I'd been trying to conceptualize for years sprang forth. I was able to channel these thoughts into images that I wanted to put into quilt form to show the ongoing struggle of African people in the Americas throughout the past five hundred years. I began what proved to be a wonderfully creative and healing experience in developing a set of quilts that I would show as my contribution to the 1992 Columbus Quincentenary celebration.

MY QUINCENTENARY QUILTS

I had developed my plans for the Quincentenary in response to a request for a quilt exhibition I had received from Springside School, a private girls' school in Philadelphia, Pennsylvania. People from the school had seen the *Stand by Me* exhibit and the related *National Geographic* article, and the school had a strong African-American presence in its parents' association. As my exhibits usually hang in museums or cultural arts centers, my first inclination was to decline their request. They invited me to visit the school, and after I did, and they were able to assure me they would provide proper insurance and security, I agreed to an opening in January 1992. Although I knew that museums throughout the Americas, from Canada to Argentina, had been planning their Quincentenary exhibits for five or more years, and I had less than one year, I developed my concept for the show and was able to book a five-site tour, with a closing exhibit at the Museum of the American Quilter's Society in Paducah, Kentucky, in the fall of 1992. I now had only a few months to create these quilts.

I labored for a week, sketch after sketch, until finally the design for the quilt called *Mother Africa's Children* lay before me. This would be the opening quilt in the exhibition (see p. 124). In the design, the large black Adam and Eve figures at the bottom symbolically represent both Africa, as the cradle of civilization, and our species'

evolution, coming out of the sea and into the bush. This bottom section uses a combination of fabric and abstract figures for these ideas. The connecting bodies across the middle of the quilt signify the "Middle Passage." The central column that extends from the bottom directly up to the middle of the multicolored mask in the center of the top provides several unifying aspects to the quilt. First, its colors represent the many races that have mixed with blacks. The two vertical strips on each side of the center mask, each of which has three small faces in it, represent the different skin tones of African Americans resulting from this mixing of blood. Second, the large circle toward the bottom of the column, repeated in the circles in the two large figures, as well as in the circles in and next to the mask, represents the spiritual core of African people, both in Africa and throughout the diaspora. The large man and woman at the bottom are holding up the central horizontal strip, and in turn the smaller figures above their heads are supporting the vertical strips above them, in order to dramatize that Black Gold (slave labor) was the foundation for the wealth and economic development of Western civilization. The mass exploitation of African people by the church, the state, and the financial world are suggested in the two upper outside panels that contain outlines of ships of discovery, African faces (a woman on the right and a man on the left), and maps (Africa on the right and the Americas on the left). In summary, *Mother Africa's Children* is meant to represent our coming out of Africa, enduring the Middle Passage, and starting a different life in this strange new land.

This quilt started my rejuvenation process. It was now clear that I had to use all the strength I could muster to consolidate my life's work. Too many people had trusted me with the intimate moments of their lives, and I had a moral obligation not to violate that trust. I started the tedious process of organizing my records and photographs, and I tried to remember things long forgotten. While looking through the many photographs I'd taken of quilters, it dawned on me that I should design a quilt as a salute to all these wonderful people. I got a call from my

Hand Me Down My Mother's Work, 1991, 62" × 62"
Designed and fabric selected by Roland L. Freeman.
Pieced and quilted by Barbara Pietila of the African American Quilters of Baltimore,
Maryland.

(4 × 5 CT)

homeboy Ja Jahannes in Savannah, Georgia. Through the worst of my illness, Ja was one of the few who had kept up a constant flow of encouragement. Among his many other talents, Ja is a poet, so I asked him to write some poems about quilts. One was called "Hand Me Down My Mother's Work." This became the centerpiece for the design and the title for my tribute quilt to African-American quilters.

> Hand me down my mother's work
> In the bright patterns that she made
> For she did keep a dream or two
> From before she was a slave
>
> Hand me down my mother's work
> And the symbols that she knew
> For I must make a patchwork quilt
> For all my children too

The creative juices just kept on flowing. One evening cousin Jeannetta Chase came to me in a dream and told me to design a quilt based on "Lift Every Voice and Sing" (see p. 110). This is a poem depicting the struggles of African Americans written by James Weldon Johnson and put to music by his brother, J. Rosamond Johnson; it has become internationally known as the African-American national anthem. As I read the poem, I realized that I needed some drawings by my good friend, artist Julee Thompson, who through my encouragement had started quilting a few years earlier (see pp. 88–89). For this quilt I wanted three simple drawings, to illustrate the first two lines of each of the three stanzas of the song. These were my ideas:

> *Lift every voice and sing*
> *Till earth and heaven ring . . .*

For this I wanted to show a person singing, full of hope;

> *Stony the road we trod,*
> *Bitter the chastening rod . . .*

For this I wanted a whip hitting a person; and

> *God of our weary years,*
> *God of our silent tears, . . .*

Finally, I wanted a picture of a face with silent tears.

I was pouring so much energy into this process that it took my mind off my illness. Once I had completed the drawing for a design, I would work out the color scheme. Then I was off to G Street Fabrics, my favorite fabric store in Rockville, Maryland, to select the material. Normally, I would have had my Mississippi quilters make these quilts, but because of the intricacies involved in these new designs, I wanted to follow their construction very closely; therefore I needed a good seamstress who lived nearby. I am a member of the Daughters of Dorcas and Sons (DDS), a quilting group of more than one hundred people in the metropolitan Washington area, and I contacted the founder and president, master quilter Viola Canady. She took one look at my design for *Mother Africa's Children* and shook her head. She started laughing. "You're real good with that pencil, but you need to learn how to sew so you can make these wild things yourself. This is going to be a lot of work, and I don't come cheap." The joking over, we settled on a price and the work began. Viola did all the piecing, and three other DDS members—Gertrude Braan, Vivian Hoban, and Joyce Nixon—did most of the quilting (see p. 111). Mrs. Canady also pieced and helped them to quilt *Lift Every Voice and Sing* for me.

Historical ideas for story quilts just kept on coming. I wanted to say something about the Underground Railroad, so I called Raymond Dobard, another DDS member. Raymond is a professor of art at Howard University, and an excellent quilter. I remembered we had once talked about how the Jacob's Ladder pattern was also known by the name Underground Railroad. This pattern is believed to date back to the 1830s, when women were most active in the formative years of the abolitionist movement. The pattern was not published as the Underground Railroad until after 1870 because of the struggle for freedom and the Civil War. Quilts with this pattern were often hung outside to indicate a safe house for runaway slaves. Because of its strong directional motif, the pattern may well have been used to indicate direction, and conceivably it also provided approximate mileage to the next station, thus serving as a true map.

Lift Every Voice and Sing, 1991, 67" × 67"
Designed and fabric selected by Roland L. Freeman.
Pieced by Viola Canady and quilted by Gertrude Braan, Vivian Hoban, and Joyce Nixon,
members of the Daughters of Dorcas and Sons, Washington, D.C.
    (4 × 5 CT)

Four members of the Daughters of Dorcas quilting *Mother Africa's Children,* an original design by Roland L. Freeman. *Left to right:* Gertrude Braan, Vivian Hoban, Joyce Nixon, and Viola Canady.

WASHINGTON, D.C., NOVEMBER 1991 (FRAME 5, 2¼ CT)

Raymond agreed to make a few squares for me, just enough to show the design. I then went through all my books looking for images related to the Underground Railroad. The first image I selected was of Frances Harper, a black abolitionist from Baltimore who went to Philadelphia to assist William Still in his project to collect oral histories from blacks who had liberated themselves. Next were Harriet Tubman and Frederick Douglass, who were from Talbot County on Maryland's Eastern Shore. After his escape, Frederick Douglass went north, educated himself, and became an international statesman, newspaper editor, orator, and author. Harriet Tubman, also called "Black Moses," is noted for her many heroic return trips to the South to lead hundreds north to freedom.

The next image showed black runaways arriving at Levi Coffin's house, which was a stop on the Underground Railroad in Fountain City, Indiana. The rest of the images were famous paintings and etchings. Then, in the white blocks of the pattern, I wrote the names of places and people that were important to this struggle (see p. 112).

I asked Barbara Pietila, in Baltimore, to quilt *Hand Me Down My Mother's Work,* my salute to African-American quilters. Barbara did a superb job of piecing this complicated design, but she told me, "Piecing this quilt really got on my nerves. It gave me headaches." I tried to make light of it, but she said it wasn't funny. We had long talks about the big slave markets that used to

The Underground Railroad, 1991, 114" × 90"
Designed and fabric selected by Roland L. Freeman.
Pieced by Raymond Dobard of the Daughters of Dorcas and Sons, Washington, D.C, and
quilted by Annie Dennis, Mississippi.
        (4 × 5 CT)

be in Maryland, and she remarked, "It's a damn shame how they did anything they wanted with us—just sold us right down the river. Think I'll make me a quilt about it." A few months later, she showed me a quilt of a white man driving off with a wagonload of black people, and an older woman gathering foxglove leaves. I said to Barbara, "You know foxglove is poisonous," and she said, "Yeah, that's right, this lady is the cook and she's not only mad, she's about to get even." Barbara named this quilt *They Sold Nettie Down South* (see p. 114). On a lighter note, we joked about growing up in Baltimore and watching the

Arabbers* sell watermelons, so Barbara made me a small and intricate quilt that depicted this whole tradition (see p. 115).

By now, it was late fall and I had to put the final touches on the exhibit. Two Philadelphia-based folklorists, Catherine Jacobs and Cassandra Stancil, generously helped me hang it at the Springside School, its first venue. At the time, Cassandra was writing her dissertation on quilts in her family. The opening was a spectacular success, and three weeks later the *Philadelphia Inquirer* Sunday magazine ran a cover story on the six quilts I had designed specifically for the Quincentenary.

A few weeks earlier, I had submitted a photograph of the *Mother Africa's Children* quilt to the

* *Arabbers* is a folk term peculiar to Baltimore for people who sell produce and seafood door to door from horse-drawn wagons.

National Black Arts Festival (NBAF) to be considered for the official festival poster. NBAF art director, Stephanie Hughley, called to tell me that it had been selected and that she wanted me to fly to Atlanta for the unveiling of the poster at their press conference initiating the publicity for the 1992 festival. I was overjoyed. At the unveiling, I announced that I was also curating an exhibit for the 1992 NBAF in Atlanta, which I called *Some Things of Value: Images of African and African-American Folklife*. This exhibit combined my photographs of culture-bearers with artifacts either used or produced by them, and it included the seven quilts I had designed for the Quincentenary.

Right after I returned from Atlanta, my Quincentenary quilt exhibit opened at the Beach Institute in Savannah, Georgia, to coincide with the meeting of the North American Pan African Congress. It then moved on to the National Civil Rights Museum in Memphis, Tennessee, to be part of the city's "Memphis in May" celebration. In planning a public forum at the Museum, I invited several local quilters, as well as Carolyn Mazloomi from Cincinnati and Hystercine Rankin from Mississippi, to participate. This museum is built on the site of the Lorraine Motel, where Dr. Martin Luther King Jr. was murdered on April 4, 1968; I thought this would be the perfect setting for Mrs. Rankin to publicly share the story of her father's murder. With several of her daughters there for moral support, this quiet gentle lady very nervously spoke of her father, a strong young black man—just like Dr. King—who was cut down in his prime for standing up for his rights and the rights of others. The audience sat speechless, moved beyond words.

There was one additional quilt I was designing for the Quincentenary, but had not completed it in time to include it in these first exhibit venues. It deals with the Maroons, and I completed it for inclusion in my exhibit at the 1992 NBAF and at the subsequent stops for the Quincentenary exhibit. I asked a Maryland seamstress, Shirley Blakely, to piece this design. Her husband, historian Allison Blakely, had assisted me with my research during the design phase. My quilt incorporates derivations from Saramaka designs, and various Maroon* statues and photographs, with the words "Maroons in the Americas, Slaves No More" in the center (see p. 116).

At the 1992 Festival of American Folklife, there was an entire section devoted to "Maroon Culture in the Americas." I had desperately wanted to participate in the fieldwork for this project, but just wasn't strong enough yet. The fieldwork was led by folklorist Ken Bilby, assisted by Diana N'Diaye, a Smithsonian folklorist. The Smithsonian agreed to bring Maroons from different parts of the Americas together in one place for the first time ever: among them, Alukus from French Guiana; Jamaicans from the Moore Town and Accompong communities; Black Seminoles from Texas and Mexico; Palenqueros from Colombia; and Saramakas and Ndjukas from Suriname. I was particularly interested in the Saramakas from Suriname, about whom I'd first learned from Richard and Sally Price's 1980 book and exhibit, *Afro-American Arts of the Suriname Rain Forest*. When I first saw the book jacket, I thought I was looking at a quilt pattern made by African Americans. As it turned out, it was a Saramaka man's shoulder cape of a patchwork design called "Aseesente." Fortunately

*"Maroons," *1992 Festival of American Folklife Program*, pp. 54–80. Reprinted with permission from the Smithsonian Institution's Center for Folklife Programs and Cultural Studies. The Maroons, derived from the Spanish "cimarron," were communities of independent, and often defiant, Africans in the New World who had liberated themselves. (Sometimes one also finds the term used to refer to slaves who escaped in America and fled south and west to live with Native Americans.) They were in the forefront of resistance to slavery, and they were also among the first pioneers to occupy and adapt to the more remote, unsettled spaces

in North and South America, and on several Caribbean islands. Their communities united people who had come from many regions of Africa and had different languages, customs, and traditions. Long before the independence struggles that gave birth to the American nations we know today, many Maroon communities fought for the right to self-determination, and several eventually forced the colonial powers to enter treaties guaranteeing their freedom and granting them partial political autonomy. Some of the better known Maroon communities that still exist are in the hills of Jamaica and in Suriname, French Guiana, and Brazil.

They Sold Aunt Nettie Down South, 1991, 60" × 60"
Quilt by Barbara Pietila.
(FRAME 4, 2¼ CT)

for me, Richard and Sally Price accompanied and presented some of the Maroons at the festival, and Sally Price helped me secure two of these Saramaka capes for my collection, as well as several Saramaka woodcarvings and small carved calabash bowls—all of which I included in the *Some Things of Value* exhibit.

My Quincentenary quilt exhibit concluded its initial tour with a showing that opened in October 1992 at the Museum of the American Quilter's Society in Paducah, Kentucky. I had insisted that a space in the exhibit be reserved to showcase the work of local quilters on a rotating basis, with a different quilter's work being high-lighted every two weeks. This helped to stimulate fresh interest in the exhibit, and it also helped the museum make new contacts in the African-American community. The museum did

a wonderful job in hanging the exhibit, and while it was there, I finally met Victoria Faoro, editor of *American Quilter* magazine, who had run a six-page spread in the 1992 winter issue featuring the quilts I had designed.

I returned to Paducah in January for the exhibit's closing during the Martin Luther King Jr. holiday weekend. As a closing activity, we held the first national African-American Quilters Forum, on January 16, 1993. This pioneering event was supported by The Group for Cultural Documentation, along with many local business, civic, and religious organizations in Paducah.

I photographed seven of the local quilters (see p. 117–20), one of whom, Catherine Monger, was a recent refugee from Liberia, West Africa. Her great-grandfather, Robert Hyatt Montgomery, was part of a movement that sent ex-slaves back to Africa and who had settled in Liberia.

Baltimore Arabber Selling Watermelons, 1991, 35" × 45"
Quilt by Barbara Pietila.
(FRAME 8, 2¼ CT)

MOVING TOWARD THE NATIONAL SURVEY

As I was regaining my strength after the worst part of my illness, I had a lot of time to reflect on how I'd use whatever time I'd still have once I could resume my work. I'd been documenting the world of African-American quilters for fifteen years, and while I'd seen interest in their quilts grow tremendously—along with a primarily scholarly, and sometimes bitter, controversy about their derivation and classification—I'd not yet seen any work based on a full consideration of their remarkable extent and diversity. I realized that I might be within striking distance of an initial systematic survey of the world of African-American quilters, their craft, and its preservation. If I could complete and publish such a survey, the subsequent study of these quilts at least would have a stronger foundation on which to build. In

addition, any study would have to take into account the full extent of our documentation about this aspect of African-American tradition and culture. And perhaps appropriate serious attention would begin to be paid to the remarkable lives of African-American quilters across the generations, and to the fact that their quilts are best understood in the context of those lives.

Let me expand and clarify how I'd developed this perspective. First, over the past thirty years, quilting by African Americans has been subject to the same influences—positive and negative—as many other areas of American social and cultural life. While there has been important growth in both interest and understanding, progress has been neither easy nor without setbacks. While professional opportunities and recognition have expanded, adherence to older perspectives has at times been surprisingly tenacious, and inclusion

Maroons, 1992, 83" × 73"
Designed and fabric selected by Roland L. Freeman.
Pieced by Shirley Blakely, Silver Spring, Maryland.
(2¼ CT)

of new learnings and the involved scholars has required more continuous a struggle than might have been anticipated. Along the way, criticism, although sometimes valid and appropriate, was also sometimes used to justify classism, racism and regional prejudices. And, the newly appreciated quilters themselves were too often exploited, and inadequately paid for their work or acknowledged in its copying or reproduction.

Despite these negatives, over the years our overall understanding and appreciation of quilting by African Americans has certainly grown; many bona fide practitioners have found artistic recognition and economic empowerment, and many of those studying and disseminating what has been learned are committed to understanding the full picture and acknowledging the complex and interrelated currents influencing these quilts

and their creation. At the same time, establishing an appropriate understanding of the world of quilting by African Americans remains an often frustrating struggle.

A SUMMARY OF FIFTY YEARS OF STUDY OF QUILTING BY AFRICAN AMERICANS

With deference to more rigorous treatment of the scholarship related to quilting by African Americans throughout this period, the following may be helpful in clarifying what had occurred by the early 1990s.

Building on earlier work in cultural anthropology by Franz Boas, Melville Herskovits, and Zora Neale Hurston, among others, Robert Farris Thompson and John Michael Vlach were among the vanguard of those engaged in the study of

African aesthetics during the 1960s and 1970s. Their general focus was cultural diffusion—how and why cultural elements change with contact among diverse groups—with significant attention to linking the cultural dynamics of the African diaspora to West African forms. They and other scholars essentially built on earlier arguments that there are cultural components among African Americans that are not mere vestiges of a past, but are living, vital evidence of an ongoing culture whose roots lay in Africa. Their work seemed timely, with the social, political, and cultural changes then occurring in the broader American society contributing to popular interest in their work.

Although these scholars' general interests were quite broad—aesthetics and aesthetic principles—one of the cultural dimensions they explored was textiles, including quilts, looking for patterns and structures that testified to these continuities throughout the diaspora. Maude Wahlman, a student of Thompson's, narrowed her focus to

quilts, building on Thompson's work on aesthetics, form, dynamics, and improvisation. Her approach was to look at a lot of quilts, seeking the actual patterns that Thompson's work had suggested would exist. In essence, Thompson, Vlach, and Wahlman laid the foundation for all the subsequent discussion of quilting by African Americans. They were the first to identify it as different from other quilting and to claim that it is informed by its own aesthetics; in short, they insisted that African-American quilting be looked at apart from other quilting traditions in this country.

When this position was first being put forward, only a limited number of quilts made by African Americans were generally available for study, and it was easy to select from these the strip (or improvisational) quilts, which were basically consistent in appearance with hypotheses of African continuances. However, starting in the late 1970s and accelerating thereafter, an ever larger number of quilts made by African Americans were

Christopher David Vaughn, who is learning to quilt from his grandmother.

McCracken County, Kentucky, January 1993 (1-66446/16, 2¼ CN)

Hazel K. Irvin.

Trigg County, Kentucky, January 1993 (7-66446/5, 2¼ CN)

being identified, and their wider aesthetic range was harder to ignore. This, combined with some of the direct responses to these scholars' work—including ongoing opposition to cultural diffusion theories, the implicit racism reflected in other people's attacks on the quality and value of the quilts the scholars were studying, and their seeming entrenchment and limiting of their focus to quilts supporting their conclusions—coalesced into an increasingly loud opposition. In addition, despite recognizing the importance of identifying these aesthetic patterns and their expression in quilts, many of the scholars' supporters began to believe that their position was overstated; that as correct as they likely were about many of the quilts made by African Americans, they were ignoring large and important parts of the tradition they were studying.

These were the issues being discussed when my first book of quilts made by African Americans, *Something to Keep You Warm*, was published in 1981. The book presented about twenty-five quilts from Mississippi, selected from the work of quilters I had documented, without consideration of the particular aesthetic they might or might not represent, and including a mixture of strip and symmetrical quilts. Although Maude Wahlman wrote part of the introduction, only some of the quilts included in the book reflected her aesthetic hypothesis.

During the 1980s, at times this debate about the continuity of cultural tradition in quilt aesthetics became incredibly acrimonious. The positions taken by individuals often affected their reputations, careers, and friendships. For whatever reasons, rather than seeking a broad framework that would accommodate the African-continuance position along with the ever greater diversity being identified in quilts made by African Americans, those studying the field became increasingly polarized around such issues as these: What should be said about all those quilts made by African Americans that don't fit the defined categories of African textile design,

Emma S. Blaine.
TRIGG COUNTY, KENTUCKY, JANUARY 1993 (1-66446/13, 2¼ CN)

Catherine Monger, quilter from Liberia.
McCRACKEN COUNTY, KENTUCKY, JANUARY 1993 (5-66446/10, 2¼ CN)

but look far more like Euro-American quilts? What about those African-American quilters who, after completing one quilt that looks like West African stripweaving, make their next to be perfectly symmetrical and ordered in every detail? What about white quilters who make improvisational quilts that look like what's been labeled as African-American aesthetics?

Though I had no answers to these questions, some things had become clear to me through my ongoing photodocumentation of cultural traditions—African-American and other— throughout the United States: I had come to learn that no community is singular; like all others, the African-American community is a host of many varied traditions, and within it there are different tastes and a remarkable variety in how these tastes are expressed. Also, what a craftsperson embodies in any given work may or may not tell us about her or his aesthetics in general, and even within a single aesthetic, one finds a lot of individual variation. In addition, our country's

history makes it inevitable for strong cultural traditions to impact each other, often in quite significant ways. For example, it would be truly surprising for the historical drive within the white world toward order and symmetry not to be reflected in every community, black and white, because it is such a dominant part of American, including African-American, culture. It is also clear that white traditions in America, especially aesthetic and cultural ones, have been affected by black traditions—as this is clear in language, music, dance, and cooking, for example, how could it not be true also for quilting? Why should it be so controversial to say that in quilting there have been reciprocal influences?

At the same time, I believed it important not to overstate these reciprocal influences; they clearly have not homogenized American quilting. While there is a definite African-American presence in the entire American quilting tradition— and similarly, a definite Euro-American presence in the African-American one—there are indeed

Pearl Smith.
CALDWELL COUNTY, KENTUCKY, JANUARY 1993
(3-66446/11, 2¼ CN)

Gracie Taylor.
McCRACKEN COUNTY, KENTUCKY, JANUARY 1993
(3-66446/9, 2¼ CN)

aspects of the tradition that seem to owe their lifeblood to African Americans and their African roots; aspects that are so strongly African American that the community recognizes them as such.

Cuesta Benberry was one of the few who seemed to understand the complexity of the issues involved and the dangers of oversimplifying the study of quilts made by African Americans. Throughout the 1980s, she was writing and lecturing extensively about quilters and quilt patterns. During her lectures around the country, she would often provide her own comment on this matter by showing slides of strip quilts comparable in design, pointing out that some had been made by white folk, and of comparable tight geometrical quilts, some of which had been made by black folk. I believe that Cuesta was responding to what she saw as the potential ghettoization of quilts made by African Americans. She understood the destructiveness of "celebrating the African-Americaness" of quilts through pronouncements

Birdie Reeves Claybrooks.
MCCRACKEN COUNTY, KENTUCKY, JANUARY 1993
(6-66446/4, 2¼ CN)

about what they need to look like if the quilter is "true" to her or his culture. Cuesta knew it wasn't as simple as that, and that African Americans could be true to their culture without doing strip quilts; that their culture was no longer so singular that it could only find one form in which to express itself; and that geometrical quilts could be as culturally valid for African-American quilters as strip quilts.

Some of these controversies escalated in December 1987, when the San Francisco Crafts and Folk Art Museum opened *Who'd A Thought It: Improvisation in African-American Quiltmaking,* an exhibit of quilts collected by Eli Leon; an accompanying catalog included a piece by Robert Farris Thompson. Some people were sufficiently irate to come to San Francisco at their own expense and voice their concerns directly at a public forum held in conjunction with the exhibit. Again, the major bone of contention was that the exhibit included only a limited range of quilts made by African Americans, and they were being presented as the only "true" African-American quilts. My telephone began to jump off the hook, partly because the exhibit built on parts of the essay Maude Wahlman had written in 1981 for *Something to Keep You Warm.* I listened carefully to what people had to say, and although by then I had seen hundreds of quilts made by African Americans and knew they could not be stereotyped, I refused to enter the debate. I was also somewhat incredulous to learn that during the time of the exhibit, some white quilters were holding workshops on how to make (what they perceived as) "African-American quilts"! And even more peculiar, though not particularly surprising, was the number of African Americans who seemed to accept the legitimacy of these definitions.

For those who could get beyond the controversies around African origins and representativeness, Leon's exhibit and catalog were thrilling. The show was extensive and contained many quilts not previously seen, some of magnificent beauty and quality. Perhaps the most important aspect of this exhibit was that Leon succeeded in mounting it. It was the largest national touring exhibit since *Something to Keep You Warm,* and it enabled a large number of people to see, many for the first time, a selection of the kind of quilts that had generated so much attention. In preparing for the exhibit, Leon had supported and worked closely with many quilters, and through the exhibit itself, the origins controversy expanded beyond the academic world to include the world of the galleries and the museums. People didn't just read about it; they saw the quilts and they could make up their own minds. To some it proved the point that forms of African culture are widespread and still observable in contemporary America; to some it didn't.

Although there were few published challenges to the origins theories, the grapevine was humming with rumors and innuendos questioning the research behind the show, particularly the "proof" that all these quilts were made by African Americans. A lot of this controversy focused on Leon's claim to have found among the fibers in the quilts, hairs that on analysis proved to be "African American." Many of his critics were disturbed by this approach and by the limitations inherent in his categorization, with its implicit assumptions about there being "black" hair, what it was, and what it meant—especially given the many decades of racial mixing in America, from intermarriage as well as from widespread miscegenation. Some accused him of "crypto-racism."

What was going on here? How could such basic facts about American history be so easily ignored? Of course, what was happening in the study of quilts made by African Americans was the same thing that had been happening (and unfortunately to a large degree continues to happen) in many areas of study related to African Americans. For whatever reasons, most of the recognized scholars accepted as authorities interpreting this field were non-black. And to be a player among those studying black culture, you had to read their books and build on their theories.

Both white and black America were continuing to struggle with appropriate inclusion and valuing of African and African-American history and culture, and what was occurring in the predominantly white museum field reflected the overall situation. It did not seem to value the few black scholars involved with African-American folk culture, and for the most part white scholars were defining how the field should be interpreted, exhibited, and positioned. In general, black folk scholars were excluded from major exhibition and publication opportunities and were limited to mounting small exhibits seen by few people, and to writing fine articles that were not widely read.

Change was accelerated following the urban rebellions of the 1960s and new federal funding guidelines, and many major museums began to seek out people of color with whom they could work. Though this resulted in some African Americans being offered jobs and/or exhibitions to curate, the numbers remained small, and the opportunities were often inherently limited by the museums' traditional operating procedures. Further change occurred in response to community activism and confrontations regarding demands for exhibitions with more relevance to demonstrators' lives. In addition to the resulting changes made by mainstream museums by the late 1960s, a black museum movement was gaining momentum. Dr. Margaret Burroughs, founder of the DuSable Museum in Chicago, and Dr. Charles Wright, founder of the Museum of African-American History in Detroit, initiated a series of conferences for black museum professionals. Their efforts eventually led to the formation of the African-American Museums Association in February 1978, and by 1988, there were already institutional members in thirty states and the District of Columbia, and individual members in thirty-one states.

The growing presence of African Americans in art and academic institutions was also seen in the quilt world; it certainly contributed to the additional attention that quilting by African Americans was receiving and to the reexamination of standing assertions related to its aesthetics, craftsmanship, and value—assertions that had gone unchallenged earlier.

Throughout the 1970s and 1980s, my own research on the world of African-American quilters often put me in the midst of these ongoing controversies. Frankly, I was often perplexed by the details of the arguments and the "evidence" brought to bear. Somehow, it seemed to me that there was room for all of these approaches. Struggling with all this both motivated my continuing work and underlined for me the core difference of what I was doing from most of what was being debated. I saw that most of the ongoing research related to quilting by African Americans focused almost exclusively on aesthetic dimensions—on criteria related to quilt structure, pattern, and form—without any consideration of the broader context in which the quilts were made. I couldn't understand this seeming blindness of many researchers to these other dimensions of quilting: the life experience and feelings of the quilter, the act of creating the quilt, and the experience of the quilt's use. It seemed both strange and ironic that so much of the research and excitement about quilts made by African Americans was taking place outside the world of the women who were sustaining the tradition. For example, quilters like Phoeba Johnson and her daughters Annie Dennis and Emma Russell, whose work I had by then been studying and collecting for more than fifteen years, were part of a four-generation Mississippi chain whose work was analyzed for these controversies. This analysis took place without any consideration being given to the fact that these quilters were totally unaware of any connections between their art and that of their African forebears, while they were quite aware of specific here-and-now connections to each quilt they made.

I realized that from childhood on, I had been fascinated by the ways quilts were used, the magic they contained, and the stories told in connection with them. I thought about my having titled my first book about quilts *Something to Keep You Warm*, underlining the importance to me of the subjective dimension. I had started with what it felt like to be under a quilt, and with how people described their individual experiences of it. The very words were something I'd heard—"Oh, the quilts, they're just something to keep you warm"—not a description of pattern or form, but of how something is experienced. For me, a full understanding of these quilts required a combination of both objective and subjective dimensions, going beyond the aesthetics to include the quilters and

the stories they tell, both about their lives and about the quilts in their lives.

THE GROUP FOR CULTURAL DOCUMENTATION

Throughout the twenty years of my folklife photodocumentation, although I usually carried out specific projects teamed with one or more of my colleagues, I had approached my work independently of any permanent corporate or organizational structure. I'd always valued the resulting freedom of action and approach, and I had been able to make temporary use of others' organizations when that was required.

Over the previous few years, however, I had increasingly become aware of the potential advantages of operating from an organizational base. First, it would contribute to permanence and continuity for my own work. Second, given the directions that my work had taken over the years, I knew that my own efforts would benefit from the perspectives and skills others might contribute through such an organization. Third, it would facilitate disseminating what I and others had already learned about cultural doc-umentation and preservation, as well as our ability to provide outreach and support to re-lated work. Finally, such a structure would facili-tate fundraising and cost-effective grant and program management.

In light of the above, and reinforced by my personal health concerns, in mid-1991, with technical assistance provided through a program of the Maryland State Arts Council, I moved ahead with establishing The Group for Cultural Documentation, Inc. (TGCD). TGCD was incorporated in November 1991, and it was recognized by the IRS in April 1992 as a publicly supported, tax-exempt 501(c)(3) organization.

In summary, TGCD's purpose is to increase awareness and appreciation of the vitality and importance of our multiple cultural traditions. Its mission is to contribute to preserving and documenting cultural traditions within and across communities, and to develop under-standing of the value provided by community and national cultural diversity. TGCD's areas of focus include documenting cultural traditions and encouraging others in local documentation and preservation; exhibiting and interpreting cultural documentation and traditions, and producing and disseminating related materials; bridging cultural gaps and building cross-cultural skills through interactive programs; and providing technical assistance and support to related efforts.

Since its establishment, TGCD has played a major role in all of my work. Through its organizational positioning, the support it has generated, and perhaps most importantly, its board members Judith H. Katz and David B. Levine, it has been invaluable to my continuing the struggle.

With my health at least holding its own, my increasing clarity about what I hoped to contribute to the world of African-American quilting, and The Group for Cultural Documentation in place, I made up my mind to transform my work into a national study. I wrote to state folklorists seeking their help in identifying African-American quilters in their respective states, activated my own informal networks, and relied heavily on Carolyn Mazloomi and the membership of the Women of Color Quilters' Network to gather the information needed to identify African-American quilters across the country.

Mother Africa's Children, 1991, 78" × 93"
Designed and fabric selected by Roland L. Freeman.
Pieced by Viola Canady and quilted by Gertrude Braan, Vivian Hoban, Joyce Nixon, and

PART TWO

MORE THAN JUST SOMETHING TO KEEP YOU WARM

*Completing the National Survey
(1992–96)*

Beverly Guy-Sheftall, standing in front of a reproduction of a Harriett Powers quilt.

FULTON COUNTY, GEORGIA, NOVEMBER 1995 (35 MM CT)

CHAPTER 5
Getting Ready (1992)

The year 1992 had begun with an important milestone in the quilt world: the simultaneous showing of six exhibits that opened in early February 1992 as part of the Kentucky Quilt Project's *Louisville Celebrates the American Quilt*. Featured African Americans included Carolyn Mazloomi, coordinator of the Women of Color Quilters' Network; Yvonne Wells, a quilter from Tuscaloosa, Alabama; and Cuesta Benberry. A significant part of this celebration was the commemoration and replication of the landmark quilt exhibition curated by Jonathan Holstein in 1971 at the Whitney Museum of Art in New York City. Many historians credit this 1971 exhibit with providing a major impetus for the subsequent attention to quilting as a serious art form.

Cuesta's exhibit, *Always There: The African-American Presence in American Quilts,* at the Museum of History and Science in Louisville, Kentucky, along with the long-awaited publication of her book of the same title, created the most excitement. The exhibit included quilts from slavery through contemporary times. Her scholarship clearly demonstrated that the diversity and magnitude of quilts made by African Americans extend far beyond the limitations imposed by viewing them through any single lens or by limiting them to any single category.

In early November, I was in Jackson, Mississippi, where the University Press of Mississippi was releasing my new book, *Margaret Walker's "For My People": A Tribute by Roland L. Freeman,* to coincide with an exhibit opening at Jackson State University. While there, I again met Beverly Guy-Sheftall, director of the Women's Research and Resource Center at Spelman College and one of the editors of *SAGE: A Scholarly Journal on Black Women*. She was curious about my quilt project and I told her it was now national in scope, but that I was in desperate need of funds to complete it. To my delight, she offered the Center's assistance. First, she explained, it was consistent with their mission of helping to document the political and cultural history of African-American women, and the Center's Anna Julia Cooper Chair (endowed by the Charles Mott Foundation) provided her some funds for research activities related to the history of black women. Second, she said that Spelman's president, Dr. Johnnetta B. Cole, was committed to the College's leadership in women's studies among the historically black colleges and had endorsed the College's association with a project that would underscore the cultural legacy of our foremothers.

Beverly also brought a personal interest in art by and about women and her own passion for collecting quilts, which had begun more than a decade ago, inspired by her reading of Alice Walker's essay, "In Search of Our Mothers' Gardens." Through Beverly's efforts, the previous year Spelman College had contracted me to locate a special quilt to give to Nobel Prize–winning, African-American author Toni Morrison, who was to give a lecture at Spelman. Although I was not able to be at the presentation, photographer Susan Ross later sent me a photograph of it. While Beverly and I were talking, it suddenly struck me that it would be wonderful to include in the survey contemporary African-American women writers who either made or collected quilts.

Florence Barnes.
WILKINSON COUNTY, MISSISSIPPI,
OCTOBER 1992 (65936/8,
2¼ CN)

MISSISSIPPI, OCTOBER AND NOVEMBER 1992 AND FEBRUARY 1993

In October, I photographed quilter Florence Barnes; and then, when I returned to Mississippi the next month, I photographed a young journalist, Deborah Diane Douglas, with her grandmother's quilt. (Mrs. Douglas has since moved to Chicago, Illinois.)

A few days later, I stopped by Mississippi Cultural Crossroads to pick up Mrs. Rankin to accompany me to Anner Brinner's house. She is a one-hundred-year-old quilter whose photograph was on the last page of my new book, and I was taking her several copies. She lived in a senior citizens' community on the outskirts of Port Gibson, and she was sitting on the front porch when we arrived. Before I had a chance to speak, recognizing me, she said, "I just finished a top for you, young man, but you got to get someone else to quilt it." Without saying a word, I opened the book to her picture, and with a big broad smile she said, "You're a man of your word. You said you were gonna put me in a book." She had made me a simple Nine-Patch out of her scraps, and I thanked her (see p. 130).

While having lunch with Mrs. Rankin and her husband, I told her about the exhibit tour and how people were responding to her quilt (see p. 85). I also shared with them a surprising occurrence, reported to me by the staff of the museum in Kentucky. A white couple by the name of Smith, from Natchez, Mississippi, upon seeing the quilt of Mrs. Rankin's father's murder, mentioned to the museum staff that Farrell Humphrey— the man who killed her father—was related to them. The staff was flabbergasted by this revelation and, at first, were a bit hesitant about letting me know. Mrs. Rankin just shook her head. "Isn't that just something for you?" Mr. Rankin asked, "You mean they just came right out and said it?"

While watching their reactions, I realized that I would like to see the road where her father was killed, so I asked Mrs. Rankin if she'd mind showing me. She hesitated for a moment, but Ezekiel said, "Sure we will, let's go now." It was a clear November afternoon as we left their home near Russum and took Highway 61 south to Fayette, and then turned on 28 east toward Union Church. About half the distance to Union Church, we turned off to the left on a gravel road which they called, "old Highway 20." Suddenly Mrs. Rankin got quiet. We passed an abandoned house on the left, and then just at the top of a little hill on the right was a two-story house with newly landscaped grounds and a pond. Mrs. Rankin whispered, "That's where that man lived who shot my father

Deborah Diane Douglas with her grandmother's quilt.
OCTOBER 1992 (1-65870/17, 2¼ CN)

down. They done fixed it up and added on to it, but they can't hide the ugly facts."

We went down a slight hill, and Mrs. Rankin said, "Pull over, it happened right in here." I asked, "How often do you come here?" and she replied, "It's been fifty-some years since I've been on this road. I was just a little girl, but I know this is the place. I never came here because I heard the old folks say that every time it rains, blood would rise up in this road. After my daddy's funeral, I had nightmares about this road. For many years, I could see the road and that house, and I believe I could even find my way to the spring where I heard the shots."

We laid the quilt top I'd just gotten from Mrs. Brinner on the road, as though we had covered the spot where her father once lay, and Mr. and Mrs. Rankin just stood there in silence for about ten minutes (see p. 131). Later I asked what she had been thinking as she stood on the road. "Looking down at that quilt, I was wondering how long after they shot him did my daddy live before he took his last breath. Maybe he could have been saved. That's what I was thinking."

We drove back to Highway 28 and continued into Union Church where Mrs. Rankin pointed out the Varnado Grocery Store. "See the name's been changed. That used to be Paul Cato's store, where that Farrell Humphrey and all them white men gathered after they killed my daddy."

Meditating: one-hundred-year-old quilter Annie Brinner.
CLAIBORNE COUNTY, MISSISSIPPI, 1992 (6-92006/7)

Then she got real quiet again and didn't have much to say until she got home. She gave me a big hug good-bye and thanked me for helping her overcome a haunting nightmare.

There is a curious postscript to this story. In the spring of 1995, the Jefferson County, Mississippi, road supervisor, a black man, was up for re-election. Campaigning very hard against him was a white man named Brown Humphrey. One afternoon in early August 1995, Mr. Humphrey pulled into the Rankins' yard to ask them to vote for him. As he made his pitch, Mrs. Rankin later told me that she just stared at Mr. Humphrey and his wife dumbfounded. Mrs. Humphrey then complimented Mrs. Rankin on her achievements in quilting, but Mrs. Rankin just looked at them, and said, "I want you all to know that my father was Denver Gray." She told me, "This was the son of the white man who killed my daddy. The very nerve of him to come here and ask me to vote for him. I

Hystercine Rankin and her husband Ezekiel Rankin pause for a moment of silence at the place where her father was murdered, on her first visit to the site since childhood.

JEFFERSON COUNTY, MISSISSIPPI, OCTOBER 1992 (FRAME 14, 2¼ CT)

just began to shake and almost cried. Ezekiel put his arm around me and told them, 'Please excuse us. She's very upset.' And we went in the house and he closed the door." Mrs. Rankin went on to tell me that she knew Brown Humphrey was just a little boy when her father was killed. But Mr. Humphrey's father had never been prosecuted for the murder. She said, "He must be crazy to think I'd ever vote for him. I stood up in church and I called everybody I knew. I didn't tell them not to vote for him, I just told them who he was. And he didn't get elected."

I returned to Mississippi in February 1993 and used the opportunity to document a group of quilters in a Mississippi Delta community called Tutwiler. I'd heard about them over the past few years, and they had been featured twice on the CBS television program, *60 Minutes*. The group was coordinated by a Catholic nun, Sister Maureen Delaney, who directs the Tutwiler Community Education Center. Since 1988, she had been encouraging local women to use quilting as a means to economic empowerment, and the *60 Minutes* show had brought in orders from around the United States.

As I passed among these quilters, I was intrigued to hear them refer to the type of quilts they were making as "African American." Then in the Center's library, I noticed there were about twenty copies of Eli Leon's book, *Who'd A Thought It*. In all my travels, this was the first time I'd come across a situation where African Americans were being trained to make

Left to right: Lady B. Lloyd and Ollie
Crawford from Tutwiler.
<small>TALLAHATCHIE COUNTY,
MISSISSIPPI, FEBRUARY 1993
(2-66807/1)</small>

"African-American quilts." The director had a dedicated team of white nuns on hand to train the women in "African-American quilting techniques." The Center has a system of inspecting each quilt as it is being made for such things as broken threads, straight stitches, and stains. If at any stage the quilt doesn't meet the nuns' standards, it must be reworked until it's correct.

Among the quilters were Lady B. Lloyd and her husband, Ollie Crawford, who quilt together, and Alberta Mitchell. While I was photographing Mrs. Mitchell, she proudly pointed out an autographed photograph of Ed Bradley, the *60 Minutes* correspondent. She said that he had been to her home and had ordered one of her quilts. Grinning like a Cheshire cat, she said, "I put a lot of good stuff in that quilt I sent him. Just think, one of my quilts is keeping that handsome man warm on all those cold nights up there in New York. Now that's something special."

LOUISIANA, NOVEMBER 1992

I headed south to New Orleans to deliver one of Mrs. Rankin's medallion quilts that some friends of mine had ordered. It was for Jean-Paul and Bernadette Pinel, an interracial couple who own La Belle Gallerie, an art gallery in the French Quarter. As they marveled at the quilt, Bernadette said, "This is not something I'm going to hang on the wall. We're going to sleep under it tonight." The next morning I photographed them in bed with their baby son and Mrs. Rankin's quilt (see p. 134).

ALABAMA, NOVEMBER 1992

I left New Orleans and headed back up through Mississippi and over to Eutaw, Alabama. I wanted to take a copy of my new book to quilters George and Beatrice Gosa, who were in it and whom I had photographed in 1986. Mrs. Gosa thanked me profusely and told me her husband was quite ill at the time; he passed the next September.

I then went to see Mrs. Nora Ezell. She had just won a 1992 National Heritage Fellowship for quilting from the National Endowment for the Arts Folk Arts Program. When I pulled into her yard, she was hammering away, building a bathroom onto her house by herself. Looking up, she started shaking the hammer at me, saying, "I'll kill you if you take my picture dressed like this." We joked for a while, and then she told me how wonderful it was to get the $5,000 award. "You see, I'm putting some of it to good use right now. I've been wanting to put this room on the house for years." She then went to change clothes so I could photograph her with the award.

My next stop was to see Dr. Sandral Hullett, who was about to make a house call, something I didn't know doctors did anymore. Dr. Hullett said she wanted me to meet an incredible woman, Mattie Lee Leftwich, who for thirty years had been caring for her quadriplegic son, Ivory Lee Smith, who had been paralyzed in a car accident. The first thing I noticed was a red and white quilt Mrs. Leftwich had over him, which she had made. She explained to me that over the years she'd made several quilts for him, but that he liked this one best. "It just seems to cheer him up." As Dr. Hullett examined him and the three of them talked

Alberta Mitchell.
TALLAHATCHIE COUNTY, MISSISSIPPI, FEBRUARY 1993 (1-66807/42)

about how he was doing, I made a few pictures and marveled at this mother's love and dedication to her son (see p. 135). In earlier years, she had worked two jobs and hired other people to help with him. Not being satisfied with the care they gave, however, in 1988 she retired to devote her full attention to him, and Dr. Hullett was using all her power to help Mrs. Leftwich obtain whatever assistance she could get. That evening at dinner with the Hullett's, it was decided that I would send back a large photograph of Mrs. Ezell with her award to add to their exhibit of the Eutaw quilters I'd taken to the Smithsonian festival in 1986.

GEORGIA, NOVEMBER 1992

The next morning I picked up Highway 80 East back into Columbus, Georgia, to follow up on a quilter named Frances Chapman. What interested me about Mrs. Chapman was that she had just shown up at the local museum with a beautiful Pine Burr quilt. She had simply said she wanted to give it to the museum if they would display it sometime, so people would know her work. In all my experience of documenting quilters, I'd never heard of anything like this. When I arrived in Columbus, I called to see if we could meet. Mrs. Chapman was a live-in maid for Mr. and Mrs. Benno and Babbet Rothschild and invited me to see her at their house. She immediately showed me her quilts and very

Bernadette and Jean-Paul Pinel and their son Mathieu Florian Pinel.
NEW ORLEANS, LOUISIANA, NOVEMBER 1992 (5-65938/34, 35 MM CN)

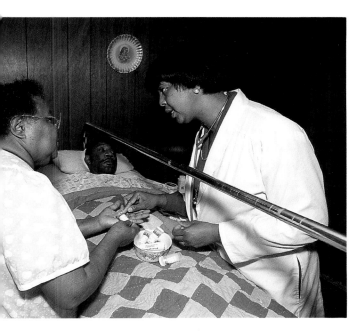

Left to right: Mattie Lee Leftwich, a quilter, her son, Ivory Lee Smith, and Dr. Sandral Hullett.
GREENE COUNTY, ALABAMA, NOVEMBER 1992 (35 MM CT)

Frances S. Chapman, a live-in maid for the Rothschild family.
MUSCOGEE COUNTY, GEORGIA, NOVEMBER 1992
(FRAME 1, 2¼ CT)

proudly pointed out a king-size Log Cabin quilt on Mr. Rothschild's bed that she'd made from his old ties. I was curious to know more about her life and how she had come to work for this family.

Well, I'm from about fifty miles from here, near a town called Weston in Webster County, Georgia. My people are just poor folk. We'd been sharecropping peanuts and corn. My husband also cut pulpwood for $30 to $40 a week, and I did some day work for $10 a week. We was raising three children, two boys and my daughter, Betty. She's the youngest. We didn't have much, but we did have love. In 1969, my husband died. The boys had finished high school and gone off to Atlanta to try to work their way through college, and I'm happy to say today that they made it. They're doing fine, and I got two grandsons.

But I was most worried about my daughter. I wanted life to be better for her. So I came here to Columbus hoping to find a live-in job so I could save more money to put her through college. I wanted her to make a living with book and pencil, not a mop and broom. So I went to this job placement office, and they only had two maid jobs open, one in Atlanta and one here in Columbus. I took the one here because it was closer to home and my mother. You see, I left Betty with Mama until I could make enough to get her started in college.

Christine King Farris standing by the bed where her brother Martin Luther King Jr. was born, and next to the crib where he slept as a baby.
FULTON COUNTY, GEORGIA, NOVEMBER 1992 (5-65977/10)

Dr. Johnnetta B. Cole, president, Spelman College.
FULTON COUNTY, GEORGIA, NOVEMBER 1992 (FRAME 4, 2¼ CT)

And these Rothschilds I work for, they're real good, understanding people. They got more than anybody I ever knew, and they're not stingy. They pay me well, and they always gave me extra money to help with Betty's tuition and books. I've been with these folks for twenty-three years, and I'm sixty-four now. I only went to the eighth grade and can't get no better job with the schooling I got, so I guess I'll just be staying here. A few years ago when I was making a little extra money helping another family with a party, I met Gertha Jones. She comes by and quilts with me, and we've become real good friends.

My sons got their families, and they still yet trying to get more education. Betty got married, lost two children, and was teaching and working on her Ph.D. when she died six years ago. These are the things I think about when I'm sitting here making my quilts. It helps to fill the empty space in my heart when I'm shut off from my family.

All the way to Atlanta, Mrs. Chapman stayed on my mind, and I enjoyed sharing her story with Beverly Guy-Sheftall. As promised, Beverly had contacted several people, and our potential contemporary writer

Darlene Jones making the quilt that Dr. Camille Cosby bought as a Christmas gift for
Dr. Johnnetta B. Cole.
JEFFERSON COUNTY, MISSISSIPPI, 1990 (35 MM CT)

interviewees now included Maya Angelou, Nikki Giovanni, Bernice
Johnson Reagon, Sonia Sanchez, and Alice Walker.

While I was visiting her office, Beverly introduced fellow faculty
member Christine King Farris, who is Martin Luther King Jr.'s sister. I
quickly asked her about quilts in her family and whether I could
photograph her with some of them. So she took me to the King family
home, which is now an historic site run by the National Park Service. I
photographed her with some family heirloom quilts in her parents'
bedroom where all the King children had been born.

I then went back to Spelman to review its quilt collection and to
photograph its president, Dr. Johnnetta B. Cole, with some of her quilts. I
was particularly pleased to see a quilt from Mississippi Cultural
Crossroads that Camille Cosby had given her, which was made by
Darlene Jones. Two years earlier I had photographed Mrs. Jones on her
front porch while she was making this quilt.

A week or so later, I was back in Atlanta, and I met Stephanie
Hughley, the artistic director of the National Black Arts Festival, who had
made arrangements for me to photograph the Reynoldstown Quilters of
Atlanta, to which both she and her mother-in-law belonged (see p. 138).

Reynoldstown Quilters in Atlanta. *Left to right:* Pearl Walker, Annie S. Heard, Annie L. Parks, Mamie L. Hughley, and Stephanie S. Hughley.
FULTON COUNTY, GEORGIA, NOVEMBER 1992 (8-66100/15, 2¼ CN)

North Carolina, May and November 1992

In May, I had the opportunity to photograph Waymon and Beatrice W. Totten in Caswell County.

Maya Angelou, Winston-Salem

Author Maya Angelou had been one of the contributors to *Double Stitch: Black Women Write about Mothers and Daughters,* co-edited by the *SAGE* editorial group, and Beverly had arranged for us to go to her home in Winston-Salem to photograph her. Our plan was to arrive at Dr. Angelou's house around 9:30 A.M., spend a few hours with her, and then drive to Columbia, South Carolina, to photograph quilter Joann Thompson on our way back to Atlanta. After warm greetings, we settled in her living room for a get-acquainted conversation. We went on to compliment each other about our respective work. I then commented that I knew she was a very busy person, and that we might want to move on to the photo session because I had another shoot that afternoon in South Carolina.

Mr. and Mrs. Waymon Totten and Beatrice W. Totten.
CASWELL COUNTY, NORTH CAROLINA, MAY 1992
(23-92008/14, 2¼ CN)

Dr. Angelou looked at us, somewhat taken aback, and said, "You mean you're not spending the night? Oh, you simply must stay overnight. I won't have it any other way. There are all sorts of wonderful things happening this weekend that you shouldn't miss. You see, the director George Faison, who won a Tony on Broadway for *The Wiz,* is here doing a new play. It's all about Billie Holiday, and Jackee [from the TV sitcom *227*] is starring in it. Tomorrow's matinee is the last performance, and I'll get you tickets. And afterwards, I'm throwing a party here for her." She smiled and asked, "You wouldn't want to miss that, would you?" Although I'd been trying to catch up with Joann Thompson in South Carolina for two years, I gave her a call and explained what had just happened. I was grateful to hear her say, "Well, by all means, stay. That's what I'd do. You can get me another time."

I first photographed Dr. Angelou with a quilt that had been a birthday present from her close friend, television personality Oprah Winfrey, who had commissioned it from New York artist Faith Ringgold. I also photographed her with another quilt in her collection that was from Liberia. During the photo session, Dr. Angelou commented on her fond childhood memories of quilting bees in her hometown of Stamps, Arkansas, and also said, "If Linus has his blanket, black women certainly have their quilts."

Left to right: Dolly McPherson, Maya Angelou, and Beverly Guy-Sheftall, with a quilt made in Liberia.
FORSYTH COUNTY, NORTH CAROLINA, NOVEMBER 1992 (31-65979/8, 2¼ CN)

Maya Angelou, author, educator, and quilter. The quilt on her wall was a gift from Oprah Winfrey, who commissioned it from Faith Ringgold.
FORSYTH COUNTY, NORTH CAROLINA, NOVEMBER 1992
(2-65979/9, 2¼ CN)

One-hundred-year-old quilter Offie E. Phillips.
CLEVELAND COUNTY, NORTH CAROLINA, NOVEMBER 1992
(2-66100/4, 2¼ CN)

The next morning, we accompanied Dr. Angelou to church, after which she returned home to prepare for the party, and Beverly and I went to the matinee with George Faison. Dr. Angelou personally fixed tons of wonderful food for the party, and we feasted shamelessly and showered her with praise—and I made pictures as people sang, danced, and talked the night away.

SHELBY

Following up on a lead from my colleague, folklorist Glenn Hinson, I drove to Shelby to photograph one-hundred-year-old quilter, Offie E. Phillips.

VIRGINIA, NOVEMBER 1992

The next morning, I headed out to Charlottesville, Virginia, to photograph Dorothy Howard Holden. I'd met Mrs. Holden in Louisville, Kentucky, when she had had a quilt in Cuesta Benberry's exhibit. Born in the 1930s in Kansas City, Missouri, she learned to quilt from her mother, Gladys

Dorothy H. Holden.
ALBEMARLE COUNTY, VIRGINIA,
NOVEMBER 1992 (3-66100/10,
2¼ CN)

Garvin Howard, who was born in Kentucky and died in 1944. However, it was her stepmother, Mattie Keys Howard, who was born in Deniston, Texas, who made quilting a summer project for Mrs. Holden and her two sisters, Sheryl Howard Clayton and Mary Elaine Howard Rice. She says that at that time, she hated quilting because she would have much preferred to be outside playing. After migrating to Virginia in 1977, her interest in quilting was revived largely through the efforts of a fellow church member and white quilter, Fern Morrison. Mrs. Holden said, "My experiences with quilting have been essentially with white quilters, and I felt like (I imagine) some troubled black American students do in their schools . . . ignored, criticized, and rebuked. However, with a background of resources—and age a big factor—I have survived." Today Mrs. Holden's work has been widely exhibited in the United States.

CHAPTER 6
California (December 1992)

On December 2, Beverly and I flew to California. Our week there would combine interviews arranged through my personal contacts, with others arranged by Beverly. I had contacted Gussie Wells and Arbie Williams, winners of the 1991 National Heritage Fellowships for quilting, both of whom lived in Oakland, and Beverly had contacted writer Alice Walker and Sue Bailey Thurman, a Spelman alumna who had contributed to their quilt collection.

Sue Bailey Thurman, San Francisco

Our first stop was to see Sue Bailey Thurman, who was born in Pine Bluff, Arkansas, in 1903. She was the daughter of the Reverend Isaac and Mrs. Sue Bailey, who had founded and run the Southeast Arkansas Academy in Dermott. Mrs. Thurman had finished Spelman Seminary High School in three years in 1921. She wanted to go to Oberlin College, Ohio—which was the first white American college to accept black students—but needed more Latin and math, which she studied during a year at Morehouse College before going to Oberlin. While at Morehouse, she met her future husband, the Reverend Howard Thurman.*

After graduating from Oberlin, Mrs. Thurman taught for two years at Hampton Institute in Virginia, and then went to New York to work on the National Board of the Young Women's Christian Association until her marriage. Among the most precious gifts she received at her 1932 wedding were five quilts from the staff at her parents' school in Arkansas. Two of these quilts were passed on to her oldest daughter, Olive, when she married in 1954. Mrs. Thurman is very proud that these cherished heirlooms remain in her family today and that though neither she nor

---

* The contributions of Howard Thurman, a much-admired American theologian, have been recognized as varied, vast, and significant. As a result of his remarkable ability to communicate with people with no formal education as well as with the most advanced scholars, his ideas are considered to have influenced thousands: laypersons, ministers, students, and scholars. After he retired from a distinguished career as minister-at-large, dean of Marsh Chapel, and professor of spiritual resources and disciplines at Boston University, the Thurmans lived in San Francisco until his death in 1981. They have two daughters, Olive Wong, a librarian and playwright in New York, and Anne Chiarenza, a journalist and attorney. (From *Major Black Religious Leaders since 1940*, by Henry J. Young [Nashville: Abingdon, 1979].)

Left to right: Anne S. Thurman and her mother Sue Bailey Thurman, quilt preserver.

SAN FRANCISCO, CALIFORNIA, DECEMBER 1992 (9-66200/7, 2¼ CN)

her mother quilted, she has been able to preserve several historical quilts.

As newlyweds, the Thurmans moved to Washington, D.C., where the Reverend Thurman was dean of Rankin Chapel and professor of theology at Howard University for twelve years. In addition to the social demands of being a dean's wife, Mrs. Thurman became an accomplished author and social historian. She was one of the original members of the National Council of Negro Women (NCNW), and she founded and edited its pioneering *Africamerican Woman's Journal (AWJ)* beginning in 1940. As editor, two of her first goals were to encourage NCNW members to collect and preserve artifacts related to Negro history, and to start an archives and eventually a museum for the NCNW.

In 1944, the Thurmans left Washington and moved to San Francisco, California, where they started the Church for the Fellowship of All People. Mrs. Thurman continued to edit *AWJ* for a few more years. These were exciting times: many African Americans had migrated west to work in the war industries, and some had settled in Marin County, California, where they mingled with newly arrived European immigrants. In this unique setting, at war's end, an integrated group were meeting regularly at the home of white artist Ben Irvin, in the name of understanding and awareness of each others' cultural values. Mrs. Thurman said of this group, "I doubt if it would have been possible to do this in any other part of the country at that time." This wasn't so much a Negro history group at its inception as it was just some neighbors and friends who wanted to share and learn from one another.

A quilt project evolved out of this climate. One of the first quilts they made resulted from Ben Irvin's fascination with the story of Harriet "Moses" Tubman, a courageous African American who had led more than three hundred slaves out of the South to freedom via the Underground Railroad. Mr. Irvin designed a quilt with an imposing figure of Harriet Tubman in the foreground; in the background in a dark sky were the North Star, which Tubman used as a guide, and an owl that denotes her wisdom and ability to travel successfully at night. Some women in the group told Mr. Irvin that they'd read in the *Africamerican Woman's Journal* about Mrs. Thurman's interest in Negro history. He already knew of the work Rev. Thurman was doing. When the Tubman quilt was completed in 1951, Mr. Irvin called the Thurmans, and they invited him to bring by the quilt that day. Mrs. Thurman immediately

Frederick Douglass Quilt, 1953, 120" × 96"
Designed by Ben Irvin.
Made by the Negro History Club of Marin City and Sausalito, California.

Harriet Tubman Quilt, 1951, 120" × 96"
Designed by Ben Irvin.
Made by the Negro History Club of Marin City and Sausalito, California.

became an advocate for the quilt and wrote about it in the *AWJ*. The quilt also won second place at the 1952 California State Fair. Because of Harriet Tubman's long history with the African Methodist Episcopal (AME) Zion Church in New York, she also wrote to then Bishop W. J. Walls of the New York Convention. He responded with an invitation for Mrs. Thurman to bring the quilt to Auburn, New York, the site of Harriet Tubman's home, where the church's officers would be meeting. After a tiring, cross-country train ride by herself, Mrs. Thurman was surprised to find that, "Even though Bishop Walls understood, I still had to sell the other dignitaries on the importance of this quilt for our history. It took some doing. A group of us took the quilt out to Harriet Tubman's gravesite, and a picture was made there to mark the occasion (see p. 146). All the local people in Auburn were fully aware of her importance, however, and the mayor eagerly posed with the quilt." After New York,

Posing with the *Harriet Tubman Quilt* in Auburn, NY, in 1953. *Left to right:* Mrs. Adelaide B. Mead; Rev. Arthur May of the AME Zion Church; Mrs. Sue Bailey Thurman; Robert A. Nelson, Mayor of Auburn, NY; Bishop William Walls of the AME Zion Church; Dickie Wellington, editor of the *Auburn Citizen* newspaper; Mrs. Margaret A. May, wife of Rev. Arthur May; and an unknown man.

(PHOTOGRAPH COURTESY OF THE HARRIET TUBMAN HOME HISTORIC SITE. B/W PRINT)

Mrs. Thurman took the quilt to be shown at the national headquarters of NCNW in Washington, D.C., and later to the commencement at Livingstone College, which is supported by the AME Zion Church, in Salisbury, North Carolina.

While this was going on, the group in Marin County finished a second quilt (see p. 145). This one was about Frederick Douglass and was somewhat more intricately detailed than the Tubman quilt. As Mrs. Thurman says, "It was more finished, with better stitching and appliqué work." In 1953, these two quilts, along with other black memorabilia, were part of a special exhibit in the sanctuary of Grace Cathedral in San Francisco.

About this time, the Thurmans bought both quilts for the Howard Thurman Educational Trust Foundation. Later, when a new library named for Robert W. Woodruff was being built to serve the Atlanta University Center (made up of five black colleges: Atlanta University, Morris Brown College, Clark Atlanta University, Spelman College, and Morehouse College), the Thurmans thought this might be an appropriate permanent home for these quilts. The Howard Thurman Educational Trust Foundation then donated them to the Robert W. Woodruff Library, where they are permanently displayed on the first floor.

HENRIETTA HOUSTON, BERKELEY

The next morning, following a lead Beverly obtained from filmmaker Carroll Blue, we went to photograph and interview Ms. Blue's aunt, Henrietta Houston, who lived in Berkeley.

OAKLAND

ARBIE WILLIAMS

Early that afternoon, I found National Heritage Fellowship winner Arbie Williams, who is best known for her "britches" quilts, working with her son in their Oakland garden. She was kind enough to take a quick break so I could photograph her. When I asked how she had wound up in Oakland, she said that her husband had family there. Once they had come out to visit and he had wanted to stay, so they did. I then asked what it meant to her to win the award, she said, "When they first called, I didn't believe it. Told them it wasn't me, they had the wrong person. So then the woman told me where I was born, how old I was, my birthday,

Henrietta Houston.
BERKELEY, CALIFORNIA, DECEMBER 1992
(7/66200/16, 2¼ CN)

Arbie Williams, a winner of the 1991 National Heritage Fellowship,
awarded by the National Endowment for the Arts Folk Arts Program.
OAKLAND, CALIFORNIA, DECEMBER 1992 (35 MM CT)

and everything. And they took me to Washington, gave me all that
money, and showed me a really fine time. I never thought anything like
that would ever happen to me."

Arbie Williams was born in Carthage, Texas, in 1916. Her mother
taught her to sew when she was eight years old. She started piecing quilts
by age ten or twelve. She married right out of school and raised nine
children. As a young woman in the early 1940s, she organized a quilting
club in a little railroad community in Beckville, Texas, where she and her
family were living. The women met in each other's houses in the summer
and did a quilt or two a week, working four hours or so on Wednesdays
and Fridays. In the wintertime they each pieced separately and kept their
work hidden, to surprise each other the following summer. Each year
they tried to make one special quilt, like a Lone Star, a Log Cabin, or an
Ocean Wave. Over the years, Williams has worked as a cocktail waitress,
maid, cook, nurse, seamstress, beautician, and farmer, in addition to
mother and housewife. She settled in Oakland in 1945. Mrs. Williams
had stopped quilting and took it up again only after her children were
grown. Sometimes a pattern comes to her in a dream and she gets up in
the night to put it together, so that she won't forget it. She gives most of

Gussie Wells, a winner of the 1991 National Heritage Fellowship, awarded by the National Endowment for the Arts Folk Arts Program.

OAKLAND, CALIFORNIA, DECEMBER 1992
(4-66200/15, 2¼ CN)

her quilts to her family, and in 1986 she gave ten quilts to her grandchildren.*

Shortly after I took this photograph, in January 1993, Mrs. Williams was one of the craftspeople invited to participate in President Clinton's inaugural "America's Reunion on the Mall." In 1994, she was invited back to Washington to join other National Heritage Fellowship winners in a special section of the Smithsonian's Festival of American Folklife. One of her britches quilts was chosen for that year's festival poster.

GUSSIE WELLS

Later that afternoon, we went to photograph Gussie Wells, another National Heritage Fellowship winner who lived in Oakland. Mrs. Wells was then ninety-one, lived with her daughter, Janell Chestra, and no longer quilted. Her daughter explained how grateful Mrs. Wells's family was that she had received such a prestigious award, and they only wished it could have happened much earlier in her life.

Gussie Wells was born in Princeton, Louisiana, in 1901. From the age of nine, she helped her grandmother quilt. At sixteen, during World War I, she went to work in the sawmills. In 1921, she moved to Galveston, Texas, where she did housework and hotel work while raising her daughter. She never made any quilts by herself as a young woman. She left Texas for New York City in 1927, where she did housework, ran a candy store, and worked at sewing machines in clothing and burlap-bag factories. In 1945 she came to San Francisco. She moved back and forth between the city and the country—she owned several houses, a restaurant in San Francisco, and ranches in Santa Rosa and Merced. She retired in 1963 and settled in Oakland in 1977. She took up quilting again in her eighties, after she met Arbie Williams, who had come to work for her to help care for Wells's ninety-four-year-old mother. Williams was making quilts and Wells began making them with her. She often donated them to her church when they had sales, or she sent them to her family in Louisiana or to missions in Alabama and Mississippi for distribution to the poor.* Mrs. Wells passed away in February 1994.

* The biographical information on Williams and on Wells is from *Who'd A Thought It.* by Eli Leon (San Francisco Craft & Folk Art Museum, 1987).

ALICE WALKER

The next day I arose early for a morning walk, and anticipating our appointment later that day with Alice Walker, my mind drifted back to eleven years before, when Alice had invited me to Sunday supper. My exhibit *Southern Roads/City Pavements* had been at the Oakland Museum, and she had accepted my invitation to be a panelist on a public forum there. However, due to an extraordinary rainstorm, she was unable to make it back to the city in time from her country retreat. She had called to apologize and invited me to come for Sunday supper a few weeks later when I was going to be back in Oakland for a workshop. When I arrived at her condo, one of the first things she pointed out were some photographs of Mississippi made by Student Nonviolent Coordinating Committee (SNCC) photographer Bob Fletcher. Then I noticed a partly finished quilt top, and she casually mentioned that making this quilt was helping her as she struggled to develop the characters for her new book. I inquired what it was about, and she said, "Oh, a lady writing letters to God." As she fixed tea, I read part of the chapter she was working on. During the evening, we shared experiences from our rural upbringings and what Mississippi had been like for each of us. Over the years, I'd never forgotten Alice, the quilt, or my first exposure to *The Color Purple*.

Beverly and I arrived at Alice Walker's Victorian row house on a pleasant, rainy Sunday afternoon. Alice has a gentle, quiet personality, and the sound of her voice is very soothing—and the peaceful aura that surrounds her also draws you in. I quietly went about setting up my lights, as Alice talked about her recent film on female genital mutilation and her new book, *Possessing the Secret of Joy*. We then spread out a few of her quilts and Alice got comfortable on her sofa. I asked Alice to talk first about the tradition of quilting in her family.

> Well, my mother was a quilter, and I remember many, many after-noons of my mother and the neighborhood women sitting on the porch around the quilting frame, quilting and talking, you know; getting up to stir something on the stove and coming back and sit-ting down. My mother also had a frame inside the house. Some-times during the winter she would quilt and she often pieced quilts. Piecing . . . I'm really more of a piecer, actually, than I am a quilter, because I can get as far as piecing all of the little squares or sections together, and sometimes putting them together into big blocks, but then I always have to call in help—spreading it out on the frame, or spreading it out on the floor and putting the batting in and doing the actual quilting.
>
> [The first quilt] I worked on [was] the *In Love and Trouble* quilt. And I did that one when I was living in Mississippi. It was during a period when we were wearing African-inspired dresses. So all of the pieces are from dresses that I actually wore. This yellow and black

fabric I bought when I was in Uganda, and I had a beautiful dress made of it that I wore and wore and wore and eventually I couldn't wear it any more; partly I had worn it out and also I was pregnant, so it didn't fit, and I used that and I used the red and white and black, which was a long, floor-length dress that I had when I was pregnant with my daughter, Rebecca, who is now twenty-three. I took these things apart or I used scraps. I put them together in this quilt, because it just seemed perfect. Mississippi was full of political and social struggle, and regular quilts were all African American with emphasis on being here in the United States. But because of the African consciousness that was being raised and the way that we were all wearing our hair in naturals and wearing all of these African dresses, I felt the need to blend these two traditions. So it's a quilt of great memory and importance to me. I use it a lot and that's why it's so worn.

Well, I actually have an essay, "How I Wrote *The Color Purple*," in which I describe how, when I started thinking about that book, I had to change everything in my life in order to write it. I had to leave my husband, sell my house in New York, sell two houses in New York, in fact, come here and try to find a place to work. I settled in San Francisco and that wasn't right, and I went north to the country and that was right, finally, although I went all over the country, this part of the country, looking for a place. I knew that in order for me to have the kind of meditative depth to the book that I needed, that I had to do work with my hands and I asked my mother to suggest a pattern that would be easy, and she said that there was nothing easier than the Nine-Patch. You know, you just get some fabric and cut up the pieces into nine blocks and you sew them together and that's it. So, I followed her advice and I went to Boonville, in Northern California, and I was with my partner, Robert Allen, and we would make big fires in the stove and go apple picking, or swimming in the river, or whatever, and then in the evenings I would work on this quilt. And as I worked on it, the novel formed.

I asked Alice about the significance of the colors she chose:

I am very deeply influenced by colors, and there are certain colors that come into my life with real persistence. And this kind of reddish or fuchsia, along with one of my old Indian dresses, black, green, and maroon stripes—these are colors that just struck me as colors I needed to give me strength to go on into the work I was doing, so that it always felt cheerful and strong and interesting working with those colors. I couldn't have written *The Color Purple* working on a brown quilt.

I asked her what happens when she sleeps under that quilt:

Oh . . . I am warm and I am secure and I am safe. I feel that I know how to create my own environment, and I know how to protect it.

Alice Walker, writer and quilter.
SAN FRANCISCO, CALIFORNIA, DECEMBER 1992 (10-66200/7, 2¼ CN)

And I know how to choose it. I realize that my quilts are really simple, and yet, they give me so much pleasure, because even in their extreme simplicity they are just as useful as the most complex. And in their own way, they are beautiful because they do express what I was feeling and they clearly mark a particular time for me.

Well, the Crazy quilt I have, by Rosie Tompkins of Oakland, is very special because unlike so many quilts, it has a lot of satin in it and what else—almost party-dress fabric—and I get under that quilt and I just feel real snazzy, and I can't be depressed but so long, lying under that. Under this Log Cabin Windmill quilt, I—it is just so lovely. I mean, I wake up and I just feel that I am sleeping under a beauty that is as complicated and as rich as the beauty I see out my window, which is nature. And so it just makes me feel all the more connected as a human being to what is created constantly in and among nature.

I mentioned to Alice that Maya Angelou had told me that when she was having trouble writing a particular book, her mother told her, "Take this quilt and go and sit on it and you won't have those problems, it will be all right." I told her that I've come across a lot of folklore within my family and others about powers and quilts, and I asked her if she had had any such experiences.

Well . . . other than to say that I feel just really good and protected and blessed, especially when I am under quilts made by my mother. But my feeling of power—because I feel myself to be in the Shaman tradition—comes from the making. The making of myself. It's the same tradition as sand painting, or carving—all of those things that people do. The power is partly about grounding yourself in something that is humble, something that is—that you can actually see take form through your own effort, and it's like seeing that you can change things and create through your own effort and in a way that you can see. This makes you realize that you also do that constantly in an unseen way. That is also the way that the world is created. There is a consciousness that is manifesting in things that you see around you. Even though you never see it, it's there. I feel really connected through the work that I do. It is such a great experience to do this while writing a book, because, you know on days when you cannot move in the narrative, you can work on your quilt! There are days when the characters just don't want to come anyway. They are off doing something else in another world. You have your quilt and you can keep going, and so one faith leads the other—the faith that you can continue making this pattern in the quilt restores the faith that you may start moving, that you can continue in the unseen—which is to draw these characters out of nothing and make them real for someone.

I asked her if she had made a quilt for her daughter.

No. I'm sure that she will make her own quilt. I'll be happy to leave her these if they are not worn out, which they will probably be, but I hope that she will make quilts for her own grounding and her own connection to me and to her grandmother and to her great-grandmother. [I've seen] quilts that my grandmother made. They tended to be very serviceable, very heavy and really for warmth, and, well of course, beautiful. [My daughter has a quilt] that she travels with. It's just a beautiful simple quilt that she loves. I gave it to her because she just feels like you can't sleep under just any old thing. It's got to be something that is congenial with your dreams—your dream sense, your dreamtime. I'm trying to think of where I got it. I think that I just bought it somewhere. I believe it is from Texas.

I asked Alice what she'd like to say to people in general about quilting.

That they should learn to do it. That they should think less about collecting quilts and give more thought to making them. Because, really, that is the power. It may do all kinds of good things, too, to collect what others have made, but I think that it is essential that we know how to express, you know, our own sense of connection. And there is no better sense of understanding our own creation than to create, and so we should do that.

And to those people who prefer to buy a quilt, saying they don't have time to make one:

Well, I think that they should restructure their lives because obviously there is a problem and we should stop actually saying that we don't have time. Time is all we do have. And really learn to do the things that matter rather than only the things we think are worth doing. Some people will immediately think that's not possible, but I think if you want to really be here, you have to be committed to being here, and to be here now is to be here at this moment. It is the only moment there is. And there is nothing like quilting to help you appreciate that, because it's very slow. It is very slow. Your life just sort of winds down to a very slow stroll. And it's wonderful because you are really there, and that's why, you know, we talk about all the reasons that people make quilts, but it's really because of that glimpse of eternity that people get. That's one of the greatest gifts—that glimpse of eternity—that fraction of eternity.

Let me try [to clarify]. Because it is easy if you've felt it, but there comes a time when you do grasp that you live in eternity. But the eternity is only in the second that you have. That's the eternity. But once you really live in it, once you really know that you can have it, you will have it forever, and that's why there is no reason to be afraid of dying. And in quilting you have moments of that where you know that this is eternity. This very moment is eternity. A bus could fall on my head at this minute and I will have had my eternity. In other words, as Martin Luther King said, "Longevity has its place." But once you really have your life, you have it, whether you have it for ten minutes, or for a hundred years. It's all about whether you are alive in the moment that you have.

And the process of quilting gives you that. Yes, as well as any-thing would, I mean, like again sand painting. I don't know if you read the article about the monks who came to the San Francisco Museum. They came to town, and they were making this elaborate mandala out of sand, and they're working and they're working, and they're working and they work for—I don't know how long—weeks to make this mandala, and just as they were about to finish, there was a woman who came, leapt over the little rope, and danced on the mandala and completely destroyed it. And what did the monks do? They stood there and smiled. And when she had completely demolished it, they gathered up the sand and started over. Because that was what was going to happen to it anyway. When they fin-ished with it, they destroyed it. So it's in the doing, you know, it is really in the doing. It's in the creation. That's where your joy is. It's a gift. Because they have gotten the gift. They're not giving anything away. They are giving you what's left. The quilt or the sand painting is what's left. And we look at a quilt, a sand painting, or any gen-uine work of art and we say, "Oh, how beautiful!" As I do every day. But I know I'm just seeing what's left. What's really amazing is what was going on when she was making this quilt. You know, I mean, boy, when she was just whoever, doing her art, what a state of being!

I asked Alice about the relation of quilting to the camaraderie of women and whether that relation fits into the whole process of creation.

Absolutely. Absolutely. And it's even higher because it's communal. It's one thing to get into eternity by yourself, but to get into it with five or six other people, all of them cooking and talking about whatever. It's really incredible. I mean, you're talking about some high states of being. We just have taken this as being completely ordinary. What's happening is very fine. Very high. I mean really evolved. And yet, the people doing this, they say, "Get out of here—What are you talking about?" But the evolution is there. Because they are creating out of the heart. But not in a precious way. And they're together on it. They're making something together. It's really quite remarkable. And when you think about that kind of creation and then you think about these rugs that you can buy from India where they literally steal these children and they beat them and force them to make these rugs . . . this is the other end of it. This is where the moment is not a glimpse of eter-nity, it is a moment of hell. I mean it's eternity in a different way. And that is what you get. You get the rug and you think that this is a beautiful design, but you can feel that it just doesn't have the life. It doesn't have that purity; that moment where you were just, as the creator, up there.

I asked her to comment on her sense of my attraction to the environment women created in quilting, one in which they were away from men.

Well, first of all, even though you thought what you wanted to hear was what they were saying, what attracted you was the feeling that they generated. You were attracted to their eternity. They had taken their eternity back from the men around them. And this was the form that they used to have their eternity. You see. And then when you get one of their quilts, you can see that this is what their eternity, externalized and made into a form, looks like, but in fact, they experienced their eternity long before you saw their quilt. They took it. God bless them. God has blessed them. Because think of the people who don't know how to steal their eternity back from people who have stolen it! And there they are without an eternity. They're mad. People who take drugs are trying to get their eternity. They're trying to have their time, their endless time of being, who they are, as they are, their eternity, and they take the drug and—they think this feels like it, you know, this feels like . . . this must be . . . this is so good it must be my eternity. But it's not. Because you don't need drugs to get it. You need creative work to get it. You need creativity to get it. You need to create just like, whoever created all of this—the earth, the cosmos—needed to create.

Edna Lee Taylor.
OAKLAND, CALIFORNIA,
DECEMBER 1992 (35 MM CT)

EDNA LEE TAYLOR

Before leaving northern California, I also photographed Edna Lee Taylor in Oakland.

LOS ANGELES

VARNETTE HONEYWOOD

On December 7, we flew to Los Angeles. I was anxious to follow up with Varnette Honeywood, a young artist whom I had met in Mississippi in 1976 while Worth and I were doing the Mississippi Folklife Project. Varnette, an alumna of Spelman, with roots in Magnolia, Mississippi, had told us of her uncle, Oza Allen, who made gravestones and concrete funerary sculpture. Worth and I had driven Varnette to an area called Progress, just west of Magnolia, where her maternal grandparents, Herman and Vera Allen, lived in a house loaded with quilts and several of Varnette's early paintings.

Left to right: Stephanie P. Honeywood (seated), Lovie Varnette A. Honeywood (mother of both), and Varnette P. Honeywood. LOS ANGELES, CALIFORNIA, DECEMBER 1992 (5/66220/4, 2¼ CN)

Over the years I had kept up with Varnette and her increasing exposure and reputation. Three important contributions to her success were: first, Carroll Blue's 1980 film, *Varnette's World, Study of an Artist*, which appeared repeatedly on PBS; second, an article about her written by her sister Stephanie in 1983 for *Essence* magazine; and finally, the use of some of her paintings as set decorations on television's *The Cosby Show*. Early in her career, Varnette formed a business called Black Lifestyles to handle the distribution of her posters and cards, which she still runs with her immediate family.

Although Varnette grew up surrounded by quilts made by her maternal and paternal grandparents and great-aunts, she says that she has never taken the time to learn how to quilt. Nevertheless, she frequently uses quilt designs in her artwork. For example, in the late 1970s, she used several traditional quilt patterns in a piece called *I Do Thee Wed*. In 1985, she used the Double Wedding Ring design in a piece that she calls *A Century of Empowerment*, which was commissioned by *Essence* magazine to celebrate its fifteenth anniversary. When her sister was attending UCLA, they met many African students, and this started her on collecting African cloth:

I became fascinated with the symbolism in the design of some Nigerian fabric and then started to incorporate those symbols into my art. Also, my family only made quilts with traditional patterns, and I thought that was the way you had to make them. In the late 1980s, I began to be influenced by the improvisational quilts that were being exhibited. This freed my mind and I thought of quilts in a new way. I had also recently discovered Adinkra symbols on cloth from Ghana, and began to incorporate both of these influences into my work.* At the same time I had just started to explore a new medium—monoprinting—using ink as paint and manipulating it with chemicals and tools on plexiglass, and then transferring it to paper to create a print. All of this led to my making what I call *Adinkra Quilts*, which are not made of cloth, but are rather a form of monoprinting on paper.

* Adinkra is a special cloth, primarily used in Ghana and associated with funerals and related occasions. The material is stamped with a pattern of traditional symbols that have been selected specifically from several dozen available.

Varnette has lately started to appliqué figures on blocks of cloth and hopes that this will lead to her first fabric quilt.

African-American Quilters of Los Angeles

In midafternoon, we arrived at the William Grant Still Arts Center in central Los Angeles to photograph the African-American Quilters of Los Angeles (AAQLA). Founded in 1986, this group was an outgrowth of a quilting class that Carolyn Mazloomi taught in the mid-1980s at the California African-American Museum in Los Angeles. Seven of the eighteen people in that class prevailed on Carolyn to consider a possible continuing quilting alliance; together, these eight formed AAQLA: Helen Braithwaite, Ouida Braithwaite, Darlyne Dandridge, Jan Emanuel, Ella Hales, Carolyn Mazloomi, Willie Mae Smith, and Joseph Syphax. Since its inception the group has grown rapidly and today has about one hundred members who participate in a variety of city and state-wide activities.

Carolyn helped AAQLA with a proposal that received funding for AAQLA member Darlyne Dandridge to work with Rachel Clark, a prominent African-American clothing artist from Northern California. She also helped secure funding for an exhibition of quilts at the William Grant Still Arts Center, located in the inner city of Los Angeles.

The following are all in the group photo (see p. 158):

Jan Emanuel was born in 1945 in Oakland, California; raised until 1956 in Detroit, Michigan; and then migrated to California at age eleven. No one in her family quilted, but all her relatives sewed for people. Mrs. Emanuel started to quilt in 1986, after seeing an exhibit at the California African-American Museum on quilting and taking the mini-workshop there with Carolyn Mazloomi. She later started her mother quilting.

Dorothy Taylor was born in 1936 in Oskaloosa, Iowa. When she was six, the family migrated from Oskaloosa to Des Moines, after her father was murdered by two white neighboring brothers with whom he had grown up. The story goes that because he was better at everything they tried, one day in a jealous rage they started trying to beat him up, and when it was clear that they were losing the fight, one of the brothers took an iron pipe and hit him in the head, killing him. The judge declared it justifiable homicide, and the brothers did no time. Her maternal grandmother Arie (last name unknown) quilted, but Mrs. Taylor learned from her mother Eddie Bolden (1902–85). Mrs. Taylor says:

> Our mother made sock dolls, made our clothes, and made fiber flowers that we sold from door to door in the white neighborhoods. She made quilts until her eyesight became so bad she could not see. I started making quilts around 1980 after I signed myself out of the hospital with a promise that I would stay in bed. I sewed the pieces by hand. Mother thought none of her children would become quilters. I had to "discover" it. I now make dolls, wearable art clothes,

African-American Quilters of Los Angeles (only twenty-one of the approximately seventy-five members are shown). *Front row (left to right):* Blanche Jones, Mary F. Cannon, Ernestine G. Offord, Barbara King, Isabel Seruby, Dora Simmons, Helen Brathwaite, Eloise Thompson, and Ozellia Crawford. *Middle row (left to right):* Sara Brandon, Jan Emanuel, Barbara Hunter, Doris Parker, A. Bernice Hilson, Lavonia North, Carolyn Pruitt, Anita Holloway, and Corrie McNeal. *Back row (left to right):* Doretha Parker, Dorothy Taylor (middle with dolls), and Dorothye Brandon.

LOS ANGELES COUNTY, CALIFORNIA, DECEMBER 1992
(2-66853/1, 2¼ CN)

> wallhangings, and quilts. To me quilting is life, and creating any
> form of art in my life is just like breathing; I have to create or die.

Mrs. Taylor migrated to California in 1969. One of her daughters, Verlee Janet Taylor (b. 1958), quilts, and Mrs. Taylor is now teaching four of her young grandchildren, two girls and two boys, who are the fifth generation of quilters in her family.

Barbara A. Hunter was born in 1935 in Valhalla, New York, and migrated to California in 1954. As a child, she saw a great-aunt and some older second cousins quilting. She had been quilting for only about five years at the time of the photo, but has always wanted to quilt and loves quilts. She is fascinated with old quilts, saying, "It makes me try and imagine the conditions the quilters lived with, the kinds of conversations they had while quilting, and how they collected the materials."

Dora Lee Simmons was born in 1934 in Fort Worth, Texas. She first came to California at the age of thirteen in 1947, when her parents divorced and her father came to work and live in Los Angeles. Growing up, she saw her mother and father, and some aunts and uncles, quilt. She explained, "I made my first quilt at age twelve. My mother taught me. Then in 1978 I started to subscribe to quilt magazines and buy quilt books to become more skillful. I have made over 160 quilts since 1978. I'm a quiltaholic."

Corrie McNeal was born in 1923 in Hankamer, Texas, and migrated to California in 1943. As a child she saw her mother and grandmother quilt. She first started to quilt at age nine, loves both sewing and quilting, and is now teaching her grandchildren.

Ozellia Mosely Crawford was born in 1927 in Benton, Mississippi, and migrated from there to California in 1953. She says, "My family was a family of quilters—my mother, grandmother, and aunts—and I was inspired by my grandmother. I learned to sew in homemaking classes in high school and majored in home economics in college. I taught myself to quilt, but have also participated in workshops with the AAQLA. God reveals [quilting] designs to me, also fabrics to use, because I pray and ask for direction in my life and in my quilting."

Arlilura Bernice Hilson was born in 1932 in Alligator, Mississippi, and migrated to California in the 1950s. Growing up, she saw her grandmother and great-aunts quilt, but she did not start quilting until she was an adult.

Carolyn A. Pruitt was born in 1949 and is a native of Los Angeles, California. She says, "My mother was a seamstress and my maternal grandmother was a quilter. I watched my grandmother quilt for many years, but I was more motivated to play sports than anything else. When my mother died in 1980, I realized that it's most important to leave a legacy. I decided after having a daughter and son that I wanted to make the kids a quilt out of their baby clothes, and I inquired where I could take lessons. I signed up at a local quilt shop and since then have never stopped being creative."

Mary Frances Cannon was born in West Point, Mississippi, and migrated to California around 1940. Growing up, she saw family and community members quilting. As she says, "I started to quilt at a very young age. I made quilts for my dolls, and later on helped my mother piece and quilt. My mother taught me, plus I would observe her and my grandmother."

Barbara King was born in 1939 in Greenville, Mississippi, and migrated to California in 1941. Growing up, she saw many women in her community quilt, including her mother, both grandmothers, aunts, cousins, and neighbors. She explains, "As a child, I 'quilted'—but was really a go-for—for my relatives. I've since taken quilt shop classes and quilt workshops with AAQLA."

Lavonia Marie North was born in 1923 in Anahuac, Texas, and migrated to California in 1952. As a child she saw family and community members quilting. She started to quilt around the age of twelve because she liked to sew and wanted to learn.

SHIRLEY GREAR

Another Women of Color Quilters' Network member I photographed in Los Angeles was Shirley Grear. Aside from the fact that she was making some exquisite story quilts, I was also intrigued with her Asian appearance. When I inquired about this, she told me that she was raised as an African American and was very proud of that heritage. Her mother, Dolores Walker, was an African American with established roots going back to North Carolina. Her paternal great-grandparents migrated from Korea to Hawaii, and her paternal grandparents from Hawaii to Los Angeles. Her father, Mr. Lee, was born in Los Angeles and attended a predominantly black high school where he met her mother. They married when Dolores was in her early twenties and had twin girls, Shirley and her sister Sharlene. Of her mixed heritage, Shirley says:

> One of the things that damages self-esteem in American society is forcing children and adults of mixed ethnic background to select a single heritage, thereby denying the other parts of themselves. I am very proud of my black heritage, and I'm bothered by the fact that I'm always asked to deny my Asian heritage—and this mainly comes from other African Americans. All my life I've tried to figure this out, and it's caused me great pain.
>
> I saw my maternal grandmother, Mary Walker, piece two small quilts when I was about four or five years old. I also grew up watching dozens of women in my church quilt around a large quilt frame. They were part of a community service organization called "Dorcas" [named for a weaver mentioned in the Bible].
>
> In 1976, I saw a review about a quilt display in New York. With absolutely no training or idea of what I was doing, I started a Log Cabin quilt. I still have the pieces . . . it never became a quilt. Since

the age of ten, I made my clothing but always said I would never cut fabric into tiny pieces only to stitch them back together again. In approximately 1984, my twin sister showed me how to make a "speed-pieced" Log Cabin quilt, and I was hooked immediately. I taught all my friends and that began my teaching career. My mother even learned to quilt from my twin and me, by joining one of my classes. My twin sister continues to quilt, but it never became a passion for her the way it did for me.

I have quilt tops that were made by others. A group of senior citizens in San Diego meets together each Tuesday to quilt. Their families are not quilt lovers, and so they have given me their quilt blocks and tops. Everybody seems to have somebody who will take a quilt, but tops and blocks can disappear with one disinterested generation. I have a small collection of quilts, as well as a number of quilt tops and blocks.

Shirley Grear.
LOS ANGELES, CALIFORNIA, JANUARY 1993 (35 MM CT)

Most of my own quilts are pieced, although some are appliquéd. I enjoy making story quilts . . . quilts that have something to say. I enjoy watching people try to interpret my quilts. It doesn't matter to me if they get the story right . . . just as long as it says something to them. Most of my quilts are original designs. I like a challenge.

My daughter, Michelle, started quilting at age five. She's twelve now and is still sticking with it. I'll soon be involving her with me in making an ancestral quilt. In making this piece, I hope not only to commemorate the spirit of my ancestors, but also to give to my children and others a new vision of the future through the window of dreams realized by past generations.

CHAPTER 7

New York to Washington, D.C., etc. (1992-93)

NEW YORK, NEW YORK, NOVEMBER–DECEMBER 1992

MICHAEL CUMMINGS

In November, Beverly and I went to New York to interview and photograph a male quilter, Michael L. Cummings (see p. 164).

Michael was born in 1945 in Los Angeles, California, and moved to New York City in 1970. No one in his early life had quilted; he began quilting in 1973. Largely self-taught, he learned through quilting books and by attending quilt exhibitions around New York. I had first met Michael about twelve years earlier when he lived in Greenwich Village and showed me his work on cloth. We had stayed in touch, and I'd watched his development over the years. He was now being recognized for some of the fabulous pieces he made, which were selling for $5,000 to $10,000. Michael says:

> The role quilting plays in my life is phenomenal. I have always wanted to be an artist. It was a dream I carried from childhood. I thought painting was the purest form of visual art, although through art history books and exhibitions from around the world I did see many other art forms. Romare Bearden* influenced my art-work. When I made a banner in the early 1970s, a window opened in my mind. I transferred the collage format to a quilt format, and the appliquéd quilt format has enabled me to transcend the collage and still maintain the rich color and tactile surface. This appliquéd format also allows me to work with narrative, and I see the politics of our cultural reality in my quilts.
>
> When completing several quilts with human faces that were life-size, I have experienced a queer feeling in my studio. It was as if there was another life force in the room. In some of my *Jazz Series,* and especially with one of my quilts, *I'll Fly Away,* I had to

---

*Romare Bearden, 1912–88, an African American born in North Carolina, is valued among America's premier artists. Much of his painting represented African-American lives and traditions, and incorporated collage, photomontage, and other media. His work is included in the twentieth-century collections of most major museums and private collections worldwide, and has been widely reproduced.

Michael A. Cummings.
NEW YORK, NEW YORK,
NOVEMBER 1992 (2-66044/15,
2¼ CN)

leave the room because the presence of something was so strong. In another quilt called *Star*, which I still don't open too often after nine years, an odd feeling is projected from the quilt image. In these quilts, I was attempting in a very detailed way to illuminate a personality, and the presence of a spirit seemed to be evoked with the love and care put into creating the quilts.

CAMILLE COSBY

In December, Beverly and I once again went to New York to meet Dr. Camille Cosby. Beverly flew directly from Atlanta; I drove up to New York City to meet her, and then we met Dr. Cosby at her recently renovated home. Its being still largely empty, except for a few pieces of antique furniture, permitted us the flexibility to create the setting we wanted. When Beverly and I arrived, the housekeeper informed us that Dr. Cosby had sent over some items for the shoot: a quilt made by her maternal grandmother; a pink chair; an end table; a photograph of her grandmother; and a bouquet of flowers to complement the quilt and the chair. Dr. Cosby arrived promptly at 11:30 A.M., and after we exchanged greetings her hair stylist went right to work. I had met Dr. Cosby once before, in August 1983 on the Mall in Washington, D.C., at the twentieth anniversary of the March on Washington for Jobs and Freedom. That day she had been with her children and her husband, and I remember being struck by how "regular" she was.

Camille O. Cosby was born in 1944 in Washington, D.C., and migrated to California in 1964, the year of her marriage. She currently spends time on both coasts. She is not a quilter herself, but has many memories of her maternal grandmother quilting. I asked her to comment on the quilt she had selected for the photo shoot, starting with some information about her grandmother:

> My grandmother's name was Clara Elizabeth Jackson Carter, and she was born in 1881 and died in 1971. She was eighty-nine years old at the time of her death. This particular quilt that you have photographed was made in 1962. The home that my grandmother lived in with my grandfather and their thirteen children, of which my mother is the youngest, was destroyed by fire in the 1950s. So all the quilts that she had made—which were, of course, very utilitarian, not decorative—were destroyed. So in 1962 when she made

this quilt, she just simply recreated what she had done prior to the fire that destroyed her home. My mother gave it to me for my birthday, about three years ago. She wanted me to have it, and actually there are only five other quilts that are left that my grandmother made before she died. One of those quilts is with my mother, and the other four are with my aunt who lives in Virginia, which is the old homestead of my grandmother.

I then asked Mrs. Cosby when she first started collecting quilts.

I think it was in the middle 1970s, when I went to Mississippi to visit Patty Crosby, who heads Mississippi Cultural Crossroads. What I did, it was an interesting thing that happened, actually, I was photographing the people down there—African-American women and men and children—for a project that I

Camille Cosby, quilt preserver, with a quilt made by her maternal grandmother, which was given to Mrs. Cosby's mother and then passed on to her.

NEW YORK, NEW YORK, DECEMBER 1992 (4-66278/2, 2¼ CN)

was working on for my master's studies at the University of Massachusetts. And I decided to give each person a copy of the photograph that I had taken. Well, after I did that, they rewarded me with a couple of quilts, and that was really the beginning of the quilt collection. Then later on I paid them to make quilts for me and my family and for friends.

And then I contacted a gentleman by the name of Joseph White (see p. 189), who was recommended by Dr. David Driscoll, because I wanted to have some quilts that were made by African-American men. And this gentleman, at the time, was in his seventies and he was blind in one eye. But his quilts are massive, and are really very colorful, lots of reds and greens and yellows, and once again not any particular pattern—very utilitarian, running stitches, such as my grandmother stitched, framed with color. But neither one used a framing device. My grandmother certainly didn't, and I don't think that Mr. White did either, because it didn't look like he did. But I just love the colors and the fact that they are utilitarian, rather than something that's decorative.

I have one quilt made by artist Faith Ringgold. It's an anniversary quilt that I commissioned her to make as a surprise for my husband for our nineteenth wedding anniversary, which was ten years ago.

I asked Mrs. Cosby what she eventually expects to do with her quilt collection.

New York chapter of the Women of Color Quilters' Network. *Left to right:* Yvette L. Walton, Valarie Jean Bailey, Marie Wilson, Peggie L. Hartwell, Hazel R. Blackman, and June Bridgeforth.

NEW YORK, NEW YORK, DECEMBER 1992 (1-66278/9, 2¼ CN)

I expect to always keep them, and I hope our children will enjoy them long after we are gone. I just want them to be there for posterity in our family and to be used in the manner that my grandmother used them, to provide warmth. And we use them on our sofas and sometimes as bedcovers. All kinds of things, you know. And we give them as gifts.

I then inquired if she had ever talked to her grandmother about quilting.

I never did, but I have spoken to my mother and her sisters and brothers about her, and they remember my grandmother quilting by a kerosene lamp in the evenings. She would use the fabrics from flour sacks, leftover pieces from sewing curtains or clothing, or whatever. She also ordered them in bulk from a magazine, which I clearly remember, called *The Progressive Farmer*.

I was curious if Mrs. Cosby's mother ever mentioned anything about particular quilts having any particular powers.

No. She never did. She never discussed that. As far as feeling something special, I think that my mother does, I know that I do, because I was very close to my grandparents. I feel very comfortable when I put the quilt on me. I just feel that my grandmother is with me. Her spirit is in that quilt. Sometimes, if I'm really agonizing over something, I'll just go and get the quilt and just put it on me to feel her warmth and protective spirit. It is a connection to her, a connection to my roots, to my grandmother. I know that she spent a lot of time, although the quilt looks very simple, but there was a lot of labor and her will of love that went into the making of the quilt. Now none of my children quilts, but I've given all of them quilts and they love them.

New York Chapter, Women of Color Quilters' Network

After leaving Mrs. Cosby, we had a quick lunch and then headed over to Peggie Hartwell's apartment on Central Park West to meet some of the members of the New York chapter of the Women of Color Quilters' Network (NYC/WCQN). Everyone was very excited about a large quilt the chapter was making to commemorate the twenty-fifth anniversary of the Dance Theatre of Harlem. This quilt was completed in March 1993 and unveiled at the New York State Theater in Lincoln Center; it is now at the Dance Theatre of Harlem (see p. 169).

Peggie Lois Hartwell was born in 1939 in Springfield, South Carolina, and is a fourth-generation quilter. Although her family migrated to Brooklyn, New York, when she was seven, she returned to Springfield each summer to live with her maternal grandmother, Annie Brown Tyler (1888–1988). Growing up she remembers seeing many women quilt— her grandmother Tyler's mother Fannie Brown Woodard; her mother, Rose Tyler Hartwell (b. 1910); her mother's seven sisters (Eloise, Kilsey,

Samella, Lottie, Elmira, Dorothy, and Fannie) and other relatives and community members. Mrs. Hartwell still treasures quilts that her grandmother made, and she told me this very special story about her:

> Whenever I work embroidery stitches into my quilts, I always think of my grandmother. She stitched the very first cross stitch I ever remember seeing—on the back of a young chicken! During an electrical storm, the lightning struck one of my grandmother's young chickens, knocking off all of his feathers, except two or three around his neck and two or three on his tail. The lightning also cut a long gash on his back—almost the entire length—and in addition, dislocated one of his legs. However, the chicken survived, but what a mess he was. My grandmother, who generally performed "certain surgical procedures" on her farm animals, took a long needle with heavy black thread and stitched very beautiful cross stitches on the back of a very frightened, kicking, pecking, clucking chicken. During the summer as I watched the chicken limp all over the yard sporting his embroidered back, I could not help but smile and marvel at this walking piece of art. Quilting today is everything to me, especially since I began creating a "childhood memories series." Through my quilting I am in constant touch with my past.

Peggie is involved in research, teaching, exhibiting locally and nationally, and is very active in the New York chapter of the WCQN.

Valarie Jean Bailey, another of the quilters we met at Peggie's, was born in 1949 in Lillington, North Carolina. As she relates:

> I moved to Elizabeth, New Jersey, at age four to live with a maternal aunt, Lillie Mae Hamer (1909-?), after the death of my mother. Then in 1964, I was sent back to Lillington to live with my father. My stepmother was a seamstress and milliner, and I learned a lot of sewing skills from her, but not quilting. I have no recollections of relatives quilting when I was a young child, although I'm sure some of them did. We were tobacco and cotton farmers. When I started quilting, my maternal aunt, who raised me, told me that the women in my family quilted, and she recalled how they "would beat the cotton down with sticks to put between the quilts." I remember the heavy quilts of my country relatives, but much to my chagrin, I don't recall them being made.
>
> I made my first quilt in 1975 as an accessory for a doll that I was making. I had a line of dolls called *Chocklat Chips*, which I custom-made for people. I just made simple scrap quilts, but I didn't know anything about the traditional ways of quilting at that time. In 1980 or 1981, I was commissioned by Ntozake Shange to do a quilt for a reading of *Cypress, Sassafras, and Indigo* she was performing at the Public Theatre. I had made a doll for her after seeing *For Colored Girls* . . . some years before, and she remembered. So I set about making this quilt. I had seen other quilts and was especially attracted to trian-

Tableau, 1993, 10' × 14'

This quilt was created to commemorate the New York City engagement of the Dance Theatre of Harlem at the New York State Theater of Lincoln Center in March 1993. Nine members of the group participated in producing the quilt. The dances shown and the quilters who made them are as follows. *Clockwise from bottom:* nine dancers in "Giselle," by Mary Ellen Webb; couple (man in red and woman in white) in "Streetcar Named Desire," by Yvette Walton; couple (both in white) in "Forces of Rhythm," by Hazel Blackman; at the top, seven dancers in "Dougla," by Valarie Bailey and June Bridgeforth; couple in "Song for a Dead Warrior," by Marguerite Hatfield; woman (in red dress) in "Medea," by Mauline Powell; and in the center, woman in "Firebird," by Peggie Hartwell.

Photo courtesy of Theobald G. Wilson.

(35 MM CT)

gles and patchwork. I was flying blind and didn't really have any good reference books on quilting. The quilt was okay; it was just that when they hung it on the stage, it shrunk! So after that experience, I decided to learn the traditional ways of quilting. I started taking classes at the Quilt Center. My first instructors there were Dee Danley-Brown, Jeff Gutcheon, Leslie Levison, and I got to know some of the quilters around New York. But I read a lot also and through a subscription to *Quilter's Newsletter* magazine learned of the Women of Color Quilters' Network—and have become active in that group as well as several other local guilds. So, in a sense, I'm a bit self-taught, and then I was exposed to some pretty terrific quilters in my family, and [learned] through my associates after I sought them out. I started going to quilt exhibits such as the Great American Quilt Festival and learning all I could about the craft. I quilt now, and also have taught a little, because I love it. It is a passion that fulfills a lot of my emotional and feminine needs.

I have collected some quilts from flea markets and such, but nothing of any great value. However, I purchased a quilt from Fannie Roberts Chaney, formerly of Meridian, Mississippi, in 1989 after we met through the Eldercraftsmen, Inc., a nonprofit senior organization, and I consider this to be a valuable quilt. Since that time I have gone through an apprenticeship program with Ms. Chaney, funded through the New York State Council on the Arts and sponsored by the Eldercraftsmen, Inc.

Quilting means many things to me. It is a way of expressing myself through my art and craft. It is a connection to my ancestors and their ancient properties. It is therapy and relaxation after a long day at work. (And I must say here, as with many quilters, I too have a "9 to 5" and quilt mostly in the midnight hours; sometimes I work all night long, shower and go to work, then if the rhythm is there, I go home and work some more.) It's a place to go when I feel like a motherless child, whether that means working on a quilt and shutting out the world or curling up under one for warmth. Quilting is a way for me to further validate myself as artist, as contributor, as warrior.

Working on the Dance Theatre of Harlem quilt with eight members of the NYC/WCQN was a spiritual experience of sorts. I had to pray a lot to continue with the project. I was tempted and I was tried. But I survived the experience and learned a great deal about working on group quilts and helped to produce a spectacular piece of art.

The Quilters Guild of Brooklyn is a multiracial, multicultural group that started in May of 1993 with 53 members and has grown to about 105. The *Quilt Brooklyn* exhibit was a multicultural show. The African-American quilters exhibiting at Borough Hall were myself and Virginia Hall. There was another part to the exhibit called *Windows on Bridge Street,* where quilts were exhibited in the windows of the New York Telephone Co. on the Bridge Street side. There were two African-American quilters in that exhibit, myself and Djamillah Samad. So I felt extremely proud of being able to represent my people in that way. Not to mention that Virginia Hall's and Djamillah Samad's quilts were also outstanding. The African-American quilt aesthetic was well defined in this show.

Marie Wilson was born in 1923 in Gary, Indiana. She was raised in Chicago and migrated to New York in 1943 with her husband, a New Yorker. Her mother, Josie Myers Dowell (1893–1984), from San Marcos, Texas, was a traditional quilter, but she didn't begin quilting herself until 1976, as an experiment. She is self-taught. She explains:

> Since 1976, I have been engaged in the design and production of needlework projects for retail and corporate clients, needlecraft magazines, and individuals. My primary works are narrative wall-hangings, which I call *Contemporary Tapestries*. They have been sold in New York and Florida boutiques and displayed nationally in gallery and museum exhibitions. Several of my designs were converted into fabric by M. Lowenstein & Sons. I have designed and executed prototypes of needlework for instruction and for future mass production. Corporate assignments have come from DuPont, the American Can Company, The Gap, and Banana Republic. In 1982, I designed *American Beauty Appliqués* for the Bloomingdale's fall promotion of American designers and craftsmen. In the previous year, I created miniature window treatments and textile furnishings for a traveling exhibit of a miniature country house, sponsored by the Hobby Industry of America.
>
> During 1985, I designed the setting and coordinated the assemblage of a *Weaver of Dreams* quilt. The quilt is composed of blocks made by students in thirty-five Martin Luther King Jr. schools throughout the country. It was dedicated in Atlanta on the first national observance of his birthday and hangs in the Rosa Parks Room of the King Center. The project was underwritten by the American Can Company. In 1988, I served as exhibition chairperson for the twentieth anniversary exhibition of the Manhattan Chapter of the Embroiderers' Guild of America. In the fall of 1992, I designed a quilt to commemorate the 1993 spring engagement of the Dance Theatre of Harlem at Lincoln Center.
>
> I conduct "hands-on" workshops and give slide presentations on design concepts and needle skills for organizations. The organizations include: American Craft Museum; Museum of American Folk Art; Embroiderers' Guild of America; Spencer Art Museum of the University of Kansas; Stony Brook University; and the Eldercraftsmen Training Studio.

Hazel Rodney Blackman was born in 1929 in Kingston, Jamaica, West Indies. She migrated to New York in 1944 and has become a famous artist and designer. She owned Manhattan's African Tree House boutique and was the principal designer there, specializing in the use of African fabrics and African designs, which she adapted to the practicalities and demands of American life and the local market. She has received numerous awards for her contributions to the fashion industry. Her

Faith Ringgold in her studio.
NEW YORK, NEW YORK, DECEMBER 1992 (5-66278/7, 2¼ CN)

artwork has been influenced by her studies in Jamaica, the United States, and Africa, and her paintings and sculpted figures have been exhibited in galleries and museums worldwide. She has researched the background of traditional African cotton prints, and in particular Khanga, the Swahili name for an East African cloth that is stamp-printed, predominantly in reds, oranges, and yellows. Quilting, however, was the last thing this pioneering designer learned. As she says:

> In 1968 while traveling as a consultant with the Federation of Southern Cooperatives, we went to see several quilting groups from Atlanta to Mississippi, New Orleans, and San Francisco. With my designing and craft background, I became interested in quilting. I started piecing, bought some books, and now it's a strong personal interest—I love it!

Yvette Walton was born in the Bronx, New York, and had just started learning to quilt when I took this picture. She was primarily a knitter and made only one block for the Dance Theatre of Harlem quilt.

Sonia Sanchez, writer and quilt preserver
DELAWARE COUNTY, PENNSYLVANIA, DECEMBER 1992 (1-66303/11, 2¼ CN)

FAITH RINGGOLD

After leaving Peggie's and the NYC/WCQN members, we headed downtown to meet internationally known artist Faith Ringgold. Beverly is a close friend of Faith's daughter, the author Michele Wallace, who was also meeting us there. Faith was busy with a new book for Walt Disney, and spreads of the work-in-progress lined the walls. She had just returned from Paris, where she had unveiled her latest quilt, a piece showing ten American expatriates who had gathered at the Paris home of Gertrude Stein and Alice B. Toklas.

Faith was born in 1930 in Harlem, New York, and now resides in New Jersey. She has been a painter since the 1950s. In the 1970s, she began to work in soft sculpture, collaborating with her mother, Willi Posey Jones, a fashion designer and dressmaker, who has had a major influence on Faith's interest in quilts. Willi Posey described watching her grandmother, Betsy Bingham, boil and bleach flour sacks to line the quilts she sewed. Susie Shannon, Betsy's mother, was a slave in antebellum Florida who made quilts as part of her duties.

Forty-six members of the Daughters of Dorcas and Sons. *(Rows are listed from back to front.) Back row (left to right):* Pansy Lee Lovelace, Jeanette E. Ford, Gertrude Braan, Mary B. Turpin, Cleo F. Kendall, Geraldine M. Curry, Frances M. Henry, Marie Banks, Evelyn E. Salinger, Hazel A. Beatty, Jackie Mosely, Melba T. Thalley, and Anita M. Wilkinson. *Second row (left to right):* Elsie M. Upshur, Deborah A. Draughn, Alberta M. Perry, Regenia Spears, Lucy E. Robinson, unidentified woman, Theresa T. Pinckney, Bessie E. Sharpe, Selma G. Lee, Isabelle C. Davis, Frances M. Boyd, Evelyn F. Greene, Sarah E. Rollins, Maria R. Goodwin, and Sarajane C. Goodwin. *Third row (left to right):* Mae Carter Hill Bolden, Alice Burton, Wilma L. R. Gordon, Mildred B. Ridgley, Annie M. Strivers, and Pattie H. Brew. *Fourth row (left to right):* Joyce B. Nixon, Carmel S. Washington, Vivian J. Lucas, Viola V. Canady, Muriel W. Drew, Ruth T. Campbell, and Vivian E. Hoban. *Front row (left to right):* Bertha J. Morgan, Doris R. Payne, Raymond G. Dobard, Ruth H. Stokes, and Roland L. Freeman.

WASHINGTON, D.C., JANUARY 1993 (1-66425/13, 2¼ CN)

Faith is best known for her "story quilts," works that combine painting, quilted fabric, and storytelling—sometimes autobiographical —and now sell for $30,000 and up. She has exhibited internationally and has published several award-winning children's books.

PHILADELPHIA, PENNSYLVANIA, DECEMBER 1992

SONIA SANCHEZ

On our way back to Washington, D.C., we stopped in Philadelphia to photograph Sonia Sanchez with some of her quilts. Sonia has quilts in every room of her house (see p. 173).

> I am saying physically and initially, something happens when you put a quilt on your bed. And wow, when you sleep under it, it's like you are sheltered, like nothing can happen to you. Maybe what I'm saying is you feel protected, and I mean it's like what some people call "ooga booga" stuff. These quilts can be a form of intellectual nourishment. When I look at some of these quilts, I see the blood, I see the tears, and I see the sweat. I see women who could not say what I say on paper—but they certainly say it loud and clear in their quilts. You can hear the spirits of the sisters moaning, moaning, moaning. They're not crying, they're just moaning. And all I'm saying is, in these quilts, there is life that gives love.

Chekesha W. Rashad and her mother Johari M. Rashad.
WASHINGTON, D.C., JANUARY 1993 (35 MM CT)

WASHINGTON, D.C., JANUARY 1993

I started 1993 by photographing several local quilters. I went to the home of Johari M. Rashad, a long-time volunteer at the annual Festival of American Folklife. A Washington native, Ms. Rashad was born in 1951. No one in her family quilted, and as she said, "I had admired quilts for years, having sewed since 1966, but I'd never made one. I was inspired to quilt by the Alabama quilters at the folklife festival, and especially by Mrs. Canady from Washington, D.C., who was also demonstrating there. I designed and made my first quilt by myself. I can lose myself for hours at my quilting frame—I get to spend time with my creative and spiritual self." Ms. Rashad made a quilt for her daughter, Chekesha Rashad, who had been a troubled teen. This quilt was for her to take to college at Louisiana's Grambling State University. As Johari told me, "After I made the quilt for my daughter, . . . I bathed and put on one of my favorite oils. I slept naked in the quilt so that it would be infused with my scent, so that when my daughter got it, it would have my scent, my spirit, in it."

THE DAUGHTERS OF DORCAS AND SONS

I also used this opportunity to photograph the local quilting group, the Daughters of Dorcas and Sons, of which I am a member (see p. 174). The Daughters of Dorcas and Sons exemplify the long tradition of American quilting by doing what quilters have done for centuries: working together and teaching others. Meeting weekly at Calvary Episcopal Church at 820 Sixth Street, N.E., they share ideas and techniques as they work individually and jointly. Chartered in 1980 with the National Quilting Association, the Daughters of Dorcas and Sons—named for the Biblical seamstress, Dorcas—was founded by nationally recognized quilter Viola Canady and Etta F. Portlock (now deceased). Beginning as a small circle of African-American women, the 114 members now include three "Sons." Although the members are predominantly of African-American ancestry, the Daughters of Dorcas and Sons derives designs, fabrics, and ideas from a variety of ethnic backgrounds and fabrics using traditional patterns of American quilting, in addition to more innovative designs, materials, and techniques. On January 12, I photographed forty-six members with a quilt they were making for the headquarters of the National Council of Negro Women, entitled *Black Family Reunion Quilt*. This quilt incorporated an original design with photo transfer and original quilting. Along with other quilts by members, it was later shown at the National Council of Negro Women conference in October 1993.

Viola V. Canady, president of this group, was born in 1922 in Goldsboro, North Carolina. She learned to quilt primarily from her mother, Lila Grady (1897–1932), and her mother's mother, Ava Grady (1867–1953), both of whom were from La Grange, North Carolina. As she says, "We had to quilt to keep warm. There was no money to buy blankets. I learned to sew clothes, and sewed and quilted before I went to school." She also saw her paternal great-grandmother, Lil Newman (1858–1951), from Pink Hill, North Carolina, quilt, and told me the following story about her.

> I never will forget this old lady. She lived to be 93, and if I live to be 193 I'll still remember her. She liked her corn liquor and she bossed around everybody in the family. She had this big stick and wasn't afraid to beat anybody with it, children and grown-ups alike. She'd let loose on the grown-ups if anyone ever took her liquor or wouldn't go get her some when she wanted it. And she gave me the worst whipping I ever had.
> It all started when me and my sister and two cousins was making these grass dolls. See, you pull up some long grass with the roots still on it, wash the dirt out of the roots, and then you

would turn the grass upside down. About two inches from the roots you'd tie a piece of string around it and that would be the doll's head, and the roots would be the hair. About four to five inches down from that, you'd tie another piece of string and that would be the waist. Well, we wanted some clothes for these dolls, so we went in my great-grandmother Lil's trunk where she had all these quilts and quilt tops. I'm talking about some fancy quilt tops. And we decided to cut some of these real pretty blocks out of the tops she'd pieced up to use as dresses for our dolls. When this old lady found that out, she plumb went crazy. We were just girls, but she took two good swigs of liquor and made us lie down in a row on the porch and show our bare behinds. Then she took her favorite whipping stick and beat all four of us so bad that we couldn't hardly walk, much less sit down.

Raymond G. Dobard.
WASHINGTON, D.C., JANUARY 1991 (2-91001/16)

In 1945, Mrs. Canady migrated to Washington, D.C., where she continues to quilt. She received a $5,000 individual fellowship from the D.C. Commission on the Arts and Humanities in 1990, and represented Washington, D.C., at the Smithsonian's Festival of American Folklife on the Mall. She became nationally known after completing a quilted wallhanging of the Sumner School Museum, which was commissioned by this historic site located at 17th and M Streets, N.W., in Washington. She is presently working on a second such wallhanging of the Franklin School Museum, another historic building in Washington. Having taught quilting for many years, Mrs. Canady specializes in the "stained glass" appliqué technique (which means creating the effect of looking at a stained-glass window by arranging colored pieces of fabric between thin strips of black material). Her How to Quilt piece appeared in the Smithsonian Institution's Anacostia Museum exhibit on African-American quilts, and her ideas about quilt-making appeared in the November 1993 issue of Quilter's Newsletter magazine.

Gertrude Braan—another member of the Daughters of Dorcas and Sons—was born in 1932 in Brooklyn, New York, and migrated to Washington, D.C., in 1966. Growing up she did not know any quilters, but she did learn to sew clothes at an early age. She has made most of her children's and her own clothes since then. As she explains, "On my

Twins Kristi and Kimblee James.
CLAIBORNE COUNTY, MISSISSIPPI,
FEBRUARY 1993 (3-66853/11,
2¼ CN)

lunch break in 1984, a co-worker of mine, Carmie Smith, was sewing some pieces of fabric together for a quilt. I said, 'Gee, I'd like to learn how to quilt.' The next day she brought some fabric, etc., and my lessons began. I still have my first project, a pillow, that was the result of my first lessons."

Alice Burton was born in 1917 in Fairmont, North Carolina, and migrated to Washington, D.C., in 1941. While growing up, she saw her mother, Iva Boone (1885–1932), who was from Holland, Virginia, and her mother's friends quilting. She simply says, "I saw my mother quilt, and I liked what I saw."

Raymond G. Dobard (see p. 177) was born in 1947 in New Orleans, Louisiana. He left New Orleans in 1970 in order to attend graduate school at Johns Hopkins University in Baltimore, Maryland, and in 1975 moved to Washington, D.C. No one in his family quilted, but he says:

My Aunt Freda [Alfreda Ruiz Gilyot] did crochet, and I was spell-bound watching her turn thread into geometric creations. I began quilting in the fall of 1985 after visiting an antique show and wishing to have a Log Cabin quilt. I purchased the book *Better Homes and Gardens' American Patchwork* and taught myself how to make quilts. A year or two later, I joined the Daughters of Dorcas and Sons quilt guild and furthered my knowledge and skills. When I am lost in making a quilt, I am in contact with myself and my spirit feels free. To me, quiltmaking is comparable to meditation. On a very personal level, I feel in contact with my late Aunt Freda.

Vivian E. Hoban was born in 1922 in Troy, North Carolina, and migrated to Washington, D.C., in 1941. Growing up she saw her mother, Annie Jane Townsend Lambert (1882–1980), who was also from North Carolina, quilt. She says: "I began quilting in 1987. I learned by joining the Daughters of Dorcas and Sons. Quilting has given me another opportunity to share with others the pleasure it brings to me and to pass on the art to a younger generation."

Pansy L. Lovelace was born in 1936 in Lawndale, North Carolina. Her parents migrated to Chase City, a small town in southern Virginia, where she resided until 1958, when she moved to Washington, D.C. She recalls seeing both her paternal grandmother Ophelia Polen Hector (1868–1955), and her father's sister, Patty Jean Hector (1900–91), quilt,

Quilt, 24" × 48", made by twins Kristi and Kimblee James, guided by the Mississippi Cultural Crossroads quilters.
CLAIBORNE COUNTY, MISSISSIPPI, FEBRUARY 1993 (FRAME 2, 2¼ CT)

both of whom were from Oconee County, Georgia. She explains, "My Aunt Patty was a very prolific seamstress and quilter, and she would either quilt or tack her common quilts. I'm not sure what year I started quilting, but I guess it was around the age of eight. We wanted to make quilts for our doll bed, and I learned by watching the older ladies."

Annie M. Strivers, a native of Washington, D.C., was born in 1929. No one in her family quilted, and she says, "I started to quilt in February 1990. Quilting was something that I decided to try after retiring. I knew the basics of sewing, and the Daughters of Dorcas were wonderful teachers."

Ruth H. Stokes, another native of Washington, D.C., was born in 1933. She learned to quilt from her mother, Josephine Elizabeth Sendall Perry (1904–53), who was from Charles County, Maryland, and her mother's sister, Alberta Sendall Proctor (1912–67), and also from other family members. As she puts it, "I am still learning from the Daughters of Dorcas."

Mae Carter Hill Bolden was born in 1920 in Franklin County, Georgia, and her family moved to Washington, D.C., when she was six months old. Growing up she saw her maternal grandmother, Caroline Reeder Knox (1882–1968), quilt. Then, as she said, "Quilting was something that I always wanted to do, and one day I saw adult classes advertised. That was nine years after I retired, and I took many classes and joined three quilt clubs." She then told a fascinating story.

 I received a commission to make a Double Wedding Ring quilt for the wife of the ambassador from Saudi Arabia in June 1991. I had been

Mississippi Cultural Crossroads quilting bee: elders teaching the young.
CLAIBORNE COUNTY, MISSISSIPPI, FEBRUARY 1993 (35 MM CT)

diagnosed with carpal tunnel syndrome, and my shoulders and arms ached all week. I was on my way to a meeting when a woman stopped me and said that she was hungry. I fumbled in my purse—my arms were so sore—until I found a ten-dollar bill and then gave it to her. She said, "Thank you, this is my birthday. May I hug you?" We hugged, and my pains left me and have never returned. I had received a blessing through this woman. And that is why as I quilted this quilt—it took seventeen months, sewing ten to twelve hours a day—I exposed it with nothing but love. I turned off the TV when news came on. It was a joy to quilt with absolutely no pain. And as a thanksgiving, I now put money into the hands of any homeless whom I meet.

Mrs. Bolden has since moved to Oregon where she started a chapter of the Daughters and Sons of Dorcas at her church.

MISSISSIPPI CULTURAL CROSSROADS, FEBRUARY 1993

I made a quick trip back to Port Gibson, Mississippi to photograph a quilting bee; in this case, one where the tradition was being passed on to

Enoch Thompson and his four sons. *Left to right:* Hakiba, Jajaf, Janali, and H'Cone.
WASHINGTON, D.C., MARCH 1993 (FRAME 5, 2¼ CT)

the next generations through the guidance of the Cultural Crossroads
master quilters (see pp. 178–179).

JULEE DICKERSON THOMPSON AND ANN S. DICKERSON

On March 3, I continued this documentation by photographing two local
women whom I had known for years and had commissioned to work on
some of my original quilt designs (see pp. 81–83, 88–89). Julee
Dickerson Thompson, a native of Washington, D.C., was born in 1955.
No one in her family quilted, although her mother, Ann S. Dickerson,
loved crafts. She explains, "A soft-sculpture class in college led me into
quilting as a fabricated form of art. I have picked up additional
techniques from my mother, her friend Roz Watkins, and books. My
quilting work with senior citizens has been wonderful, and reflective of
the quilting tradition—stories were shared, especially concerning the
subject of each quilt. The sessions became wonderful history lessons for
me. If only I could have gotten them on tape! Quilting to me is an artistic
expression celebrating the fabric of life."

Ann S. Dickerson, Julee's mother and also a Washington native, was born "in the late twenties." She told me that growing up she "had no direct association with anyone doing quilting. I developed an interest from casual exposure: musems, people's homes, and magazines. I started hand-sewing when I was fourteen. My first serious work with quilting began in 1971 with a girls' recycling boutique, and I am self-taught. To me, quilting means perpetuating culture and heritage; recycling; developing a meaningful craft; and it is inspiritional, exciting, and fulfilling."

I also photographed Julee's husband, Enoch, reading a bedtime story to their four sons under a quilt that she and Ann had made together (see p. 181).

CHAPTER 8
The Cross-Country Voyage
(March–June 1993)

I spent the next three months on the road, leaving Washington on March 10 and returning on June 17, 1993. During that time I documented quilters in thirty states: in many, for the first time; in others, following up on earlier work. The results of this trip are presented chronologically, following my progress on this journey.

North Carolina, March 10, 1993

From Washington, I went to Charlotte, North Carolina, and after a quick stop at the Afro-American Cultural Center for the opening of my quilt exhibition, *More Than Just Something to Keep You Warm,* I continued to South Carolina.

South Carolina, March 11–16, 1993

Columbia

In Columbia, I met with Joann Thompson. Joann had made an all-black quilt that I wanted to see, but it was in a touring exhibit, so I made her picture in front of what she had. I was excited to hear about her doctoral dissertation project, which was to use quilts to help a multiethnic group of students improve their language skills (see p. 184).

Conway

I met Worth in Georgetown, South Carolina, where we stayed with the family of Vanessa Greene, a local arts person. Her family helped show us around the area. Worth and I first went to Conway to meet a quilter, Leola Hicks Burroughs (see p. 185). The local newspaper had done a front-page story of Worth's work in this area, and Mrs. Burroughs was one of the people featured. With a broad smile and warm hugs, Mrs. Burroughs welcomed us into her home. She was seventy years old, and told us she was born in an old "pole house" (a log cabin) in Georgetown County. As she says:

> I ain't never known nothing but farming, cooking, raising children, and making quilts. I first married a Hicks, then a Burroughs. I've had twenty-two kids, including three sets of twins. I've been a mid-

Joann E. Thompson.
RICHLAND COUNTY, SOUTH
CAROLINA, MARCH 1993
(FRAME 14, 2¼ CT)

wife for forty-nine years and waited on myself for seven of my children. I've been quilting since I was a young girl. I just take what I got and put them together. I don't have time to make anything fancy.

Her first husband had a stroke and couldn't work. She took her family Bible that had all the dates of her children's birthdays in it, and as she says,

I went off to see the Social Security people to get some money. I needed help. Didn't have no birth certificates and they wouldn't believe what was in the Bible. Went to several other places but didn't have no luck. I was scuffling around here, and one day this white lady showed up and said she could get me some help if I'd sign all the land, almost one hundred acres, over to her, except for two acres around the house. My mother-in-law told us don't do it, whatever you do hold on to the land. The Lord will make a way somehow. So we got everybody together and put up a "prayer stick." And we came out of them prayers and built another little place on the house and I went to cooking and selling meals to folks, and then white folks started to come and get me to cook all sorts of stuff for them—cakes, pies, barbecues, etc. And when I wasn't doing that, I was quilting. And between my cooking and quilting we got by.

PAWLEYS ISLAND

I next went to Pawleys Island to meet Carrie Grate Coachman, who in 1989 had won a South Carolina Folk Heritage Award for her quilting. Since she lived close to the water, we decided to take a couple of her quilts to the beach (see p. 186). While I was arranging one of them in the sand dunes, I noticed she had wrapped herself in the other one. Mrs. Coachman, a native of Georgetown County, is a quiltmaker whose work well represents styles seen along the South Carolina coast. She grew up in a traditional quiltmaking community and learned her sewing skills principally from her mother. Her quilts are marked by an eclectic adaptation of different concepts of quilt patterning. Like most quilters in her region, she often uses many small pieces of cloth, but she improvises color combinations into patterns that she has designed herself. Describing herself as an American quilter, she draws on the string and block pattern concepts to create personal artistic statements that synthesize diverse traditional elements in her own personal style. She is recognized within her community as a fine quiltmaker, and she teaches her skill to others.

Vanessa Greene's father was showing me around Pawleys Island, most of which is developed. When driving south along Highway 17 toward Georgetown, I noticed a several-mile stretch of forested land. He told me that this was part of the Arcadia Plantation. I asked if he knew anyone who lived there and whether we could visit them, and he said, "Sure I know lots of folk out here. I used to come out here a lot when I was a kid." I wondered aloud, "Why were you coming to a plantation as a kid if you didn't have to?" He answered, "Oh man, used to be big doings out here on the 4th of July and Christmas. This place would be flooded with folks." We turned right off Highway 17 onto a gravel road, and the first thing we saw was a huge "No Trespassing" sign. Mr. Greene assured me it was all right as long as we were going to visit someone. There were many houses of different sizes and a few trailers set among the trees along a horseshoe dirt road, with the majority clustered at the end of the loop.

Leola Hicks Burroughs.
HORRY COUNTY, SOUTH
CAROLINA, MARCH 1993
(FRAME 4, 2¼ CT)

On the right just before the cluster was a unique brick church with a big bell tower, and I stopped to read several plaques set at intervals in the wall. They explained the history of this site. The plaque closest to the rear said that the original wooden structure was erected by Major Huger of the Revolutionary Army during the eighteenth century and was used as a hospital for slaves until the close of the Civil War in 1865. The middle plaque read: "St. Anne's School Private Erected and Supported by Anne Preston Emerson in 1927 for the children of the colored people employed on the Estate of Arcadia." The plaque on the front said, "St. Anne's Church rebuilt by Capt. I. E. Emerson owner of Arcadia Estate Dedicated to God 1927" (see p. 187).

We then met Martha German who was coming out of the church, and she explained to us that the building connected to the back of the church was once a school that her grandparents had attended. She also told us that no one on the plantation quilted anymore. The only quilt she had was literally falling apart. It had been made by her grandmother, Susan Alston Smalls, who was born on Arcadia Plantation in 1896 and had raised her. Mrs. German gladly went and got her grandmother's quilt and

Carrie Coachman.
PAWLEYS ISLAND, GEORGETOWN
COUNTY, SOUTH CAROLINA,
MARCH 1993 (35 MM CT)

obituary. She gently placed the quilt on a table in front of the church altar (see p. 188) and handed me the obituary to read, which included the following poem:

(see p. 188)

> She lived—this is the way she lived,
> with Christian love and a smile on her face,
> she never met a stranger,
> and in her heart, each found a place.
> She died—this is the way she lived
> and when her breath was done
> she calmly turned to those she loved
> and headed for the sun.

Being in this place and seeing this worn-out quilt, I suddenly felt I was stepping back in time. Before I could make a picture, I had to sit down and ponder the situation. Even though this old quilt was indeed worn-out, it still had a lot of life in it; it made me stop and think about the hands that made it, and the love that went into it, and the warmth it provided. Its maker was born, had died, and was buried on this land. I looked around the church, and her granddaughter pointed out where Mrs. Smalls used to sit. She told me that quite often she had come here with her grandmother when no one else was around, and her grandmother would just sit and hum and talk to the old ones.

As I glanced around, on the left back wall behind the pulpit, I saw a plaque that read "Arcadia Plantation Honor Roll." Among the names listed were some of America's richest industrialists, including George and Alfred Vanderbilt. Sensing my interest, Mrs. German asked if we would like to meet some of the other people who lived there, so we went to Maybelle McColl's house, where we were joined by four other people who lived on the plantation. For the next three hours, they told me about the history of the plantation and what their lives had been like. Most of the talking was done by a seventy-seven-year-old retired man, Andrew Smalls Jr., who was one of Mrs. Smalls's three children. He remembered his grandfather, Joseph Alston, who was born around 1823. His grandfather said that his mother had been sold three times, first to the Alston family in Charlotte, North Carolina. After he and his mother were freed, they were walking toward the ocean and were picked up by some relatives of the Alston family whom they had just left, and were brought to Rose Hill Plantation in South Carolina.

At that time, there was a whole row of plantations coming out on this island, starting with Rose Hill, then Lawn Oak, Clifton, George Hill, Prospect Hill, Fairfield, Oak Hill, and then Mackie. You see, they had this boat they brought down from Baltimore called "Arcadia," and that's why they named all this Arcadia. Right here, which used to be Prospect Hill, was owned way back by Major Huger during slavery times, then by the Wards, and then Emerson had it. And somewhere up in there is the Vanderbilts who moved here. And then Margaret Emerson married a Vanderbilt, and he drowned on the Titanic—I'm sure you heard about that, that was the big luxury ship all them rich folks died on back in 1912—and he left her with three children. Her oldest son Alfred is the one who had the famous race horse, Native Dancer. George Vanderbilt was the second son, and his grandfather gave him the plantation because Alfred didn't like the country. They also had a sister Gloria. We called her Mamie, but her name was Gloria. The lady who lives in the big house now is Mrs. Lucille Pate, and she's George's only child. She was raised here, but she was born in Honolulu, Hawaii.

Pre–Civil War church on Pawleys Island, which was used at different times as a school and hospital.
GEORGETOWN COUNTY, SOUTH CAROLINA, MARCH 1993
(FRAME 2, 2¼ CT)

I asked Mr. Smalls how he remembered all of this so clearly.

You see, I traveled all over the world with them. I did the valet, chauffeuring, and bodyguarding. You see, these are my people.

I asked him what he meant by "these are my people."

Well, we all growed up right here together, and me, momma, and all of us worked in the big house. Even my daughter works there today. In World War II, Mr. [George] Vanderbilt went in the navy and I went in the army, and he tried to get them to put me in the navy with him, but they'd sent me to Europe already. And after the war, I went right back to working for him.

I asked if he had any of his mother's quilts.

No, the only quilt left is the one my niece, Martha, brought up to you at the church. You see, most of that old-time stuff is played out. No more blacksmith shops, making baskets, growing rice, no more, no more. Was a time when somebody died, they'd blow this big conch shell, and this one will blow that conch shell, the next plantation will hear it and get it, and he'll sound off and he will blow, the next plantation will get it; and that passed the word on down the island. Today they ring the church bell.

Martha S. German with quilts made by her grandmother Susan Alston Smalls (1896–1989).

PAWLEYS ISLAND, GEORGETOWN COUNTY, SOUTH CAROLINA, MARCH 1993 (FRAME 4, 2¼ CT)

I then asked, "Mr. Smalls, as you travel throughout the world, how do you refer to this place?" He asked, "Do you mean my home, this plantation?" "Yes, what type of reaction do you get when you tell people that you live on a plantation on Pawleys Island, South Carolina?"

Don't get no reaction, except they want to know if I got any land to sell them on the water. Everybody wants some beach-front property, especially white folks. They love to be by the water. But I'm comfortable right where I am.

It's an historical fact that many African Americans can trace their ancestry back to some plantation, but there is deep-seated bitterness and resentment about that period of our history—and a lot of distrust of people who write about it. Much of the same attitudes are held about modern-day plantation life, and I realized the importance of my accurately observing what I saw, while acknowledging the complexity of its historical evolution.

As I learned from these quilters and expanded my own understandings of their social backgrounds, I was able to relate what I heard to three major sequential periods in our history: first, the Middle Passage, combined with the forced migration from the Upper South to the Lower South for the cultivation of cotton; second, the post–Civil War migration from plantation to plant, or field to factory; and third, the current migration back to the Southern homeland. Some of those now heading South are successful black professionals and retirees making a positive choice as to where they want to live. However, for far too many, the dreams of a better life have died in the urban canyons of the North. At the same time, many of their families have sold their land in the South, some have been cheated out of it, and some have been hopelessly run off. Now, old and weary, and longing for home, they are retiring to a new South. But, not only is it hard to erase the psychological scars of the past; in many cases their family land is no longer there for them.

Over time, what some people came to realize was that the plant was just a workplace, whereas their family farms or the plantation— regardless of circumstances—had been a living place; it had been home. The Southland was where your roots were, and you were tied to it because it was home. It didn't matter if the land was sold; that didn't change the fact that it was home. Folks would say, "My people are buried here, my blood is here." And the churches and graveyards for many were revered as holy places. They had brought down the spirit, and it resided there.

Most African-born ancestors of U.S. African Americans arrived before the American Revolution, between 1710 and the 1770s, and their descendants are seventh- or eighth-generation Americans. As the generations went by and families no longer had specific geographical or ethnic anchors in Africa, the Southland became the home base for the extended family. And most people will be as surprised as I was to discover isolated instances in which the descendants of slaves still live as tenants on the plantation where their ancestors had been slaves.

Eighty-six-year-old quilter Joseph White.

BERKELEY COUNTY, SOUTH CAROLINA, MARCH 1993 (FRAME 11, 2¼ CT)

CHARLESTON

I left Georgetown and headed south on Highway 17 toward Charleston to follow up on a lead that Camille Cosby had given me on Joseph White, a male quilter. He was an eighty-six-year-old retiree who was born on Wadmalaw Island and raised on Johns Island. As a young boy, he learned to quilt from his mother, Victoria White, but stopped in his teens. He didn't return to quilting until after he retired. As he said, "I needed something to do beside look at television. So I got me a sewing machine and started putting together scraps." His wife, who doesn't quilt, thinks what he does is beautiful. Most of his neighbors don't know he quilts, and he likes it that way.

ALABAMA, MARCH 20–21, 1993

BIRMINGHAM

Back on March 10, when I had stopped in Charlotte, North Carolina, I'd seen Wanda Montgomery, the new director of the Afro-American Cultural Center there, with whom I'd worked at the Smithsonian. She had suggested I talk with her receptionist, Jane Lewis, who had a special quilt in her family. Mrs. Lewis had informed me that the quilt had come down through four generations of women in her family, and that she had recently passed it on to her niece, Gloria Cockerham, who lived in Birmingham. So we had called her niece and made arrangements for me to go and photograph her with it. After I arrived, Mrs. Cockerham brought this lovely quilt out of an old trunk. While I was making photographs, Mrs. Cockerham explained the history of the quilt. It was made by her great-great-grandmother, Lizzie Chambers Barber, who was born around 1857, a few years before the Civil War, in Red Spring, South Carolina, and who died in 1955. Gloria had never met Lizzie, but said that Lizzie's daughter—her great-grandmother, Janey Barber Marrow Kirkpatrick—who lived until 1972, had been her link to the past:

> My history teacher in my last year of high school impressed upon us the importance of learning our history from the elders in our family, and today I'm really glad I did that. We called Janie "Big Momma," and she remembered things that her mother Lizzie told her. Parts of the quilt were made from old dresses and some of her husband's clothes. Lizzie passed the quilt on to her daughter, Janie ("Big Momma"), as a wedding gift. From Janie, it skipped her daughter, Vivian, who was my grandmother, and went to her grand-daughter, who is my Aunt Jane Lewis, the lady you met in Charlotte. She kept the quilt for a very long time, and even once thought about getting rid of it. When she mentioned the quilt to the director at the arts center where she was working, she was asked to bring it in and they put it on exhibit. It was only then that she began to truly appreciate what a significant family treasure this was. Then Aunt Jane, who had one son and no girls, decided to pass the quilt on to me.

I then asked Mrs. Cockerham if she had slept under the quilt.

> Yes, when I first got it. I kicked my husband out of the bed so I could see what kind of vibes I got from it. And I put a five-genera-tion picture on my bedstand—all women but my older brother; he made up the fifth generation. And I got some other memorabilia from my two grandmothers and my great-grandmother, handker-chiefs and stuff like that, and put it all in the bed with me. And the vibes were nice. I made a connection with all those good spirits. This quilt comes down on the woman's side, and it's the thing that really meant something to the women who came before me. I'll cherish it the rest of my life, and see that it and the stories are passed on.

Tuscaloosa

The next morning I left Birmingham and headed for Tuscaloosa, where I had an appointment with quilter Yvonne Wells. Mrs. Wells's quilts had been widely exhibited around the world, and much had been written about her. I had first met her and her artistic representative Robert Cargo at the Museum of American Folk Art in New York City at the opening of Dr. Gladys-Marie Fry's exhibit, *Stitched from the Soul: Slave Quilts from the*

Antebellum South. I had seen her again in 1992 when she and Carolyn Mazloomi shared an exhibit in Louisville, Kentucky, as part of the *Louisville Celebrates the American Quilt* conference.

Mrs. Wells, a native of Tuscaloosa, had seen her mother quilting when she was a child, but didn't quilt until she taught herself in 1979. From the outset, she varied traditional patterns with some abstract ideas, and she was quite reluctant to show or exhibit her quilts. However, she was encouraged by a friend, Robert Cargo, to enter an exhibition in 1985, and she cites that experience as the turning point in her career. I asked Mrs. Wells to describe the three quilts that best conveyed the message she was trying to give to people through quilting.

Gloria R. Cockerham with quilt made by her great-grandmother.
SHELBY COUNTY, ALABAMA, MARCH 1993 (35 MM CT)

> One would be the *Crucifixion,* and you know the story of the Crucifixion. The next would be the sociopolitical, and that's *Martin Luther King* and the Civil Rights movement in the South; and the third one would be *Picture This,* with no particular story behind it, just artistic beauty.

I then asked her to explain the two large identical quilts that were hanging behind her in the photograph I had taken (see p. 192).

> Those are called *Portrait of the King.* Martin Luther King is standing in that quilt. He's standing up and he has his arm outstretched with a Bible, a purple Bible, in it. We know that he was a minister, and he is delivering a message, and believe it or not, I have him with a pipe in his mouth, but the pipe is not producing smoke. From this pipe is coming heart shapes and he is talking about love. If you remember, Martin Luther King was nonviolent. He preached love during all these things that were happening. So I have him preaching with the Bible in one hand, and his voice is producing love as he speaks. And his out-stretched arm—you can imagine him waving that arm, just back and forth—and he's showing all of the events that are happening.
>
> Some of the events in there are the burning of the church in Birmingham, where we had the "little girls" who were killed in Sunday school. We have George C. Wallace standing in the door at the University of Alabama to prevent Vivian Malone from entering. At that time "Bull" Connor was the sheriff who used dogs to sic on the marchers as they were marching around and singing. At the bottom you will see a lynching. This is quite prevalent, was quite prevalent

Yvonne T. Wells.
TUSCALOOSA COUNTY, ALABAMA, MARCH 1993 (FRAME 1,5, 2¼ CT)

during the Civil Rights movement, and you see a black man just hanging from a tree. There is another section where three guys who were in Mississippi trying to get people to register to vote—that was Goodman, Scherner, and Chaney—and we know that they were killed and dumped into a ravine or gully, where they were buried, so that's where they are and it is shown there. Also there are water fountains that were "white" and "colored," because that was the sign of the day during that time.

I then asked her to talk about the quilt in the middle in the background, with the two black men.

This is called *Brother, My Brother.* I made this quilt last year because there was a lot of killing going on among the black guys, and I wanted to show some institutions that are instrumental in changing things. The church, the school, and the home—those are at the bottom, and if there is anything to be changed, these institutions must step forward and make a change so that we can change our way of living and seeing things. If you will notice, and you have to look real hard to find her, there is a little lady in there, which maybe is what the fight is all about. A lady in the background, plus these guys are drunk. You notice one has a gun and he shot, but the bullet went the opposite direction and he lived, but the other guy walked past him and just stabbed him in the chest and the blood flowed down. And they were standing beside a rocky pond and you see a fish in the rocky area there. But at the top of the quilt, I have used a traditional pattern called Drunkard's Path, and it fits very well with the thing that I was trying to convey.

My next question was about the quilt that was right behind her, the one with a lot of women next to one another.

That quilt, I just finished that about a month ago. It hasn't been shown. You are the first person, other than my agent, who has seen it. The quilt . . . I got started two years ago, but I couldn't get it in my mind. Usually I can make a quilt and go directly through it, but something about this quilt; I had to pick it up, put it down, pick it up, and put it down, but I knew that I wanted it to be transformed from African to American and from American to African. These are women who are singing and they could be singing any song that they want to be singing. Or it could be something to do with freedom, but they just sing. They are soul sisters singing, so they could be singing, "His Eyes Are on the Sparrow," which is a very close piece to me, and I have made several pieces on that. But these ladies are singing, and they have been singing from Africa to America and America to Africa. And they are just dressed-up ladies. Each has her own microphone, and this shows individuality, not just as a group—they are as a group—but by them having their own microphones and doing their own solos, it gives them a sense of being

Thelma W. Williams with family heirloom quilts.
ADAMS COUNTY, MISSISSIPPI, MARCH 1993 (35 MM CT)

Margaret Page with her four daughters by two different partners.
Top, left to right: Lettye Wheaton, Margaret Page, and Mattie
Wheaton. *Bottom, left to right:* Ida McGuire and Marguerite
McGuire. Marguerite is the mother of Thelma Williams.
Photo courtesy of Thelma Williams's family archives.
ADAMS COUNTY, MISSISSIPPI (FA-8)

somebody—individually, but collectively, as
a person.

Finally I asked if there was anything she wanted to
say to her fellow sisters and brothers who quilt.
She answered, "The only thing is that I would
hope they would continue to quilt, and not be
swayed by any outside influence as to what to
quilt."

MISSISSIPPI, MARCH 22–27, 1993

PORT GIBSON

I was coming back to be one of the judges for the
sixth Annual Quilt Contest and Exhibition. This
yearly event sponsored by Mississippi Cultural
Crossroads had grown tremendously, and I was
again very proud to be a part of it. First, we sorted
the quilts into different categories. On the second
day, I was joined by the two other judges: Mary
Lohrenz, curator of collections for the Mississippi
State Historical Musem, and Martha Skelton,
master quilter. After we selected the winners in each
exhibit category, we had one day for Dave Crosby
to design and develop the exhibition program,
while I designed and hung the exhibit. The third

Left to right: Irvin Jones Jr., his mother, Valerie Jackson Jones, and his sister Sylvia Jones.
ADAMS COUNTY, MISSISSIPPI, MARCH 1993 (35 MM CT)

afternoon, we held a public forum and announced the winners, and we concluded the event with a buffet prepared by all the Mississippi Cultural Crossroads quilters.

NATCHEZ

On March 27, I left Port Gibson and headed for Natchez to see Thelma Williams, who directs Project Southern Cross, which as part of its program operates the Mostly African Market, a gallery and store. Thelma is one of those delightful, informed world travelers who is very comfortable to be around. Thelma has traced her Mississippi roots back to the Stanton plantation in Adams County near the Jefferson County line. She knows that her great-grandmother Stanton was partnered with an Irishman named W. William Page, by whom she had three children: Tom Page, Ida Page, and Margaret, who is Thelma's grandmother.

Margaret was born in 1860. Her first partner was a white man named Wheaton, and they had two daughters, Lettye Wheaton and Mattie Wheaton. They lived together, and the records clearly show that before his death in 1886, Wheaton signed over his house in Natchez to Margaret. Margaret then married Miller "Pony" McGuire, an African-American blacksmith from Natchez, and together they had a son, Willie McGuire, and two daughters, Ida McGuire and Marguerite McGuire. Marguerite married William Wallace of Shreveport, Louisiana, and there they raised two children, William and Thelma. After graduating from St. Augustine's College in North Carolina, Thelma Wallace migrated to New York and married. When her husband died in the mid-1980s, she

Louise Williams.

migrated back to the South and settled in her grandmother Margaret's house in Natchez.

Her great-grandfather W. William Page leased a Louisiana plantation, and he and another white family named Orr jointly owned a plantation of bottom land twelve miles south of Natchez on the Mississippi River. Called "Poverty and Destruction Plantation," it is still jointly owned by the descendants of the Orr family, and of Ida Page and Tom Page.

Among the many heirlooms left by Thelma's grandparents, parents, and aunts are five red-and-white quilts (see p.194). She fondly remembers spending most of her summers in this house and recalls seeing a quilting frame, but has no recollection of people quilting. She says her mother and aunts all sewed beautifully, and assumes that either they or the women who worked for them made these quilts.

LOUISIANA, MARCH 28, 1993

BATON ROUGE

On Sunday morning, March 28, I headed south on Highway 61 toward Baton Rouge, Louisiana, to meet Thelma's cousin Valerie Jackson Jones. I had met Valerie and her family at the first Delta Blues Festival back in 1977, and over the years we had become as close as brother and sister. Valerie shared my passions for genealogy and for the Mississippi River; she often said she couldn't imagine being away from the Mississippi for any extended period of time. Even when she went North to college, she chose Viterbo College in La Crosse, Wisconsin, which is right on the river. And after her marriage, she settled in Baton Rouge, which is also on the Mississippi. She was now working at Southern University and was involved in a study of the river's ecosystem. I met Valerie and her son and daughter for lunch, and afterwards we went off to explore the Spanish Town section of Baton Rouge (see p. 195).

There we met ninety-seven-year-old quilter Louise Williams. She tearfully told us that during a recent stay in the hospital, folks thought she was going to die, and someone broke into her house and stole most of her valuables, including all of her quilts. She was so distressed by all of this that she couldn't bring herself to do any more quilting. Even though she had no quilts left, she and her granddaughter, Janelle Wilson, insisted that I photograph her for the project.

Over the years, Valerie and I had spent many weekends exploring the plantations and antebellum homes to which she had traced her family. Every spring, thousands of people come to the area between Vicksburg and New Orleans to tour these homes, but seldom are they told of the African Americans whose labor made it all possible. Valerie grew up listening to her maternal grandmother, Daisy Green, talk about her parents, who were the children of mulatto women who came off two different plantations. These people of mixed blood became what Valerie calls the "black aristocracy" of Natchez, and she has spent countless hours documenting their genealogy and accomplishments.

Daisy's paternal grandmother, Emily McCurran, was a mixed child, and was a cook on the Melrose Plantation in Natchez. Today Melrose is the only antebellum home designated as a national park. In the 1850s, Emily married Washington Miller, who was a slave on a neighboring plantation owned by James Hagen Miller, and they had several children. James Miller then took Washington with him when he went to California during the Civil War, and there Washington bought his freedom. After the Civil War he returned to Natchez and, with money he had initially saved to buy his wife's and children's freedom, he was now able to buy a house and a livery stable and started a hack (horse and carriage taxi) service. His former master had promised to give him a cow if Washington would name one of his sons after him, which he did. He then took the money he made from the cow's milk and sent this son, James Hagen Miller, to Tougaloo College and then to medical school in Illinois. Dr. Miller returned to Natchez to practice medicine and married Irene Virginia Davis, who became his nurse, and they had three girls. One of their daughters was Daisy, who married William Hillard Green, a school principal and businessman in Greenville, Mississippi. Their daughter, Sylvia Green, married Greenville businessman Bill Jackson, and their daughter is Valerie Jackson Jones.

Daisy's maternal grandmother, Sinia Surgett, also a mixed child, was the daughter of a Frenchman, Frank Surgett, who owned plantations on both sides of the Mississippi River from New Orleans to Arkansas. Born in 1850 on one of his plantations, by the age of seven Sinia was being picked on so badly by other slaves that her father took her to Natchez and had her educated. She became a seamstress and he set her up in her own home. After marrying another mulatto, William Minor Davis, she died in

Della B. Collins.
HARRIS COUNTY, TEXAS, MARCH 1993 (FRAME 14, 2¼ CT)

Albert Sams.
HARRIS COUNTY, TEXAS, MARCH 1993 (FRAME 12, 2¼ CI)

childbirth at the age of thirty-five, leaving behind three young daughters, one of whom was Irene Virginia Davis. It was Irene who married Emily's son, Dr. James Hagen Miller, and they had Valerie's grandmother Daisy.

Over the years I had observed a very warm and close kinship between Valerie and Thelma, but I was often confused when they tried to explain how they were cousins. Four generations back, Valerie's great-great-grandfather Washington Miller had a sister named Miami, and she was the mother of Thelma's grandfather Miller "Pony" McGuire.

TEXAS, MARCH 29–31, 1993

HOUSTON

The next morning, I headed for Houston, where I met Della Collins (see p. 197), a Women of Color Quilters' Network member who also arranged for me to meet several other quilters in the area. Mrs. Collins was born in Lake Charles, Louisiana, in 1925. She married in 1942 and then joined the U.S. Army in 1943, which gave her a chance to travel across the country. She remembers seeing her mother, aunts, and neighbors quilt in the small mill town of Deweyville, Texas:

My mother quilted for a short time during the depression, when women weren't able to work, and we had to move from Beaumont, Texas, to Deweyville as a matter of survival. The women didn't have to work there, because the sawmills was running. The men did all the work, and the women quilted, so that was the only time I can remember her quilting. Other than that, my mother had to really work for a living; my daddy wasn't very supportive of the family. So she had to work away from home. I had a grandmother who sewed a lot, and my grandmother taught me how to make clothing, because that is what she specialized in, but I've always had in the back of my mind that I wanted to make quilts.

But raising a family as a single parent, I haven't had time to devote to quilting as much as I'd like to, but I have been actively involved with the quilt guild, and I do programs on the diversity of Afro-American quilts for guilds covering this entire area. I have been to San Antonio, to Galveston, College Station, and Crosby, Texas. I do programs on the quilt, which is a slide-and-lecture program. And then I do have some quilts. I have several old quilts that have been given to me. I have a friend who quilts, who uses nothing but scraps. She has small, wallhanging-size quilts. So I have two of her quilts, and then I have a slide collection that I photographed of African-American quilts.

As a child I always loved fabric, and when I made something I collected all the leftover pieces, and combined them to make one-of-a-kind clothing. And I collected the smaller pieces to someday make a quilt. I machine-pieced my first one from a found *Workbasket Craft* magazine in the early 1970s. I didn't make any more quilts until I got tired of the likes of Eli Leon and Maude Wahlman saying what black-made quilts look like and why. I knew it was a one-sided theory, and I was mad about it. Being a charter member of the International Quilt Association, I asked the organizer to let me do an exhibit of black quilters, and my Houston friends told me I had to have a quilt in the exhibit, so in 1989 I made *A Child's World*, my first real quilt.

Rosyne S. Wimbish.
HARRIS COUNTY, TEXAS, MARCH 1993 (FRAME 14, 2¼ CT)

She cherishes the two quilts she has that her mother made during the 1930s. The kinds of quilts she likes to make most are appliqué, and she enjoys doing her own thing. She makes theme quilts, novelty quilts, and variations of traditional patterns. Mrs. Collins has now retired from Baylor Medical School where she worked in the pathology lab as an histologist, and she plans to devote her time to quilting. I photographed her with two of her quilts.

That evening I photographed two other quilters, Alfred Sams and Rosyne Wimbish, who came to my motel room. Albert Sams, who is thirty years old, grew up in a sewing tradition. His mother was a seamstress, and his grandmother quilted; he's kept some of her quilts as family heirlooms. He started quilting at twenty-four and has made quilts for each of his three daughters. He said of quilting that it has brought him "peace of mind." He continued, "To me, quilting is an individual thing that brings out a personality within, that a lot of people never know and never see." Rosyne Wimbish was born in San Antonio, Texas, in 1952, and she later migrated to Houston. Growing up, she saw her grandmother and other family members quilt, but her mother never quilted. In 1973, she got some quilt books and started to quilt. She likes to make traditional patterns, and since 1992 has belonged to the Bay Area Quilt Guild of Houston, Texas.

The next morning, I photographed Minerva King Mitchell (see p. 200). Minerva was born in 1904 in the Pleasant Hill community in Victoria, Texas, and fondly remembers the stories her great-granddaddy Walker Thomas told her. Walker was four years old in 1852 when his

Minerva King Mitchell.
HARRIS COUNTY, TEXAS, MARCH 1993 (35 MM CT)

mother was sold, and he never saw her again. He was seventeen when word came to Texas on Juneteenth Day (June 19, 1865) that the slaves had been freed. He married twice, had eight children, and died in 1930 at the age of eighty-two. His oldest daughter, Ada, is Minerva's grandmother, and she taught Minerva to quilt when Minerva was seven. Minerva cherishes a patchwork feedsack quilt made by Ada. Minerva married, and migrated to Houston in 1945. Minerva's mother, Joretta Brown King, was a skilled seamstress, and was deaf from the age of thirteen. She spent most of her life cooking and making clothes for white folks. Minerva took care of her grandmother until her death in 1969, and then cared for her mother until her death in 1974. She is very proud that she cared for both of them in her house and that they didn't die alone in an old folks' home. Childless at ninety-one, Minerva has faith that God will take care of her.

LONG BRANCH AND BECKVILLE

On March 31, I headed north from Houston to Nacogdoches and then to Long Branch. I had come there to see two teachers I had first met in 1992

Onnie Mae Davis (1911–93).
PANOLA COUNTY, TEXAS, MARCH 1993 (35 MM CT)

at my quilt exhibit at the National Black Arts Festival in Atlanta. They had offered to locate some local quilters for me. I met them in mid-afternoon at their school, and we left immediately to go see Onnie Mae Davis, who had been born in Long Branch in 1911 and still lived there. My photographs of Mrs. Davis were the last pictures made of her before her death a month later on April 26, 1993.

Eddie Mae Jones has lived her whole life in Beckville, Texas, where she was born in 1923. As a young girl, she learned to quilt from her mother, and she does traditional patterns. She says that quilting is a hobby she loves because it keeps her occupied, keeps her mind challenged, and is a "company keeper." I photographed her with her granddaughter Sharonda LaSha Jones, whom she has raised and to whom she hopes to pass on the tradition (see p. 202).

ARKANSAS, APRIL 1–3, 1993

HOPE

The morning of April 1, I headed north to Texarkana, Arkansas, to meet Dr. Jan Rosenberg, the folklife coordinator of the Texarkana Regional Arts

Eddie Mae Jones and her granddaughter Sharonda L. Jones on the left.
PANOLA COUNTY, TEXAS, MARCH 1993 (FRAME 6, 2¼ CT)

and Humanities Council. She was taking me to meet two quilters whom she had interviewed in Hope, which is the birthplace of President Bill Clinton. The following information is quoted, with permission, directly from her unpublished fieldnotes*:

> Lillie Mae Smith was born on September 26, 1913, one of twelve children to Ed and Emma Thomas. The Thomases farmed in Homer, Louisiana, up to 1925. Then they moved to Hope where they worked on area farms. The family was self-sufficient, up to the coverage they used to keep warm at night while sleeping. Mrs. Thomas made her own quilts, piecing blocks of scrap from clothing, etc., by hand and quilting the tops to batting and bottom cloth on a frame suspended from four nails in the ceiling of the house. Lillie Mae Smith watched her mother make quilts, and observation gave way to imitating quiltmaking and finally mastering the skills and quilting on her own.

Lillie Mae Smith.
HOPE, ARKANSAS, APRIL 1993
(FRAME 12, 2¼ CT)

Mrs. Smith continues to use remnants of cloth to make her quilts. Some of the material is very heavy, like a thick curtain. Other material is very light and airy. Her color choices vary from prints to solids, but all of the colors are bright. The bright cloth is not shockingly bright. The eyes are opened and brightened by the pinks and reds, golds and blues.

Mrs. Smith's patterns come from many sources. Family memories, quilt pattern books, friends, and the imagination are all resources for Mrs. Smith's quilting decisions. She will piece blocks by hand, or she may incorporate colors and pieces of larger cloth to create a top. Mrs. Smith will then quilt the quilt top on a hoop frame or a floor frame supported by sawhorses.

In the past year, Mrs. Smith's quilting has diminished. She has trouble with her hands and wrists—they can't hold things any more like they used to. As a result of this ailment, Mrs. Smith has, for now, stopped quilting.

Mrs. Smith has made many quilts over the years, giving them to her children (four boys and a girl). She misses quilting for the same reason she likes it. Quilting, for Mrs. Smith, occupies her time and keeps her from thinking negative thoughts. Or, in the words of blues/jazz man Jack Cannon (who lives near Mrs. Smith), "Quilting occupies the time and satisfies the mind."

* Interviews with Jan Rosenberg, March 9 and 18, 1993.

Dessie Lee Benton.
HOPE, ARKANSAS, APRIL 1993 (35 MM CT)

Dessie Lee Benton was born in 1927 in Emmet, Arkansas, the seventh of thirteen children. Hers was a farming family that made everything they needed, grew their vegetables, and raised their food animals. A part of their subsistence was making clothing and sewing quilts.

Mrs. Benton's mother, Rebecca Hunter, pieced quilt tops from remnants of material and made her cotton batting from cotton grown in their fields. Oftentimes women from the community would meet at the Hunter home to help Mrs. Hunter quilt quilts, using a frame that was suspended from the ceiling. It was a time, Mrs. Benton feels, when there was more love between people, and more love led, in a way, to more time to help your neighbors with all kinds of chores.

Mrs. Benton recalls playing under the quilts as the women quilted. She would play until the activity caused the quilters—including her mother—to prick their fingers too many times as they rocked the needle in and out of the cloth and cotton. Then Mrs. Benton would be scolded and told to play somewhere else. And she did.

Mrs. Benton doesn't recall exactly how she learned to quilt, but it was her mother who taught her to cut material scraps and piece them to make tops and then put the top together with cotton batting and an undersheet to make a quilt. Pattern names were not passed on, but a sense of color coordination and stitching were. Mrs. Benton likes to use pleasantly bright colors for her tops today, pieced and quilted with small stitches. In fact, a good quilt, in Mrs. Benton's mind, is one that is well put together—in color and in stitching.

Mrs. Benton married and moved to Texarkana. She had five children of her own, all girls. Mrs. Benton sewed her daughters' clothes, and by using remnants, was never lacking for quilting material. When Mr. Benton died in a car crash in the 1950s or 1960s, Mrs. Benton chose to move to Hope to begin anew. She carried her quilting with her.

Today Mrs. Benton likes to piece quilts, and she quilts them, as time allows, on a sawhorse frame. She may

Justine C. Ross, quilter, with her husband, Jesse Ross, and granddaughter Sean Antoinette Washington in the background.
GARLAND COUNTY, ARKANSAS, APRIL 1993 (FRAME 8, 2¼ CT)

piece a quilt pattern from what she sees in a quilt pattern book, but the identities of the patterns are not all that important. Mrs. Benton chooses her own colors, based on the remnants she has saved over the years. She quilts and pieces alone, for she has found that not many people are interested in quilting groups these days. Sometimes, however, she has joined Lillie Mae Smith, her next-door neighbor, to quilt with her.

Right now, one of Mrs. Benton's favorite quilt tops is a Grandmother's Flower Garden that she will continue to piece until it covers the bed. Although Mrs. Benton's quilts are intended for twin beds, she makes them full-size so they can provide the user with a comfortable sleeping cover.

HOT SPRINGS

On April 2, I headed toward Hot Springs, following a lead I had received from Florene Dawkins, a native of Hot Springs who now lives in Columbus, Georgia. I'd called ahead and talked with Justine Ross, who informed me that she and her good friends had set aside the afternoon and were all ready for me.

Mrs. Ross was born in 1926 in New Jersey, and migrated to Buna, Texas (near Beaumont), in 1942, and then to Hot Springs. She grew up watching her mother, Oda Crockett, and grandmother, Cynthia Westbrooks, make string quilts. She didn't really start quilting herself

Dorothy Hunter.
GARLAND COUNTY, ARKANSAS,
APRIL 1993 (FRAME 10, 2¼ CT)

until 1987 when she became jealous of the beautiful quilts her friends were making. Since then, she says, "I've gotten the bug real bad." She has made mostly traditional pattern quilts for her whole family.

Dorothy Hunter was born in 1931 in Forrest City, Arkansas, and came to Hot Springs in 1950. She grew up on a farm, and neighboring women would gather at the family home for quilting bees, producing mostly string quilts. She was always fascinated by the quilting frame that was raised and lowered from the ceiling. Both her grandmother, Lulu Ferguson, and her mother, Margaret Atkins, were quilters. Mrs. Hunter started quilting after her marriage and has made quilts for all her eight children, eleven grandchildren, and other family members. Several of her daughters are seamstresses, and she hopes they will eventually pick up the tradition.

Florence Polk was born in 1923 in Preston, Arkansas. Her mother taught her to quilt when she was a young girl. She fondly remembers quilting bees, because it was a time when women were so preoccupied with conversation they didn't want the children to hear, that the children were ordered to go off and play somewhere else. She never had any children of her own, but raised two kids who are now in their forties, and she has made quilts for them, their children, and many other relatives around the country.

Zeola Hale was born in 1931 in Louisiana and grew up on a sharecropping farm. She came to Hot Springs in 1946. As she says, "I learned to quilt from my mother, Katie Williams, who is eighty-five, and she quilted up until a few years ago. She had to give it up because of diabetes and bad eyesight. For me, quilting is just like taking a dose of medicine. It makes you feel good. I love it. I don't like to use dull colors, but I can make a quilt with them. I like loud colors; it makes the quilt more beautiful."

Her husband, Tracy Hale, who was born in 1926 in Oklahoma, is also from a sharecropping family. He told me, "I started quilting when I was in my teens. My mother, Connie Hale, would be quilting and I'd try to help her out. I'd make some shells, and she'd make me stop because the stitches were too long. But I'd keep trying, because I loved it. When I got married, I'd help my wife set up the quilt, and we still quilt together." Both retired, they have made quilts for all their children, grandchildren, and other family members (see p. 208).

OKLAHOMA, APRIL 4–5, 1993

LANGSTON

On Monday morning, April 5, I headed north from Oklahoma City to Guthrie and then northeast into Langston, which is another all-black town. It was named for the illustrious nineteenth-century black leader, John Mercer Langston, who was poet and author Langston Hughes's great-uncle. Langston University, an historical black land-grant college founded in 1897, is the lifeblood of this town. Driving past the university, the first thing I noticed was the Melvin B. Tolson Black Heritage Center, and remembered that my cousin, Mariann Russell, had written a book about Tolson and his poetry* While exploring the town, I met Margaret Norris, executive director of the Langston Housing Authority, and she introduced me to quilter Amanda Gross, who worked part-time in her office.

Florence L. Polk.
GARLAND COUNTY, ARKANSAS,
APRIL 1993 (FRAME 4, 2¼ CT)

Mrs. Gross was born in 1914 in Logan County, Oklahoma, southeast of Langston, and has lived here all her life (see p. 209). In the 1890s, her great-uncle S. J. Favis, who had a white father, came out to Oklahoma from Georgia. As she tells it:

> He then sent back for his mother, Dealsie Puckett, and his brother, which is my grandfather Hudson; his wife, Sarah Moriah Hudson; and their children. Their daughter Amanda—that's my momma— says she was just a little girl then. Momma married a Peter Franklin from Austin, Texas, and all of us was raised here. I had ten children, and now I'm trying to put all this history on my Family Tree quilts. And you know, my great-uncle Favis later bought some land in Guthrie, built a school on it, and gave it to the city.

Lula Mae Brown was born and raised on the south bank of the Cimarron River in Silver City, Oklahoma, about fifty miles east of Langston. She learned to quilt from her mother, who was a midwife (see p. 210).

---

* Mariann is a professor at Sacred Heart University in Fairfield, Connecticut, and her book is entitled *Melvin B. Tolson's "The Harlem Gallery": A Literary Analysis.* It explores the relationship between this poem and the real Harlem.

Left to right: Mr. and Mrs. Tracy T. Hale and Zeola Hale, both quilters. The quilt behind Mr. Hale was made by his mother, Connie Hale, and that behind Mrs. Hale by her mother, Katie Williams. In the foreground are their respective quilts.

GARLAND COUNTY, ARKANSAS, APRIL 1993 (FRAME 15, 2¼ CT)

I wanted to find some more quilters in Oklahoma, but I had arranged with Anita Knox, another WCQN member, to take me around the Dallas/Fort Worth area, and she was leaving town on Good Friday, April 9. So on Tuesday morning, April 6, I headed south to Fort Worth.

TEXAS, APRIL 6–13, 1993

FORT WORTH

Anita G. Knox was born in 1953 in Oklahoma City, Oklahoma. She came east to study at Howard University in Washington, D.C., and while in graduate school at the University of Texas in Arlington, she met her future husband. She started quilting in 1982 when he introduced her to Fort Worth quilter Irene Jones. She says, "Immediately I started thinking about how I could transfer some of my images from canvas onto fabric. Ever since, I've been making quilts for my family and friends, and occasionally I do special commissions. I think quilting is such a personal thing that it's kind of hard to explain, but quilts become so much a part of you that they are almost like family members or children." Anita has been exhibited widely around the country, and her work is in several permanent collections. Anita asked to be photographed at the Bill Pickett statue in Fort Worth (see p. 211). He was a famous black cowboy (1860s–1932) who created a style known as "bulldogging," where while chasing a steer at a full gallop, he would jump off his horse and grab the steer by his horns and mouth and pull him down to the ground. (This evolved into rodeo's "steer wrestling" event.) Bill Pickett is the only African-American in the National Cowboy Hall of Fame.

My next stop was Cherry's Quilt Shop in the Glen Crest area of Fort Worth. Cherry Henderson was born in 1928 in Fairfield, Texas. She said that her great-great-grandmother, Liza Hayes, was an ex-slave who was raised with Indians. Liza was about one hundred years old when she died in Buffalo, Texas, in 1930. Liza's daughter, Laura Collins, taught Cherry's mother, Jane Hayes, to quilt, and Cherry learned to quilt in turn from her mother. However, she said, "My mother's mother, Ella Hayes, didn't quilt. She was a guitar-playing blues singer. I don't know if she ever made any records, but she was a well-known singer around east Texas." Cherry and her husband, Rev. Robert C. Henderson, opened this shop in 1985, where she is constantly commissioned to make quilts (see p. 212). "When I'm doing my quilting, I meditate on the Lord. I can put the Bible right next to me and get my Sunday school lessons done."

Amanda Gross.
LOGAN COUNTY, OKLAHOMA,
APRIL 1993 (FRAME 2, 2¼ CT)

DALLAS

Anita then took me to Dallas to meet Karella Shaw, who was born in 1917 in Marshall, Texas. Her maternal great–grandmother, Amy Scott; Amy's daughter, Prinie Mitchell; and Prinie's daughter Lizzie Wilder—who is Mrs. Shaw's mother and taught her to quilt—were all from Marshall. As a young adult, Mrs. Shaw migrated to Dallas, where she raised her five children. "My daughter in California says she wants to learn to quilt. When I asked her could she use a thimble, she said no. I said, well, you can't quilt then." All of her children have several of her quilts. Mrs. Shaw's work has been shown around Texas and in several national touring exhibitions (see p. 213).

BRACKETTVILLE

For many years I'd read articles about the black Seminole Indians from Florida. In a saga that spans more than one hundred years, the short of it is that from Florida to Texas, some nineteenth-century blacks used perseverance, courage, and skills as weapons in a battle against slavery. At the 1992 Festival of American Folklife, several black Seminoles from Texas were featured as part of the Maroon section. I had talked at length with Charles Emily Wilson, a black Seminole from Brackettville, Texas, and she had informed me that there were quilters in their community. So on Good Friday, April 9, I left Dallas on my way to Brackettville, which is near Del Rio on the Texas-Mexico border. Late that afternoon I located Miss Wilson with about a dozen people at the campground, planning the 1993 Juneteenth celebration activities.

Lula Mae Brown with her quilt and her daughter Ruby Jean Brown on the right.
LOGAN COUNTY, OKLAHOMA, APRIL 1993 (FRAME 7, 2¼ CT)

I had first heard about Juneteenth Day while in the U.S. Air Force back in 1955, when my first sergeant informed me that I had the next day off. When I asked why, he said, "It's Juneteenth Day. Go ask your colored buddies about it." They explained to me that Juneteenth Day marked the day when slaves in Texas first learned that they had been freed. The history of Juneteenth, a name derived from the slang combination of June and nineteenth, dates to June 19, 1865, when Union General Gordon Granger landed in Galveston, Texas; declared U.S. sovereignty; and announced the freedom of the state's 250,000 slaves by reading President Lincoln's Emancipation Proclamation. This was two and one-half years after the date the Proclamation had officially taken effect (January 1, 1863)! When Granger arrived in Texas, the Civil War had been over for seventy-one days, and Lincoln had been dead for sixty-five. But Texas was the last Confederate state to yield to the Union, and word that slavery and the war had ended was slow getting there. While there is a legend among black Texans that the message was sent from Washington by a slow-stepping mule, historians attribute it to the slow-moving bureaucracy. The revival of Juneteenth began in 1979 when state representative Al Edwards of Houston steered a bill through the Texas legislature declaring June 19 an official state holiday. Today Juneteenth Day is celebrated by many groups of African Americans from coast to coast.

After the meeting at the campground, they took me out to their cemetery. They proudly pointed out the four Congressional Medal of

Honor winners among the approximately seventy Seminole Indian scouts buried there. Back at Miss Wilson's that evening, several neighbors joined us for dinner and told me the story of their black Seminole ancestors. It was an odyssey that started with runaway slaves from the Carolinas, Georgia, and Florida who lived among the Seminole Indians, and for many years fought the U. S. Army and slave-catchers. Eventually forced out of Florida for resettlement in Oklahoma, and then betrayed by the U.S. government, they had to fight the same battles again as some of them retreated into Mexico. The struggle continued, and after the Civil War the U.S. Army sought their services as scouts in the Indian wars. With government promises of land, but not in writing, some came back across the border and settled near Fort Clark at Brackettville. However, after they'd given many years of heroic service, the government again defaulted on its promise and ran them out of the village near the fort, and they had to move into the town of Brackettville, where many of their descendants live today.

Anita G. Knox with her quilts and a statue of Will Pickett, the black cowboy.

TARRANT COUNTY, TEXAS, APRIL 1993 (FRAME 11, 2¼ CT)

For the next two days, I photographed these proud people. Miss Wilson chose to be photographed with a Fan quilt that was made by her maternal grandmother, Mary July, who was mixed Creek Indian and black Seminole. I also photographed Ethel July Warrior and her husband, William Warrior, with a Double Wedding Ring quilt made by William's niece Pat Raspberry. Next I photographed Augusta Ann Pines and her sister's daughter, Windy Nichole Goodloe, holding a quilt made by Windy's paternal grandmother, Cerella Factor Daniels (see p. 213). Finally, I photographed Billy Joe Pierce, the great-great-grandson of John Warrior Ward, one of the four black Seminole scouts awarded a Medal of Honor in 1875, with a quilt his grandmother made for him.

Filled with conflicting emotions, I had trouble sleeping that night. I was bothered by the strange turns that history takes in people's struggles for freedom. The history here was of enslaved African people in America fighting for their freedom, and teaming up with indigenous Native Americans who were fighting to protect their land and families; the white power structure was viciously ripping off both of them. Then these same black Seminoles from Florida were used by that power structure to help commit genocide against other Native Americans in the Southwest. Now I had come along, working my way through this strange history, looking

Rev. Robert C. and Cherry Henderson.
TARRANT COUNTY, TEXAS, APRIL 1993 (35 MM CT)

for quilts they had made and being very disappointed when I didn't see anything unique!

Along the way, I had also learned that the black Seminole scouts once worked with the black "Buffalo Soldiers," so I now went off looking for the quilts that I presumed would be found among their artifacts. Because I had seen an image of a black cavalryman on a flyer advertising historic Fort Stockton, Texas, I decided to go there first. On Monday, April 12, I left Brackettville, heading west on Route 90 to Sanderson, and then went north on Route 285 to Fort Stockton to research quilts at this historic preservation project and museum.

FORT DAVIS

Much to my dismay, this historic site was still in the early stages of development, and there were no quilts in its small collection of artifacts. However, the director told me there was a fully restored barracks of the Tenth Cavalry at Fort Davis, Texas, and he clearly remembered seeing quilts on the bunks. We then called to confirm this, and spoke with Elaine Harmon, the curator of the Fort Davis National Historic Site. She agreed to let me photograph the barracks, so I immediately left for Fort Davis, which

Karella Shaw.
DALLAS COUNTY, TEXAS, APRIL 1993 (35 MM CT)

is in the foothills of the Davis Mountains. On the way, I checked my cassette tapes and was pleased to find the Persuasions' *Street Corner Symphony,* with its song "Buffalo Soldier." This romantic version of their story is nice, but the historical facts are that, although largely denied access to the riches of the West, African Americans were given an opportunity to help the white man conquer the Native Americans of the region. African-American troops had performed exceedingly well during the Civil War (some fighting in regions west of the Mississippi), and it was logical, therefore, to recruit African Americans to do some of the white man's fighting in the Plains and Southwest.

In 1866 legislation was adopted that allowed African Americans to serve in the regular peacetime army in up to six regiments of segregated troops. By 1867, several units were operational and were assigned to garrison duty in Oklahoma and Kansas. Thereafter, and until 1891, they fought with

Left to right: Augusta Ann Pines and Windy Nichole Goodloe.
KINNEY COUNTY, TEXAS, APRIL 1993 (FRAME 12, 2¼ CT)

great courage and ultimate success against Indians in New Mexico, Arizona, West Texas, Oklahoma, Colorado, and the Dakotas, earning the nickname "buffalo soldiers," bestowed upon them by their native enemies. It was the Cheyenne Indians who called the black troopers "buffalo soldiers," noting the resemblance between the fur on a buffalo's head and the soldiers' hair. The nickname showed respect, as the buffalo was an object of veneration among the Plains Indians, and the black soldiers proudly adopted it for themselves.

More than twelve thousand African Americans served in the Indian wars of the West, constituting one-fifth of the cavalry assigned to that struggle, and including many of the troops that actively fought the Apaches. Their heroism and fortitude never received just recognition at the time, nor, of course, has Hollywood chosen to portray correctly the racial character of the "Indian-fighting" Army in the multitude of western motion pictures produced.

Early on the morning of April 13, I met Mrs. Harmon and explained my quilt project. She was most informative and extremely accommodating. I was so thrilled to be standing in one of the barracks of the famous "buffalo soldiers"—Fort Davis housed Troop H of the Tenth Cavalry, a combat-tested company first organized at Fort Leavenworth, Kansas, in 1867—and I was especially pleased to see

Ft. Davis National Historic Site. One of the barracks of the buffalo soldiers with historic quilts on the beds.
JEFFERSON DAVIS COUNTY, TEXAS, APRIL 1993 (35 MM CT)

quilts everywhere. Most of the antique quilts were made from the sample materials carried by traveling salesmen and are thus called "suit sample" quilts. About one fourth of the quilts were contemporary and had been made by the local Davis Mountain quilters.

I left Fort Davis that afternoon feeling very good, and went back up Route 17 to Interstate 10 and headed west to El Paso, Texas, and into Las Cruces, New Mexico, for the evening. It was here that I had one of the strangest experiences on my trip. I had called ahead twice to arrange a meeting with a quilter, and I had explained the project in great detail. Upon seeing me, however, this quilter said, "I don't believe you. Black folk don't do this kind of research, and I'm not letting you in my house." I was disgusted beyond words.

New Mexico, April 14, 1993

When I called home that night, my wife gave me a message from a friend, Beverlee Bruce, in New York. I had known Beverlee when she

Rosa Brown with one of her quilts on the right, and one by her mother, Dollie Lloyd (1898–1972), on the left.
VALENCIA COUNTY, NEW MEXICO, APRIL 1993 (FRAME 6, 2¼ CT)

Catherine Gill. The Sunburst quilt *(left)* was made by her mother, Classy Blaylock (1901–60), from Decatur, Mississippi.
COCONINO COUNTY, ARIZONA, APRIL 1993 (35 MM CT)

was directing the honors program at Howard University. When I called her, I related what had just happened and asked if she knew any people in New Mexico who either quilted or preserved family heirloom quilts. She gave me the name of her sister-in-law, Brenda J. M. Hollingsworth-Pickett, who lived just south of Albuquerque.

BOSQUE

The next morning, April 14, I called Brenda, who said she had only one quilt, and that it didn't look like much. It had been made by her deceased father-in-law, Leroy Smiley, from Alabama. We agreed to meet that afternoon, and in the meantime she was to check with some of her neighbors. Just south of Albuquerque at Los Lunas, I turned south on Route 314 to Bosque. There I made a picture of Brenda. She told me she was able to find only one person on short notice, and that I needed to hurry because she was leaving in two hours. So I continued on to Belen, just a few miles north of Bosque, to meet Rosa Brown.

Left to right: Dollie Mealey Johnson Calvin and her daughter Vera Johnson Peeler. Dollie, who is from Woodville, Mississippi, married Phoeba Johnson's son Grover and migrated to Arizona.
COCONINO COUNTY, ARIZONA, APRIL 1993 (FRAME 4, 2¼ CT)

Nancy J. and Owen W. Justice with quilts made by their respective grandmothers in North Carolina.
CLARK COUNTY, NEVADA, APRIL 1993 (FRAME 9, 2¼ CT)

BELEN

Mrs. Brown was born in 1919 in Jasper, Georgia, and migrated from there to Detroit. She married a union man, Henry Brown Jr., and upon retirement they moved to New Mexico. She learned to quilt from her mother, Dollie Lloyd (1898–1972). By the time I arrived, Mrs. Brown had laid out two quilts with which to be photographed: an old quilt made by her mother, and a Dutch Girl pattern of hers (see p. 215).

ARIZONA, APRIL 15–16, 1993

My initial plan had been to leave Las Cruces and continue on Interstate 10 West to Tucson, Arizona, where some WCQN members lived, but now that I'd traveled north to Albuquerque, I didn't want to backtrack. Checking the map, I saw that Interstate 40, which runs through Albuquerque, goes to

Jerome M. Jackson Jr.
CLARK COUNTY, NEVADA, APRIL 1993 (FRAME 4, 2¼ CT)

Willie Mae Smith (1933–93).
CLARK COUNTY, NEVADA, APRIL 1993 (35 MM CT)

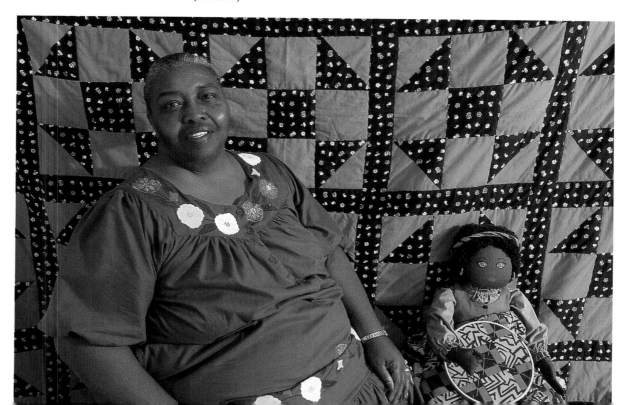

Flagstaff. Then I remembered that back in Mississippi in 1975, I had met Phoeba Johnson's son, Curtis Johnson, who had migrated to Flagstaff, Arizona, so I called his sister, Annie Dennis, in Mississippi. She informed me that although Curtis's wife didn't quilt, the wife of his brother Grover, who also lived there, did. Annie said, "Dollie is good Mississippi people, and she knows that we done adopted you into this family, so I'll call and tell her you're on your way and to take good care of you." That evening, after a wonderful down-home meal, Dollie's daughter and her husband, Vera and Jim Peeler, insisted that I stay with them.

FLAGSTAFF

Dollie M. Johnson Calvin was born in 1909 in Woodville, Mississippi, where she married her first husband, Grover Johnson, and they had two children. She learned to quilt from her mother, Rosa L. Mealey (1880–1975), and in turn she taught her only daughter Vera, who was born in 1939. Dollie's maternal grandmother, Emma Laneheart, also a quilter, died around 1911 at the age of 80. Dollie migrated to Flagstaff, Arizona, in 1955 with her husband, Grover. Vera migrated to Flagstaff one year later in 1956, and first married a Reeves, but is now married to Jim Peeler. She has five daughters who all have quilts made by either her or her mother or their great-grandmother, Phoeba Johnson. Even at age one hundred, Phoeba still had been prolific, and could machine-piece a quilt top in two days. After Phoeba's funeral in 1984, Vera took six of Phoeba's tops and brought them back to Flagstaff, where she and her mother then tacked them and gave one to each of her five daughters (see p. 216).

Nettie Mae Washington.
CLARK COUNTY, NEVADA, APRIL 1993 (35 MM CT)

On April 16, Vera Peeler took me to meet Catherine Gill. Mrs. Gill was born in 1932 in Decatur, Mississippi, and married a local man. They migrated to Flagstaff in 1949. Her mother, Classy Blaylock (1901–60), was a quilter and a skilled seamstress. Classy had eight girls, and she made six quilts for each of them. She also taught all of her daughters to sew well, but only two of them took to quilting. Mrs. Gill still has three of the six quilts her mother gave her, and has made more

Girtia Lukes.
CLARK COUNTY, NEVADA, APRIL 1993
(35 MM CT)

Gloria Y. Binford.
CLARK COUNTY, NEVADA, APRIL 1993 (FRAME 6, 2¼ CT)

than three hundred quilts herself. Only one of her two daughters is interested in learning to quilt. Mrs. Gill belongs to several quilting guilds, teaches quilting at Yellow Park College, and she has been exhibited nationally. She also supervises a local Head Start program (see p. 215).

NEVADA, APRIL 17–21, 1993

LAS VEGAS

On April 17, I left Flagstaff, picking up Interstate 40 West to Kingman, Arizona, and then turned north on Route 93 into Las Vegas. Nancy Justice, an art collector, had offered to put me up. I had first met her in 1990 in Oakland, California, when I was traveling across the country as

Raymond and Girtia Lukes.
CLARK COUNTY, NEVADA, APRIL 1993 (35 MM CT)

Nelson Mandela's photographer. As Las Vegas was not on Mandela's tour, Nancy, like thousands of others, had come to Oakland to catch a glimpse of him. Nancy and her husband, Owen, are from Hillsborough, North Carolina. They migrated to Las Vegas in 1976, and Nancy manages Owen's dental practice there. The photo of them (p. 216) shows several heirloom quilts they have from their respective grandmothers: on Nancy's side, her maternal grandmother, Sudie Wade (1882–1934), and her paternal grandmother, Fannie Jones (1890–1990), and Owen's maternal grandmother, Grace Mack (1893–1993), whose daughter Luna is his mother. Grace taught all five of her girls to quilt. All of these quilters were from Hillsborough, North Carolina.

I had several leads from WCQN members, and they in turn introduced me to others, and for the next two days I photographed quilters in the greater Las Vegas area. On April 19, I photographed Jerome M. Jackson Jr., who was born in 1922 in Du Quoin, Illinois (see p. 217). His Irish mother, Cecilia Young, and African-American father, Jerome Jackson Sr., married and had five children. Jerome was in the middle. His two older sisters didn't quilt, but he started trying to quilt with his mother at about five years of age. He made his first Nine-Patch block when he was six. Commenting on his white appearance, Jerome says, "I was born a Negro, and they changed it to black all of a sudden when I was about twenty. And now they've changed it to African American, without even notifying me." He has quilted sporadically over the years, having moved to Chicago and San Francisco before settling in Las Vegas in 1985. He has made more than two hundred quilts, and he says the only thing he likes better is to hang out in the casinos.

Willie Mae Smith (1933–93) (see p. 217) was born in Warren, Arkansas, and her family first moved to Las Vegas, then Portland, Oregon, and finally settled in Pasadena, California, when she was twelve, where she lived until returning to Las Vegas late in life. She remembers her maternal grandmother, Alice Callum, quilting, but her mother, Naomi Callum Johnson, did not. However, she fondly remembers learning most of her quilting from her great-aunt Alice Callum

Left to right: K. Fleeta McNair and her mother, Rosa L. McNair, with baby quilts. The tops were made by Rosa's great-grandmother and quilted by her grandmother Amanda Waters and mother, Dolly Waters Lewis.
CLARK COUNTY, NEVADA, APRIL 1993 (FRAME 16, 2¼ CT)

Clara F. Henderson.
ROY, UTAH, APRIL 1993 (35 MM CT)

Cleo Myles.
OGDEN, UTAH, APRIL 1993
(35 MM CT)

McClane. Mrs. Smith was one of the founding members of the African-American Quilters of Los Angeles. Mrs. Smith related:

> Aunt Alice had twenty-two children, but when she came to California she took up with that cult leader Jim Jones. And he was the one who took those people over to Guyana in South America, and they had that mass suicide over there, and this was in 1978. She was eighty-two when she died. She'd been trying to get me to quilt all my life. It was all over the television when those people died, and it hurt me so, I just picked up her quilting patterns and I've been quilting ever since. It's just like she came back and grabbed me, and I haven't stopped from that day to this.

Nettie Mae Washington (see p. 218) was born in 1917 in Okmulgee, Oklahoma, and grew up on a farm where two quilting frames were constantly in use. Her mother, Della Mae Randolph, had five girls and taught all of them to quilt:

> Momma would be quilting while we were in the field working, and in the evenings and all winter we'd all be quilting. We made all kinds of pretty patterns and some "ducking" quilts. They was made out of scraps of cotton sacks, jeans, khaki pants, overalls, you know, and we just called that kind "ducking" quilts. My husband and I have two kids of our own, eight grandchildren, fourteen great-grandchildren, and one great-great-grandchild. I made quilts for all of their beds, and those that got married, I made a fancy quilt for their wedding gift.

Girtia Lukes was born in 1933 in Macon, Mississippi, and was raised on a cotton farm until the age of ten, when her family migrated to East St. Louis, Illinois. She made her first quilt block when she was four. She remembers ladies coming to her parents' house in the fall and staying for two to three weeks for a continuous quilting bee. Her mother taught all eight of her daughters to quilt, but today Mrs. Lukes is the only one still quilting. She says, "You get addicted to quilting, and once it gets hold of you, you can't stop." She and her husband moved to Las Vegas in 1985 to be near some of their children. She now teaches quilting, belongs to several quilting guilds, and has been exhibited throughout the region (see pp. 219 and 220).

Gloria Binford was born in 1944 in East Moline, Illinois. Her mother quilted, but Mrs. Binford learned by taking classes at a local quilt shop.

African-American Quilters and Collectors Guild, Denver. *Front row (left to right):* Lois M. Watson, Clara Kirven, and Rosie Smith. *Back row (left to right):* Juanita Gray, Carolyn R. Hogan, Barbara Lyons, E. Juanita Freeman, and Rose E. Shipp. The mudcloth quilt in the background and the quilt at the front left are by Rose Shipp, the center quilt is by Rosie Smith, and the quilt at the front right is by Juanita Gray.

DENVER, COLORADO, APRIL 1993 (FRAME 10, 2¼ CT)

The Rankin Family. *Back row (left to right):* Lee and Bonnie Rankin Jones, Debra Rankin holding her one-month-old son, Kelly, her daughter, Ashley, held by Ashley's great-uncle Walter Gray. *Front and center:* Ezekiel Rankin holding his son Jeremy Rankin. All the quilts were made by Hystercine Rankin of Claiborne County, Mississippi, who is Ezekiel and Bonnie's mother and Walter's sister.

DENVER, COLORADO, APRIL 1993 (FRAME 14, 2¼ CT)

She migrated to Las Vegas in 1985, where she belongs to several quilting groups (see p. 219).

Rosa Lewis McNair was born in 1951 in Jackson County, Florida. Her maternal grandmother, Amanda Lockett Waters (1871–1950) quilted, as did her mother Dolly Waters Lewis (1911–77). Some of her most prized possessions are three quilts that she used as a baby, and which she has also used with her children (see p. 221). These baby quilts were pieced by Laura Williams (1854–1964), who was part of Rosa's extended family, and whom she grew up calling "grandmother."

UTAH, APRIL 21–23, 1993

Nancy Justice called a friend of hers, Belle Cope, in Ogden, to see if she knew of any African-American quilters. She did and agreed to introduce me to them if I would come the next day, as she was about to leave town. So on the morning of April 21, I left Las Vegas and headed to Salt Lake City.

OGDEN

I drove straight through to Ogden, which is just north of Salt Lake City, where Mrs. Cope had me to dinner. She had located two quilters, a man and a woman. On April 22, I went to meet Clara F. Henderson. Mrs. Henderson was born in 1931 in New Boston, Texas, and started quilting with her mother when she was eight. Her family sharecropped in Texas and Oklahoma. She married and had several children, but her husband died in 1964, and she says, "I raised my kids on up then myself, and I refused to go on welfare to do so. I worked sixteen hours a day to support my children and all of them got through high school, and all of them went to college. While my last two were at Langston University in Oklahoma, I came out here to visit another daughter in 1972. She helped me get a good job so I could help them get through college, and that's the reason why I'm still here now." With Clara's help, her mother made her last quilt in 1978, before she passed in 1982 (see p. 221).

Cleo Myles was born in 1921 in Brookhaven, Mississippi. He grew up watching his maternal grandmother, Pashie Rauls (1866–1956), quilt, but his mother didn't quilt. He learned to sew from his sister, Kathareen Wright. He joined the U.S. Army in 1942 and was sent to Utah. There he met and married Bada B. Miles (1899–1986), who was from Tulsa,

Left to right: Hazel J. Whitsett, Annie M. Watkins, and Shanika N. Whitsett.
DENVER, COLORADO, APRIL 1993 (FRAME 7, 2¼ CT)

Nell B. Smith.
COLORADO SPRINGS, COLORADO, APRIL 1993 (FRAME 14, 2¼ CT)

Oklahoma. She was a quilter, but they never quilted together. Mr. Miles said, "I don't like TV much, and I do most of my quilting at night. About ten years ago, I started doing a lot of cross-stitch work, and it really pacifies me, especially after my wife died" (see p. 222).

COLORADO, APRIL 23–26, 1993

My next stop was in Denver to meet with the African-American Quilters and Collectors Guild. I'd been communicating for a few years with its president, Rose Shipp, and she invited me to join them for their meeting that Saturday, April 24. So on the morning of April 23, I left Ogden on Interstate 15 South and picked up Interstate 80 East which goes through Weber Canyon and takes you across the mountains. I stayed on Interstate 80 through southern Wyoming, passing Rock Springs, Rawlins, and Laramie. At Cheyenne, I stopped for a late lunch and contemplated where I was going to spend the night. Then it dawned on me that Hystercine Rankin had some family in Denver, so I called Mississippi to get their numbers.

Denver

Mrs. Rankin's youngest daughter, Bonnie, had just married and moved to Denver. I called her right after lunch, and by that time Mrs. Rankin had called both her and her son Ezekiel. From Cheyenne, I went south on Interstate 25 into Denver. They both lived in Aurora, a suburb of Denver, and when I arrived they were arguing about which one was going to put me up. They treated me so well that I didn't want to leave.

On Saturday, April 24, I attended the meeting of the African-American Quilters and Collectors Guild at the Ford Warren Library in Denver. After exhaustive questioning about my project, they allowed me to photograph them (see p. 223). The genesis of this group was a tea in honor of Martin Luther King Jr. in January 1988, and an exhibit during Black History Month in February 1988. These events paved the way for organizing the guild, and a group of women who shared an interest in promoting and recognizing the achievements and heritage of African-American quilters in the needle arts continued to meet until they formally organized in 1988.

Pearlena O. Moore.
GRAHAM COUNTY, KANSAS, APRIL 1993 (35 mm ct)

Early that afternoon, I went to photograph quilter Hazel Whitsett with her mother, Annie M. Watkins, and daughter, Shanika N. Whitsett, at her home in Denver (see p. 225).

On Sunday, April 25, the whole Mississippi crowd gathered at Ezekiel Rankin's house for a barbeque. We did some heavy relaxing and I made a picture of him, his wife, their three children, his uncle Walter Gray, Bonnie, and her husband Lee Jones, with some of the quilts Mrs. Rankin had made for them (see p. 224). They were all very happy about her increasing recognition as a master quilter.

Colorado Springs

Later that afternoon I called Juanita Freeman in Colorado Springs. She was in the group photograph I had made the day before. During the show-and-tell period, she had presented a *Desert Storm* quilt that a neighbor of hers in Colorado Springs had made for her son, who served in the Persian Gulf War. Juanita arranged for me to meet the quilter, Nell Smith, the next afternoon.

Left to right: Vera M. Wells, NedRa Bonds, and parents Mr. and Mrs. Patton.
WYANDOTTE COUNTY, KANSAS, APRIL 1993 (35 MM CT)

So, on Monday, April 26, I headed south, and after stopping briefly at Colorado College to catch folklorist Adrienne Seward for lunch, I met Mrs. Smith (see p. 226).

Nell B. Smith was born in 1948 in Suffolk, Virginia. She was one of three girls who made up the fourth generation of known quilters in her family, starting with her great-grandmother Alice Butler Parker (1885–1965), then her grandmother Purlar Moring (1892–1973), and her mother, Dessie Moring Boone, who was born in 1920; all of them were from Gates, North Carolina, near the Virginia border. Nell met her husband, Al Smith, who was in the U.S. Air Force, in Virginia and traveled the world with him. In 1972, his last assignment was in Colorado Springs, where he retired. Nell is a prolific quilter like her grandmother Purlar Moring, but thinks the family tradition will end with her generation, as her daughter and nieces have no interest in quilting. Nell and her husband insisted that I spend the night, and I gladly accepted. On April 27, I left Colorado Springs and headed for Nicodemus, Kansas, which I had first visited in August 1988 (see pp. 78ff.).

KANSAS, APRIL 27–30, 1993

NICODEMUS

Pearlena O. Moore was born in 1929 in
Nicodemus, Kansas, and her mother, Margaret
Williams Napue, died giving birth to her. Mrs.
Moore was raised by her maternal
grandmother, Elizabeth Risby Williams
(1890–1954), who was born in Abilene,
Kansas. Elizabeth's parents, Samuel and
Margaret Risby, were Afro-Canadians from
Alberta, Canada. Elizabeth raised twelve
children of her own plus Pearlena. She taught
all the girls to sew, but Pearlena is the only
one still quilting (see p. 227).

Mrs. Moore introduced me to Rosa L. Stokes,
who had settled there four years earlier. Mrs.
Stokes was born in 1924 on a farm near
Bogue, Kansas. Traveling in a horse-drawn
covered wagon, her maternal grandmother,
Annabelle Slaughter (1885–1972?), came to

Rosa L. Stokes.
NICODEMUS, KANSAS, APRIL
1993 (35 MM CT)

Kansas from Gary, Indiana, as a little girl. In Kansas, she met her
husband, Dave Cannon, whose parents were from Kentucky, and they
had a daughter, Mary Cannon (1891–1966), who is Rosa's mother.
Mary and Rosa's father, Schuyler Jones (1884–1964), were married
sixty-three years and had nine daughters, all of whom learned to quilt.
Mrs. Stokes remembers going from farm to farm for all-day quilting
bees with German and French neighbors. Today Rosa's only remaining
sister has stopped quilting. Rosa returned to Kansas City after high
school to work in a munitions plant, then moved to Denver, Colorado,
and Los Angeles, California. In 1989 she returned to Kansas and settled
in Nicodemus. She says, "I came back here because it's quiet and
peaceful, no drugs and no crime." She has passed on the quilting
tradition to her only child, Norma Lois Willis, who lives in Anaheim,
California, and now makes quilts for her grandchildren, great-
grandchildren, nieces, and nephews.

Right after lunch, I left Nicodemus and took Interstate 70 East on my
way to Kansas City, Kansas, to meet some WCQN members there.

KANSAS CITY

I arrived at Georgia Patton's house about midafternoon. Mrs. Patton was
born in 1924 in Plattsburg, Missouri. She learned to quilt from both her
mother, Virginia Payne Goff (1903–65), and her maternal grandmother,

Kyra E. Hicks.
CLAY COUNTY, MISSOURI, MAY
1993 (FRAME 11, 2¼ CT)

Mary Lucy Sidney Payne (? –1934), both of whom were also from Plattsburg:

> You see, my mother did domestic work, and I spent my days with my grandmother Mary Lucy. And she taught me to do everything: we gardened, we canned and preserved, we fished, and we quilted every day. I heard talk about Mary Lucy's mother, Armetta Sidney, but I never saw her and don't know much about her. I also learned quilting from my daddy. You see, Momma and Daddy quilted together, and Daddy also smocked. He smocked all of the yokes of our dresses, and also embroidered the Peter Pan collars on our dresses. I also used to really enjoy the big quilting bees at the AME church every Wednesday night. We'd all go—Grandma, Momma, and Daddy. It never seemed to bother him, he was the only man quilting. He seemed to really love it.

Among Mrs. Patton's most prized possessions are several quilts that have been passed down through her husband's family. William Patton was born in Armstrong, Missouri. He doesn't quilt, but his mother, Juanita R. Patton, who was also born in Armstrong, was a prolific quilter. Juanita learned from her mother, Josie Sidney Watts Richardson (1872–1957), who was born in Armstrong, Missouri; Georgia has five quilts that were made by Sidney Richardson. Sidney's mother, Annie Hargrove Watts (1847–1943), was born in Buchanan County, Missouri, and in 1866 she married a Baptist preacher, Rev. Isaam Watts (1836–1938), who was born in Audrain County, Missouri. Right after he died in September 1938, the good reverend was featured in Ripley's "Believe It or Not" because by age 102, Rev. Watts had preached a sermon every Sunday for 71 straight years.

The story that has been passed down is that Ann Watts was half Cherokee, and as Georgia relates, "She'd go to the woods, get the bark off certain trees, bring it home and boil it, and make her own dyes. She'd use whatever materials she had, and she'd dye those and make her quilts and curtains. Around 1930, she made a real fine quilt out of sateen [polished cotton] and made a design using cross-stitch. That's been handed down over the years, and I now have it."

Georgia and William Patton married after World War II and settled in Kansas City to raise their five children—NedRa, Winifred, Michael, Candy, and Cedric—all of whom she taught to quilt (see p. 228). Georgia proudly said, "Of all my girls, it's NedRa and Winifred who are still quilting the most. But I've taught Candy's two boys to quilt, and they've just finished their first top. That makes six generations of us quilters." The Patton family quilters have been widely exhibited, and are included in the Kansas State Quilt Survey.

Mrs. Patton jokingly says of her family:

> If you're looking for the American melting pot, you can find it right here. We're right in the middle of America, kind of like the crossroads. And all those different people who came to this country, when they got right here in the middle, they started fraternizing with one another, and you got people like me and my husband. We're all-American. We're mixed up with African, Indian, Scotch-Irish, Japanese, and Polish, but my girls and I are called "African-American quilters."

Mrs. Patton's oldest daughter, NedRa Bonds, was born in 1948. Speaking of her early childhood and learning to quilt, she says:

Georgia M. Patton.
WYANDOTTE COUNTY, KANSAS,
APRIL 1993 (35 MM CT)

> When I was six years old, my grandmother told me I needed to start my "hope chest." She taught me to stitch using the first joint of my finger as the measure for my work. She demanded ten stitches within the space between the tip of my forefinger and the first joint. She made me take it out if it wasn't done right. I teach art appreciation and use quilts as examples of universal symbolism. My quilts, they speak to me of experiences, and in many ways they are "the fabric of life." And like all the women in my family, I want to pass this joyous experience on. I look forward to teaching my granddaughter. I'm also really excited about an invitation I just received to go to Africa and teach quilting in Kenya.

MISSOURI, MAY 1–2, 1993

KANSAS CITY

On Saturday, May 1, I met Kyra Ethelene Hicks, another WCQN member, who lived right across the river in Kansas City, Missouri. She had told Carolyn Mazloomi to tell me she had her guest room on reserve for me. Kyra was born in 1965 in Los Angeles, California. She

Sherry Whetstone-McCall.
CLAY COUNTY, MISSOURI, MAY 1993 (FRAME 2, 2¼ CT)

came East at age sixteen to attend Howard University, spent a year in London, and, in 1991, while in graduate school at the University of Michigan, was recruited by Hallmark, and subsequently moved to Kansas City. Her father, Richard Wayne Hicks, sewed, and she took a sewing class in seventh grade, but Kyra was inspired to start quilting after seeing a storytelling quilt show in 1990 (see p. 230). She says, "I call [this quilted wallhanging] *He Took His Time*. I wanted to show how a woman felt. I hope that when people look at it there's a universal feeling of sensuality, which is how I felt to have someone make love to me. I don't mean it to be pornographic, because that's generally what is thought when you see people unclothed. This is just meant to express a very nice feeling."

Another of her quilts was inspired by frustrations shared by many young African-American women, and it is called *Single Black Female*. On the wallhanging are the words "SBF [single black female] Praying for SBM [single black male] to Share My Quilt." Kyra said she was far too modest to place such a personal ad in the newspaper, but instead soothed her loneliness by expressing this feeling in a quilt. This same quest for an eligible, desirable bachelor led to a third quilt she was doing for her thirtieth birthday, entitled *No Fairy Godmothers,* which she said represents a common dilemma facing many of her contemporaries who are "waiting for either their Prince Charming with the slipper, or a knight in shining armor to come and rescue them."

Kyra took me to meet Sherry Whetstone-McCall, whose quilts incorporated an innovative use of textiles for a three-dimensional effect. Sherry was born in 1957 at Fort Sill, Oklahoma. As far as she knows, no one in her family quilted. As she says, "I'm an army brat, so I lived in many states until I was ten or eleven years old. We then settled in Oklahoma, and I attended Oklahoma State University in Stillwater, married in 1980, and moved to Liberty, Missouri. I started quilting because I thought it was an intriguing, disciplined, and creative art form. After a short time, I found traditional patterns a bit boring, and I started to create my own designs. What I make is a combination of Crazy quilts and 3-D wallhangings." Sherry now teaches quilting and has been exhibited throughout Kansas and Missouri.

Emily J. Harris.
OMAHA, NEBRASKA, MAY 1993
(FRAME 17, 2¼ CT)

NEBRASKA, MAY 3–5, 1993

OMAHA

Kyra had saved a newspaper article she thought I'd want to read, which was about Bertha Calloway, director of the Great Plains Black Museum in Omaha, Nebraska. Because I had no quilters in Omaha, I called to see if she knew of any. She did know one quilter, Della Littlejohn, and said there were a few quilts in the museum's collection. So on Monday, May 3, I left Kansas City and took Interstate 29 North to Omaha. I had called Mrs. Littlejohn, and she had invited me over that afternoon (see p. 234).

Then ninety years old, Mrs. Littlejohn was born in 1903 in Newport, Arkansas. Looking for better employment, her family migrated to Omaha in 1913. She said she was fourteen when she was actually twelve so she could go to work in a meatpacking house. She learned to quilt from her mother, Ella Wilson Marrill, who was born in Little Rock, Arkansas, and died in 1974 at the age of seventy. Della had a son and daughter by her first husband, and in 1929 she married Nathaniel Littlejohn, who adopted her two children. They bought a home in an area of North Omaha which, because it was so far from downtown, was jokingly called

Della Littlejohn.
OMAHA, NEBRASKA, MAY 1993
(35 MM CT)

"Plumb Nearly"—meaning it was out of the city and nearly out in the country.

Later that afternoon, Mrs. Littlejohn introduced me to a neighbor of hers, Rose Z. Huntley, who, though working in her garden, stopped for me to photograph her with one of her quilts.

That evening I called Bertha Calloway, the director of the Great Plains Black Museum, who invited me to visit the museum. Mrs. Calloway and her staff were extremely helpful, and I was able to make a photograph of some quilts in their collection.

The Omaha Quilters Guild had given me the name of Emily J. Harris, who agreed to be photographed (see p. 233). Mrs. Harris, who lives in South Omaha, was born in 1943 in Eutawville, South Carolina. She learned to quilt from her mother, Bessie Davis, who was born in 1919 in Eutawville, and her maternal grandmother, and says, "I can remember the quilting bees and a lot of food. This was an all-day affair. I started quilting at an early age, making small blocks for my dolls." Today Mrs. Harris is a prolific quilter, and has her work displayed in every room of her house.

SOUTH DAKOTA, MAY 5–6, 1993

FLANDREAU

Mrs. Calloway also referred me to a Ted Blakey, who is the official African-American Historian for South Dakota, and he gave me a lead on a quilter in Flandreau. I called and arranged a meeting with Catherine Teer. On the morning of May 5, I left Omaha and took Interstate 29 North through Sioux Falls, and then turned East on Route 34 to Flandreau. Mrs. Teer was born in 1923 in Butler, Alabama. Her mother, Lucy Ellen Ruffin Allen (?–1954), and father, Benjamin Allen (?–1967), were both from Butler; together they had ten children. Catherine says, "I'm the fifth girl and the tenth child. My father was a real family man, and he liked to do things with the kids. He taught me how to crochet and piece quilt tops. But the actual quilting I did with my mother."

Around 1933, the family migrated to East St. Louis, Illinois, and it was there that Catherine met and married Cornelius Teer Jr., who was from Greenwood, Mississippi. They migrated to South Dakota in 1952 when he came to teach with the Bureau of Indian Affairs. After raising her four children, in 1987 Mrs. Teer founded the Wholeness Center in Flandreau, which is a shelter for abused women and children; she started quilting classes there as a form of therapy. Mrs. Teer has several family heirloom quilts, one of which was made by her mother-in-law, Lottie Perkins Teer (?–1966), who was from Shuqualak, Mississippi. None of Mrs. Teer's four children is interested in quilting, but she has made quilts for all of them and for her seven grandchildren (see p. 236).

Vermillion

Mr. Blakey had also told me about a lap quilt made by one of the early black residents of Sioux Falls, South Dakota, that was at the William Henry Over Museum in Vermillion. As fate would have it, I wasn't going to arrive in Vermillion until after visiting hours, so a member of the museum staff arranged for the quilt to be borrowed for the night. And that's how I encountered a quilt at the Allen Chapel AME Church in Yankton, South Dakota.

Illinois, May 8–10, 1993

East St. Louis

After a stop in Kansas City, I continued to East St. Louis to visit Reginald and Edna Petty. Edna had recently returned from Senegal, West Africa, where she had fallen in love with African cloth. Edna Willis Patterson-Petty (see p. 237) was born in 1945 in St. Louis, Missouri. Her mother, Alberta Hicks, who was born in 1925 in Rolling Fork, Mississippi, migrated to St. Louis, married, and had seven children. Edna, her oldest child, says:

> I'm not sure you can call what I do quilting. I am a fiber artist using mixed media as well as found objects. Within the last two years I have been doing large tapestries with some quilting techniques. I fit in with the quilters of the nineties genre. Originally I did a lot of hand-stitching, but now I use my sewing machine because it's faster and easier on my hands. I watched my mother make quilts, and she would let me help her cut the fabric. She didn't do any fancy designs as I see in a lot of traditional quilts. She used old clothes, etc., and I helped to trim the material.

Rose Z. Huntley.
OMAHA, NEBRASKA, MAY 1993
(35 mm ct)

Catherine Teer.
FLANDREAU, SOUTH DAKOTA, MAY
1993 (FRAME 12, 2¼ CT)

Elizabeth D. Moore was born in 1929 in Centreville, Illinois, in an area formerly called "Fireworks Station." Her mother, Pauline Peters Dunn, was born in 1903 in Enterprise, Mississippi, and migrated to Centreville, where she raised her family. Mrs. Moore learned to quilt from her mother and has taught her seven girls to sew, but none of them took up quilting. She has made quilts for all of her thirteen children, twenty-three grandchildren, and three great-grandchildren.

Beatrice Nebraska Neely, who says she is "seventy-few" years old, was born in Metcalfe, Mississippi. Her parents migrated to East St. Louis in the 1920s, and her mother taught her to quilt at a young age.

MISSOURI, MAY 10–11, 1993

ST. LOUIS

Vivian L. McCullin Smith (see p. 238) was born in St. Louis, Missouri, to which her parents had migrated around 1913. As she explains:

I moved to Chicago, Illinois, from St. Louis in the late fifties to further my education and to work as a teacher in the Chicago Public School System. I moved back to St. Louis in 1986 to care for my mother, who was unwell and losing her eyesight. I saw no one quilting in my family. When I was a small child, I saw my mother sewing to make clothes for my sister and me using an old Singer sewing machine she had converted into an electric-pedal machine. Mother was very skilled and creative, doing many types of needle-work, crocheting, tatting, weaving, knitting, and embroidery. This is one of the incidents mother told us about her childhood. When she was twelve years old, she made dresser scarves from Indian head linen and sold them for $1.50. Outside of my family, I saw Mrs. Sue Redman quilting when I went to her home to learn handloom weaving from her daughter, Jane Redman. I did my first quilt called Nine-Patch, a tie quilt, under her supervision.

I learned much more about quilting in 1986 when I came to St. Louis. I enrolled in a quilting class of the Kirkwood Library sponsored by a community college. The class was taught by Mrs. Lois Mueller, a well-known quilter in the St. Louis area. After completing the course, I enrolled in various quilt workshops to enhance my knowledge and skill in this art form. I took a class as a private student at the home of Barbara O'Connor, a well-known

Edna W. Patterson-Petty.
EAST ST. LOUIS, ILLINOIS, MAY 1993 (FRAME 10, 2¼ CT)

quilter who was in the St. Louis area at the time. In 1987, I was invited by quilter Nancy Kollmar to the Sutter Presbyterian Quilters Group to quilt each Wednesday. It was there I met twenty other quilters, many of whom were skilled and outstanding quilters. Their ages ranged from late twenties to seventy. I gained so much from them by listening, observing, and following gentle directions.

I have written and illustrated a little quilt book called *My First Quilt Workshop* for a children's workshop for ages kindergarten through eighth grade. This book was used for three workshops. Each child who participated in the workshop was given a copy of the book.

Mrs. Smith's brother, James Mark McCullin Jr., was the first black pilot killed in Europe during World War II. Killed in 1943, he was a member of the highly decorated 99th Aviation Pursuit Squadron, an all-African-American group of pilots known as the "Tuskegee Airmen." They have the unique distinction of being the only group of flyers that never lost a bomber they escorted during air raids over Germany. Mrs. Smith is now making a small quilt to honor her brother.

Vivian L. Smith.
ST. LOUIS, MISSOURI, MAY 1993 (FRAME 14, 2¼ CT)

INDIANA, MAY 12–14, 1993

I left St. Louis and crossed Illinois into Indiana to meet some quilters identified through Emilye Crosby, the oldest daughter of Dave and Patty Crosby of Mississippi, and her roommate at Indiana University, Kathy Connelly, who was from Terre Haute.

INDIANAPOLIS

Nellie Leona Redmon Tyler was born in 1902 near Seelyville, Indiana, in an area called "Lost Creek Township." As she told me, "I started quilting around twelve years old. My mother taught me, and she required that we do something constructive in our so-called 'free time.' Everybody quilted then, family and community members. I moved from Lost Creek to the city of Terre Haute in 1942, and then I moved to Indianapolis in 1992, and I still quilt." That afternoon I went into Terre Haute and spent the night with Pam and Steve Connelly, who had arranged for me to meet with several quilters in the area.

Karen Yvonne Anderson was born in 1957 in Terre Haute, Indiana. She remembers starting to quilt around five under the tutelage of a community elder, Mrs. Campbell. Her mother, Erneita Anderson Phillips, doesn't quilt, but her father, Leo Franklin Phillips, has a quilt made by his mother, Cecil Phillips, who was from Lost Creek (see p. 240).

A fourth-generation quilter, Cleta Ross Harris (see p. 241) was born in 1922 in Otter Creek Township, Indiana, and in 1940 moved to the adjoining township of Lost Creek. Her mother, Louella Hathecock Ross (1893–1955), was a seamstress and made "yarn tie" (tacked) quilts out of material that was too heavy to quilt otherwise. Mrs. Harris's maternal grandmother, Mary Alice Stewart Hathecock (1855–1937), was born in Otter Creek, but her great-grandmother, Charlotte Stewart, was from North Carolina. Mrs. Harris has five daughters, none of whom quilts, so she makes quilts for them and for her eleven grandchildren.

Nellie Tyler, formerly of the Lost Creek area.

MARION COUNTY, INDIANA, MAY 1993 (FRAME 17, 2¼ CT)

I was very curious about the name "Lost Creek" and how this community of light-skinned African Americans had come about. Shortly after leaving Mrs. Harris's house, I spotted an official state marker that read, "Hoosiers Homestead Farm, Owned by the Same Family for over 100 Years." I stopped to investigate, and met Dr. Geneva A. Ross, born 1927, and her sister Dorothy M. Ross, born 1923. They were not only natives of Lost Creek, but also had documentation and photographs to substantiate that their ancestors had founded it back in the 1830s. They had eight family heirloom quilts—made by their mother, Ema Anderson Ross, their grandmother Armeania Stewart Anderson, their great-grandmother Elizabeth Malone Walden Stewart, and a great-aunt Cassie Anderson Stewart. We immediately got busy setting up the quilts and family photographs around the historical marker. This unusual set-up stopped afternoon traffic and attracted a small crowd of onlookers. After making the photographs (see p. 242), I was invited to dinner and given the fascinating story of the "Lost Creek Township Community" of freed blacks.

These two sisters' genealogy is unlike that of the majority of African Americans, as they can go back four generations through their mother's mother, and five generations through their mother's father—eight generations from their grandchildren back to the late 1700s. The Ross sisters gave me a written summary of the oral history gathered by their ancestors in Lost Creek. It states that in 1824, "Bowen Roberts, a lone scout, set out on

Left to right: Erneita Phillips, her daughter Karen Y. Anderson, and her husband, Dr. Leo F. Phillips, of the Lost Creek area. VIGO COUNTY, INDIANA, MAY 1993 (FRAME 8, 2¼ CT)

horseback to seek a haven from persecution for himself and other freed slaves in North Carolina. He passed through Lost Creek Township and was greatly impressed. His report back to his people was 'fat hogs are roaming the forest with knives and forks in their backs.' Soon a caravan of six families—Andersons, Archers, Chavises, Roberts, Stewarts, and Trevans— were on their way on foot and by ox cart. History tells us that African Americans were not allowed to travel freely, especially in the South, so how was it possible for this small caravan to cross four states? Part of the answer is found in a document this family possesses. It is an original document, dated August 21, 1826, from Wake County, North Carolina, stating that Dixon Stewart Sr. was born and raised there, 'was born of free parents, and had conducted himself in an honest and orderly way.' "

We can safely assume that since Dixon Stewart Sr. was born of free parents in 1801, his parents were born probably fifteen to twenty years earlier, and were mulatto offspring of white plantation owners and slave women. What's even more rare, Dixon and the others somehow were able to purchase what they needed to make the journey, and they had enough money left to buy large plots of land when they got to Lost Creek. These families purchased land from the government, cleared it for cultivation,

Cleta Harris of the Lost Creek area.
VIGO COUNTY, INDIANA, MAY 1993 (35 MM CT)

and built log cabins. In a very short time, they established a thriving community, and by 1832 they had built their first church and school. In 1840, an AME Church was organized, and in 1850 a Missionary Baptist Church. The AME Church also joined with local Quakers to make Lost Creek a stop on the Underground Railroad (marked with a plaque erected in 1974), and there was a secret hiding place on George Anderson's land. When Dixon Stewart Sr. died in 1889, he had acquired 1,040 acres of land, and was one of the community's wealthiest men.

GARY

I left Lost Creek and headed up Highway 41 into Gary. My colleague Jerrilyn McGregory's parents lived there, and her mother had located some quilters for me. My first stop was to see Lucy Jones Jackson, who was born in 1917 in Lynchburg, Virginia. As a child, she'd seen her mother, Nanny Jones, quilt, but didn't learn from her. In 1937, she migrated to Chicago and worked as a seamstress, and in 1958 she married her second husband and migrated to Gary. As she says, "I started quilting in 1976 after my husband died. I'd always wanted to quilt, but I was so busy working, and me and my

Lost Creek quilters. *Left to right:* Dorothy M. Ross, Dr. Leo F. Phillips, Beulah Edwards, and Geneva A. Ross.
VIGO COUNTY, INDIANA, MAY 1993 (FRAME 5, 2¼ CT)

husband had two children, and I was taking care of the children, and I had too much to do. Then my husband died. One day I was looking in a book and I saw a quilt, and I said, 'That's what I think I'll do.' And I just went out and bought some material and came home and started quilting, and I've been quilting ever since."

Katharine Walton (see p. 244) was born in 1922 in Forrest City, Arkansas, and migrated to Gary in 1980. She learned to quilt from her mother, Ethel Anderson, and her father, W. H. Moore, who were both from Arkansas. Mrs. Walton said, "My father had his own special thimble, and when he wasn't away preaching, he'd be sitting right there at the quilting frame with us women. He was more particular than we were." As early as she can remember, she was trying to help her mother quilt, and she pieced her first top at twelve. She also quilted with her aunts Eliza Smith and Ruthie Smith, and her grandmother Annie Anderson. "I have two girls, Annie and Arlene, and I taught them both to quilt, but since they're grown, they've stopped."

Lucy Jones Jackson.
LAKE COUNTY, INDIANA, MAY 1993 (FRAME 2, 2¼ CT)

GARY COMMUNITY QUILTERS GUILD

Cheryl L. Tolbert, founder of the Gary Community Quilters Guild (see p. 245), was born in 1956 in East Chicago, Indiana. Her family moved to Gary in the late 1960s, after "Gary elected a black mayor, and white flight made affordable homes more accessible and obtainable." She has very vivid memories of some of her relatives who quilted:

> My paternal great-grandmother, Safronia Williams [1899–1984], from Hurtsboro, Alabama [Russell County], would sit and "piece." She would come North usually once a year and piece to keep her hands busy. I never saw her actually quilting, nor did I see her quilting on a frame. My father remembers seeing her work, but always using the bed as a support or foundation, and generally working at night after completion of her domestic chores. I began quilting after my great-grandmother died in 1984. I had asked her to teach me, but she said that quilting wasn't something young people needed to know. After her death, I inherited several unquilted tops and pieced squares. My maternal grandmother, Lucille Sly Thomas, who was born in 1915 in Russell County, Alabama, and paternal grandmother, Mittie Lee Williams Tolbert, who was born in 1912 in Hurtsboro, Alabama, also quilted. I have tried self-instruction, mini

Katharine Walton.
LAKE COUNTY, INDIANA, MAY
1993 (FRAME 15, 2¼ CT)

informal courses at local schools and community centers, and lastly guild-sponsored programs. I have learned by trial and error mostly, and really haven't decided which format has been most beneficial.

I have several special quilts. One was made by our local guild, which I received as the guild's founder. I have my paternal great-grandmother's quilt, and my maternal grandmother's unfinished top. The latter is OK, but my great-grandmother's quilts or unquilted tops I have acquired by default. No one else quilts, so my mother, my sister, and I received numerous tops, not as gifts, but as scraps no one else had use for. When my great-grandmother died, her quilts simply vanished. We asked about them at the funeral, but no one knew who had them or where any of them were hiding. My great-grandmother traditionally sent quilts North every year and made baby quilts for her grandchildren's kids. Surprisingly quilts were somehow misdirected or re-routed on their journey North. Often Grandma would ask us about quilts that never arrived in Indiana. About five years after her death, these tops started to surface and finally we received something she had pieced.

Sarah A. Lowe was born in 1935 in Gary, Indiana. She said, "When I was a little girl, my Aunt Inez Williams, who was born in 1914, and my grandmother Sarah Johnson [1889–1963]—she came up here from Opelika, Alabama, before I was born—would make me cut blocks to keep me busy. I hated quilting, because it interfered with my playing. However, they taught me, and I didn't appreciate it until I got married. When my grandmother passed in 1963 at age seventy-four, the other family members argued over her quilts, so I stayed out of the arguments and made my own." Mrs. Lowe has one daughter and three sons; she quilts only for her family.

Donna Jean Vessel-Barksdale was born in 1956 in East Chicago, Indiana. She moved to Gary, Indiana, in 1988 after she married. She explained, "I started quilting in 1992. I wasn't working and I love to sew and do all kinds of crafts. I saw an ad in the newspaper and thought that would be interesting to do. Actually one of the quilters in the group showed me how to quilt. I already knew how to sew, so it wasn't hard to learn how to quilt."

Myrtle Marie Jones was born in 1933 in Kansas City, Missouri. She migrated to Gary in 1950 after her marriage. She started quilting in 1991

Gary Community Quilters Guild. *Back row (left to right):* Georgi A. Williams, Gwendolyn Keaton, Donna Vessel-Barksdale, and Myrtle M. Jones. *Middle row:* Cheryl Tolbert. *Front row (left to right):* Sarah A. Lowe and Barbara N. Cole.

LAKE COUNTY, INDIANA, MAY 1993 (FRAME 7, 2¼ CT)

Jim S. Smoote II.
COOK COUNTY, ILLINOIS, MAY 1993 (FRAME 5, 2¼ CT)

after seeing some quilt books and television programs, and she also took quilting classes. She makes quilts for her family.

Barbara N. Lee Cole was born in 1934 in Newark, New Jersey. Although her mother did not quilt, her maternal grandmother, Edith Askew (1902–85), from Baltimore, Maryland, did, but Mrs. Cole did not learn from her. When she was two, her family migrated to Philadelphia, Pennsylvania, and in 1990 she migrated to Gary, Indiana. She started quilting in 1993 and is self-taught.

ILLINOIS, MAY 15–17, 1993

CHICAGO

Still following leads from the WCQN members, I went into Chicago to meet another male quilter, Jim Silas Smoote II. Jim was born in 1950 in Grenada, Mississippi, and learned to quilt from his mother, Vernia Purnell Smoote, who was born in 1926 in Duck Hill, Mississippi. As Jim says:

> When I was younger, my mother would occasionally take us (my brother, sister, and myself) to quilting bees when we lived in Missis-

sippi, and again when we visited in the summer. The quilting was usually done by older female relatives and friends. In 1956 when I was five, my family migrated to Chicago.

I discovered at a very early age the aptitude for drawing, an ability that was recognized and supported by my parents and instructors. At the School of the Art Institute of Chicago, I studied under two weavers, and I developed an interest in African and folk textiles, as well as the printed fabrics from the twenties and the thirties. I gravitated toward the medium of surface decoration of fabrics, because it offered me more flexibility as an artist. For almost twenty years, I have been exploring the mask and the fetish image through the infinite applications of the fiber and fabric media. Now however, I primarily produce quilted pieces applied with acrylic paint mixed with various traditional and nontraditional techniques and materials. My work has provided me with pleasure and enjoyment and has afforded me the opportunity to travel and exhibit not only here in America, but also in Africa, South America, and Europe.

NEEDLES AND THREADS QUILTERS GUILD (AFRICAN-AMERICAN QUILTERS OF CHICAGO)

The Needles and Threads Quilters Guild (see p. 248) was founded in 1992 by Julia M. Howard. Mrs. Howard was born in 1934 in Hattiesburg, Mississippi, and migrated from there to Chicago in June 1952. She was mentored by a community elder who was affectionately called "grandma" by everyone, and whom she observed making utility (scrap or string) quilts. Mrs. Howard always liked needle arts, and her father's family were all skilled seamstresses. She started quilting in 1985 and is self-taught, having learned from quilting books and magazines:

> In February 1992, I founded the Needles and Threads Quilters Guild. Our original members were—and all of them are in your photograph—Bessie L. Blake, Charlean K. Byrd, Mildred Hopkins-Calender, Jewell Dooley, Juanita Graham, Ethel Harrelson, Mildred Johnson, and myself. I find it very rewarding that I am playing a small role in keeping the creative art of quilting alive in the African-American community. Quilting has been and is a time where I find quiet, peace, joy; a time when I can leave the world's problems outside, and it's just me and my quilt.

Onetta Johnson was born in 1934 in Bristow, Oklahoma, and her family migrated to Chicago in 1943. As a child, she saw her mother and grandmother quilt, as well as other community members in Oklahoma:

> My mother still quilts, now more than ever. I did several quilt tops as a teenager. I became interested because sewing and quilting were done as a necessity, and I did as much by watching older women, but mostly family members. Quilting reminds me of home, when

Needles and Threads Quilters Guild of the greater Chicago area. *Back row (left to right):* Marian L. Hayes, Vera Durham, Mildred L. Johnson, Mildred Hopkins-Calender, and Charlean K. Byrd.

Middle row (left to right): Jewell A. Dooley, Bessie L. Blake, Juanita Graham, Julia A. White, and Tarliece Edmonds. *Front row (left to right):* Julia M. Howard, Ethel L. Harrelson, and Onetta Johnson.
COOK COUNTY, ILLINOIS, MAY 1993 (FRAME 14, 2¼ CT)

neighbors got together and helped each other finish their projects. I think there is a lot of black tradition in quilting, and I'd like to see it continued.

Mildred Hopkins-Calender was born in 1932 in Birdeye, Arkansas. She migrated to Chicago in 1950 and has lived there ever since. When she was young, she recalls seeing her mother and grandmother and other ladies in the community quilt. "I started quilting in 1986, and I taught myself. I've always liked to sew, and I like most of all colors, and mixing colors."

Jewell A. Dooley was born in 1932 in Yazoo County, Mississippi, and migrated to Chicago in 1949. Growing up she saw her mother, Leola Rennel Dillard, who was born in Bentonia, Mississippi, in 1912, and her maternal grandmother, Roxie Pikes Rennel (1890–1968), also from Bentonia, and other community members quilt. She is primarily an appreciator of quilts and loves their infinite forms of beauty.

Marian L. Hayes was born in Chicago in 1954 and has lived there all her life. As she says:

> I started quilting after I had a dream about scraps in a treasure chest. In the dream it seemed that if I used the scraps, I could become rich. My mother, Bettye Hayes Harris [from Clarksdale, Mississippi], had a barrelful of scraps, so I used them to make my first quilts. The quilts were never full-size, so when my grandmother Elizabeth Dixson Hayes saw them, she said I needed to learn how to make real quilts. My mother didn't quilt, but her brother, George Hayes, did. Ever since my dream concerning scraps, quilts and quilt-making have enriched my life. It has opened doors to places I might not have ever entered. I was able to make a reasonable income while teaching the craft, and I have met so many beautiful people. Quilting means a binding together of my people here in the United States and Africa. Quilting has enabled me to explore the history of black Americans and appreciate my ancestors.

Tarliece Edmonds was born in 1925 in Redfield, Arkansas, and migrated to Chicago in 1947. Her mother, Puella Lewis (1894–1976), and her maternal grandmother, Julia Lewis (1857–1935), both from Homer, Louisiana, taught her to quilt. Tarliece and her older sister, Cloteal Burns, who was born in 1915 and now lives in Little Rock, Arkansas, are the only two of her mother's thirteen children who are still quilting. She makes quilts for her family.

Ethel Harrelson was born in 1928 in Clarksdale, Mississippi, and migrated to Chicago in 1949 in order to find work. Her mother, Cleo Duncan Person, born in 1908 in Fayette, Alabama, taught her to quilt. At eight, she made her first quilt, an Eight-Point Star made from strings on pieces of paper.

WASHINGTON, MAY 19–20, 1993

From Chicago, I flew to the West Coast to photograph quilters in Oregon and Washington state. Although I knew no one there, I had possible leads in each, including one from Dolly McPherson, a friend of Dr. Maya Angelou, who had told me that her sister was the organizer of an historical quilt project in Portland, Oregon, and one from Gracie Lee Laskey, whom I had met in Brackettville, Texas. I flew to Portland, Oregon, rented a car, and headed north on Interstate 5 to Tacoma.

TACOMA

I first went to meet Rosie Shepherd, who was born in 1918 in Grambling, Louisiana, where her mother's ancestors helped found Grambling College (now Grambling State University). She migrated to Tacoma in 1950 and that same year brought out her mother, Rosie Gibson Wright (1894–1973), who was also born in Grambling. "When I was young, my mother taught me to quilt a little, but I didn't stick with it. I keep my mother's quilts around in remembrance of her, and have given some of them to my nieces and nephews."

Louise Thompson was born in 1944 in the black Seminole community in Brackettville, Texas. She grew up in the house with her grandmother Nancy Williams, who was born in 1910 in Nacimiento, Mexico, and her maternal great-grandmother, Mary Thompson Bowlegs (1887–1951), who was also born in Mexico. Of her great-grandmother, Mrs. Thompson says:

> She was the person who taught me about quilting, and I was her helper. I was the person who cut out the pieces and picked out the buttons. She would save buttons from clothing, you know old clothing or whatever, and she would put them in a can. And when we were ready to do a quilting project, and she was deciding on what type of quilt we were going to make, she'd let me do the sorting of the buttons for the quilt. Where they have the cording [tacks] in the quilts, sometimes she would put buttons just as a decorative effect.

Mrs. Thompson has a quilt made by her grandmother, and as she said:

> Well, a lot of the quilts they made during that time that I remember were not made with a lot of emphasis on design. You see, they were made mainly for warmth and durability, and they were made from whatever materials that were available. We migrated here in 1963 when my stepfather, who was in the Air Force, was stationed here, and we remained when he retired.

Left to right: Louise Thompson, Benji Lasky, and her son Rob Thompson, with a quilt made by her grandmother Nancy

Williams, who is a black Seminole living in Texas.
TACOMA, WASHINGTON, MAY 1993 (2-68039/[2A-3], 35 MM CN)

OREGON, MAY 21–23, 1993

PORTLAND

I drove back to Portland and met Osly J. Gates, who arranged with the Oregon Historical Society for me to photograph her with the Afro-American Heritage Bicentennial Quilt (see p. 252). This quilt was the collaborative effort of fifteen women from Portland, Oregon, who, under the leadership of Mrs. Gates, as their contribution to the 1976 bicentennial celebration, sought to commemorate the history of blacks in America. The quilt is narrated in chronological sequence beginning on the top left with Alonzo Pietro, the pilot of the Niña, and ending on the bottom right with Hank Aaron, the man of the hour in 1975 when the quilt was completed. Other people and events depicted in the quilt's blocks include the Emancipation Proclamation, the Fifteenth Amendment, and the struggle for freedom through the courts (expressed metaphorically as climbing high steps). Both political and cultural figures

Osly J. Gates with the *Afro-American Heritage Bicentennial Commemorative Quilt.* Mrs. Gates convened the group that made this quilt, and then donated it to the Oregon Historical Society.

PORTLAND, OREGON, MAY 1993
(35 MM CT)

are treated, with Louis Armstrong placed near Martin Luther King Jr., and Marian Anderson not far from Harriet Tubman.

Lillie Pearl Hawthorne was born in 1922 in El Dorado, Arkansas, and says:

> I was raised on a farm by a most wonderful man and woman who both are now deceased. My father, Alec Cobbs (1886–1943), and mother, Ida Mae Cobbs, raised a family of nine children. They had seven of their own and two adopted. I'm happy to say that them two people give us all the same love, same understanding, and the same training. My mother quilted and then my mother-in-law was a quilter, a professional quilter. Her name was Lou Hawthorne and she was born in Louisiana, but raised up there in Arkansas. She gave me the most points on mixing colors and putting quilts together than anybody did. She and my mother used to give what you called "quiltings" in the neighborhood, where you get a whole bunch of women together, and in a few hours' time they would have a quilt out. They'd call up the ones in the neighborhood and invite them over and cook a big dinner, put up a quilt and everybody get around it, and in two or three hours' time that quilt was quilted out. My husband always wanted to put his two cents and a half into the quilts that I made, that's what I call him meddling with my quilts, and my father was bad about that, too.
>
> I started quilting when I was nine, and didn't make my first whole quilt until I was eighteen and got married in 1939. My husband and I migrated to Ogden, Utah, in 1965, and then here to Portland in 1966, and I started in on my family to move this way. I had promised my father on his dying bed—he had asked me if I would please see that the family stayed together. It just pressed on my mind to do that, you know, and I kept on until I got them here one by one, two by two.
>
> I just turned seventy-one, and I said three score and ten, that's all God promised me. I'm not going to be around too much longer, and so I made up my mind to quilt everybody a quilt, including the little children. I'm making a quilt now for my unborn great-grandchild, who I've named Lillian Rose. I asked if the doctor told her what sex it was, and my granddaughter said no

Quilter Lillie P. Hawthorne *(front and center)* with her family. *Back row (left to right):* Robert E. Mitchell, LaVerne Holland, Yvette Garnett, her daughter Monique M. Dreher (girl), and Jean Lewis. *Front row* *(left to right):* Lovey Mitchell and her son Ezekiel Jones Jr. (baby), Lillie P. Hawthorne holding her grandnephew Anthony Penney, her niece Artent Mitchell (Anthony's mother), and Bertha M. Holton. PORTLAND, OREGON, MAY 1993 (FRAME 6, 2¼ CT)

he didn't, but I told them it was going to be a girl—and if it's a boy, we'll be disappointed—and the name's still going to be Lillian Rose.

These quilts I'm making are not to be destroyed. It is something that you put up and you take care of it and treasure it. You don't destroy a quilt, you handle it as careful as you would a piece of jewelry. For the simple reason somebody has put in a lot of time, and if they make a quilt and give it to you, it's because they love you. Love and care for that person, and love should be treasured. God loves us, too. We should treasure that. We don't need to worship these quilts and make a God out of them, but we should treasure them because somebody has put a lot of time into making it.

MICHIGAN, MAY 23–30, 1993

On Sunday, May 23, I flew back to Chicago, and the next morning headed out on Interstate 94 East on my way to Lansing to revisit

Marguerite Berry-Jackson, whom I had first met in 1986, when I was working in Michigan for the Smithsonian. I was really anxious to follow up on a story she had told me about her grandparents and to see several historical quilts in which her family is included (see pp. 66–67).

LANSING

Marguerite Louise Berry-Jackson was born in 1913 in Jackson, Michigan, where her parents, Mabel Porter Berry (1892–1924) and John Henry Berry Sr. (1882–1974?), were employed. Both of them were from Mecosta County, Michigan. However, as she says:

> Three months after my birth, they were called back to Mecosta because my father's father, Isaac Berry (1832–1914), had died. And so they took what little they had, which was two trunks and me, and moved back up to Mecosta County to Grandpa's log cabin on the family farm at School Section Lake. My mother and paternal grandmother, Lucy Esther Millard Berry (1838–1929)—who was born in Wayne County, New York—taught me to quilt. I first tried to make a doll quilt, like Grandmother Berry taught me. The pattern was the Nine-Patch. I was about eleven or twelve years old. I had always liked to sew. My mother had made most of my clothes, and she gave me some of the scraps. I usually picked them up from the floor where she had been sewing. And I used to enjoy looking at the quilts on Grandmother Berry's featherbed. To lie on her bed was such a pleasure. My mother had a blue and white quilt that Granny Berry had made—the pattern was Flying Geese—and I used to fancy myself flying with the geese when I laid on it. Quilting was a part of my early childhood, which didn't seem to last very long. My mother died when I was ten years old, and Granny Berry came to live with us. She kept quilts in her trunk, and often she'd air them outdoors in the summer. I enjoyed seeing them hanging on the line.
>
> Roland, in 1986 when you went up there with my sister Marie to the Mecosta County Park on the lake and saw that granite marker—well my whole family went through the eighth grade at that "Little River School." The original log cabin school was built by my grandpa Berry and some other men who came with him from Canada. And my grandmother Berry and a neighbor, Auntie Sarah Robinson—her family and the Letts and Pointers all moved up here from Ohio—were the first teachers. They had no teaching certificates. They just knew that these kids had to be educated and taught them. As the community grew, they had to get certified teachers, but you only needed six months of training to be certified in those days.

I then interrupted Mrs. Berry-Jackson to ask, "When you say that your grandparents came from Canada, were they Canadians or were they runaway slaves?" She replied:

Well, sit back, get comfortable, and I'll tell you the story of my grandparents. As I now look back, it all started in the sixth grade when I was eleven years old. A classmate told me that my grandfather had been a slave, and it just took me off my feet. All of a sudden, I realized that I was black. It was something that hadn't been discussed in my house. My grandfather had been dead for ten years, so I rushed home to question my grandmother, a stern, reticent woman who was raising me, my brother, and four sisters. I found her rocking in her favorite chair and smoking her corncob pipe, and I asked her if it was true that my grandfather was a slave. She said yes, and then I asked whether he had picked cotton. She said no, there was no cotton in the area. She was reluctant to answer any other questions—it was just like asking about the facts of life.

People wouldn't tell you much in those days, but it just made me that much more curious. Every chance I got, I'd question her, and little by little the story unfolded. My grandmother's oldest daughter, Aunt Kate [born Mary Clarissa Berry] was a lot more helpful, because she had heard Grandpa Berry many times telling stories about his life. As I got older and my interest in black history grew, I discovered that Aunt Kate had some letters and other official papers about the family. I became so obsessed with this that at one point I went to Canada and looked in the provincial records and found my grandparents and their children. But now, I know you want to know how they got to Canada.

First things first. There was this white man, Uriah George Berry, who had a plantation in Livingston County, Kentucky, in the Salt River area, south of Frankfort. And my grandfather, Isaac, was born on his plantation and was his slave. Now in Mr. Berry's will, when he died, the slaves were to be divided. He willed Isaac's mother, Mary Clara, and all her children—Isaac, his three brothers Harvey, John, and Elijah, and his two sisters Nancy and Mary—to his only daughter Juliann Berry who had married a man from Missouri by the name of Pratt. And in his will he gave specific instructions that neither Isaac nor his sister Nancy were ever to be whipped or sold. So all of them were taken to Missouri by their new mistress Juliann Berry Pratt. Now my grandfather is in Missouri, but I have to go back and pick up my grandmother.

As I said, she was born in Wayne County, New York. Her father, Nelson Millard, who was born in New York, was a minister of the Mormon faith. Her mother, Clarissa Diane Taylor Millard, was born in Vermont. Lucy had twin brothers, but I can't remember their names. She also had an only sister, Clarissa, and they were very close. When they left New York, my grandmother must have been about thirteen years old. They came by the Erie Canal up to Buffalo on a flatboat with all their worldly goods, with another brother who was also a minister. And they came down the lake, went into Ohio, I understand, and stayed a little while, then came up into Michigan to Washtenaw County. That's where Ann Arbor is right now. And my grandmother's mother, Diane Millard, died of tuberculosis there. So, after a while, these two ministers tried to set up a Mormon settlement in Washtenaw County, and there is history of that. It's in the books, but the local people didn't want that. So then my grandmother's father, after he had buried his wife—and her marker is in Washtenaw County in the cemetery there—moved to a Mormon settlement in northeast Missouri near Palmyra. This was almost due south of an earlier thriving Mormon center in Nauvoo, Illinois, on the Mississippi River, which had been destroyed. And they were there for a short time, which is when my grandparents met.

So my grandfather Isaac was still a slave of Juliann and Jim Pratt, at their home near Paris, Missouri. Now Jim Pratt was a riverboat gambler, and if he lost money gambling, he would sell a slave to pay off his debts. You see, in Missouri, the law at that time was that the women had no say about anything, including their personal property. The man of the house controlled all the money and made all the decisions. And now Jim Pratt was going to sell my grandfather to pay off another gambling debt. He'd already sold one of Isaac's brothers [Harvey] down the river of no return, reportedly saying that he was lazy and, "By gracious, you'll work down there, or they'll kill you." But Juliann said no, you cannot sell him, because that's the will that my daddy gave me. He is not to be sold. So she went to my grandfather and said, "Isaac, if you can get away, you have my permission to go. I won't help you, but you have my permission to go. But don't tell me when or anything about it. Just make your plans and go on."

You have to understand, having grown up and worked in the big house, Isaac was used to having a lot of privileges and Juliann continued them. We believe that Isaac was her half brother. And he was allowed to have his weekends free, and whatever money he made was his. Isaac played the fiddle, and Juliann allowed him the freedom to play for dances and social affairs. One of his favorite tunes was "The Devil's Dream." He'd often not return to the Pratts until early Monday morning, but they trusted him. And he had a horse and a saddle, so any weekend within ten miles he could go and play for the various engagements—and in this way he met a lot of people, a few of whom helped him later. He also hunted and sold the meat and kept the money. But Juliann's husband, Jim Pratt, wanted to sell him, you see, and even boasted he could get $2,000 for Isaac in the St. Louis slave market. In the meantime, Isaac had met Lucy, because you see the Millards had moved to Missouri.

Lucy's family didn't own slaves. As part of their Mormon mission, Lucy's father encouraged his two daughters to be kind to the slaves. She told of taking drinking water to the slaves who were sodbusting the prairie. Grandpa Berry was rented out by Jim Pratt annually to new settlers in Missouri, who were called sodbusters. Grandpa drove a team of oxen, saying they would go in a straight line for a mile, and occasionally Lucy and her sister would take water out to the drivers. Lucy and Clarissa also helped the slave women and children.

She and her sister were also allowed to go to country dances, even though Mormons are not allowed to dance, but were only permitted to do the schottische—that's a little dance where you just took each other's hand and went back and forth and did a skipping step. My grandmother taught me how to do it. So, she said that she loved to hear Isaac play that fiddle, and she said he was handsome. I presume there were more meetings because she eventually told her father she was in love with Isaac and wanted to marry him.

Her father of course said, no, that won't do. So he was going to send her away to a woman's finishing school in Springfield, Illinois, and she played right along with it. But she and Isaac had made their plans; they were both going to run away and go on their own, not together. And they planned to meet eventually in Detroit, but didn't know where nor did they know when. Lucy's father gave her some money and sent her off to school on a train to Springfield. But when she got there, she took another train and went to Detroit, with no idea of how she would find Isaac.

Marguerite L. Berry-Jackson surrounded by family photographs, quilts, and memorabilia.
CLINTON COUNTY, MICHIGAN, MAY 1993 (35 MM CT)

Now, Isaac, you understand, took off walking. He sold his horse and his saddle for enough money to put in his pocket, and took his fiddle and his razor, his revolver and knife, and some cayenne pepper, to throw the slave-catcher's dogs off his tracks. And on one Saturday in April 1859, Isaac told the Pratts he was going off to play for a dance. He had arranged with one of his colored friends to give him a ride to the Mississippi River. Also, while playing his fiddle, he had met a free colored man, Albert Campbell, who lived in Quincy, on the Illinois side of the river, and who was to help him with his escape. Once he got across the river, he made his way to Quincy where Albert charted him a route to Chicago. Isaac continued on to northern Indiana where Albert had directed him to the Purdues, another colored family, and here he got his first full meal since leaving Albert Campbell, and rested up for about a week. The Purdues then directed him to Saline, Michigan, telling him only to travel at night because the slave-catchers were thick in the area. By the time he arrived in Saline, he had worn out two pairs of shoes; one pair which he called "shaly panks" he had made by ripping out the

"Old Settler" creole quilters. *Standing (left to right):* Kittie B. N. Pointer and Ione Todd. *Seated (left to right):* Deonna T. Green, Kayla Green, and Marie L. Cross.

MECOSTA COUNTY, MICHIGAN, MAY 1993 (35 MM CT)

sleeves of his coat, cutting out some cardboard that he put inside the sleeves as soles, and then tying a knot at one end of the sleeve and tying them on his feet.

He was plumb worn-out, but Saline brought him a small blessing when he met a free colored man who helped runaway slaves. He and his wife put Isaac up, fed him, and gave him a chance to get some badly needed rest and let his feet heal. This was a small community with a number of free colored people, and they took up a collection to buy him some shoes. Once he had rested, two of these people took him down to Detroit to Finney's barn. Finney was a white man who owned a hotel where a lot of the slave-catchers stayed, but he had a hiding place in the hayloft of his barn where slaves would stay right under their noses. Late at night, slaves would be taken across the Detroit River to Canada and freedom. When Isaac got to Windsor, Canada, he looked up Albert Campbell's aunt, Celia Flenoy, who got him a room with a colored family, who in turn got him a job. And he went back to playing his fiddle on weekends.

In the meantime, my grandmother Lucy had made her way to Detroit, but hadn't the least idea how to find Isaac. But she got a place to stay and a job in a factory sewing shirts. Finally, someone told her if she was looking for a runaway slave, they wouldn't be in Detroit, they'd be across the river in Canada. So she went to Windsor, Canada, got a little job, and every day she would go out walking, hoping to see him. One Saturday evening, she was passing a dance hall, saloon-type place, and heard the unique sound of his fiddle, walked in, and there was Isaac. They got married in Windsor, Canada, in August 1859 and had six children there. They actually lived in Puce, a village near Windsor, with a John Martindale for whom Isaac worked. All [the children] were recorded in a Canadian census. It is interesting that in this Windsor census, Isaac was recorded as an African, while Lucy and the children were listed as Mormons.

Twelve years after the Civil War—along with the Stephen Todds, Amos Johnsons, and another family—they came back to Michigan, where their last two children, my daddy, John, and his sister Minnie, were born. I even went to Canada and found documentation that Isaac and his oldest son William stood up [were witnesses] for Stephen and Caroline Todd when they married in Windsor in 1874.

Grandma Berry told me that Isaac and Stephen even had known each other growing up as slaves in Kentucky, but never knew the other had escaped until they met in Canada.

It took the families three weeks to reach Ionia, Michigan, in the spring of 1877, and they said it was a good warm spring for Michigan. There was a land-grant office in Ionia where you could see what government properties were available, and my grandfather paid $1.25 an acre for eighty acres of land on School Section Lake. They joined some other people who had been settling a three-county area [Mecosta, Montcalm, and Isabella] since 1860. The area around the lake had been a logging camp and, when the loggers had finished cutting the best white pine timber, they had left some wooden shanties into which the local Indians had moved. But when my grand-parents and the other settlers arrived, the Indians were away. Needing some shelter

Deonna T. Green with her family genealogy quilt.
MECOSTA COUNTY, MICHIGAN, OCTOBER 1995 (FRAME 16, 2¼ CT)

they just moved in. The Indians returned in the fall and ordered them out. My grandfather Isaac and Uncle William and Uncle Ike had to get their guns and tell the Indians they had bought the land. The chief then asked for their "talking paper" [deed]. The government later rounded up most of the Indians in this area and settled them on some land near the Forks, an area where the East Little Muskegon River joins the West Little Muskegon River. Some Indians even intermarried with the settlers, and we went to school together before a separate Indian school was established in Mt. Pleasant.

Back in the 1890s, after the harvest every year, they would have a big picnic of all the early settlers. White and colored people from all around would come, and take the whole day off for this big picnic in August. And we still do that to this very day. A few years back, we put up a big granite marker with the names of all the early settlers on it down at School Section Lake where my grand-parents used to live. The event is legally organized and officially recognized by the State of Michigan as the "Old Settlers' Reunion Association Picnic."

I arranged some of Mrs. Berry-Jackson's quilts, including several heirlooms, and old family photographs in front of her for my photograph (see p. 257). As she stood in this setting, I asked her to explain the history of the quilts, and who were in the old photographs. To her left on the wall was a picture of her white grandmother, Lucy

Flint Afro-American Quilters Guild. *Back row (left to right):* Jean M. Elbert, Teressie May, Joseph Rolston, Jocille Johnson-Brady, Charlotte Williams, Leo McClain, Bennye Hayes, and Katharine Harris. *Middle row (left to right):* Lois Flowers, Cora Vanderson, Lucille Rolston, and Jeffalone Rumph. *Front:* Gloria D. Henley, granddaughter of Teressie May.

GENESEE COUNTY, MICHIGAN, MAY 1993 (FRAME 10, 2¼ CT)

Berry, who was a Mormon. Of the picture on the wall to her right, of two girls, she said, "That's Marie and me, made right down here in Lansing. We came to visit our Aunt Jessie, and mother took us to a studio and had that picture made." The oval picture right in front of her is of her mother, Mabel Porter Berry. In the picture just to the left of her are her Aunt Cora and Uncle Walter on her mother's side. And in the lower left foreground on the quilt is a picture of a seated man and a woman standing next to him, which are her grandfather and grandmother Berry. Speaking of the quilt that is draped over the chair under her arm, she said,

> Granny Berry made that in 1924 for my baby sister Esther Ann. I named her. My grandmother's name was Lucy Esther, so I took one of her names, and my grandmother Porter's name was Ann, so I took Esther and Ann and asked my mother if I could name my sister, and she said yes. So she made that quilt for Esther Ann.

Mrs. Berry-Jackson went on to explain that:

> The Flower Garden quilt here on the left was the first quilt I made after I was married. In the center, the quilt with the circles in it is called the Mariner's Compass, and that was a wedding gift to me from our neighbors in Mecosta, Mr. and Mrs. Ezra Knight. She had what was called the "shaking palsy," and the doctor told her she needed to do something with her hands. She said as long as she quilted, her hands never shook. In the center of the picture is a quilt square that has been framed, and that square is out of a quilt that's over one hundred years old. The piece of twisted wood is part of one of my grandpa Berry's walking sticks. The quilt with the names embroidered on it is a genealogy quilt I am making. And I'm also making this black and white zigzag quilt for my daughter, and I'm calling it *Black Lightning*.

Learning the history of her grandfather's escape from slavery had increased Mrs. Berry-Jackson's thirst for knowledge about African-American history in general. She eventually earned her master's degree in history and then taught at Sexton High School in Lansing. And in the summer of 1962, with a group of her Delta Sigma Theta sorority sisters, she fulfilled a lifelong dream to visit Africa and spent a month touring Senegal, Liberia, Ghana, Nigeria, Sudan, Kenya, Ethiopia, and Egypt. The memories are still strong, especially of a reception in Nairobi, Kenya, where the women were greeted by Dr. Jomo Kenyatta, who was then president. Mrs. Berry-Jackson said she'd written to her friends in Michigan, telling them that he was a dynamic person. She wrote that he said: "This is your home. Your great-great-grandmothers and grandfathers were stolen from their homes many years ago, and now you, their descendants, have returned. The beat of the drum, the tom-tom, and the rhythm are inborn and can't escape." She also wrote: "He says that every time he hears jazz or spirituals, his soul sings because that is what makes

us kin. Then he asked us to sing a spiritual, and before we finished singing 'We Are Climbing Jacob's Ladder,' they were all swaying and humming with us." In 1968, Mrs. Berry-Jackson initiated the first black studies curriculum in the Lansing School District.

MECOSTA COUNTY

The next morning, I took Route 27 North to Mt. Pleasant, Michigan, where I turned west on Route 20 to Mecosta to revisit Mrs. Berry-Jackson's sister Marie Berry-Cross, whom I'd met in 1986. Mrs. Cross was born in 1915 in Mecosta, and has lived there her whole life. She had brought together three other women who are descended from the original settlers. We all gathered at School Section Lake to make a picture (see p. 258) by the granite marker that lists the names of the original old settlers and their descendants from a three-county area.

Carole Harris.
WAYNE COUNTY, MICHIGAN, MAY 1993 (FRAME 4, 2¼ CT)

Deonna Todd Green was born in 1948 in Blanchard, Michigan. She learned to quilt by watching her mother, Ione Sawyer Todd (who was born in 1927 and still helps her daughter with her quilt projects), and her maternal grandmother, Wealthy Guy Sawyer (1898–1995). She said, "I started quilting in 1980. It was a family-tree quilt. I love to make family-history quilts, genealogy quilts, and ethnic quilts. I make the quilts so that my children can hold onto their African heritage" (see p. 259).

Mrs. Green has been exhibited widely throughout the United States, and in 1991 participated in the Smithsonian's Festival of American Folklife. In 1995, she received the Michigan Heritage Award and the Governor's Award, in recognition of her historical genealogy quilts. She also received a grant from the Michigan Arts Council to produce another historical quilt on the oldest black resort in the United States, which is the town of Idlewild, Michigan. Her now famous genealogy quilt depicts the story of her great-grandfather Stephen Todd, who was a runaway slave from Garrard County, Kentucky, who escaped to Indiana and joined the Twenty-Eighth Colored Infantry in 1864. After the Civil War, he came to Peppertone, Indiana, and went to work for a German farmer named Fred Kahler. There Mr. Todd fell in love with Mr. Kahler's daughter Caroline, and they ran away together to Canada where they met up with Isaac Berry (see pp. 253ff.) and his family. Mrs. Green's quilt shows Isaac and his son William Berry standing up for Stephen Todd at his wedding on August 24, 1874. The Todds and the Berrys migrated to Michigan in 1877.

Wednesday Night Quilting Sisters of Detroit. *Back row (left to right)*: Michele Lawhorn, Deborah Walton, Elaine Carter, Elaine Yancy Hollis, Shirley Gibson Bell, and Robin Phillips-Gaston.

Front row (left to right): Sarah Carolyn Reese, Brandon Wilson Lawhorn (boy), Mary Turner, and Pearl Ephrain-Cook. WAYNE COUNTY, MICHIGAN, MAY 1993 (35 MM CT)

Kittie Belle Norman Pointer was born in 1919 in Remus, Michigan. She learned to quilt mostly from her mother-in-law, Mary Berry Pointer (1864–1967), who was born in Canada and was a daughter of Isaac and Lucy Berry. She told me, "My mother, Goldie Norman [1892–1945], enjoyed quilting as a social activity, but didn't really quilt much. I started quilting when I was about twenty-five and have made at least 280—and I can remember exactly to whom I have given most of them."

That afternoon I left Mecosta and took Route 20 East into Bay City on my way to Flint. I spent the night with Joseph and Lucille Rolston, and photographed the Flint Afro-American Quilters Guild the next day (see p. 260).

FLINT AFRO-AMERICAN QUILTERS GUILD

Jeffalone B. Rumph, who organized the Flint Afro-American Quilters Guild in 1987, was born in 1929 in Eupora, Mississippi. She grew up in a family of six children, and they all helped their mother, Theretha Brown

Levi Coffin House, which was a stop on the Underground Railroad for runaway slaves. The portrait is of Levi Coffin, who was a Quaker.
FOUNTAIN CITY, INDIANA, MAY 1993 (FRAME 12, 2¼ CT)

Brantley (1908–89), also from Eupora, quilt. She also learned from her father's sister, Ora Bell Brantley Hillard, who is still living in Eupora. Mrs. Rumph migrated to Flint in 1964.

Lucille W. Rolston was born in 1921 in Kerrville, Tennessee. She learned to quilt from her mother, Mary Ann Jones Williams (1894–1986), and her father's mother, Alice Williams (1845–1937). In 1952, her family migrated from Tennessee to Flint, looking for better jobs. Now in retirement, she has taught her husband Joseph to quilt. It gives them something to do together, and it gives Mrs. Rolston a "very good feeling to know I'm now quilting some tops that my mother started seventy-two years ago."

Teressie May was born in 1932 in Ozan, Arkansas. Her mother died when she was four, and she learned to quilt at about six from her step-mother, Rosie Lee Coulter White, who was born in 1902 in Nashville, Arkansas, and who is still living in Hope, Arkansas. She also learned from her paternal grandmother, Bell Walker White (1876–1952). Mrs. May migrated from Arkansas to Flint in 1953. She still has the first quilt top she made, at age seven. Her two daughters do not quilt, but Mrs. May is very happy that her granddaughter Gloria D. Henley is learning to quilt.

Bennye Hayes was born in 1933 in Carthage, Mississippi. She learned to quilt primarily from her mother, Violet Johnson Morris, who was born in 1905 in Walnut Grove, Mississippi, and also from her father's sister, Daisy Morris Henry (1870–1935), from Carthage, Mississippi. Mrs. Hayes said, "I'm proud to say that my mother and father were able to send eight kids from the red hills of Mississippi to college, and they've all finished. But only two of us are still quilting, me and my sister Eva McCloud, who was born in 1937 and has migrated to Maryland." Today Mrs. Hayes is retired from thirty-two years of teaching and is busy making quilts for her family.

Leo McClain was born in 1937 in Muldrow, Oklahoma, and learned to quilt from his mother, Bellzora Pettis McClain (1893–1990), who was born in Charles, Arkansas. He also learned from his paternal grandmother, Nellie Starr McClain (1872–1971), who was born in the Indian Territory of Oklahoma near Muldrow. Quoting from an article called "Quilting Man" in the *Flint Journal* of May 9, 1993:

In a household of eleven boys and four girls, Leo McClain's family didn't subscribe to the theory that certain chores were off-limits to boys. Raised on a farm in Muldrow, Oklahoma, the fifty-six-year-old retired General Motors worker said his mother insisted he and his brothers learn how to maintain a home by teaching them cooking, cleaning, gardening, and quiltmaking. Now he practices his hobby as the only male member of the Flint Afro-American Quilters Guild. For McClain, his introduction to quilting began when he was seven or eight, and he enjoyed it despite the fact he knew no other boys outside of the family doing it. McClain maintained a hold on one family heirloom, a Yo-Yo quilt made by his mother. His mother used the quilt only to decorate the guest bed on Sunday, a time for visitors. McClain continues that tradition of simply admiring its beauty, saying it is much too valuable to be put to any other use.

Helen O. Epps.
FRANKLIN COUNTY, OHIO, JUNE 1993 (FRAME 15, 2¼ CT)

Cora Lee Vanderson was born in 1929 in Hamburg, Mississippi. She was taught to quilt by her mother, Getty Smith Allen (1900–63), who was born in Fayette, Mississippi, and by her father's sister Cora Jones from Franklin County, Mississippi. Her family migrated to Flint in 1956 to work in the auto industry. As she says, "It makes me feel good to know that my children cherish the quilts I've made for them."

Lois H. Flowers was born in 1924 in Newbern, Tennessee. She learned to quilt from her grandmother Mary Jordon (1880–1960). She says, "I would love watching my grandmother quilting. I was always told I was too little to quilt. By the time I was old enough, I had lost interest. A number of years later, having gotten a degree in home economics with a specialty in sewing, and married and started a family, at night I would put the children to bed and then start quilting. I would quilt until my husband got home from work at 1:00 A.M." Mrs. Flowers migrated to Flint in 1952 when she married. Neither of her two daughters quilts; she's making a quilt now for her grandson.

Jocille Wickware Johnson was born in 1927 in Ishire, Indiana. Her family migrated to Flint in 1929 when she was two. As she tells it:

> My mother, Vergie Mae Givens Wickware [1907–83], who was from Ishire, too, and my maternal grandmother, Ida Givens Young

Wyrelene S. Mays with her granddaughter Keitiaunna W. Howard.
FRANKLIN COUNTY, OHIO, JUNE 1993 (FRAME 16, 2¼ CT)

[1888–1962], who was born in Central City, Kentucky, started me quilting with the Nine-Block at the age of four. We were taught how to straight-stitch and back-stitch, and how to lock our stitches at the end of a row. I have eight children and forty grandchildren, and all of them have quilts of some kind. I am trying to make a quilt for each grandchild, so they can have something to remember me when I am gone. I also teach them how to wash the quilts, so they will last many years. I love to work with all the colors mixed up. I call my quilts, "colors running crazy."

Precious Miller-Holston was born in 1925 in St. Louis, Missouri. She migrated to Flint in 1971. She simply stated, "I started quilting in 1980 while caring for a son who was ill and in a body cast. At that time, I had not had any lessons; I began with only what I remembered seeing my grandmother do."

DETROIT

After photographing the Flint group, I took Interstate 75 South into Detroit and went straight to the Hartford Memorial Baptist Church to revisit the Wednesday Night Quilting Sisters (see p. 263), a group I'd first met and photographed in 1987 (see p. 69).

Carole Harris (see p. 262) was born in 1943 in Detroit, Michigan, where she has spent her whole life. She said:

> I taught myself to quilt. Quilting is not a difficult task. If you can sew, you can quilt. I have been sewing and making my own clothes since I was a teenager. My earliest form of needlework was embroidery, which I was taught by my mother around the age of six or seven. I made my first quilt in 1966 as a functional piece, intended for my impending marriage that same year. For me, quilting is a very personal and necessary form of expression. Cloth is the medium which I have chosen, or which has chosen me, as the channel for impressions of my feelings and life around me.

Mrs. Harris has been exhibited widely throughout the United States.

INDIANA, MAY 31–JUNE 1, 1993

FOUNTAIN CITY

After the Memorial Day weekend, I set out for Fountain City, Indiana, where I wanted to investigate the quilts at the Levi Coffin House. For

Mary L. Dobson.
FRANKLIN COUNTY, OHIO, JUNE 1993 (35 MM CT)

years I kept coming across reproductions of a painting by C. T. Webber called *The Underground Railroad,* which showed a wintry scene of fourteen escaped slaves being welcomed at the home of the Coffins, an Indiana Quaker family. I had gotten permission from the Cincinnati Museum of Art to include this image on *The Underground Railroad* quilt I had designed for the Quincentenary (see p. 112). This stop on the Underground Railroad is now a privately owned historic site, and the staff was very accommodating and stayed after hours to assist me in making my photographs (see p. 264). None of the quilts brought there by slaves had survived, and I was told that the quilts they had on display were made locally in the 1800s by the mother of a Nancy Parker.

OHIO, JUNE 2–3, 1993

COLUMBUS

The next day I headed east again on Interstate 70 into Columbus, where Carolyn Mazloomi had arranged for me to meet Catherine T. Willis. Mrs. Willis in turn had lined up a group of quilters, including some young

Barbara Payne and her daughter
Makeba A. R. Payne.
FRANKLIN COUNTY, OHIO, JUNE
1993 (FRAME 5, 2¼ CT)

women with whom she was working on a quilt project. Ms. Diane Newsum, manager of the Martin Luther King branch of the Columbus Metropolitan Library, permitted me to use their meeting room to photograph the quilters (see p. 265–68).

Helen O. Epps was born in 1925 in Youngstown, Ohio. Her mother was a seamstress, but did not quilt. It was her aunt Brookie Robinson (1898–1972) who influenced her. Mrs. Epps's daughter is not interested in quilting yet, and she has no grandchildren, so she quilts for her personal interest. However, she has passed the tradition on to young people through school projects.

Wyrelene S. Mays was born in 1922 in Newnan, Georgia. Before she was two, her mother died and she was brought to Chattanooga, Tennessee, and reared by her paternal grandparents, but she often visited her maternal grandparents and relatives. In her quilting, she was influenced by three women, all from Georgia: her paternal and maternal grandmothers and her mother's sister. Respectively, they were Maggie Strozier (1871–1956); Nellie Couch (1862–1943) from Luthersville; and her aunt Lucille Bowen (d. 1992) from Curtisville, who also gave her quilts. She recalls, "I sat at and under the quilting frame of my paternal grandmother as she and her friends quilted. She said my stitches were too long, but she encouraged me to keep trying to quilt. I became the needle threader. I treasure a quilt that my maternal grandmother made and sent to me about 1943 while I was a student in a school of nursing. It is a Postage Stamp scrap quilt." In 1978, Mrs. Mays made a "Memories" quilt, which reflects her family life and the joyous experience of raising her children. Today she hopes to pass this tradition on to her granddaughter Keitiaunna W. Howard.

Mary L. Dobson was born in 1927 in Murfreesboro, Tennessee. Her quilting was influenced by her mother, Mary Carney (1916–55), and her maternal grandmother, Lue Carney (1877–1942), both from Murfreesboro, Tennessee. She says, "I tried to help them cut pieces when I was about twelve years old. There was quilting in our home with the neighborhood people on certain nights of the week."

Barbara Holt Payne was born in 1950 in Thomaston, Georgia. In talking about whom she saw quilting, she said, "I watched and learned from my

Sacred Sisters and Brothers Mentoring Group. *Back row (left to right):* Debra Brittman, Catherine Willis, and Angela Tanyhill. *Middle row (left to right):* Donna Brittman, Anna Brown, and Andrea Sullivan. *Front row (left to right):* Arika Woodruff, Alex Brown.

FRANKLIN COUNTY, OHIO, JUNE 1993 (35 MM CT)

mother, Sally Emma Holt [1910–58], and my sister Beulah Holt Tysinger [b. 1935], and from my two aunts Laura Bell Johnson [1904–89] and Katie Pearl Green, all of whom were from Thomaston, Georgia. I came to Columbus in 1969 to attend Ohio State University, and really didn't start quilting much until after I graduated in 1974." Today, Mrs. Payne belongs to several quilting groups, and in her home is teaching her ten-year-old daughter, Makeba Payne, and one of Makeba's friends to quilt.

I next photographed a delightful group of young women who are part of the Sacred Sisters and Brothers Mentoring Group of Columbus. They had worked on several quilting projects coordinated by Catherine T. Willis.

CINCINNATI

The next morning I headed south on Interstate 75 to Cincinnati to see Dr. Carolyn Mazloomi, coordinator of the Women of Color Quilters' Network. After warm hellos, the first thing she told me was that the

Left to right: Damian P. Mazloomi and his mother, Dr. Carolyn Mazloomi, founder and coordinator of the Women of Color Quilters' Network.
CINCINNATI, OHIO, JULY 1993 (FRAME 2, 2¼ CT)

WCQN hotline had really been humming. "Everyone's talking about your cross-country trip and wanting to know how they can help. I hear they're even taking up collections in church for you." She was right. A lot of people were contributing to this effort, and I was very grateful. However, I was still thinking about all those folks I hadn't yet photographed. Carolyn fixed me a wonderful meal and brought me up to date on everything. I then converted her living room into a quilt gallery and photographed her and her oldest son, Damian Patrick Mazloomi (b. 1977), who designs quilt patterns and also helps his mother. As Damian says, "I'm not really a quilter, but my role in quilting makes me feel important. My mother, knowing that I'm helping her out and giving her suggestions as to what the quilt will consist of—the colors, the design— that is very important to me. It makes me feel special that I'm a big part in that aspect of my mother's life."

Dr. Carolyn Stuart Mazloomi was born in 1948 in New Orleans, Louisiana. No one in her family quilted, and as she explains:

> I started quilting in 1980. I taught myself to quilt after seeing a quilt for the first time at the Dallas Trade Market. The quilt was a traditional patchwork quilt with an American eagle in each corner. I simply could not believe that something so beautiful could be made by hand. It called out to me to "touch it." At that point, I was hooked. Most of my quilts deal with social, political, or religious themes that affect people of color. Many of my fellow WCQN members say that these types of quilts are too "hard edged." However, I will keep making them, for the simple reason that we as black folk have many stories to tell. The truth is not always pretty.
>
> I am especially interested in teaching young African-American kids how to quilt. I've been working with one group of children from the [housing] projects in Columbus for five years now. In 1989 the first quilt they ever made was exhibited at the Taft Museum in Cincinnati. A nonprofit organization, Friends of Art for Community Advancement, hired a bus to bring the kids to see the show. I will never forget the look on those kids' faces when they saw their quilt hanging in a museum. They were so proud. This boosted their self-esteem through the roof!
>
> Quilting has given me an artistic outlet in which I can express my views about the society I live in. Since my work is Afrocentric, it has allowed my black audiences to see something of themselves portrayed in what I have created. Quilting means carrying on a craft form that my ancestors have taken an active role in for hundreds of years, and it helps to validate my own existence on this planet.
>
> In 1986 I was diagnosed as having a brain tumor. Before having surgery for its removal, I had a dream about "life after death." I survived the surgery, and went on to create the quilt I saw in my dream. The title of that quilt is *The Homecoming*. It's called that because death takes you to your true home; this earthly realm is just a temporary way station.

Sandra German and her daughter
Meredith German.
CINCINNATI, OHIO, JUNE 1993
(FRAME 16, 2¼ CT)

My quilts have been used to teach young children African-American history. Many of my quilts deal with the struggles of the African American. These quilts are cultural documents that vividly depict our lives in this country as well as in Africa. I believe in "color therapy." Color is life-giving. I made a series of quilts for my brother, who was dying of AIDS at a hospice in Houston. I wanted him and the other patients to be surrounded by color, in hopes that the vibrancy would help infuse life into their dying bodies. I would like to think that the color kept them alive just a little longer and helped ease their pain.

Dr. Mazloomi migrated to Cincinnati in 1988 and today is a prolific quilter, as well as a quilt collector and dealer. She is widely published and exhibited, and through the WCQN which she founded in 1986, she continually communicates with quilters around the world. In light of this, I was quite interested in her views about African-American quilting in general. I first asked what the world of quilting meant to her:

Well, a lot is going on here. I am first of all happy that finally African-American quilters are getting the recognition they so richly deserve. Being a contemporary quilter myself, I'm more concerned with the acceptance of the contemporary quilts that are made by African Americans today. So often quilt appreciators and collectors will look at the traditional quilts that African Americans have made and not so much the contemporary quilts, because of the prominence and publicity that the traditional quilts have gotten. So the contemporary African-American quilters are truly coming into their own right now, and people have seen—especially in the past two years—that all the quilts African Americans create are not improvisational quilts. The quilts that we create are as varied as the race of people themselves. It's not just relegated to one definitive style, and I'm glad that this arena is opening to include the contemporary African-American quilter who makes use of our cultural heritage in order to produce a quilt that will, years from now of course, become a cultural document and give people a glimpse into how we've lived as African Americans in this country. This is important to me.

Most of my story quilts are appliqué pictorial quilts. They utilize social and political themes. This is important. I think some of the pieces that we create must carry a message. And what better venue than the museum or gallery circuit to let people know how we the artists feel about what's happening with the world today. Maybe we can impact somebody who's looking at these pieces by talking about the Middle Passage, or the plight of black men in America today, or the plight of the Haitian people, the boat people, or the Chinese refugees coming into this country. If in that way we're able to impact anyone, to create an aura of justice, this is well done. I think people truly underestimate the power of an artist. An artist has a special station. Even in God's world, the artist has a special station. In the Baha'i faith, we firmly believe the artist is a special person—has the power to convey so much. And the power to make a difference. When people see social commentary or political commentary in our work, this sends a message and hopefully it will be a positive one. It will make people stop and think what they can do to inflict a positive change for the good of mankind.

And there are many quilt movements today, such as "Green Quilts." A Green Quilt is a quilt that addresses environmental issues such as pollution and saving the animals. Right now I'm working on a Green Quilt, and its theme and title is *Endangered Species*. I have all the endangered animal species on it, but they are surrounded by the human species because I figure we can't save the damned animals until somebody saves mankind. We have to be saved first. To me, man is the first endangered species and then we save the animals. If we can't save ourselves, we're in bad shape. So hence up until now, all of the Green Quilts that have been made have addressed environmental issues, animal rights, recycling, pollution. Nobody's saying anything about mankind. So my quilt addresses man.

I then questioned Carolyn further what she meant by "improvisational":

I think that every artist is dealing with improvisation. When many collectors think of improvisation, they think of geometric improvisation—being able to make a quilt block without using patterns, that random flow of the patterns. Many people have seen those same improvisational quilts in Kentucky that are made by white folks, Appalachian people. But again we're coming into the stereotypes. The haphazard patterning, the random stitches, big bold stitches, and the coloration.

I want to say one other thing. In this improvisation, a lot of stylers and a lot of collectors have gone out of their way to connect what we create with African patterning. We have people in this network, from [ages] twelve on up to over ninety-five, many of whom knew their grandparents, and many of whom knew their great-grandparents. Not many people have any recollection of any African connections.

What we are creating today comes about from a conscious effort of studying our culture. I don't know anything about West African

Juanita G. Yeager.
JEFFERSON COUNTY, KENTUCKY,
JUNE 1993 (FRAME 4, 2¼ CT)

masks; I don't know anything about Adinkra symbols; I have to go and study that. Even if I ask my father or my grandfather, they can't tell me this. You know we have many religious symbols (and I speak for my family) that I can trace back to the Caribbean, and perhaps trace back to Africa—some of these traditions—but when you talk about random patterning, looking like the Dahomey, or the Fon, or whatever, I don't know what the hell you're talking about. We have many people in this network, many contemporary quilters, whose quilts look like West African weavings. But this is from a conscientious study of West African woven fabrics to make them look like quilts. These people have done it on purpose so that they can reach back and relate something in their lives to their culture, their African heritage. It is not something inherent. It is something that we had to study. So it really upsets me when people want to relate and define everything that we do back to Africa.

Everybody wants to explain what we do and justify what we do. It has to be some scientific study for everything. So this is good when I find in your cursory study that you've actually gone and seen these quilters and you talk with them. You actually talked to them and valued what they said, and you didn't try to interpret and put a label on it. The mainstream collectors and the historians have yet to fully discover the ramifications of African-American quilting because heretofore, prior to Cuesta's 1992 show (see p. 127), there was not inclusiveness of the contemporary African-American quilter. We are still trying to find our place. This is so because collectors and scholars have concentrated on the stereotypical quilt because they use a set of criteria in describing the African-American quilts based on this old school that goes back to John Vlach—criteria of bold colors, improvisational haphazard piecing, large stitching, random strip piecing.

That does not form the criteria of the main body of African-American quilts. This is from a certain era, a certain region, a certain socioeconomic level, and within the body of this network, it's just two or three percent. It represents maybe three percent of what the people are creating in this network.

Sandra German (see p. 272) was born in 1948 in Cincinnati. She edits the WCQN newsletter and teaches and exhibits widely. No one in her family made quilts, and growing up, she'd noticed them only in passing. Although she always loved "wonderful fabrics, textiles, and textures," she didn't pay close attention to quilts until she was thirty-five and went to a quilt show:

> I enthusiastically and joyously viewed them, but perceived that it took someone close to a saint to make them. My concept was of a quilt taking two years, and little old ladies with bleeding fingers. As the mother of five young children, I knew I didn't have the mindset or environment that allowed one to sit and stitch. It took me a couple years to realize that it wouldn't take two years to make a quilt, and to date I estimate I've made about one hundred. I used to make them for my children but don't anymore, and they are jealous when I sell them.
>
> One special quilt that I made in 1989 was after one of my daughters was involved in an attempted rape. I spent a whole night in the emergency room—and the way I chose to express or release my emotions of anger, love, and concern, was by creating this face on a quilt. It only took two days. It was in honor of all my children, to let them know how much I treasured them and wished for their continued safety. I feel a special power from my quilts, but most are not made to be slept under. I create quilts to give a message of hope; there is always a spiritual message in them: keep the faith, look to that which is greatest in the human spirit and that which helps us overcome (see p. 272).

KENTUCKY, JUNE 4, 1993

LOUISVILLE

The next morning, I left Cincinnati for Louisville, to meet another WCQN member, Juanita Gibson Yeager. Mrs. Yeager was born in 1943 in Louisville and has lived there her whole life. As she says:

> I started quilting in the winter of 1984. My children were nearly adults, my days of chauffeuring kids to and from scouts, shopping, and other activities were over, and I had free time to pursue my own interests. I wasn't aware of quilts until by chance I saw a quiltmaking program on a public education station. I was looking for something to relax me. My first attempts at machine-piecing were unsatisfactory. Machine sewing seemed too production oriented. I am basically a very impatient person, and I was in a hurry to get that first quilt completed, so I went to the library and checked out several books on the subject, which were written for quilters who made quilts by hand. I taught myself to hand-piece and loved it. A year or so later, I enrolled in an adult education class to further my knowledge.
>
> I have an observation to share. For a very long time, I didn't know other quilters of color and most of what I learned or used as examples of quilting was garnered from books and the quilters in my local guild, all of whom were Caucasian. As the only [African

Claire E. Carter.
MONROE COUNTY, WEST VIRGINIA, JUNE 1993 (35 MM CT)

American] among them, I was never made to feel unwanted. I have traveled from Texas to Maine because of my love of quilts, and I learned that quilters speak a common language that sees no color differences other than those in the patches of quilts. I have been in homes of millionaires and on farms with outhouses, in cities and towns and boroughs I would have never ventured into if it was not for quilting. Nothing in my life, my marriage, raising four children, or working as a registered nurse for over twenty years, has given me the opportunity to really know such a diverse group of people, in terms of race, economics, culture. Some I have come to truly love like sisters, and many more I call true friends.

Quilting is a very important part of my life. It's that part of me that gets the accolades that I never heard because I was a good wife, a good mother, a good nurse. Quilting fulfills that creative part of me that for years wanted to be an artist, a painter of pretty scenes on canvas. I am a happy person, and I think my quilts express my joy. I don't have any drums to beat, so consequently I don't do narratives with stories to tell people. I just like for people to look at my work and smile and be happy, because the colors make me happy. I can't see myself doing anything, you know, depressing or with a whole lot of thought. Maybe that is a little shallow of me.

West Virginia, June 5, 1993

The next day I left Kentucky for Charleston, West Virginia, en route to Gap Mills in the rural southeast part of the state close to the Virginia line, to meet Claire Carter, another WCQN member.

Gap Mills

Claire Elizabeth Dunlap Carter was born in 1920 in Detroit, Michigan. She said:

Claire E. Carter's paternal grandparents' bedroom.
MONROE COUNTY, WEST VIRGINIA, JUNE 1993
(35 mm ct)

> Even though I grew up in Detroit, we were sent to Gap Mills here to spend our summers, where I saw my patenal grandmother, Mariah Jane Ross Dunlap [1863–1954], who was from Gap Mills, quilting. My grandfather Eligah Dunlap [1857–1932] was born in Red Sulphur, West Virginia. There's something strange going on with them that I've never been clear about. I was always told they were born free, but it was during slavery time. What is even more confusing is that Eligah's father, my great-grandfather, was a Jew with a Scottish last name, Dunlap, and he had a farm in Red Sulphur and owned slaves. He had a child, my grandfather Eligah, by a slave woman whose name we don't know, and he sold this woman when Eligah was two or three years old. Eligah was then raised by another black woman, whose name we also don't know, whom he called "grandmother." All of these unknowns really hang me up sometimes. I'm all mixed up with African, Indian, Jewish, and white, and I can't account for it. I also have great-grandparents on my mother's side who were called "free French slaves," and nobody knows where they came from.

Mrs. Carter first showed me the old family home and the quilts of her paternal grandparents. She explained that she first tried to quilt when she was eight or nine years old:

> I tried to copy a doll quilt given me for Christmas, a Double Nine-Patch. As a teenager I asked my paternal grandmother for a quilt, and was told I was big and ugly enough to make my own. I did make one the year I was twenty-five. I am self-taught. My grandmother lived to see this quilt, but I only wish she had lived to see my work now. In my paternal grandparents' bedroom, there are three photographs. The family portrait is of Eligah and Mariah Dun-

African-American Heritage Quilters Guild of metropolitan Pittsburgh. *Front and center:* Brigette Bethea. *Back row (left to right):* Mary Jo Miller, Julianne McAdoo, Geraldine Benton, Sandra Ford, D. Michelle Brisker, Sandra Godfrey, Frenchie O. Richardson, and Carolyn N. Streater. *Middle row (left to right):* Alice Ried, Delores Rodriguez, Natalie Joy Mays, and Bobetta B. Johnson. *Front row (left to right):* Christine McCray-Bethea, Ruth A. Ward, and Michaeline Reed.

ALLEGHENY COUNTY, PENNSYLVANIA, JUNE 1993 (FRAME 13, 2¼ CT)

lap and their seven children and dog. The large portrait on the wall is of my Aunt Bertha Dunlap Key, their oldest daughter, and the small photograph next to hers is of my grandmother Mariah Dunlap and her younger sister Fanny.

Quilting means many things to me. It is my way of showing my artistic ability. It is my "Linus blanket" when I'm depressed or in the dumps. Before I retired as a supervisor, after a nerve-shattering day, quilt pictures, magazines, books, or working on a project would calm my nerves and bring me back to my normal self. To a degree, I always find the question of what quilting means to me hard to answer. Quilt-related things do have a very special place in my life.

Beatrice H. Mitchell, poet and quilter.
RAVENNA, OHIO, JUNE 1993
(FRAME 8, 2¼ CT)

PITTSBURGH, PENNSYLVANIA, JUNE 6, 1993

AFRICAN-AMERICAN HERITAGE QUILTERS GUILD

The AAHQG began as a small group of friends who met informally to quilt and to socialize. The group began to grow and in 1989 formally established itself. The membership then was about thirty, beginners and professionals, many artistically talented and stylistically unique, both traditional and contemporary quilters. The members feel that it is the joy of quilting, the sharing of their heritage, and the fellowship with each other that make their participation in the guild worthwhile.

Ruth A. Ward was born in 1933 in Barbourville, Kentucky. Her family migrated to Pittsburgh when she was eight. Both of her maternal grandparents were quilters from Kentucky: Hanna Ellen White (1877–1939), born in Knox County, and William Charles White (1862–1943). Her grandfather was also a weaver, and after retiring from farming, he made a loom for rugs that he sold. As Mrs. Ward said, "I started sewing when I was in the seventh grade and have been sewing all of my life. I began seriously quilting about five years ago, after an illness that compelled me to give up my job as a personnel officer. A friend, Costella Woods, sparked my interest in quilting. We joined the AAHQG, and we took some classes from Guild members as well as at local quilt shops."

Gerry Benton was born in 1946 in Pittsburgh and has lived there all her life. Her earliest quilting influence was her maternal grandmother, Rose Salter (1887–1952), who was born in Damascus, Georgia. After she was

Magnolia K. Owens, quilter,
surrounded by family photographs,
memorabilia, and a selection of
antique quilts made by her mother,
grandmother, aunts, and sisters.
STARK COUNTY, OHIO, JUNE 1993
(FRAME 11, 2¼ CT)

grown, Mrs. Benton says, "I went to an exhibit of African-American quilts, and this inspired me to want to learn how to quilt. I started quilting in September 1989, and learned from AAHQG members and other local teachers. I have been learning advanced skills from international teachers ever since 1991."

Bobetta B. Johnson was born in 1926 in Henderson, Kentucky, and her family migrated to Pittsburgh when she was seven. She credits her paternal grandmother, Luvenia Brooks (1880–1967), from Brookstown, Kentucky, for sparking her interest in quilting. She explained, "Quilting has opened a new area in my life. I had always wanted to quilt. I thought quilts were really beautiful. After I retired, I went to a Log Cabin class. I was the only Afro-American student. I took several other classes, and again was the only Afro-American. I had a friend who also took some classes, and we finally connected up with other Afro-American quilters. Their artistic talent really blew my mind. Then I began to see the real beauty in an old quilt that I have."

Julianne McAdoo was born in 1949 in Pittsburgh, has lived there all her life. She never saw anyone in her family quilting, but was told that her great-grandmother Emma Johnson made quilts. She began quilting in Pittsburgh in 1984, and was taught by Michaeline Reed, a member of the Guild.

Natalie Joy Mays, born in 1960 in Pittsburgh, has lived there all her life. She started quilting when she was sixteen, because "I liked sewing and seemed to have a lot of scraps. No one I knew quilted, so I was self-taught."

Frenchie O. Richardson was born in 1921 in Dublin, Georgia, and came North with her parents in 1922. She was introduced to quilting by a Bible class teacher in the early 1930s. For her, she says, "Quilting is a quiet-time activity. I had no professional lessons until the late 1950s. I am basically self-taught. I have not sold any of my quilts, and only give them to family members and friends as gifts."

OHIO, JUNE 7–8, 1993

RAVENNA

From Pittsburgh, I returned to Ohio to see quilter Beatrice Hunter Mitchell (see p. 279) in Ravenna, who was born in 1929 in Cincinnati,

Ohio. She moved with her family to Georgia when she was two, and they returned to Cincinnati when she was seven. In Georgia, she saw three members of her family quilt: her mother, Birdell Cox Hunter, who was born in 1904 near Athens; her maternal grandmother, Emma Cox (1862–1945); and her father's mother's sister, Cindy Griffin, who was born in Commerce and died in the early 1940s. She explained how she happened to learn from her Aunt Cindy:

> The reason Aunt Cindy was in our home was that when a woman, an older woman, was either an old maid, widowed, or just separated from her husband, she didn't have any place to live but with relatives, so Poppa's Aunt Cindy came and lived on the farm where we were sharecropping. She came and lived with us in our little house. And she and my mother would be quilting. I am told before Aunt Cindy passed, she had

Left to right: EdJohnetta Miller and her daughter Ayisha Kishili Miller.
HARTFORD, CONNECTICUT, JUNE 1993 (FRAME 15, 2¼ CT)

really lost her sight, but at that time, I guess she needed glasses and didn't have them, so she would get me to thread the needles. And I would watch and see how they quilted, cause you can't quilt without a thimble. You'd stick your fingers. And a lot of young women never learned to use a thimble. But I would watch them then, to see how they pushed that needle with the thimble. And so I learned real early how to use a thimble and actually make my stitches fairly small.

And even after we moved to Cincinnati, there was an old woman that lived down the street, and another girl and I would go down and ask her for quilt pieces. I think that she had worked at someplace where they made clothing. She would have a lot of scraps and she'd give them to us. And I would sit and make a doll quilt, and once I got a piece made so big, Momma put in into a bigger quilt. Just added it to the real quilt. Because I just kept going with it, you know? And then as a young girl, I used to make my clothes, so I always had scraps.

I retired early. I was forty-nine. I should say that I "quit tired." I was doing practical nursing, and it looks like that spring—I don't know whether I was starting to go through menopause or whatever—[I] was just short-tempered. I quit work. But quilting soothes me. I didn't know it at the time, but I can come home all hyper and upset and get that needle and start quilting. Before you know it, I am just calm as I can be. Well, I say there is peace in quilting, that's what I say. I guess I started writing poems about the same time I

Hattie M. Henry.
HARTFORD, CONNECTICUT, JUNE 1993 (68123/9, & 2¼ CT)

Left to right: Dorothy Christie, Blanche M. Nelson, and Hattie M. Henry.
HARTFORD, CONNECTICUT, JUNE 1993 (35 MM CT)

started quilting again. I'm trying to quilt now with the poems that I made.

Quilting has made my retired years busier than I was when I was employed. But it has also made me happy, meeting new people and going places, to shows where quilts are displayed. It is also a connection to my past. And because I have made quilts for many family members, I feel that my presence will be around long after I am no longer among the living.

CANTON

From Ravenna, Mrs. Mitchell took me to Canton to meet quilter Magnolia Kinney Owens. Mrs. Owens was born in 1916 in Statham, Georgia, and migrated to Canton in 1940. She learned to quilt from her mother, Charlotte Kinney (1885–1960), who also was born in Statham; she also saw her mother's sisters Mary and Betsy quilt. Her maternal grandmother, Mary Kinney, also a quilter, died in 1916 shortly after Magnolia was born. As she tells it:

Maybe I was six or seven years old, something like that, because Mom had quilting frames—you know, back then they had quilting frames in the spare room, they'd put up quilts in there. They wouldn't quilt it all in one day, just space it until they got it done. At first, we weren't allowed to quilt, 'cause our stitches were too long. But later quilting became a chore. When Momma put up a quilt, if we were going to school, when we got home, like a lot of kids go out and play, we had to go to quilting.

Now what I was wearing in that picture you took of me (see p. 280), that was my mother's hat. She made me a hat. That's the hat she wore when she got dressed up to go to church, and the black dress and the blouse, she made all of it. She didn't buy. She bought the material and made it.

Margaret L. Penn, quilt preserver.
HARTFORD, CONNECTICUT, JUNE 1993 (FRAME 15, 2¼ CT)

Mrs. Owens has a collection of quilts made by her grandmother, mother, aunts, and sisters, as well as her own. As to the importance of these quilts in her life, she explained:

It has meant the great beyond, because if it didn't mean anything to me, the quilts would have been gone. I like to preserve, whether it's quilts, or something of my mother's. And if you ain't got nothing, you got the memory there, and you'll never forget the memory anyway. And the things that you went through growing up. And what you did. But then, these memories, when I look at this, and I go back, it still does something for me. 'Cause if I didn't have it and didn't see it, all I would have was the memories, but see I got this stuff. And that's why I hang on to it. And I think this is why sometimes I worry. And I shouldn't. Because once you leave this world, you are gone and they might not want them. If they don't want them, what's going to happen to them?

Although I felt ready to get home, I decided to stay on the road to complete at least some of the New England survey. I called a WCQN member, Edjohnetta Miller, in Hartford, Connecticut, and she agreed to put me up and coordinate my visit there.

CONNECTICUT, JUNE 9–10, 1993

HARTFORD

EdJohnetta Miller (see p. 281) was born in 1945 in Spartanburg, South Carolina. She and her husband migrated to Buffalo, New York, in 1966,

Marian E. Brown.
SPRINGFIELD, MASSACHUSETTS, JUNE 1993 (FRAME 12, 2¼ CT)

Mr. and Mrs. Joseph Hudson and Laura Mae Hudson.
FORESTVILLE, CONNECTICUT, JUNE 1993 (35 MM CT)

and then to Hartford in 1972. Growing up, she saw two women quilt: her maternal grandmother, Ruby Johnson (1895–1985), who was also from Spartanburg and her father's brother's wife, Dora Fowler (b. 1928) from Greenville, South Carolina. Mrs. Miller is a professional weaver and silk painter, and she also collects quilts. Four years previously, through the encouragement of Carolyn Mazloomi, she had started quilting. She is now hoping to pass on the tradition to her daughter, Ayisha Kishili Miller.

I stayed the night with EdJohnetta's family, and the next day we photographed three quilters at a senior citizens' center (see p. 282). Blanche M. Nelson was born in Hartford, Connecticut; her parents had migrated there from the South. Dorothy Christie was born in 1927 in Hartford, Connecticut. She learned to quilt at age eight or nine from her mother, Eva Matthews Mendes (1900–42), who was from Fort Gaines, Georgia. Her mother migrated to Hartford where she met Mrs.

Christie's father, who was from the Cape Verde islands off the northwestern coast of Africa. Mrs. Christie also remembers seeing her mother's sisters and two aunts, Cornelia Dawson and Zora Snellings, quilt.

Hattie M. Henry (see p. 282) was born in 1921 in Edgefield, South Carolina. Her family migrated to Washington, D.C., in 1930, where she grew up, and she migrated to Connecticut in 1969. As she describes her early memories of quilting:

> As a child in South Carolina, my mother, Catherine Jones Morgan (1895–1981), and her friends had a quilting bee that met at our home, and we had fun crawling under the quilting frame. But after we moved to Washington, that is when my exposure to quilting ended. When I retired from the federal government after thirty-six years of service, I wanted something to do that was creative. My sister Sallie Jackson, who lives in Washington and is a member of the Daughters of Dorcas quilting guild, suggested that I learn to quilt. I have been quilting since that time.

Arma Carter.
DORCHESTER, MASSACHUSETTS, JUNE 1993 (FRAME 4, 2¼ CT)

Margaret L. Penn (see p. 283) was born in 1939 in Paris, Kentucky. She migrated to New York City in 1957, and then to Hartford in 1971. Growing up, she saw her mother, Mary Penn (b. 1920), who was born in Richmond, Kentucky, and also her stepgrandmother and aunts quilting. She cherishes her family heirloom quilts. As she says, "I don't remember all the stitching that I see so much. They used to do only so much stitching and then they would tack it together, with all kinds of thread. So we used to be allowed to tack and cut the thread, that yarn-like thread or something."

BRISTOL

EdJohnetta took me to the Forestville section of Bristol, Connecticut, to meet Laura Mae Bufford Hudson. Mrs. Hudson was born in 1920 in Opelika, Alabama, and is part of a four-generation quilting chain. She learned to quilt from her mother, Willie Lee Bufford (1902–68), and grandmother, who were also from Opelika. At age fourteen, she made her first complete quilt. She remembers quilting bees where church and community people would meet at different homes in Opelika. In 1945, Mrs. Hudson migrated to Connecticut with her husband Joe, who was

Mabelle C. Barnette.
ROCKINGHAM COUNTY, NEW
HAMPSHIRE, JUNE 1993
(FRAME 5, 2¼ CT)

born in 1918 in Birmingham, Alabama, and who helps her quilt. Mrs. Hudson has taught all three of her daughters to quilt. In 1995, Mrs. Hudson received a $5,000 individual grant in the craft category from the Connecticut Commission on the Arts for her quilting (see p. 284).

MASSACHUSETTS, JUNE 11–12, 1993

SPRINGFIELD

The next morning I left Hartford and stopped in Springfield on my way to Boston. In Springfield, I photographed Marian Brown (see p. 284), born in 1921 in Lancaster, South Carolina. Growing up she saw her mother, Sally Brace Coleman, and her paternal grandmother, Lulu Coleman, quilt. She started quilting at age nine or ten.

BOSTON

Arma Carter (see p. 285), a WCQN member, was born in Empenada, California, and gave her age as sixty-two. As a young child, she moved in and out of Massachusetts with her military family, before settling in Boston as an adult. She remembers seeing her grandmother, other relatives, and neighborhood friends quilt. As she tells it, "I am a clothing and textile teacher, so when the scraps and small pieces of fabric were left, it seemed sacrilegious to throw them away—so I decided to make quilt squares and let my students make them into quilted tops and pillows. Then I started piecework of the long, skinny strips, which were later made into vests and skirt trim."

NEW HAMPSHIRE, JUNE 13, 1993

ATKINSON

From Boston, I drove north to New Hampshire, and stopped in Atkinson to photograph WCQN member, Mabelle Barnette. Mrs. Barnette was born in 1929 in Boston and she related:

> Growing up, I'm sure there was quilting going on in my community, but I had little knowledge of it, or what they call black quilts today. I don't remember any of my family quilting, but I'm now making a quilt for my grandson that has the African liberation colors in it—red, green, and black. I want to do another quilt about the diversity of black people and our experiences in this country, but I am bothered

by certain historical facts. When I start digging in my family background, I realize how difficult it must have been for Alex Haley to find his black roots, because as soon as you get back to slavery, you start finding these white men who are your great-grandfathers. It is very confusing, and it just makes you mad, and it also makes me appreciate Haley's research that much more. Too many of our people have lost their black roots, and society makes fun of us when we try to identify with Africa.

Mrs. Barnette migrated to New Hampshire in 1986 for "peace and quiet," and started quilting when she broke her leg around that time. "My daughter Celeste Barnette, who lives in Boston, is an excellent quilter, but she's not going to let you photograph her."

Francelise Dawkins.
GLENS FALLS, NEW YORK, JUNE 1993 (FRAME 13, 2¼ CT)

NEW YORK, JUNE 14, 1993

GLENS FALLS

From Atkinson, I headed to Glens Falls, New York, to meet WCQN member Francelise Dawkins. Francelise Dawkins was born in 1951 in Paris, France. She spent eleven years there in an experimental community for children of artists, monitored by art therapists. After marrying an American from Louisiana, she migrated to the United States in 1976. Of her mother, Hortense Thomas, who was born in 1924 in Baie-Mahault, Guadeloupe, in the Caribbean, she says:

> She was a prodigy. She was tailoring men's suits and had her own shop at the age of twenty. She migrated to Paris where I was born. When I came over here, my husband's mother, Mary Dawkins, who was born in 1907 in Monroe, Louisiana, gave us a quilt under which we sleep nightly. I am a textile collage artist, and I use free stitching, appliqué, and some quilting techniques in my work. I don't call it quilting, because they are so small. I am now teaching my children to do textile collage.

CONNECTICUT, JUNE 15, 1993

GREENWICH

I then returned to Connecticut to interview Mary Randall Scott in Greenwich. Mary Randall Scott, Esq., was born in 1941 in New York, New York. As she told me:

Mary Randall Scott, Esq.
GREENWICH, CONNECTICUT, JUNE
1993 (FRAME 9, 2¼ CT)

My introduction to quilting was quite serendipitous. While my Aunt Tess, with whom I spent long hours as a child, had been a dressmaker and tailor, I never learned to sew. I eventually learned to construct some garments and household items as a young mother but had never done needlework of any consequence, and had no interest in pursuing further involvement of any consequence. Several years ago, my newly acquired sisters-in-law (Jo Countley and Gwen Scott) came up to Greenwich from Philadelphia to visit and brought along materials for a quilted jacket. Although I was anxious to please and show my appreciation for their gesture, I was quite daunted by the task. What started as an apprehensive process (I had to find my sewing machine instruction book since I had forgotten how to thread the machine) turned out to be a turning point in my life. We layered the pieces together in what looked to be an unremarkable garment and to say the least I was less than impressed at what we had accomplished. Then the quilting began. I was awestruck by how the layers of cloth came alive under the foot of the sewing machine. What had been three flat layers of cloth just a few moments before took on a depth and a wonderful new dimension. It was as if I had entered another universe, one in which I could control line, form and dimension.

The need to learn more about this wonderful form was born. Greenwich High School offered a quilting class, but the beginning date was months away. Meanwhile I haunted fabric shops buying up remnants, bought what were possibly the few quilting books designed to discourage, rather than encourage a rank beginner, and floundered about waiting for the class to begin. One day I was in a local art shop when I came across a flyer advertising a workshop in reversible log cabin quilts given by Emiko Toda Loeb, and sponsored by the Silvermine Arts Center. I brought the flyer home and showed it to my husband John, and laughingly said that perhaps by next year I could attend something like this.

Several days later he told me that he had registered me for the class and that the information would be along shortly. I went to the workshop with much trepidation and while I'm not certain what I took away from that workshop, it confirmed for me the fact that I had found a new focus and that my life had changed forever. Since that time I have taken many, many classes including those given by Harriet Hargrave, Mary Mashuta, Joen Wolfrom, Elly

Sienkiewicz, Sherry Sunday, and others. Additionally, Emiko Toda Loeb, my first professional workshop teacher, who frequently travels between the States, Japan, and Europe and whose extraordinary quilts have appeared in many publications, is now a regular part of my learning experience. I attend an ongoing monthly class, presided over by Emiko, which is limited in number so that each person can develop their quilting identity and pursue new experiences in design, form, and color.

Quilting is a new focus in my life. Prior to my marriage almost six years ago, I had been practicing law in a small town in northern Connecticut. I had returned to school at mid-life, received my BA from Trinity College in Hartford, Connecticut, and then law school at the University of Connecticut. I had intended to continue practicing law once I had completely settled into my new marriage, home, and life. This new discovery, this quilting, came between me and a new law practice. Through this art form, I found all that I had been searching for as a means of a real connection to life, people, and community.

I find a deep satisfaction in color, form, art, utility, and beauty which cements the connection between man, God, and the universe. I had very good skills as an attorney and I helped solve the problems of those who sought my help, but there are many out there who can perform those tasks. I realized that somehow God had bestowed upon me at this time of my life a gift, a passion to attempt to create beauty as well as order. I know that my need and desire to make the life of those around me, as well as those whom I shall never meet, a source of positive fulfillment will be more perfectly accomplished by those objects which I create and share with others.

I truly believe that this new focus is the result of the wellspring of love, strength of character, spiritual depth, and sense of honor and purpose which dwells in my husband John. His very goodness has helped make my being a fertile ground in which to create and accomplish. At this moment, I have no idea as to whether the gift I have received is great or small, but whatever its dimensions, I shall seek to share it with others from day to day.

Charlotte McCane.
BERGEN COUNTY, NEW JERSEY,
JUNE 1993 (FRAME 18, 2¼ CT)

RIDGEWOOD

I left Greenwich, Connecticut, crossed New York and the Hudson River, and headed for Ridgewood, New Jersey, to meet another WCQN member.

Charlotte Antoinette McCane (see p. 289) was born in 1934 in Washington, D.C., where she grew up. Her mother was a Radcliffe graduate, and her father taught at Howard University. No one in her family quilted. As she tells it:

> In the late 1960s, many white communities were looking for black teachers. In 1969, through the urging of a friend I'd met on a trip to India via a Fulbright grant, I applied and was accepted for a job teaching history in Ridgewood, New Jersey. Inspired by a television program and friends, I started quilting a few years ago. In my teaching of world and U.S. history, I also decided to do a quilt project with my classes.
>
> I use quilting as a form of relaxation when I get home from work. And I also view it as a means for African Americans to tell their stories of struggle and their hopes for the future.

It was early evening as I left Ridgewood and headed south and home to Washington, D.C. It began to dawn on me how much I had accomplished over these months—and how much more had to be done to follow up on the many new leads that had been generated. I arrived home on Thursday, June 17, having driven a zigzag loop around America that covered roughly seven thousand miles.

CHAPTER 9
Filling In the Gaps
(1993-96)

While over the next month I reassessed the status of the project and prepared to move ahead, I realized how much I had left to do if the resulting touring exhibit and book were to be ready by late 1996. As museums plan their schedules two to three years in advance, both the book and the national exhibit had to be fully conceptualized now, even though I did not yet know where we would get the implementation funds. Also, when I reviewed my photographs and interviews from the cross-country trip and my prior work, there were still significant gaps—new places to visit, and others to revisit—but time and a lack of funds would limit what I could do over the next two and a half years.

Bessie Jo Jones.
ALLEGANY COUNTY, MARYLAND,
JULY 1993 (35 MM CT)

MARYLAND AND WEST VIRGINIA, JULY 1993

In the middle of July, Delton Allen—a friend and a former Peace Corps volunteer who had continued to live in the southern African country of Lesotho and work with development projects—was in Washington for a visit. He mentioned that he was on his way home to West Virginia for a few days, and after we discussed my project, he had his aunt arrange for me to meet quilters in western Maryland and West Virginia.

CUMBERLAND, MARYLAND

On the morning of July 21, Delton and I headed to Cumberland. There we met Bessie Jo Harriston Jones, who was born there in 1934. At the age of five, she went to live with her aunt and uncle, and she first saw quilting when her aunt Violet Harriston took her to a Pentecostal church. As she told me, "When my aunt died in 1986, I moved here to Cumberland. I've been quilting for about twenty years. A whole lot of people ask me why don't you get a sewing machine, but I'd

Left to right: Nellie Redmon and her daughter Carol Thomas.
FISHER, WEST VIRGINIA,
JULY 1993 (FRAME 13, 2¼ CT)

rather do with my hands because it's coming from my heart and my soul. Because the Lord gave me that talent to do. He didn't give me no machine or anything like that."

FISHER, WEST VIRGINIA

We then headed to West Virginia to meet Nellie Redmon, who was born in 1929 in Wheeling, West Virginia. Her family moved to Fisher when she was about one. As a young girl, she remembers tacking quilts with her mother, Freda Spiller Gilmore (1898– 1991), who was born in Petersburg, West Virginia. Her mother had learned to quilt from her mother, Nellie G. Spiller (1858–1946). She said, "I'm retired now and I've been quilting about twenty-five years. I just make plain quilts like my mother did, nothing fancy. I make up a bunch of tops and just tack them together. I taught my daughter Carol Thomas (b. 1951) to quilt, and she is teaching her special education students how to make quilted pillows."

KEYSER, WEST VIRGINIA

The next day I went to Keyser, West Virginia, to meet Mrs. Winnie N. Hollingsworth. She was born in 1936 in Piedmont, West Virginia, and moved to Keyser when she was married. She said:

> When I was a little girl, there weren't that many cars, and we didn't travel that far. I never remember seeing my mother or any of my neighbors quilt. But I did see quilts that were made by my maternal grandmother, Winnie Watts [1880–1945], who I was named after, who was from Davis, West Virginia. My mother's brother's wife had several quilts in her family and she was not interested, so she gave them to me. And I found several quilt tops in a drawer at my mother-in-law Mary Smith Hollingsworth's house after she had passed, and they had been pieced by her mother, Anna Beckwith [1897–1977], who was from Petersburg, West Virginia. I learned to quilt when I joined an extension homemakers club at the age of forty, and I've taught my daughter to quilt.

NORTH CAROLINA, JULY AND AUGUST 1993

HILLSBOROUGH

After a stop in Cincinnati, I proceeded toward Hillsborough, North Carolina. Upon my arrival, I checked into a motel, and made some calls to set up my photo shoot for the next morning.

Grace W. Mack (McMannen) is the maternal grandmother of Owen Justice whom I had photographed in Las Vegas with some of her quilts (see pp. 216 and 220). Born on March 15, 1893, in Hillsborough, Mrs. Mack moved to Durham County after she was married. She learned to quilt from her mother, Mollie Wilson Watlington (1858–1943), her maternal grandmother, Nannie Wilson Roundtree (1835–1914), and her aunt Emma Halls, all of whom were from Hillsborough. She and her husband, John Wesley McMannen, raised thirteen children, six of whom were girls, and she taught all the girls to quilt. Four of them joined us for the photo session (see p. 294). I was particularly struck by the gentle, loving way these women went about preparing their mother and her room for this photograph. I made some test shots so they would be fully aware of how the photograph would look, and after examining it carefully, they agreed that even though their mother didn't look her best, they wanted her to be part of my project. Mrs. Mack was more than one hundred years old when I photographed her. She had enjoyed quilting until ninety-five years of age, with the help of her daughters, and had made quilts for all of her children, grandchildren, great- and great-great-grandchildren. Seventeen days after the photo session, on August 12, 1993, Mrs. Mack passed away quietly in her sleep.

Winnie Hollingsworth.
MINERAL COUNTY, WEST VIRGINIA, JULY 1993 (FRAME 14, 2¼ CT)

CREEDMOOR

On August 3, I went to Creedmoor, to photograph Ruth Grissom Bullock (see p. 295), the grandmother of Leonard Satterwhite, whom I had met in Colorado Springs back in April 1993. Mrs. Bullock, who was born in 1911 in Granville County, North Carolina, is a third-generation quilter. Her maternal grandmother, Lucy Green Harris, passed the tradition on to Ruth's mother, Maggie Harris Grissom (1887–1977), three of whose daughters still quilt: Lucy Grissom Ferrell, who lives just south of Raleigh; Norsey Grissom Herbert (b. 1918), who lives in Franklinton; and Mrs. Bullock. Mrs. Bullock said that she learned from her mother, but her strongest quilting influence was her paternal aunt, Nancy Grissom Mayo (1885–1988), who died at the age of 103. Nancy was a prolific quilter who gave quilts to everyone in the family, and left a house full of quilts in Wake Forest when she died. This

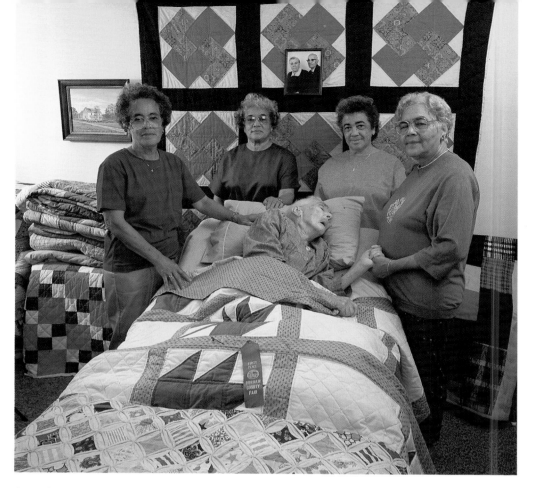

Center: Grace W. McMannen (1893–1993) surrounded by four of her daughters, all of whom she taught to quilt. *Left to right:* Pearl M. Holman, Ruth M. Pridgen, Juanita Shaw, and Ollie M. Roberts.

ORANGE COUNTY, NORTH CAROLINA, JULY 1993 (FRAME 6, 2¼ CT)

aunt, Ruth's mother, and her sisters made so many quilts that the next generation feels it doesn't have to make any. Ruth says:

> Quilting means a whole lot to me. See, when you're lonely, you sit and quilt and it brings a lot of joy to you. And that helps somebody. When you give your grandchildren, or give your great-grandchildren, or give some lonely person a quilt, that brings joy to you. You know you're doing something for somebody else. I got four children, sixteen grandchildren, and eight great-grandchildren, and I've made quilts for all of them. And I just keep on quilting, so when they have more children, I'll have plenty of quilts to keep them warm.

VIRGINIA, AUGUST AND OCTOBER 1993, JUNE 1994

HAMPTON

On August 5 and 6, I photographed several Hampton quilters (see p. 296). Lillian W. Lovett was born in 1930 in Lynchburg, Virginia. In 1934, her family migrated to Newport News, where she was raised and has

Ruthie Grissom Bullock.
DURHAM COUNTY, NORTH CAROLINA, AUGUST 1993 (FRAME [5-6], 2¼ CT)

lived ever since. Neither of her grandmothers quilted, and her mother only crocheted. Mrs. Lovett is the director of Newsome House in Newport News, which is a restored Victorian-period home of a prominent African-American attorney and newspaper editor, now listed on the State and National Registry of Historic Sites. Among other activities, the Newsome House has sponsored the African-American Quilters Guild of Hampton, Virginia since 1993. The Guild got its start from a quilting workshop that Mrs. Lovett arranged and joined during Black History Month of that year. The Guild had its second quilt show in 1996 as part of the centennial celebration of Newport News.

JoAnne Newman Cramatie was born in 1950 in Newport News. Growing up she saw several women in her family quilt: her mother's father's mother, Annie Cecilia Bryant Hines (1872–1972), who was born in North Carolina; her maternal grandmother, Mattie Christine Newman (1913–71), who was born in Charles City County, Virginia; and two of Mattie's sisters. Mrs. Cramatie treasures several of her great-grandmother Hines's quilts and sleeps under them. However, as she says,

African-American Quilters Guild of Hampton, Virginia. *Clockwise from lower left:* JoAnne N. Cramatie, June C. Robb, Gwendolyn Brown-Sinclair, Lillian W. Lovett, Sandra F. Randolph, and Patricia W. Johnson.

YORK COUNTY, VIRGINIA, AUGUST 1993 (FRAME 8, 2¼ CT)

I started to quilt about a year ago because I have always thought that the art and needlework was beautiful. I am learning by trial and error. When I was a very young girl, I can remember trying to get those small stitches perfect. Now I wish that I had listened a little more closely. Perhaps now with my own quilting, my stitches would be better, but of course that is hindsight. Quilting is a very strong link to my past, and it has caused me to embrace my heritage a little more.

June Craig Robb was born in 1937 in Fort Smith, Arkansas, and moved from there to Williamsburg in 1956. As she relates her quilting background:

My playmate's grandmother was a quilter. She used scraps provided by a seamstress and old clothes. Additionally, ladies in my Methodist church in Fort Smith, Arkansas, were quilters, and in 1949 I saw them work on a quilted robe. As a fundraiser, a long robe was constructed to fit the pastor's wife. Donations were solicited, and a patch was made for each donation that was received. The money was placed on the robe and the patch was appliquéd [quilted] over the money. The robe became a "coat of many colors." It was very heavy. When the robe was completely covered with the patches, it was a quilted garment. Slits were made in the wrong side of the robe, and the money was removed so that the quilted garment remained intact.

Jeanette H. Anderson.
YORK COUNTY, VIRGINIA, AUGUST 1993 (35 MM CT)

I started quilting in March of 1993. I am a crafter and I love new and rewarding experiences. I have always wanted to quilt, but I didn't take on the challenge until my retirement. I am learning to quilt from information in quilting books, videos, and from people who quilt.

Sandra Frye Randolph was born in 1940 in Washington, D.C. She left in 1957 to attend Hampton Institute, and as she says,

I have never returned to live there permanently. I never saw anyone in my family or community quilting. I started to quilt in 1976 while in Germany, and I'm self-taught. I always admired the quilts that my grandmother Eugenia Jones Kerrick [1880–1982], who was

Loretta M. Craig.
NORFOLK, VIRGINIA, AUGUST
1993 (FRAME 1, 2¼ CT)

born in Tom Brook (known today as 'TB'), Maryland, had made, and I really enjoyed having them. Quilting is a wonderful hobby to me. I also view it as an art form—and I want to teach my grandchildren this art form.

Patricia W. Johnson was born in 1929 in Brooklyn, N.Y., and migrated to Hampton in 1980:

> I had never seen anyone quilt until I moved to Virginia and started going to craft shows and fairs. I started quilting in the early 1980s. I sew and became interested in quilted clothing. I also love collecting fabrics, and quilting is a good way to use unusual fabrics. I have taken lessons through the Golden Thimble Guild [another quilting group in the area], a craft gallery called On the Hill in Yorktown, and with Newport News Recreation. To me, quilting is a means of artistic expression. I have always wanted to be an artist. Painting, dancing—something! But I had no talent. Using fabrics as you use paints has really released whatever artistic skills I might have.

Born in 1933 in Clayton, Delaware, Gwendolyn Brown-Sinclair migrated to Newport News in 1956. There was no quilting tradition in her family, and Mrs. Brown-Sinclair did not become aware of quilts until 1980. She is a seamstress and craftsperson, but had considered quilting too time-consuming, and traditional patterns not that interesting. Upon discovering the story and pictorial genres of more contemporary quilting, she became inspired to quilt using a sewing machine. Since starting in 1993, she has made about four quilts per year.

Jeannette H. Anderson (see p. 297) was born in 1917 in Norfolk, Virginia, and remembers seeing her grandmother "tack" comforters. She learned to quilt at meetings of the Golden Thimble Guild.

Loretta M. Craig was born in 1940 in Suffolk, Virginia. "At the age of seven, I moved to Norfolk, although weekends and summers were spent in a rural environment where quilting was done. I am a third-generation quilter. My grandmother, mother, aunts, and many family members, and also neighbors, were quilters. In 1990, I started a quilting business as a revelation from God. My mother guided me through the quilting steps and told me the history of the pattern we used."

Moses B. Gordon was born in 1941 in Chesapeake, Virginia. When he was young, he saw his mother, Rena Silvers Gordon (1897–1965), quilt. In the late 1980s he decided to start quilting and is self-taught.

WILLIAMSBURG

In October, I traveled to Williamsburg to photograph a group of retired women who gather weekly to quilt and socialize. I had learned of these quilters from Joseph Cauthorn, whose mother, Pauline Cauthorn, belonged to the group and had seen my quilt exhibit at Hampton University (previously named Hampton Institute). Five members of this quilting group met at the home of Martha Graham for the picture (see p. 300).

Mrs. Graham was born in 1930 in Delco, North Carolina. Growing up she saw her mother, Virginia Fields Webb (1899–1981), quilt, and also an aunt, Viola Davis, but wasn't really interested herself. She and her husband and children migrated to Virginia in 1960. She started quilting with some church members and tried to start a group there, but it did not succeed. Soon after, a friend suggested trying to get together with some other neighbors, and this time a group gelled. They started working with some old blocks and gradually taught themselves. Mrs. Graham's husband, Brady, built the quilting frame that they use.

Moses B. Gordon.
YORK COUNTY, VIRGINIA, AUGUST 1993 (35 MM CT)

Pauline Daniels Cauthorn was born in 1936 in Wakefield, Virginia. Her mother, Rebecca Daniels (1913–82), who was from Surry County, Virginia, was a quilter. Mrs. Cauthorn's daughter Jean Brown Canaday (b. 1951) occasionally helps her quilt.

As a postscript to this visit, from April to August 1994, my quilt exhibition *More Than Just Something to Keep You Warm*, was at Hampton University as its last stop on the Quincentenary tour. I used one spot in the exhibit to feature a different local quilter each week, and as part of the interpretive component, we also held the first African-American Quilters Forum in the Tidewater area.

NIKKI GIOVANNI, CHRISTIANSBURG

On June 1, 1994, when I drove to Christiansburg to photograph the well-known African-American author Nikki Giovanni at her home there, her

Williamsburg quilting group. *Front (left to right):* Edna B. Haywood and Pauline Cauthorn. *Back (left to right):* Essie M. Edmonds, Ethel H. O'Farrow, Lucile Williams, and Martha W. Graham.

YORK COUNTY, VIRGINIA, OCTOBER 1993 (FRAME 8, 2¼ CT)

mother was visiting her (see p. 302). Ms. Giovanni was born in 1943 in Knoxville, Tennessee, and was reared in her father's hometown of Cincinnati, Ohio. I asked who were the first people she saw quilt when she was young:

> Actually, my grandmother. She didn't belong to a quilting bee, but she had friends who quilted. And I would say ninety percent of the blankets on my grandmother's beds were quilts. We always slept under quilts. I mean winter and summer. We had winter quilts and we had summer quilts. It's warm today, and about two or three weeks ago I had changed over to my summer quilts. Summer quilts are much lighter in weight. I don't ever find myself without a quilt on the bed. And of course I read and I have a dog whom you've met—her name is Wendy—and I will take that Alabama quilt that you saw, though it's heavy 'cause my feet are always cold, and I take that out on the deck and stretch out and wrap my feet up. And Wendy and I will sit on the deck in the sun.
>
> Now my mommy never did quilt. My grandmother, her name is Emma Louvenia, was born in 1890 or so, and she grew up of course as the quintessential housewife. As for me, I started to quilt when I was expecting Thomas—but I didn't know it was Thomas—when I was expecting a child. I'm very futuristic. So I said to myself, "If I have this child and everything is all right (which I sincerely hope it will be), what are going to be my responsibilities?" I thought, "Okay. You have to be a parent, but there's no school for parenting. But it's easy to figure out how to be a grandparent because grandparents—at least in my opinion—bake bread, make cobblers, and give you a quilt." So I thought I should really make a quilt because the quilt that I have, in fact, was made by my great-grandmother Cornelia Watson, whom we called Mama Dear, and my mother had given it to me.
>
> Now I remember my grandmother doing a number of things, but I don't have a recollection of her sitting and quilting per se. But she would tell me stories of her mother quilting, and I watched her repair things. But when I made my quilt, when I was expecting Thomas, I forgot the one thing that she had always stressed about it. She had laughed about people who messed up making quilts and had to start again, because you start at the center, not at the ends, and I had started this quilt that I made for my son at the ends.

I then asked her about how she started collecting quilts:

> I've always liked quilts and of course, if I had real money, I would have quilts from the 1820s, because all those 1820 quilts are basically African American. The mistress of the house did not sit around and quilt. Some of them are more beautiful than others, and you can see those that were quilted for the slaves and those that were quilted for the big house. But there's no question of who did the work. I mean, there's no question . . . it's the same thing with folk art. If you ever get over to the Rockefeller Folk Art Exhibit in D.C.,

Yolanda W. Giovanni and her daughter Nikki Giovanni discussing family heirloom quilts.

MONTGOMERY COUNTY, VIRGINIA, JUNE 1994

(35 MM CT)

almost any artwork that you see that's not signed is slave work. Of course you'd know that because you've studied the materials. A lot of people don't. "I wonder who painted that." I don't wonder who painted it; it was somebody black. A lot of that kind of work was simply done by black people who were not allowed to . . . they didn't own it, they didn't own themselves.

I asked whether she had ever written about quilts:

I have used quilts as a metaphor. That's because I have a line in a poem called "Hands" which is a poem I wrote for Mother's Day. It says, "Quilts are the way our lives are lived. We survive on the scraps, the leftovers from a materially richer society." Quilts are such a—what's the word I'm looking for— banner to black women. Because what they ended up taking was that which nobody wanted, and making something totally beautiful out of it. Making something in fact quite valuable. At least to this day. But that's like the spirituals. We took a bad situation and found a way to make a song. So it's a definite part of the heritage.

I then asked what quilting meant to her, and if she'd had any special experiences connected with quilts:

If I have a choice of a quilt or a non-quilt . . . you know how you go into somebody's house, and if you see a quilt on the bed or you see a quilt on the couch, you have a different feeling. I'm not saying that the lack of a quilt means that you think the person is a cretin, but you do have a different feeling. I don't like wallhangings—and I shouldn't be that way and it's not personal—but I'm not happy to go into a home and see quilts hanging from the wall. I think that they should be used. Which eventually means that they will be, I suppose, somehow used up. But one year my mother and I—I lived with Mommy for ten years while my dad was sick—one year Mother and I made a "frontier pot." I don't know if you know a frontier pot, but you start off . . . We had a vegetable stew or bean stew or something going, and then we started to add to it, and we realized we had been adding to this for like two weeks. So we just thought we'd see how far we could go with adding to it. So every time we'd do something else—we both like okra—so you boil your okra and you pour your okra, you know the juice is left, then you add to it and we kept it going almost all winter.

And I think of quilts the same way. So when the quilt I have, which you see is worn, when it finally dissolves, there will be a few pieces—and that would be a couple more generations presumably—what you hope is your great-grandchild will then say, "Well, I'll take these pieces from Grandma Nik's quilt, which she got from Mama Dear, and make another quilt and start the pattern all over again." It will be modern, I mean it will probably have materials we don't even know, because that quilt is 100 percent cotton—and you see quilts now they are going to have rayon in it, they are going to have linen, silk, you know, you do different things. But I think it's a nice thought to think that in [the year] 3000, a piece of a quilt . . . you know the quilt can survive if you use it. On the other hand, if you don't use it, what's the point of its survival?

I think quilting, in particular, teaches you patience. Because you can't do it in a hurry. There's probably nothing worse than a quilt that's machine-made. I don't even know how to say it; it just goes against the whole nature of a quilt. Why would you do that? I mean, if you're good (which I am not) you're supposed to take a single thread, and you can really see those little stitches you can barely see. Mine was done with double thread. Mama Dear's was done with single thread, and that's good sewing. But it teaches you just to stop and think about all the little ways. But my house is a quilt. I mean you're sitting here, and I think if you could take the top off of it and photograph it, you know you could actually make this and anybody who looked at it would say, "Oh, that's Nikki."

LOUISIANA, SEPTEMBER AND OCTOBER 1993, FEBRUARY AND MARCH 1995

BATON ROUGE

On September 10, 1993, I flew to Mississippi for a speaking engagement and rented a car to photograph Daisy Anderson Moore in Baton Rouge. She was born in 1917 in Bastrop, Texas, and raised in Palestine, Texas. She migrated to Baton Rouge in 1953. Her maternal grandmother, Amelia Barnett (1846–1936), was born a slave in Alabama. As Mrs. Moore told her story:

> On the day the slaves was freed Amelia was about nineteen, and she belonged to a very mean master and he told her that she had to be off of his place by sundown. He told all of them that or else he was going to kill them. She had a little sister named Frances, about two, and she said she put her on her back and started walking down a dusty road and a white gentleman passed her and asked her where was she going. She didn't have anywhere to go so she told him that she would go and cook for him. He took her in

Daisy Anderson Moore, founder of the Red Stick Quilters.
EAST BATON ROUGE PARISH, LOUISIANA, SEPTEMBER 1993 (FRAME 8, 2¼ CT)

and she cooked for him until she met a man named Charlie Barnett. And she was a Barnett too, but they belonged to two different people because that was their slave name, and she married Charlie Barnett. And she had a large number of children but I only knew three, my mother, her brother, and her sister, because the others were all dead when I grew up. I was a sophomore in college when she died. She used to visit us every summer and she often told us stories about slavery. She even showed us some stripes on her back where she got whippings when she was a girl belonging to this master, as she called him.

Her husband, Charlie Barnett, ran the ferry across the Colorado River. Their home was on the banks of the river which runs down through Bastrop and Austin and all down that way east of San Antonio. And he ran the ferry for years until he died. My mother was her youngest daughter. My mother and father both finished high school in 1905. My sister has their high school diploma and it was a full accredited high school because she said the Northerners came down and set up Emile Academy, a training school there in Bastrop, and it had eleven grades, which was equivalent to what my high school had at that time. A lot of high schools didn't have twelve grades, but they

Georgia Farris (1891–1980), who taught Daisy Moore to quilt.
(PHOTO COURTESY OF DAISY MOORE. FA-10)

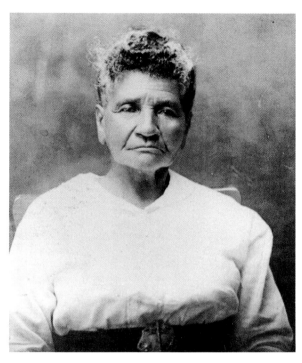

Amelia Barnett (1846–1936), Daisy Moore's grandmother.
(PHOTO COURTESY OF DAISY MOORE. FA-9)

got all their subjects in. My dad was a good mathematician and my mother had had physics, she had had math and all the courses that I have had. They graduated from high school in 1905 and married in 1909. My dad was valedictorian and my mother was salutatorian of their class. They had six daughters and two sons. The oldest was my brother Noland H. Anderson, who was a medical doctor. He practiced in Marshall, Texas, for about thirty years. My oldest sister is the only one who lives in Palestine today. All the girls are living, but my brother, who was under me, has passed now. And of the six girls, only me and my oldest sister Mary Anderson McClellan [b. 1912] quilt.

Now my mother, Lucinda Barnett Anderson [1885–1946], made quilts, but not consistently. I remember when my older brother got married, she pieced them a quilt for their wedding. But she sewed. She was a very good seamstress. The reason I say that is she made six girls' clothes all the time, and when we'd go to college she'd spend the whole summer sewing up our wardrobe for us to enter college. I had an aunt, my daddy's sister, Clara Pendergrass [1882–1962], and she made quilts—and each one of us who went to college she sent us a quilt to take with us.

Now, the way I got into quilting was, I lived next door to a lady when I was a little girl and she quilted all the time. Her name was

Georgia Farris [1891–1980], and she was a native of Palestine. Her daughter Asaline and I played dolls all the time, and Mrs. Farris would give us scraps to play with. And I always said when I get to be a lady like Mrs. Farris I'm going to quilt. Well, I had that in my mind when I first married, but when you have five children growing up and then in between working and teaching you never get to fulfill these dreams. Even before I retired I started making a quilt. That old red, white, and blue quilt you see. I did piece that when my first husband was overseas in World War II. As a girl, I was inspired by this lady that lived next door to me, Mrs. Farris, and when I went to see her daughter—whom I will see in October when I go to my high-school class reunion—she gave me an old quilt. She said, I think Mama must have made this when we were girls, and she also gave me a quilt top that her mother made. It was something about quilts that fascinated me. You may have read this book called *The Romance of the Patchwork Quilt*. I have read that book several times. I just enjoy reading that. It has nice little poems at the end. One I like very much has to do with the first patchwork quilt. It was the one that the robins made out of the fallen leaves. I've forgotten how it goes. I bought that book. It has about five hundred different patterns of quilts in it.

I've made something I call a "memory quilt," which has pictures on it. I wanted to make a quilt that would say something about me without my writing what meant a lot to me in my life, and the idea came to me to make a quilt. Each block in that quilt means something to me. First I think I said—I don't know where I started—but I love the state of Texas. Like they say, once a Texan, always . . . so I said I'll put a Texas map. I sat up in the science class and while the children were taking a test—I never will forget—I told a friend of mine I say, I was sitting up there designing my quilt, what I was going to put in each block, and I said I'll put my grandmother's, my mother's, and my dad's picture, so when I'm gone the children can see it and then they will know that my daddy chewed tobacco and he wore a polka-dot tie all the time. And then I wanted to say something about where I finished college and that's why I put Wiley [College] on there, and my high school. It finally boiled down to my sorority. They were just high points in my life.

And I used to love for my daddy—my daddy ran on the railroad for thirty-seven years, he ran from Palestine to Houston on the train and he'd come in every other day. He always brought two shopping bags of fruit. That's why I have that fruit on the quilt. The kids in the neighborhood knew he was going to bring fruit and we would be in the backyard playing, and we would go in the house and get these big plums and big peaches and things that we didn't have in Palestine. But there was a farmers' market, he said, near the railroad station in Houston and he would buy two big sacks of fruit, and we'd give all the neighborhood children some of the fruit that he bought. And that stood out in my mind and that's why I put that fruit there on that quilt.

Oak Alley Plantation near Vacherie, from the River Road levee on the Mississippi River, south of Baton Rouge. Oak Alley was built in 1837–1839 by Jacques T. Roman's craftsmen and slaves. This fine example of Greek Revival architecture is famous for its "alley" of twenty-eight evenly spaced live-oak trees believed to be at least one hundred years older than the "Big House."

ST. JAMES PARISH, LOUISIANA, OCTOBER 1993 (35 MM CT)

Now the pink and green quilt is my Alpha Kappa Alpha quilt. We were the first Negro sorority organized on Howard University's campus. I have three sisters that are AKAs, so including myself, that makes four. My three daughters are AKAs and I have five or six AKA nieces at the last count. When I made the quilt, fourteen members of my family were AKAs, but since then my granddaughter finished Grambling and she's an AKA, and then I had another little niece to finish Prairie View and she's an AKA. I have to put their names there but I have all the members of our family that are Alpha Kappa Alpha women. But I have one little niece that's a Delta and her mother is an AKA.

I then asked Mrs. Moore if she ever felt anything special sleeping under her quilts and she answered:

Well, with my memory quilt, I feel a kind of spiritual connection when I sleep under it, with my mother. I feel like, it just brings her closer to me, and the fact that she is still here in spirit, that's the way I feel. I get a gratification out of knowing that I made this just like other pieces of art. I like to make things and I guess that's why I'm always dabbling in different forms of art. And I certainly enjoy giving them to my grandchildren. My little granddaughter in Shreveport has two, and the one that finished Grambling has the *Colonial Lady* I did for her when she finished high school. I said, now don't let anybody have these quilts. And my little grandson's going to get (he's eight)

Gladys Wicker *(center)* with two of her sons, Charles C. Wicker *(left)* and Larry E. Wicker *(right),* both of whom she has taught to quilt.

EAST BATON ROUGE PARISH, LOUISIANA, OCTOBER 1993 (FRAME 3, 2¼ CT)

that quilt with the little jean overalls. I'm going to try to get it quilted before Christmas. It's a certain legacy that goes along with handing things down like that. I didn't have anybody to do it for me but I hope they will. I hope they will keep it.

Mrs. Moore has also started a local group, the Red Stick Quilters. I asked her to tell me about that:

> Well, I just decided after I retired from teaching in 1984 that I liked quilting enough and I wanted to interest others in the art and so I contacted a few ladies. About five or six of us got together and I think in all there were about ten of us and we decided that we would just quilt, make quilts for our-selves and for our children and socialize while we were making them. Quilting has helped me greatly to adjust to the idea that my husband is gone, and that my only son followed him in death only five months later. I don't know what I would have done if I didn't have my quilting to focus on.

OAK ALLEY

In October 1993, folklorist Joyce Jackson and I went to meet several of her first cousins who were male quilters. Joyce teaches at Louisiana State University in Baton Rouge, and after picking her up there, we continued to Oak Alley Plantation (see p. 307) across the Mississippi River. All day long, I'd been envisioning myself shooting from the top of the levee with the evening sunlight shining through these stately oak trees—and with quilts hanging over the fence on each side of the entrance gate. My last visit to Oak Alley had been on a dreary, cloudy day, and I had been very disappointed then that there was no Spanish moss draped from the branches of the grand oak trees that lined the driveway to the plantation house. Much to my amazement, on this day the whole scene had changed.

As we drove up, the first thing I noticed was that the fence and gate I remembered were gone. Also, the high bank of the levee from which I had planned to shoot was full of transplanted sugar cane, and on the river side of the levee, people were hard at work building an old-fashioned dock—complete with barges loaded with bales of cotton! I soon learned that this site was to be one of the settings for the movie *Interview with the Vampire,* and Hollywood had changed everything, including putting Spanish moss back on the trees. I told Joyce I hadn't come this far not to get my picture, and just then spotted a crew of men. Much to Joyce's surprise, I directed them to put back the fence and gate so I could make my photograph— and they did—assuming I had some kind of authority!

ZACHARY

The next day, October 12, Joyce and I drove back up to Zachary to see her aunt, Gladys Wicker, who told us, "I taught all my children to quilt. The girls have all moved away." But she added, beaming with pride, "All my boys built their homes right here." Two of them, Larry Ellis Wicker and Charles C. Wicker, who still quilt, came to be photographed with their mother.

Anna Williams Jones.
EAST BATON ROUGE PARISH,
LOUISIANA, FEBRUARY 1995
(FRAME 11, 2¼ CT)

BATON ROUGE

I returned to Baton Rouge with Joyce in February 1995 to document quilter Anna Williams Jones. Although we had tried to meet her on each of my previous trips, she had not been available. Finally, on February 9, 1995, we were able to catch up with her. We arrived at Mrs. Jones's home at about 6:30 P. M. She had just come in from work, and warned us that she was tired and wouldn't be long for the bed.

Anna Williams Jones was born in 1927 on the Kleinpeter plantation (a dairy and farm) in East Baton Rouge Parish, Louisiana. She is a third-generation quilter, having learned from her mother, Mary Rose Johnson Williams (?–1980), and her maternal grandmother, Othelia Johnson (?–1949), both of whom were also born on the Kleinpeter plantation. As Mrs. Jones said:

> We all worked on the plantation. We bagged Irish potatoes, sweet potatoes, picked strawberries, peanuts, corn, cut a lot of cane, and picked a lot of cotton. My mother, sister, and me used to pick about nine hundred pounds of cotton a day, and between the age of eight and ten I could pick about one hundred pounds myself. In the evenings, my grandmother and mother would make a lot of patch-work quilts out of old pants. And then we'd have these quilting

bees. We'd go from house to house, all twelve of them in a row. They were good times, laughing, joking, and eating. I used to do those kinds of quilts until I left Kleinpeter at nineteen years old with my husband, who was in the service. We traveled all over the place, but I got lonely for home and came back.

I do mostly housework around these parts, and I've been working for Katherine Watts for thirty-some years. You see, it's like this. I was telling her about my quilts, so she told me to bring some so she could see them. And when I did, she bought them from me. She'd give me $25 to $40 for each one. And then this lady Nancy Crow came and saw my work, and after that they started getting my exhibits everywhere. Mrs. Watts, she handles all of that for me, and when she sells quilts she puts my share of the money away for my retirement. Now I'm just inventing all kinds of new designs with my string quilts. I do the tops and Mrs. Watts gets her friends to quilt them. She's now writing a book about me, and sent a white photographer. That man photographed every room in the house, the hallway and all. I can't wait to see this book they're doing on me.*

I asked Mrs. Jones if she had made any quilts for her children. She answered, "My daughter Mary Louise Ringo, who lives in Texas, had been wanting to come to one of my exhibits." Joyce then interrupted to explain, "In the early 1990s, we brought the Smithsonian traveling exhibit *Black Women: Achievement Against the Odds* to Baton Rouge at the Louisiana State Archives Building, and we added a component to honor black women in Louisiana. Since I was handling the folklife section, I contacted Mrs. Watts and arranged to include Mrs. Jones's quilts." Mrs. Jones continued, "My whole family was so proud, and my daughter went out to Mrs. Watts's house to get one of my quilts to take home. I reckon when I die, my part of the quilts that's left will go to my family, and my seven boys can get some of them. Mrs. Watts takes every one I make now, 'cause we need them for all these shows she's having. And she told me, if anybody comes to my house trying to buy one, don't let them have it."

CLOUTIERVILLE

In late March 1995, on my way to Mississippi for the eighth Annual Quilt Contest and Exhibition in Port Gibson, I stopped in Cloutierville to follow up on two previous visits to the Melrose Plantation, in west-central Louisiana on the Cane River, south of Natchitoches. This is the same plantation where folk artist Clementine Hunter once lived, but

---

* Katherine Watts, *Anna Williams: Her Quilts and Their Influence* (Paducah, KY: American Quilter's Society, 1995).

Clementine Hunter's quilt. Mrs. Hunter (1887–1988) was a world-famous folk painter and a quilter, whose home was on the Melrose Plantation where she lived and died.

NATCHITOCHES PARISH, LOUISIANA, FEBRUARY 1995 (35 MM CT)

what most fascinated me was that it was established by an ex-slave named Marie Therese Coin Coin.

The following is based on information provided at Melrose. In 1742, Marie Therese was born a slave into the household of St. Denis, first commandant of the post at Natchitoches. Over the years, she had fourteen children, four of whom were black, the remaining ten of Franco-African lineage. Her son Augustin is the "grandpere" through whom Cane River descendants trace their ancestry to her. After the deaths of St. Denis and his widow, Marie Therese and her Franco-African children were sold to Claude Thomas Pierre Metoyer, a Frenchman who may have been their father. In 1780, Metoyer freed her and eventually her children, and deeded her a small grant of land. A larger grant on Old River was deeded to her from lands held in the name of the Spanish king; and, in 1796, her son Louis was granted what is now Melrose Plantation, which presumably Marie Therese held for him until he was free and thereby permitted to own property.

Melrose historian Francois Mignon wrote in his *Plantation Memo*, "Among other sterling attributes, Marie Therese was endowed with

Cane River Creole Quilters. *Seated (left to right):* Rosaline Metoyer, Rosalie Wright, Alberta Byone, and Adlitha Bonnette. *Background:* Elizabeth R. Metoyer.

NATCHITOCHES PARISH, LOUISIANA, MARCH 1995 (FRAME 13, 2¼ CT)

unusual energy and intelligence. This resourceful woman, her sons, and her slaves worked valiantly, clearing the land, cultivating tobacco, corn, and other crops, raising cattle, to achieve a successful plantation operation."* Marie Therese did not forget her black children. This remarkable woman worked to purchase the freedom of two of them and at least one of her grandchildren. She lived past the age of seventy-three, to see her grandchildren prosperous and living good lives.

By the early 1800s, her son, Augustin Metoyer, had become one of the wealthiest men in Louisiana, an incredible accomplishment for a black person at that time. He founded St. Augustine Church in Isle Brevelle, Louisiana, which I believe to be the only Catholic church in the United States that was founded, independently financed, and built by people of color for their use. In June 1803, in a letter to a friend after his return from a trip to France with his father, Augustin wrote: "In one way or another, I am sure that having a house of God in our midst, our people will live a better life." He engaged the services of his brother Louis, an accomplished builder, to construct the church on land that he donated. It was completed before the end of 1803, and named in honor of his patron saint. The church became a center of communal activity and a haven of religious and cultural stability. Its expressed purpose has never been relinquished, and it remains, nearly two centuries later, the nucleus around which the community draws inspiration and spiritual sustenance—and the majority of the creole families who attend St. Augustine Church today claim descent from Marie Therese.

On my earlier visits to Melrose Plantation, I had photographed the home and quilts made by Clementine Hunter (see p. 311), and the "African house" (c. 1800), which was the slave-fort and provision house of the plantation. Its lower story is of brick baked on the place, while the upper story is fashioned from thick hand-hewn cypress slabs. The walls of the upper story are entirely covered with Clementine Hunter's creations. I had also photographed a small group of the direct descendants of Marie Therese in the dining room of the plantation home, which was begun by Louis Metoyer and completed by his son in 1833. This was my third visit, and I was there primarily to photograph five area quilters at the home of Elizabeth R. Metoyer, one of these descendants.

Elizabeth R. Metoyer was born in 1963 in Pineville, Louisiana. She learned to quilt from her mother, Lillian Coutee Rachal (b. 1932), who is from Saline, Louisiana, and her maternal grandmother, Mary Metoyer Coutee (b. 1911), who is from Cloutierville. Mary Coutee was also a master seamstress and was able to create patterns by herself. Mrs. Metoyer started to quilt at age fifteen when she took a job working at the Community Service Center, where older ladies in the area would come together for quilting bees.

* Reprinted from "Melrose Plantation Homes, Melrose, Louisiana," a handout given to plantation visitors.

Left to right: Fannie Lee R. Chaney and Ruth Howard Chambers. Mrs. Chaney is the mother of civil rights worker James Chaney (portrait on the left), who was murdered in Mississippi in 1964 with two other men, Mickey Schwerner and Andrew Goodman (picture of all three on the right).

NEW YORK, NEW YORK, SEPTEMBER 1993 (FRAME 16, 2¼ CT)

Rosaline L. Metoyer was born in 1912 in Ward 10, Little River, near Cloutierville. She was born and raised on land that had been in the family for generations, at least as far back as her grandmother Cephalide Metoyer, who died in 1894, and was a direct descendant of "Grandpere Augustin." She learned to quilt from her mother, Cecile Rachal Lacour (1881–1964). Since the 1970s Mrs. Metoyer has demonstrated quilting as part of the annual tour at Melrose Plantation, which takes place the second Sunday each October.

Rosalie Coutee Wright was also born in 1912 at Little River. She learned to quilt from her mother, Mary Louise Bayonne Coutee (1889–1980), and her maternal grandmother, Mary Agnes Bayonne (1850–1943).

Adlitha Coutee Bonnette was born in 1933 in Mamou, Louisiana, and her family moved to Cloutierville when she was a baby. She learned to quilt from her mother, Rosalie Coutee Wright (see above), and started piecing quilts as a teen. She also remembers seeing quilting bees at her grandmother Mary Louise Coutee's house. After her marriage, she became very involved in quilting. So far, her two daughters have not shown any interest in learning this family tradition.

Alberta Byone was born in 1926 and is a native of Cloutierville. While growing up, she saw family members quilting and learned to quilt at the age of ten from her grandmother.

NEW YORK CITY, SEPTEMBER 24–25, 1993

Worth Long had told me that Fannie Lee Roberts Chaney, the mother of James Chaney, one of the three civil rights workers who had been killed in Mississippi in 1964, was a quilter, and was currently living in New York City. He put me in touch with Ruth Howard, who in the 1960s had worked with the Student Nonviolent Coordinating Committee (SNCC), who in turn arranged a meeting. I scheduled some additional documentation for New York, and on the morning of September 23, I left Washington for what I anticipated to be my final trip to New York for the project.

Fannie Lee Roberts Chaney was born in 1921 just outside Meridian in Lauderdale County, Mississippi. Her maternal grandmother, Mattie

Culbert, quilted, and she in turn taught Mrs. Chaney's mother, Kelly Culbert Roberts (1892–1957). As Mrs. Chaney says:

> I helped Mama quilt more times than a little, and I think I made my first quilt when I was about eight. Mama and Aunt Lucy would make all kinds of patterns—Bird Nest, Nine-Patch, Eight-Patch, Spinning Wheel, and sometimes just squares. I've had ten children, but only four are living, and none of them quilt. But I've been teaching friends of mine, like Ruth Chambers, to quilt. I first met Ruth when the Civil Rights movement was in Mississippi during the early 1960s, but I didn't really get to know her well until I moved to New York, which was after my son James Chaney was killed.
>
> He was murdered in 1964 with those two white boys, Mickey Schwerner and Andrew Goodman. That's them in the picture over my sofa. After they murdered my son, they wouldn't stop threatening me and my family. It got so bad I couldn't live there anymore. They were calling me, telling me what they were going to do to me and my other kids, and I couldn't get a job there anymore. Nobody would hire me. They went so far as to desecrate my son's grave, and they continue to do so until today. So then the Goodman family helped me move up here in 1965.
>
> My youngest son, Ben, was twelve when James was killed, and he took it really hard. Seems like to me it made him grow up too fast. He felt like he wanted to take his older brother's place, and tried to get into everything he could, which eventually landed him in jail in Florida. It was right after that when Ruth started coming to my apartment. Him being in jail down there in Florida upset me so, I went to quilting steady to help settle my mind. Then I started selling quilts to help pay for my trips to Florida. Making those quilts I was just thinking about going to see him and thinking about how to get him out and who to see, who to talk to, whatever. I'd just sit up here at night and quilt. It helped my mind, looks like, to not be just always thinking about what to do for him—it gave me something to keep me together. Now I'm teaching Ruth to quilt like I was taught. My mother, aunt, and sisters were all quilters, but it looks like now I'm the only one in the family that is really keeping this quilting going, and I'll do it as long as I'm able.

Ruth Howard Chambers was born in 1942 in Washington, D.C. As she explained:

> My maternal grandmother, I believe she quilted, but I don't have any quilts of hers. My mother doesn't really have any today. But my father's mother quilted, and I have some of her quilts. In fact I have a top that my father's mother made, and Mrs. Chaney then quilted. As Mrs. Chaney told you, I got interested in quilting in the early 1970s when I started visiting her regularly. I guess I finished my first one around 1975. I don't have any children, but I'm making quilts for all my nieces and nephews. Quilting relaxes me. I find that I

don't have a drive to make a lot of quilts, but I enjoy fabric. I used to work with clay and make pots, but when I started teaching in the public schools in 1983 I stopped working with clay. And that's when I really started piecing more.

In December 1992, I had photographed six members of the New York chapter of the Women of Color Quilters' Network at Peggie Hartwell's apartment. Since that time, I'd heard from several other quilting groups in New York who wanted to be included in the project, so I contacted Peggie and Valarie Jean Bailey. They agreed to coordinate a photo session of all interested African-American quilters in and around New York City, and prepared a handsome and informative flyer about my project. And so we met on Saturday, September 25, at the National Black Theatre in Harlem. Forty-one people showed up—thirty-nine women and two men. Some of them were members of more than one of the six groups represented: the Ebony Quilters of Southeast Queens; the Empire Quilters of New York City; the Long Island Quilters Association; the New York chapter of the Women of Color Quilters' Network; the Quilters Guild of Brooklyn; and the Rockdale Village Quilters of Jamaica, New York.

Glendora Simonson was born in 1957 in Irvington, New Jersey. No one in her family quilted. As she says, "Two years ago in the fall of 1991, I took a class at a local adult school. Prior to this, I had explored many crafts and art media (painting, drawing, and silk screen). I also have thirty years of extensive sewing experience." Mrs. Simonson has taught and exhibited locally.

Olivia Betty Ford was born in 1920 in Asbury Park, New Jersey, and moved from there to New York City in 1945. She remembers seeing only one great-aunt quilt when she was young. "I started quilting in 1981. I had been sewing for myself for years, and quilting became a logical extension of sewing. After retiring from teaching, I had more time to follow this interest." She exhibits and teaches in the metropolitan New York area, and belongs to four quilting guilds. Her quilt *African Mosaic* is hanging on the left in the background of the photograph.

Ruth E. Gibson was born in 1915 in New York City. No one in her family quilted, but after retiring she joined an arts and crafts class and learned to quilt. She is a member of several local quilting groups.

Marguerite Hatfield was born in 1909 in White Plains, New York. After retiring, she joined a senior citizens' center and took a course to learn to quilt. She says, "It has filled so many hours that otherwise would be quite empty and lonely."

Ora M. Kirkland was born in 1918 in Orlando, Florida, and migrated to New York in 1943. As a child, she remembers seeing her grandmother

Forty-one quilters from six different groups in the greater New York City area gathered at the National Black Theatre in Harlem. *(Rows are listed from front to back.) Front row (left to right):* Peggie L. Hartwell, Diane Pryor-Holland, Quassia Tukufu, Lynn Carrington, and Judy-Lynne Peters. *Second row (left to right):* Glendora Simonson, O. Betty Ford, Hazel R. Blackman, Ruth E. Gibson, Marguerite Hatfield, Eulaine R. Cannon, Khary Holland (boy), Eugenia Kirnon, Wanda C. Young, Willa Jackson, Ora M. Kirkland, and Agnes B. Morris. *Third row (left to right):* Karima Tawfiq, Maureen Wallace, Geraldine M. Hazel, Emma E. Green, Dorothy Desir-Davis, Sylvia Hodge, M. Elizabeth Williamson, Aline V. Moyler, and Djamillah Samad. *Fourth row (left to right):* Catherine White, Agnes Tuitt, Doris E. Prouty, Lethia Robertson, Winifred Sanders, Deborah St. Clair, and Carolyn D. Djokoto. *Fifth row (left to right):* Jacqueline Johnson, Carene W. Boykin, Carolyn Lewis, Lauren Johnson, Ruth Howard, Michael A. Cummings, Jennifer L. Johnson, and Valarie Jean Bailey.

NEW YORK, NEW YORK, SEPTEMBER 1993 (FRAME 1, 2¼ CT)

and mother quilt. She started to quilt in 1983 because "I wanted a beautiful handmade quilt, so I took classes and taught myself. It is a great hobby for anyone, but is especially good for retired people. Quilting is my mainstay. Except for the fact that I think quilts take on a life of their own, and they çan communicate with viewers, I've had no other spiritual experiences with them."

Karima Tawfiq was born in 1951 in New York City. She didn't see anyone quilting while she was growing up. "Because of a lifelong interest, I started quilting in 1987. I cherish a quilt made by my grandmother, who is from North Carolina." Ms. Tawfiq enjoys the camaraderie of the women in the quilt guilds to which she belongs.

Maureen Wallace was born in 1961 in Barbados, West Indies, and says, "I never did any quilting in my native country. After moving to New York, Mrs. Carolyn Lewis was the first to ask if I was interested in quilting. Seeing that I've always loved sewing, I found it to be very challenging."

Emma E. Green was born in 1941 in Waynesboro, Georgia. Her family left Georgia when she was a baby, and she knows of no quilting tradition. "I am the only member of my family who exhibits a need for self-expression through needlework. I started quilting about three years ago, and I am self-taught."

Aline V. Moyler was born in 1936 in Darlington, South Carolina, and belongs to two quilting guilds:

> My parents migrated North in the early 1940s for better working conditions, but my mother returned South to have her children. I don't remember seeing anyone in my family quilt, even though I'm told that it's a Southern tradition. I made one or two quilts in the early 1970s but they were poorly done. I only made them to use up scraps left over from sewing for my two daughters. I found myself the victim of a job merger and taught myself to quilt—with the help of books—in the winter of 1988–89. It's hard to say what quilting means to me. The word everything is inadequate. Creativity unleashed can't go back in the genie's bottle.

Djamillah Samad was born in 1952 in the Bronx. She knows that her maternal grandmother, Moriah Lee Crews (1874–1930), from Union Mills, North Carolina, quilted. She remembers that her paternal grandmother, Sarah Darkas Barber, from Waynesboro, Virginia (d. 1956), was a prolific quilter and made quilts for all of her nine children and many grandchildren. Ms. Samad teaches, exhibits, and is active in several quilting guilds. She said:

> I started quilting about five years ago, because of a dual interest in fabric and geometry. My skills are self-taught, with the help and stories from my parents whose mothers were both quilters. My

father's side of the family made quilts of newly bought material, whereas my mother's side made quilts out of used scraps.

For me quilting fulfills two needs: the soliloquy of my private thoughts and meditations; and the dialogue of experiences and solutions (both to life and sewing) of others. I can be alone *and* part of the greater picture at the same time within my quilting. Day to day I teach health, nutrition, and breastfeeding to young mothers, while pursuing a life in the ministry. My father's mother was a country midwife and a quilter. She died when I was about four. May the circle be unbroken.

Doris E. Prouty was born in 1947 in New York City, and moved to Gloucester, Massachusetts, in 1968 when she got married. Although still living in Massachusetts, she's a member of the New York groups—to which her two sisters, Carolyn Lewis and Lauren Johnson, also belong (see p. 322)—and came for the photo session. No one in her family quilted, but she has a Pineapple quilt that was probably made in the 1930s by her husband's grandmother. She started quilting after taking a class in 1978. "To me, quilting means quiet time."

Audrey Bland Howard (the spirit figure) at the grave of Ulysses Davis (1913–90), a master folk woodcarver, and his wife Elizabeth Davis (1917–84), a quilter. The quilt on the grave was made by Joseph White of Charleston, South Carolina.

CHATHAM COUNTY, GEORGIA, OCTOBER 1993 (FRAME 5, 2¼ CT)

Carene W. Boykin was born in 1940 in Charleston, South Carolina. Her family migrated to New York City in 1952. As a child, she vividly remembers watching community members making quilts at large quilting frames set up on their front porches. She added:

> I made three quilts about twenty years ago, for myself and my children, motivated by the challenge and accumulation of scraps from making our clothes. I am self-taught. A year ago, I bought a quilt from a department store for a few hundred dollars, which wasn't worth the price, and I returned it and decided that I could do better. I later took a course in Crazy quilting, and have been Crazy quilting since.
>
> I recently received a copy of my great-great-grandfather's will, dated 1887. Listed among the inventory and appraisement of his personal property, dated September 14, 1896, was "One lot quilts—$2.50." I was heartbroken. Where are the quilts? What happened to them? My legacy? I am very pleased to be teaching my nine-year-old grandson, Francois Espinosa, who was born in New York, to quilt at his request. He made three potholders by hand, and completed two

Mary Ann Mitchell (1887–1991), quilter, who was a cook and housekeeper on Pebble Hill Plantation for seventy-two years. Her quilts are under her family Bible. THOMAS COUNTY, GEORGIA, OCTOBER 1993 (FRAME 4, 2¼ CT).

rows of six-inch blocks for a twin-bed quilt, which I plan to finish for him.

I have been a passionate knitter for over thirty years, but never dreamed anything could take its place. (I also occasionally did needlepoint.) Quilting has! As I quilt, though, ideas for combining the two keep creeping up in my mind, so I'm sure in the near future there will be a quilted/knitted jacket or coat—wearable art—another form of quilting that I like. Why have I wasted all these years? There aren't enough hours in the day. I have a never-ending desire to quilt, quilt, quilt! I want to learn all there is to learn. It's a fascinating art, and I'm thrilled to be involved.

Winifred Sanders was born in 1932 in New York City. Her family migrated to New York from James Island, South Carolina. She was raised by two women on her father's side who were both quilters: her paternal grandmother, Delia Deas Smalls (1886–1980), who was born in Charleston, South Carolina, and her father's sister, Anna Smalls (1908–80), who died two days after her mother's burial. She says:

> Watching my grandmother, learning to quilt was natural for me. I am a dressmaker by trade, so I always have scraps of fabric on hand. It's a good way to use small pieces of fabric. I cherish a Yo-Yo quilt that my mother Mattie Chisolm Smalls [born in 1911 on James Island] made. I'm getting ready to return to my roots, and I'm moving back to James Island. I'm getting all the knowledge I can possibly acquire about quilting. I plan to make quilts, wallhangings, and pillows when I move to supplement my income. To me, quilting is a way of passing something on to my children and theirs.

Carolyn D. Djokoto was born in 1945 in Brooklyn, New York. No one in her family quilted, and she started in 1973. "I taught myself how to quilt. At the time, quilting was a natural extension of fashion arts and textiles. I have a home economics background with an emphasis on fashion design, tailoring, textiles, and costume history. By joining the two quilting groups, I am able to network with quilters frequently. I gain information, get ideas, as well as share my work and obtain valuable feedback."

Jacqueline J. Johnson was born in 1957 in Philadelphia, Pennsylvania:

> I did not know about quilting as a child, but while I was in college a friend from Detroit was laying out a quilt for a baby. She in turn

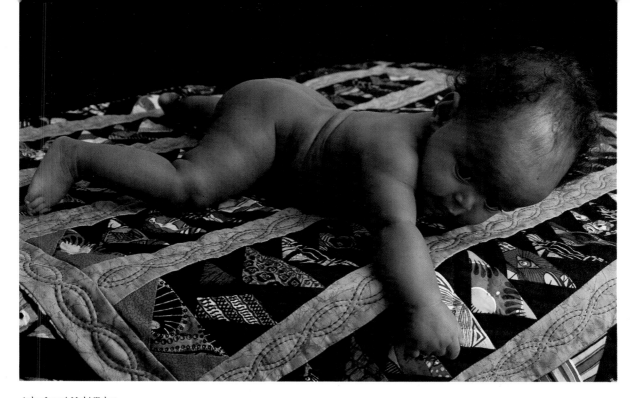

Asha Imari Haki Tyler.
FULTON COUNTY, GEORGIA, OCTOBER 1993 (35 MM CT)

Darlyne Dandridge *(left)* with her daughter Asha Imari Haki Tyler and Asha's father Thomas E. Tyler.
FULTON COUNTY, GEORGIA, OCTOBER 1993 (35 MM CT)

showed me what she was doing. I also remember seeing a quilt at my grandma's house, and it was an old North Star quilt. Later in 1983, I learned to silk-screen, and I made Adinkra cloth. One day, I had a piece left over and I decided to make a quilt. I didn't know what I was doing— but I made a baby quilt using the double-headed crocodile of the Ashanti. Since that time I've made baby quilts. In 1992, I also received formal training at the Quilters' Passion, and now I belong to several quilting groups. Being a cloth worker has made me an ambassador to people of all races and ages. Beauty to me is the common denominator, beauty of the quilt or cloth, and craft and skill. I meet so many people through quilting, it is incredible. Quilting and cloth work, like tie-dying, silk-screening, and needle-work, have given me the confidence I need to lift up my writing. I have learned they both feed from the same source, and my quilting helps the writing and vice versa.

Huisha Kiongozi.
FULTON COUNTY, GEORGIA, OCTOBER 1993 (FRAME 11, 2¼ CT)

Martha A. Dudley.
FULTON COUNTY, GEORGIA, OCTOBER 1993 (FRAME 11, 2¼ CT)

Carolyn Lewis was born in 1944 in Harlem, and around 1955 moved to Long Island City, New York. The quilting tradition in her family was begun by her and her two sisters, Doris Prouty (see p. 319) and Lauren Johnson, "I am a dressmaker and I thought it would be interesting to take up quilting. I learned from friends."

Lauren Johnson was born in 1946 in New York City. The tradition of quilting in her family is starting with her and her two sisters, Doris Prouty and Carolyn Lewis. As she says, "I started quilting as an adult. I made my first square at a workshop with my sister Carolyn. For me, quilting is a time to be with and share with other females, and it also produces a useful product."

GEORGIA, OCTOBER 1993

SAVANNAH

I began a couple of weeks of fieldwork in October 1993 in Savannah. First, I went to pay my respects to folk woodcarver Ulysses Davis (1913–90). Standing at his gravesite, I reflected on this remarkable man's legacy. He had owned and operated a barber shop in Savannah for more than fifty years, but he will be best remembered as a remarkable and prolific African-American woodcarver. At the time of his death, he still owned about ninety percent of all his artwork. One of his last requests was for a friend and cultural preservationist, W. W. Law, to keep his life's work together and in Savannah. In 1989, Dr. Ja A. Jahannes—an old friend and homeboy, currently a writer, psychologist, social critic, and minister in Savannah—had directed a project called, *Ulysses Davis, Roland Freeman, and the Documentary Process,* which had allowed me to come to Savannah and spend about a week and a half with this wonderful man. That January, I had spent ten intensive days photographing Mr. Davis and documenting his entire inventory of woodcarvings.

Back then I had inquired as to whether his wife made quilts, Mr. Davis said, "Well, Elizabeth don't make quilts anymore, but if you'd like to meet her, this is the day I go to visit." Right after lunch, he took me to the graveyard. Pointing to a double tombstone, he said, "Her body is resting here, her soul is in heaven, and her spirit is still with me." Her tombstone read, "Wife and Mother, Elizabeth W. Davis (1917–84)" and the adjoining one, "Husband and Father, Ulysses Davis, born June 3, 1913." Mr. Davis took his pipe out of his mouth and stood there in silence for a few moments. I stepped back and quietly made a photograph. That evening, he gave me one of her quilts.

Wanda G. Pierson.
FULTON COUNTY, GEORGIA,
OCTOBER 1993 (FRAME 1, 2¼ CT)

Now almost five years later, I had come again to this sacred place, where his body now also rested, and I could feel the presence of his spirit. I wished I had brought his wife's quilt as I wanted to make a photograph that expressed my reverence for these people and that would reflect a spiritual presence—and so I spent that evening and night creating such an image (see p. 319).

THOMASVILLE

Jerrilyn McGregory, a folklorist with whom I'd now periodically worked over the past decade, went with me to Pebble Hill Plantation near the town of Thomasville. Mary Louise Gilmore was born on this plantation, but had gone to work in New York City for most of her adult life. Now ailing and in a wheelchair, she had returned home. Mrs. Gilmore showed us a number of quilts made by her grandmother, Mary Ann Mitchell (1887–1991) (see p. 320). Mrs. Mitchell had lived her entire life at Pebble Hill Plantation, working as a cook and caring

Jannie C. Byrdsong.
FULTON COUNTY, GEORGIA, OCTOBER 1993 (FRAME 11, 2¼ CT)

Mr. and Mrs. Dorothy B. Williams and Robert Lee Williams, both quilters.
ORANGE COUNTY, FLORIDA, OCTOBER 1993 (FRAME 10, 2¼ CT)

for the owner's children. Mrs. Gilmore proudly showed me a photograph of her grandmother and a certificate of award she had received in December 1977 from the owner, Elizabeth Ireland Poe, for seventy-two years of loyal service at the plantation. And, as much as I have traveled around the South, I again was amazed at the persistence and strength of the bonds to these plantations that some African Americans still retain.

ATLANTA

Later that month, I went to Atlanta to meet Women of Color Quilters' Network member Darlyne Dandridge, who had arranged for me to photograph a group of quilters at her apartment. It was a pleasure to finally meet the friendly voice I had known only through telephone conversations. Darlyne Charlotte Dandridge, born in 1955 in Los Angeles, California, migrated to Atlanta in 1991 for a personal and professional life change. Though she saw members of her uncle's family quilt while she was growing up, Darlyne started quilting around 1985, largely through the influence of two women. The first was Ollie Douglas, then a ninety-two-year-old retired schoolteacher from Houston, Texas, who was the aunt of one of Darlyne's college friends. Darlyne had long admired the quilts Mrs. Douglas had made for this friend, and when she finally met her in 1985, she told her of her great fascination with them. Mrs. Douglas then had Darlyne buy some fabric, which she took back to Houston and with some friends fashioned into two quilts, which she sent to Darlyne in Los Angeles—charging only the price of the fabric, which was $35. When Darlyne protested and wanted to pay her more, Mrs. Douglas replied that she quilted only for the love of it and not for money.

Six months later, Darlyne met her second major influence, Carolyn Mazloomi. Carolyn was facilitating a quilting group in Los Angeles at the African-American Museum, which Darlyne joined as a novice; this involvement led to her later becoming a founding member of the African-American Quilters of Los Angeles (see p. 157).

While I was there, Darlyne was busy mothering her newborn daughter, Asha Imari Haki Tyler. I first photographed Asha on her baby quilt, and then, as Darlyne nursed her, both of them along with Asha's father, Thomas Tyler (see p. 321).

Rhonda Mason *(right)* with her quilt, and her husband Kenneth M. Sabia and son Kevin M. Sabia.
SEMINOLE, FLORIDA, OCTOBER 1993 (FRAME 16, 2¼ CT)

Huisha Kiongozi, a friend of Darlyne and another WCQN member, came over that afternoon with some of her quilts (see p. 322). Mrs. Kiongozi was born in 1960 in Los Angeles, California, and moved to Atlanta in 1990. Growing up she saw her mother, Geraldine Benson Jordan (1931–85), quilt. She started quilting herself in 1991 and learned from Darlyne. She has now started teaching her oldest daughter, Kamali Kiongozi, to quilt. She says, "To me, quilting means keeping the dream and craftsmanship of our great and talented foremothers and fathers alive with each stitch that is handsewn into scraps of fabric, making something more beautiful and strong out of it."

The next day I photographed Martha Ann Dudley (see p. 322), who was born in 1940 in Alexander City, Alabama. After living in Connecticut for one year, she married a noncommissioned officer and traveled with him over the next eighteen years, within and outside the United States. While growing up, Mrs. Dudley saw quilts made by her maternal grandmother, Copie Burns Meadows (1873–1958); she also saw her husband's aunt Ida Brooks (1903–77) quilt. Mrs. Dudley's mother, Harvey Meadows Justice (b. 1904), did not quilt but remembers seeing her mother, Copie, quilt. Mrs. Dudley related that Copie's mother, Mary Burns, was a white Pennsylvania

Left to right: Dorothy J. Johnson and Betty J. Carter.
HILLSBOROUGH COUNTY, FLORIDA, OCTOBER 1993
(FRAME 2, 2¼ CT)

Georgianna Linzy with her great-granddaughter Heather Breanne Williams.
STUCKY, FLORIDA, OCTOBER 1993 (FRAME 2, 2¼ CT)

Dutch woman who migrated to Alabama and married a Burns who was mixed white, Indian, and African American. Mrs. Dudley started quilting around 1983 after learning to sew and quilt through a college-level sewing course in California. She says that "quilting is the way I capture the creativity I dream." Although none of her own children quilt, she is very pleased that two of her son's daughters, Ami and Ashley Dudley, are learning to sew, and she hopes to pass the tradition on to them.

While in Atlanta, I also photographed two other quilters, Wanda G. Pierson (see p. 323) and Jannie C. Byrdsong (see p. 324).

FLORIDA, OCTOBER 1993

ORLANDO

Although I had completed some documentation in nothern Florida in 1990, including that of the Collinses (see p. 331), I wanted to build on what I had, and so made Florida a major part of my southern swing in October 1993. I started with Orlando, to meet quilters Dorothy B. and Robert Lee Williams (see p. 324), whom I had learned about in a newspaper article sent to me by Sherry DuPree, a friend and librarian in

Gainesville. Dorothy B. Thomas Williams was born in 1927 in St. Augustine, and soon afterward her parents migrated to Havana, Florida, where she was raised. She learned to quilt from her mother, Mayrosa Fulger Thomas, born in 1907 in Georgia, and her grandmother Rosetta Fulger Thomas (1862–1943). In 1976, she married and migrated to Orlando. She started to quilt at seven years of age. Now retired, she quilts with her husband, Robert Lee Williams, born in 1924 in Havana, Florida. As a young boy, he learned to quilt from his mother, Seresa Williams (1894–1954), who was also from Havana. He migrated to Orlando in 1951. As he says, "Quilting is something my wife and I enjoy doing together. We don't make anything fancy, just simple block quilts. I do the piecing on the sewing machine, and she does the tacking. It must not be many husbands and wives quilting together, because the newspaper *Orlando Sentinel* is always making a big fuss over us."

Fannie L. Rivers.
SUMTER COUNTY, FLORIDA,
OCTOBER 1993 (FRAME 9, 2¼ CT)

TAMPA AND SURROUNDING AREAS

From Orlando, I headed for the Tampa–St. Petersburg area, to the town of Seminole, to meet WCQN member, Rhonda Mason. Mrs. Mason was born in 1948 in Brooklyn, New York. Growing up, she spent her summers in South Carolina where she saw her grandmothers quilt. Both her paternal grandmother, Halyard Singleton (1890–1972), and her maternal grandmother, Caroline Girlee Breland Brabham (1886–1962), were from Ehrhardt, South Carolina. Rhonda's mother, Lizzar Brabham Singleton (b. 1919), also learned to quilt from her mother. Rhonda migrated to Connecticut in 1989, and then moved to Seminole in 1991, where her husband, Kenneth M. Sabia, became a hospital administrator. As she says, "In 1976, I began my first quilt, a Crazy Quilt, which I completed in 1990. I began to quilt seriously in 1988, taught by some Mennonite women. In 1989 when I moved to Connecticut, I spent a year refining my skills and the following year finding my 'quilting voice.' I find quilting a wonderful way to connect—with friends as we share in quiltmaking, with relatives, and with the past" (see p. 325).

That evening, Mrs. Mason invited two quilters from Tampa to come and meet me at her home. Dorothy J. Johnson was born in 1951 in Dade City, Florida, and migrated to Tampa in 1977:

> My mother, Dorothy Johnson [1918–51], who was a seamstress, died when I was born. She didn't quilt, but my two sisters and I

Wilma B. Stewart *(center)* with *(left to right):* Nyron L. Bradley, Jonathan E. Bradley, John D. Stewart, Andrako D. Bradley, Demetrius T. Anthony, Reginald Craig Bradley, and Andranique N. Bradley. Just as Mrs. Stewart retired and was preparing to travel with her husband, misfortune hit family members, obliging Mr. and Mrs. Stewart to care for these great-nieces and great-nephews.

ALACHUA COUNTY, FLORIDA, OCTOBER 1993
(FRAME 18, 2¼ CT)

inherited her sewing skills. Since my childhood, I have always done some form of needlework—sewing, knitting, crocheting, crewel, embroidery, needlepoint, and cross-stitch. In 1982, I tried quilting and fell in love with it. I have been quilting ever since. I am mostly self-taught, but have taken a few specialty classes over the years. Quilting has played and continues to play a vital role in my life. Since I started quilting, and especially since I joined the Quilters' Workshop of Tampa Bay, I have learned so much about life, other people, and myself. It's been quite an adventure. I have served as an officer in the Quilters' Workshop, in which I am the only African American among eighty members. Making the quilts and learning more about quilts and quilting has been fun!

Betty J. Carter was born in 1941 in Opelika, Alabama. Growing up, she remembers seeing two family members quilt: her paternal grandmother, Georgia Harper Stenson (1896–1961), and her paternal grandfather's sister, Elizabeth Tolbert (1902–92), both of whom were born in Orbin,

Alabama. She cherishes a scrap square quilt made by her great-aunt "Liz" Tolbert. Mrs. Carter explained, "In 1960 I moved to Syracuse, New York, and from there I moved to Izmir, Turkey, in 1978 for two years. While there I was going to learn quilting, but never did. In 1980 I moved to Tampa where I still live, and in 1990 a quilting friend, Joyce Kimbrell, encouraged me to learn to quilt."

GAINESVILLE AND SURROUNDING AREAS

From Tampa, I headed to Groveland where Mrs. DuPree had arranged for me to meet Georgianna Linzy (see p. 326). Mrs. Linzy was born in 1914 in Stucky, Florida, where she has lived her whole life. She learned to quilt from her grandmother. According to Mrs. Linzy:

Sallie Jones.
COLUMBIA COUNTY, FLORIDA,
OCTOBER 1993 (FRAME 14,
2¼ CT)

> Quilts are very good to use in big families with small children, because they can go through washings better than blankets. And they are warmer on cold nights. I can't quilt nowadays. I have arthritis in my fingers, because I am also a seamstress and dressmaker. I started sewing at a very early age, and made sewing my career. I taught my daughters to quilt and gave them all quilts. Lately my great-granddaughter Heather Williams has shown an interest in quilting, and I've been trying to show her how.

After spending the night with Mrs. DuPree and her family in Gainesville, we set out to photograph the paternal grandmother of Kenyatta Rivers, one of her church members. We would later photograph his maternal grandmother, Janie Moore, in Tuskegee, Alabama (see p. 338). We met his father's mother, Fannie L. Rivers (see p. 327), outside of Wildwood, Florida. Mrs. Rivers was born in 1915 in Dawson, Georgia. She is a fourth-generation quilter:

> Quilting in my family started with my great-grandmother Gertrude who was brought from Africa and sold in the slave market in Wilmington, North Carolina, to the Newkirk family. Gertrude had two daughters, Lizza and Alice, who was my grandmother. Alice had my mother, who was Emma Newkirk Crowley [1870–1969], and she was born in Shellman, Georgia, and taught me to quilt when I was a little girl. My family moved here in 1926, and I've been quilting ever since, making them for my children and grandchildren.

We then went to Micanopy to meet Wilma Bradley Stewart. Mrs. Stewart

Carrine M. Porter.
JACKSON COUNTY, FLORIDA, OCTOBER 1993 (35 MM CT)

was born in 1927 in Grouland, Georgia. About 1938 her family migrated to Florida, where they have lived ever since. Mrs. Stewart learned to quilt from her mother, Janie Bradley (1900–77), who was born in Claxton, Georgia. As she says, "My mother taught me when I was about eight years old. I learned to sew and also helped her with her quilting." She treasures a quilt made by her mother.

From Micanopy, we continued north to Lake City to meet Sallie Jones (see p. 329). Mrs. Jones was born in Hamilton County, Florida, and migrated to Columbia County when she married. She learned to quilt from her mother, Sophie Newsome Dye, who had sixteen children, and also from her many aunts, cousins, and other family members. As she told it:

> I started piecing quilts when I was about seven. I didn't quilt one up for myself until just before I married at eighteen, and ever since then I been quilting. And for my fifteen children, I make quilts and

Mr. and Mrs. Leola Collins.
JACKSON COUNTY, FLORIDA, NOVEMBER 1990 (35 MM CT)

just give them to them as they leave out. I had to have plenty of
quilts in the house. Now, I went to school up until I was sixteen,
but I didn't learn very much because my mother was sickly. You see,
I'm the oldest child. She wasn't sick a long time, but she was puny
after having all those children. She wasn't strong I say in a way like
the Lord made me. She was lucky to be around her people when
she had her children.

When you ask what quilting has meant to me, well I would say I
call myself a workaholic. See I used to do any kind of work I wanted
to do. If I wanted to cut yards, I got out and cut them. If I wanted to
cut wood, I went and cut it. If I wanted to dig me a place to plant, I
went and did it. If I wanted to put a window in or put some boards
on the house or whatever it needed, I did it. If I wanted to build
something, I did it. If I wanted to move everything around in my
house, I did it. But now, I can't do nothing. It aggravates me and so
now I've gone back to quilting full-time to keep my mind from
wandering. And then I just give them to my family or whoever else
needs them.

Bascom

In Bascom, following another lead from Jerrilyn McGregory, I met Carrine M. Porter, born in 1929 in Calhoun County, Florida (see p. 330). As she says, "I learned to quilt from my mother Mamie Pollock [b. 1909]. I always watched her quilt, and told myself if she can do it, I can too. She would give me the leftover scraps to put in my playhouse, so I took those scraps and sat down and put them together and made a baby quilt out of them. I started quilting at the age of twelve, and I've been quilting fifty-two years now."

Alabama, October 1993

Alberta and Gee's Bend

I was excited by the opportunity finally to photograph members of the Freedom Quilting Bee (FQB). On my way there, I thought about the first Smithsonian Festival of American Folklife in 1967, which had featured four women from Alberta, Alabama's FQB: Estelle Witherspoon from Alberta, who was managing the Bee, and Lonzie Pettway, Joanna Pettway, and Betty Bondolph from Gee's Bend, a geographically and culturally distinct farming community on a peninsula formed by the Alabama River in Wilcox County. Father Francis X. Walter, a white Episcopal minister, had driven them and their quilts to Washington in a van. I had heard about these quilters and their efforts to empower themselves economically, and I was very pleased to meet them, though disappointed that I didn't get a chance to photograph them. I was looking forward to doing that when they returned for the second Festival in 1968. Four members were again expected: Mrs. Witherspoon, Mrs. Bondolph, and two other members, Callie Young, who was then president of the Bee, and Jencie Whitt. However, our 1968 meeting was not to be. Shortly after Dr. Martin Luther King Jr.'s assassination on April 4, I had left for Marks, Mississippi, to photograph the historic mule train that was bringing poor people from the Mississippi Delta to Resurrection City in Washington, D.C., and I then stayed with the mule train until its arrival in D.C., which was after the end of the Festival and the departure of the Alabama quilters. So this opportunity was more than twenty-five years in the making!

After passing the Freedom Quilting Bee sign, south of Alberta, I drove to Estelle Witherspoon's house. By now Mrs. Witherspoon had retired as FQB manager. In our recent telephone conversations, she had told me that many of the present members had grown weary of the numbers of people coming through to photograph and get information from them—and then making money from that with no money going to FQB. She said, however, that she would welcome me in her home and help me as much as she could because I was one of the few African Americans doing such a project.

After I shared a wonderful meal with her, Mrs. Witherspoon showed me around the community, and the next morning took me to the FQB office and sewing center. She introduced me to the new manager, Carrie Williams, and they both in turn introduced me to the ten women working there that day. They agreed to be photographed outside with the FQB sign, and later that afternoon I interviewed Mrs. Witherspoon.

Mrs. Witherspoon was born Estelle Abrams in 1916 in Rehoboth, Alabama, the second of six children, and is known as "Stella" to many of her friends. Her mother, "Mama Willie" Abrams (1897–1987), quilted, as did her maternal grandmother, Dinah Walker (1882–1970), and great-grandmother Jennie Walker (1850–1930), who was from Dallas County, Alabama. The following is adapted from Nancy Callahan's 1987 book, *The Freedom Quilting Bee,* published by the University of Alabama Press, a definitive study of this quilting cooperative, its members and communities. Twenty-seven pages of the book are devoted to Mrs. Witherspoon.

> Her childhood memories include her great-grandmother, Jennie Walker, whose home was next to what is now Pine Grove Baptist Church, and who raised and taught Mrs. Witherspoon's own mother the art of making a quilt. As a child, Estelle Abrams thirsted for education. She attended Pine Grove School; some of the classes were held in the church and others in the adjacent school building.
>
> One of the students Estelle met during her time in the ninth grade was Eugene Witherspoon [he died in 1976]. Born [in] 1907, in Rehoboth, the young man lacked two months of being nine years her senior. They were married on February 26, 1936. He was almost twenty-nine; she was twenty. "He was almost ten years older than I was but he was a dear husband. I liked him." During their forty years together, Mr. Witherspoon, a farmer, not only sought to bring out the many talents of his wife but was also her strong right arm as she supervised the first decade of the Freedom Quilting Bee.
>
> By the time Estelle Abrams was married, she possessed four quilts, including *Pig in the Pen, Grandmother's Dream,* and *Monkey Wrench.* She proudly asserts:
>
>> I made 'em myself. Mama made me make 'em. Mama and Aunt Liza Jane and all of us got together and quilted. When I got ready to marry, the quilts that was still good, they gave 'em to me. We put everything in 'em—old dresses, old shirttails, and old everything. We didn't care what color they were. If you got a new dress, you'd put pieces of that in the quilt. So I wasn't picking no colors then. I was just loving everything. Just wanted me a quilt.

But who is this good-natured, country woman, a product of one of the most obscure places in the South, whose leadership changed the course of history for a group of her peers and their families? She and her husband were respected. They both could read, and people knew that if the Witherspoons read a document to them, they would tell the truth. There is so much backbiting and deception in all small, ingrown communities, but the Witherspoons managed to overcome that.

I don't know exactly how she does it, but Mrs. Witherspoon could wade through cliques and disagreements that would tend to tear organizations apart. She could work and mediate among the Gee's Bend ladies, the upper-Alberta ladies, and the up-the-highway Alberta ladies in an incredible way. Yet she also could see to it that competent people she was related to and owed things to were rewarded. She just has exquisite tact.

On April 8, 1968, Mr. Witherspoon rode with Father Walter [he helped found FQB] to Atlanta, where they represented the Freedom Quilting Bee at the funeral of Martin Luther King Jr. While there, he presented Dr. King's widow with a king-sized, multicolored Double Star quilt, a gift from members of the co-op. [Mrs. Witherspoon says:]

> I'm not altogether satisfied but we've come a long ways with the Lord's help and I'm just thankful to the Lord. Just in this area the quilting bee has come from selling quilts for $10. Now we can sell 'em for $400 and $450. An average job is $300. We can make $300 like that.

She snaps her fingers. "But we was really glad to get that $10." Mrs. Witherspoon can look at a woman's hand and tell whether she is a maker of quilts. She says that over time, the little finger takes on a darker color than the others, in the shape of a strip. "I can tell whether she been quilting or not. I've did it so much myself." *

Mrs. Witherspoon told me, "When the Freedom Quilting Bee started, it was a Godsend to most of the women in this area. It put lights in our houses, food on our table, and refrigerators in our kitchens. And it helped us clothe and educate our children better, and gave us all something to be really proud of." Quoting again from Nancy Callahan:

> In 1983, the Freedom Quilting Bee books showed $200,000 in sales, three-fourths of which came back home in wages. Estelle Witherspoon is "an economic heroine."
>
> When the Freedom Quilting Bee was chartered, Estelle Witherspoon was pushing fifty. "You know," she says as she looks back, "that was kind of old to try to help start a business. See, I was willing and the Lord just gave me the courage to go on, and I had a husband who would push me. He was willing to help me with anything he thought would uplift fallen humanity. So that's just the way I felt about it." *

* Adapted with permission from *The Freedom Quilting Bee*, Nancy Callahan, pp. 215–40.

Of the eleven women at the FQB sewing center that morning, Pattie L. Irby was the only one who took the time to talk with me. Mrs. Irby was born in 1954 in Alberta, Alabama. As a child, she often watched her mother, Liza Williams (1906–78), and her maternal grandmother, Pattie Williams (1884–1970), quilt, and when she became a teenager she often quilted with her grandmother Williams. As she says, "I started quilting when I was about thirteen. I liked doing the things my parents did, and it was a time when we could talk about all sorts of things: family, future, past, or present. My grandmother taught me to use a needle and thimble. To me, quilting means a bonding between family and friends and community, and sometimes competing to see who will have the prettiest stitches in the end. It's the joy of seeing artwork being finished." Mrs. Irby raised her brother's daughter, Jennifer L. Roberson (b. 1972), and taught her to quilt, and today they're both employed by FQB.

Lucy Marie Mingo, another quilter associated with FQB, had asked me to recommend an agent to help her sell her quilts, and I put her in touch with Carolyn Mazloomi, coordinator of the Women of Color Quilter's Network. Mrs. Mingo was born in 1931 in Gee's Bend, Alabama, and is part of a four-generation quilting chain. Growing up, she saw three women quilt: her mother, Ethel Irby Young (b. 1910), from Gee's Bend; her maternal grandmother, Nellie Irby (1864?–1952), from Uniontown, Alabama; and a family friend, China Grove Myles (1888–1976). She and her husband, David, have raised ten children, seven of them girls, but only one of her daughters—Polly Young Mingo Raymond (b. 1948)—quilts.

Nancy Callahan writes about Mrs. Mingo in *The Freedom Quilting Bee* as follows:

> Among the names on the Freedom Quilting Bee's articles of incorporation is that of Lucy Marie [Young] Mingo . . . Lucy Marie Young did not learn to quilt until she married David Mingo, but she pieced her first quilt top on the sewing machine at age fourteen:
>
>> My mother would say, "You piece your own quilts so when you get married, you'll have 'em yourself." My mother learnt me how to do *everything*. Some days, I felt like she was too hard on us but since I got grown and got out on my own, I was very proud because she learned us how to do everything. But there was one thing I really didn't learn how to do—sew and make dresses.
>>
>> She said, "Baby, you need to learn how to sew, because you don't know who you're gonna marry, and lots of times, what you have, you have to make it." I said, "Mama, I ain't gon' learn how to make no dress because whoever I marry, he's gon' buy what I want." I regretted that because I had seven daughters.

By the time the Freedom Quilting Bee had been established, Mrs. Mingo excelled as a quiltmaker, so she joined it and was called on to teach many of the other members. One of her specialties was the

Chestnut Bud. "I was the only person that knew how to make that quilt and I learnt the other ladies how to do it." The Chestnut Bud is deep-seated in Wilcox [County] quilting. Mrs. Mingo obtained the pattern from her cousin of an older generation, Pankey Pettway:

> I was always going to cousin Pank's house. She was seventy or eighty years old and had all kinds of quilts. One time I was at her house and she was making this quilt. So I got the pattern from her.
>
> See, when these people came in, we had all types of pattern blocks and that was the one they picked out. They liked it the best. That pattern is twenty-something years old with me, and cousin Pankey said she had it over twenty years. The pattern had gotten so old, it was wearing out. It's one of the oldest in this area. The oldest quilts the quilting bee is putting out right now are the Grandmother's Choice and the Bear's Paw. My mother made a Bear's Paw for me before I got married.

Perhaps more than any other quilter, Mrs. Mingo is a link to China Grove Myles, with whom she shared uncountable quilting hours. Her life is the cultural continuity between that legendary figure from the past and the future of fine craftsmanship in Gee's Bend, as evidenced by her own Pine Burr that she and daughter Willie Dell proudly take outside and exhibit. A masterpiece showing every hue of the rainbow, this regular-sized composition contains ninety blocks. Each block has 265 square pieces. The number of pieces in the entire quilt totals 23,850. "Now, that's a small quilt," she offers, "It's not a king-size."*

Although I wasn't fully satisfied with my time at FQB, I was very happy to have finally gotten there. I didn't realize I'd be returning in a week!

A few days later, in Atlanta, I met Tamara Jeffries, a young writer and art historian who was taking beginning quilt lessons from Darlyne Dandridge in Atlanta. Tamara was from Virginia, had graduated from Hampton University, and worked in Tennessee before migrating to Atlanta. She saw herself as now coming into her own as part of Atlanta's young literary and art scene. She had won first place in the 1991 *Essence* magazine Fiction Contest, and had recently done a piece for a magazine on the Freedom Quilting Bee in Alabama.

That night I lay awake, still thinking about the FQB photograph I had recently taken. The next morning, I called Carrie Williams, the FQB manager, and asked if she thought the women would have felt better about my photographing them if they'd had advance notice and been able to dress and do their hair. She sort of laughed and said they definitely would have, and I then asked if I could come back in a couple of days and re-shoot the group. She agreed, and I then invited Tamara to

---

* From *The Freedom Quilting Bee,* Nancy Callahan, pp. 182–85.

Freedom Quilting Bee, Alberta, Alabama. *Front row (left to right):* Annie Williams, Louella Pettway, Estelle Witherspoon, Mary Spencer, and Mensie Pettway. *Back row (left to right):* Jennifer Abrams, Fannie McGuister, Felicia Moseley, Ruby Young, Carrie Williams, Lucy Pettway, Pattie Irby, and Jennifer Roberson.
WILCOX COUNTY, ALABAMA, OCTOBER 1993 (35 MM CT)

accompany me, so that she could actually meet the FQB women. We again stayed at Mrs. Witherspoon's, and she and Tamara really hit it off and talked late into the night.

We first met Nellie Young Abrams and her granddaughter Shaquetta M. Young. Together, we went to meet Mrs. Abrams' mother, Annie Mae Young (b. 1930), and Shaquetta's mother, Irma Young, from whom I learned of this family's six-generation quilting chain. Annie Mae Young's mother, Lula Pettway (1890–1960), from Primrose, Alabama, and her maternal grandmother, Mary Jane Pettway (1857–1939), had taught her to quilt. Night was coming on fast as I photographed these generations of women quilters (see p. 338).

The next morning, in a joyful mood, thirteen FQB members gathered for a group photograph in the sewing center. After we all had lunch together, Tamara and I left to return to Atlanta.

Annie Young and her great-granddaughter Shaquetta Young.
WILCOX COUNTY, ALABAMA, OCTOBER 1993 (35 MM CT)

TUSKEGEE

In between these two sessions with the FQB, I stopped in Tuskegee, and photographed Janie Moore, the maternal grandmother of Kenyatta Rivers, whom I had met in Florida (see p. 329). Mrs. Moore was born in 1920 in Tuskegee and learned to quilt from her mother, Jennie Mae White (1901–71).

SOUTH CAROLINA, OCTOBER 1993

CHARLESTON

In Charleston, I met WCQN member, Marlene O'Bryant-Seabrook. Mrs. Seabrook was born in 1933 in Newberry, South Carolina, and her family moved to Charleston when she was a few weeks old. No one in her family quilted, and as she says, "In 1982, I bought a raffle ticket for a quilt with cross-stitched scenes. When I realized that I hadn't won, I decided to take a quilting course. During the eight-week quilting course, I was shown several quilts that were over one hundred years old. I was totally fascinated with the thought that future generations could learn

Janie Moore.
TUSKEGEE, ALABAMA, OCTOBER 1993 (35 MM CT)

something about me and my times from my quilts. The choice of my fabrics and ornamentation is always made with longevity in mind." She explained that one of the quilts she has collected is a "throwover."*

Because several of Mrs. Seabrook's quilts deal with the folklore of Charleston, I decided to photograph her in different settings in the city (see pp. 340–41). She had made a quilt called *Porgy and Bess Re-visited* (part of her Gullah Series I), based on the famous George Gershwin folk opera, which depicted life on Catfish Row in Charleston. Today there are two boutiques called Porgy and Bess right at the entrance to the narrow street Catfish Row, now an upscale community in historic Charleston, so we went there for the picture with that quilt. I also shot her with her first quilt, called *Record of a Rich Heritage*, which depicts famous African-American Charlestonians.

Even though Mrs. Seabrook is the only quilter in her immediate family,

*"Obatrow," in Gullah, refers to the small pieces left after the completion of patchwork quilts that were folded in triangles and sewn to a burlap ("crockersack") backing to provide small colorful quilts that were then "thrown over" the foot of a bed or the back of a chair.

Marlene O'Bryant-Seabrook showing her quilt outside St. Michael's Episcopal Church at the Corner of Four Laws in Charleston, an area where people come to sell their sweet grass baskets.

BERKELEY COUNTY, SOUTH CAROLINA, OCTOBER 1993 (FRAME 8, 2¼ CT)

she told me a fascinating story of her father's first cousin, Maggie McFarland Gillispie (1912–76), and her only child, John Gillispie Jr. (1936–76). Among her most treasured possessions are several quilts that were made by Mrs. Gillispie and her son, John, who was paraplegic, having been critically injured in an automobile accident while a teenager. For approximately twenty years, they quilted together. John died only ten days after his mother's sudden death. Mrs. Gillispie's mother, Mary McFarland, who was born in Chesterfield County, South Carolina, and died around 1945, was also a quilter. Mrs. Seabrook has named a pattern they created "Gillispie Diamonds."

In 1995, the American Quilt Study Group accepted for publication and presentation a paper that Mrs. Seabrook wrote about these two relatives entitled "Symbiotic Stitches: The Quilts of Maggie McFarland Gillispie and John Gillispie Jr."*

WASHINGTON, D.C., MAY 1994 AND OCTOBER 1995

In May 1994 and October 1995, I completed this survey's documentation of Washington, D.C., African-American quilters.

BERNICE JOHNSON REAGON

Bernice Johnson Reagon, one of my primary mentors in folklore and a close personal friend as well, finally found a mutually convenient time for me to photograph her.

Bernice is widely known and admired for her cultural and political leadership. Strongly rooted in the Civil Rights movement, she became founding director of the Smithsonian's Program in African-American Culture, and her work and writings there and elsewhere have been recognized in her designation as a MacArthur Foundation Fellow and in her receipt of the Charles Frankel Prize from the National Endowment for the Humanities. The general public probably knows her best through "Sweet Honey in the Rock," the *a capella* singing group she founded and leads, and which has recorded and toured nationally since the mid-1970's.

*Published in *Uncoverings 1995*, Volume 16 of the Research Papers of the American Quilt Study Group, pp. 175–98 and presented by Mrs. Seabrook in September 1995 to the Sixteenth Annual Seminar of the American Quilt Study Group in Paducah, Kentucky.

Marlene O'Bryant-Seabrook holding her *Porgy and Bess Revisited* quilt at the entrance to Catfish Row, Charleston, South Carolina.

BERKELEY COUNTY, SOUTH CAROLINA, OCTOBER 1993 (FRAME 1, 2¼ CT)

Dr. Reagon was born in 1942 near Albany in Dougherty County, Georgia. As I photographed her piecing a quilt at home, she shared a remarkable history with me.

> At that time, there were three girls—me, Mae Frances [1944–85], and Fannie [Johnson Dunson, b. 1938]—and my mother, Beatrice Wise Johnson [b. 1920] from Worth County, Georgia. (My other sisters, Deloris and Mamie, weren't born yet.) She made all our clothes. Momma learned to sew from her mother, Frances Hill Wise [1896–1952], who was also born in Worth County, Georgia. Momma said that she could sew, but that her mother was a seamstress. She said that our grandmother could cut cloth for any kind of outfit without measuring it. People would bring her a picture of a dress and she knew how to cut the cloth so that it would come out right. And she never used a pattern.
>
> Momma called these "piece quilts." She never threw away cloth after she finished making our dresses. She would take the pieces leftover and fold them up and put them away until it was time to make quilts. Then she would pull out her quilt piece box and call us

together around the fireplace. My mother would be in a chair and my oldest sister, Fannie, would be in a chair, and Mae Frances and I would be sitting on the floor.

First, my mother would cut the cloth into strips, if possible across the grain or on the bias. The strips would be put in piles according to lengths. The longest strips would be about fifteen inches long and the shortest would be about three to four inches long. The pieces would be at least two inches wide. Once the strips were made, then Momma took newspaper and cut it into squares about a foot square. When she thought she had enough, she would give each of us a needle, number eight thread, and once we got our needle threaded with a good knot in the end, we would begin.

We would take two of the longer strips, right side facing each other, lay them catty-corner across the newspaper square, and hand-stitch one side to the newspaper. Then we would open up the two stitched pieces and see the beginning of the design. My mother let each of us pick our pieces. I can remember picking up strips and laying them next to the two pieces and asking, "Is this good?" My memory is that my mother would look up from her patch (that's what we called the squares we were making) and look at my choice and what it was laying next to, and she always seemed to think that what I had picked was real pretty. I would look in the pile and see if I could see a strip that would go with what I had and that was the length I needed for the next strip. I liked it when there was a mixture of prints, flowers, stripes, and some solids. I was so surprised that I could put together a strip with flowers and stripes and plaids and that they would match on a quilt but you wouldn't be caught dead with it as an outfit.

Now the newspaper never leaves the quilt. Every strip is sewn onto a newspaper square and the newspaper lives in the quilt. I never thought it was strange. I never knew people made quilts any other way. I was so surprised to find when I met quilters or people who collected quilts and would ask, "Do you put newspaper in your quilt?" Most people would look at me so strange and say, "Newspaper?" Most of them said no, some have heard tell of such, but few have ever actually used this method of quilting.

I remember looking at quilts that had the same fabrics in a clear design, like a Star, or Double Ring, or such, and thinking that those quilts were too proper and they didn't have any excitement. With our quilts you never knew what you would find next to go onto your patch.

After we had a big pile of patches, then we would carefully trim around the edges of all of the strips that were overlapping the newspaper square. I remember being careful to hold down the pieces on the corners because they were usually small strips and if you were not careful, you could cut them wrong and have a mess. Yes, sometimes we had to take out the stitches and do a strip over if we left a gap. Anyway when all the squares were trimmed, we had another time to design, because we got to pick what squares went together in a nine- or twelve-square section. I remember looking over to see what Mae Frances was doing to be sure she wasn't copying off me.

When we got the sections done, my mother took wider strips of solid cloth about four inches wide. Some strips were long enough to go down the entire length of the quilt, and other strips were long enough to go across. She used the solid four-inch strips to frame the nine-patch sections to make the quilt top. Then she laid that face down on the bed. All you could see was stitched up newspaper with neat raw edges of the seams showing all over the quilt. Then my mother would unfold or unroll cotton she had bought and match it to the quilt top. Then she put the quilt backing on top of the cotton. Next she turned the quilt so the strip squares were facing up. Now we were ready to do the top stitching.

We quilted on the bed, and I have seen my mother with her quilt in her lap draped on the floor. We never had a frame. When I first heard people talking about quilting frames, I didn't know what they were talking about. Growing up, I never even saw a frame. And we would just lay it on the bed. And each one of us would start with a corner. Momma would decide the shape of the stitching, whether it was straight across or whether it was to curve, whatever it was. And she'd just say, "Don't make those stitches too big."

When Momma had finished the quilt, she would hang it on the clothesline and our Aunt Dorothy and Aunt Fannie could come over and see it. They would say, "Bea! Look 'a here. It sure is pretty!"

Me, what I loved the best was getting into bed under the new quilt. Every time you moved, the quilt would be crackling because the newspaper was still inside. That would last one season, because every spring before we put the quilts away, we washed them and then the quilts would not crackle any more.

On this quilt I am making, these are my scraps left over from me making stuff. Well, this African print is a dress I wore at the African Diaspora Program presentations at the Smithsonian Bicentennial Festival of American Folklife. This turquoise is my "Motherdust" dress. "Motherdust" was a workshop of black women singers I had for two years [1977–79]. I had stopped working at the D.C. Black Repertory Company, but I missed working with singing in a group so I started the workshop. I named it "Motherdust" because it was a group of black women who loved singing and wanted to have it in their lives, which were really centered on their families and jobs. "Motherdust" is a phrase I learned in the prayers I heard my people pray in church. There was a standard way to beginning the prayer. In southwest Georgia, we would begin with "The Lord's Prayer" and then instead of saying "For thine is the kingdom, and the power, and the glory, forever," with an "Amen" at the end—we would say, "For thine is the kingdom, the power and the glory are thine. Lord, here come me your meek and undone servant, knee bent and body bowed to the Motherdust of the Earth." I loved that phrase, "Motherdust of the Earth," so I used it to name the workshop.

Bernice Johnson Reagon.
WASHINGTON, D.C., MAY 1994
(35 MM CT)

Now this is a Sweet Honey [in the many of our costumes. If you look at our record *B'lieve I'll Run On,* you will see me in an outfit made out of this material.

When I start to lay the pieces across the newspaper square, all the while I'm stitching, I am thinking about the colors I have and what I am going to lay down next. Then my eye seems to see the next strip and on and on. After a while I notice I am working in clusters, there are a group of patches that all have this turquoise and this African print, and I wonder if that is going to tie together one section of the entire quilt. Then there is another group that has two other strips moving through the patches. So as I am stitching and deciding on the strips for a square, I am looking for the feel of the entire quilt.

Quilting is great work. It rests me so, because I cannot let up from what I am doing. Because if you are not talking with yourself about it, you will mess around and have the wrong strip in the wrong patch and have to take it out or put it aside until it can get some company. It's a lot like the way I make music. I am inside the song, looking for the rest of it and working my way out to the end. I never saw anybody else quilt other than my mother, and I really never saw my mother's mother. She saw me, but I was a baby. I remember learning the word "never" in school, and my teacher Mrs. Daniels asked me to write a sentence using the word, and I wrote, "I have never seen my grandmother." Mrs. Daniels said that that was very sad and that Mrs. Bea ought to take you to see your grandmother, but I never saw her quilt.

My father's mother, Emma Johnson [1878–1958], who was from Calhoun County, Georgia, made quilts out of big pieces of cloth, old skirts, and shirts that had worn out. You just hand-stitched together whatever clothes in the family were falling apart, you put your cotton down, lay the backing on and then stitched it together, and you've got a quilt. It was not considered a thing of beauty, but it did keep you warm in the winter.

There were five girls in my family, but I think Momma only taught three of us to quilt. I made quilts with her when I was in elementary school. I don't think she has any of her quilts. We wore those things out. And she started to go to work. We were farming during that time, sort of working in the field. So winter time she would have more time. When she started to clean house, she stopped quilting and started buying blankets, and so, my younger sisters, Deloris and Mamie, didn't quilt. I think I was about eight when I started, I can't really remember. I might have been older or younger. And we washed those quilts until . . . and the thing I remember about them is that every year they would fade. So I don't know where they are now.

Then I made my first quilt by myself the first year I was married, in 1964. When my mother saw it, she said, "Your stitches are too big!" In 1975, I took off four weeks and went on a fast to deal with my arthritis and during that time I began a new quilt. But I didn't finish that quilt on the fast, so when I got back [to work] I put it away. One of the things you need in order to quilt is time. And with me it was always a contest between sewing and reading, and these days reading always wins out.

When you called about your project, I had not been quilting, but I thought I could go to storage and pull out my quilt box and pull out my unfinished quilt. When I got the box home and opened it, it was not my unfinished quilt, but it was a box of strips and scraps that I had put together for a new quilt and forgot about. So what you are looking at is what I have been doing yesterday and today. I don't know when I am going to finish this. To do a double-bed quilt, I need six of the nine-patch sections; to do a queen-size I need nine of these nine-patch sections. And I have just started on the third section.

In thinking about this, what's interesting to me is the way the designing works. When I was doing it, I knew what I was doing. I knew without working too hard how to put the pieces together. What pieces to put next. And I can't clearly explain to you why in one patch I put certain strips together, but as I put them together I fell into the pattern that knew how to put them together. I've been really looking at it because I don't quite dress like this, but when I sew it I know it's going to match up. Then I open it up and I say, "Yeah, that's it."

When I think about it—and this comes to me every time—I think about what's missing for many young people today. Because I have this picture in my mind of these sisters with my mother. And we're on the floor and all of us are quilting. So sometimes I think, well, what I really would like to do when I stop running around is like teach young children how to quilt like that. And I have this image of them having this newspaper and having these strips and me teaching them how to quilt.

There was something about sitting in that space, we weren't doing too much talking, but a real strong image of what our relationship was about. So the quilting for me is really sewed up in there. And it was time spent with my mother, who was busy all the time. She was always doing something. And this was one time when I remember us being in this girl/woman space that was ours, and all of us were making this one thing. But it's that sitting time where you're working on something and everybody's together but each one of us could still do our own thing. It was really an amazing experience for me. A real basic piece of my grounding is in that quilting time with my mother and my sisters.

When I think about singing and its role, the singing I grew up doing in school, in church, in the yard. That stuff is central to my ability to be in the world and to be sane and functional, to deal with challenges, to be able to survive. Well, making a quilt with my mother is a piece of that same thing. Very much a part of why I am able to survive, and I can't really break it down a lot, except it's very central for me. I never saw my mother quilt with anybody else. She only quilted with us.

OTHER WASHINGTON QUILTERS

Joyce A. Ladner, whom I photographed in October 1995, was born in Battles, Mississippi, and raised in Hattiesburg, Mississippi. She is a fifth-generation quilter, and traces her quilting roots back to her maternal great-great-grandmother, Clarisa Powe, who was born in 1824 in South Carolina, and her great-grandmother, Charlotte Powe (1862–1924), who was born in Wayne County, Mississippi. As a young girl, Dr. Ladner and her sisters helped their mother, Annie Ruth Ward Woulard (1921–95), and maternal grandmother, Martha Gates Woulard (1896–1969), quilt.

Dr. Ladner said, "My mother quilted what I would call functional quilts. They were not fancy designs. For her they were comforters for warmth. They sort of demonstrate her no-nonsense approach to life, as they were large squares and fabrics. She didn't have the patience—neither do I—to do the tedium or little intricate designs. I think that part of it also was, as she got older it was not only comforters—because she could certainly afford to buy blankets and she certainly had many of them. It was a way of spending her time, whiling away her time."

I had photographed Dr. Ladner with one of her mother's quilts, and I asked if she remembered sleeping under this kind of quilt when she was little. She replied:

Sure. Where we grew up there was no central air or heating in the house. We had space heaters in each room, and at night Mother was always so afraid that the house would catch on fire if we left the gas heaters' jets on all night, that she turned them off and we got out and piled on lots and lots of covers, so much that you could barely turn over. We slept in flannel pajamas and flannel gowns, sometimes socks to keep warm, and the only thing that was sticking out was your head. So I sure slept under a lot of these quilts as I was growing up. Mother would sit hours on end, tacking them, as she called it, and my stepfather's mother, grandmother Ida, we called her "Bi-Ma," who has been dead for many years, did the same kind of quilting.

I then asked if she noticed other women in the community making the same kind of quilts:

A lot of them made the same kind of quilt. I used to own a quilt like this that was much more colorful than the one Mother gave me. It was made by a Miss Della Gassaway. Miss Della made it for me in

Dr. Joyce A. Ladner.
WASHINGTON, D.C., OCTOBER 1995 (FRAME 5, 2¼ CT)

about 1974–75, but I gave it away because it was too heavy to sleep under. I believe her name was actually spelled Galloway, but we called her Miss Della Gassaway. She made these quilts all the time. I remember I was living on Roosevelt Island in New York when Mother said, "Your quilt is ready. Miss Della is sending it to you." And then I got this big box, and I opened it and it was so beautiful. The color—there was a red backing on the quilt, and lots of designs—but it was too heavy to sleep under. It was like a sheet of lead. So I kept it for quite a while; it lit up the room because it was so bright with colors, beautiful fabrics, stitched together. But I gave it away. I wish I had kept it now, just for a keepsake.

Dr. Ladner and her older sister, Dorie Ladner Churnet (b. 1942), were both expelled from Mississippi's Jackson State University for their civil rights activities. She finished her undergraduate studies at Tougaloo College, in a suburb of Jackson. In 1971, she came to Washington, D.C., to teach at Howard University and, after working and traveling throughout the world, returned to Howard in 1981. In 1994–95, Dr. Ladner served as interim university president. Now on sabbatical, she dreams of retiring and opening an art gallery to share her international

Front: Jennifer Latifa Johnson, her husband Abdel-Gadir Adam, and son Ousman Adam. *Back (left to right):* Yassin Ibrhim Adam, Khalafalla M. Bashir, and Mohamed Elradi. *Two women in background:* Aisha Ibrhim Adam and Aster (*surname unknown*).

WASHINGTON, D.C., OCTOBER 1995 (35 MM CT)

collection. Among the more interesting quilts in her collection are examples of storytelling quilts from Zimbabwe, in southern Africa.

Jennifer Latifa Johnson was born in 1950 in Asheville, North Carolina. Her first six years were spent in Kentucky and North Carolina, and she then lived in Washington, D.C., until migrating to New York in 1978. She returned to Washington in 1994. While a child in North Carolina, she remembers seeing neighbors quilt. Her mother, Jessie Johnson (1927–84), embroidered but didn't quilt, and her maternal grandmother, Irene Askew (1904–93), who was born in Union, South Carolina, quilted until she moved North and considered quilting "old-fashioned" or "out of fashion." However, this grandmother did preserve two quilts made by her mother, Luvina Askew (1864–1947), also from Union, which have now been passed down to Mrs. Johnson and are two of her most treasured possessions.

Although she, too, embroidered, Mrs. Johnson did not begin quilting until:

> Right after my brother Hugh Johnson was killed in a plane crash in Ethiopia in 1989. You might remember this crash—it was the same one in which Texas Repre-

sentative Mickey Leland died. I desperately needed something to calm my nerves, and quilting was it. I actually started while in Washington, D.C., and learned the basics at a Quilt and Stuff shop in Alexandria, Virginia. I made my first large quilt while waiting to be cleared to adopt a child three years ago. The next quilt I made was pieced by me and quilted by me and my new husband, and in 1993 I brought our adopted son home from the orphanage in a quilt.

I joined the New York chapter of WCQN, and since moving to Washington in 1994, I've continued to quilt with my Sudanese husband, Abdel-Gadir Adam. He was born in the village of Kassala in eastern Sudan near the Ethiopian border. Traditionally his family has been weavers and tailors, and I'm happy to say that today we spend many joyous hours quilting together. We are working now on a "charm" (patchwork) quilt, and this style is a tradition going back to my great-grandmother. To me quilting is a way to create something useful that is beautiful for my home. It is also a stressbuster and a connection with my past in the United States and Africa.

Left to right: Kenja S. Hassan and her mother Sondra B. Hassan.
WASHINGTON, D.C., OCTOBER 1995 (FRAME 2, 2¼ CT)

Sondra Barrett Hassan was born in 1945 and is a native of Washington, D.C. No one in her family quilted, but she learned to sew from her mother and her maternal grandmother. She explained:

> I really started quilting in the early 1970s. I was expecting and I wanted to have a quilt for my first child. And then I made a quilt for my second daughter, and I've been quilting ever since. Much later I took some classes. The first person I got to know as a quilter was a woman named Viola Canady (see pp. 176–77), and she is just such a positive person, just such a good spirit and just such a wise soul, so generous and so energetic, that she just inspired me so much. And what I saw that she could do with these little teeny tiny stitches that she could make, that look invisible, was something I couldn't do, that I wasn't even close to, still can't do. In fact, she did a form of quilting—appliqué stained glass—that was never my style, was never going to be my style, but I watched how she did it and just watched her do it. I was actually mesmerized.

I then asked Mrs. Hassan what quilting meant to her:

> Quilting means a lot. Quilting for me is in fact a kind of therapy, and I say that kind of guardedly. But it is a kind of therapy for me.

I'm not a patient person, and it's funny because people say, "Oh, to be a quilter you must have a lot of patience." Well, I quilt because I don't have that. What I have is a lot of energy, and quilting is a way of centering me, of focusing that energy.

Now I have taught both of my daughters—Aisha Nicky Hassan, who's twenty-four, and Kenja Siobhan Hassan, who's twenty-two—to quilt. Kenja quilts and she also paints. She's an artist, and has always been an artist. Everything in her approach to life is with the eye and the sensibility and the sensitivity of an artist, to the extent that she actually did a piece for a geometry class in high school. And then the geometry teacher passed it on to the art teacher, who then put it in competition in an art show for District students, and that person put it in a competition at the Smithsonian—and that piece won first place in the Smithsonian's Women's Art competition, or something like that. I mean I can't remember the title of that exhibit, but it started off as a geometry piece and it was a project to show that on a flat surface you could show both depth and dimension. And we still have that piece, it's the quilt there on the wall with the cubes on it.

Pennsylvania, June 1994

Quilters of the Round Table, Philadelphia

Folklorist Cassandra A. Stancil Gunkel, who had helped me install my 1992 Quincentenary quilt exhibition in Philadelphia, had told me of the newly formed Quilters of the Round Table, of which she was a member. I went to Philadelphia to photograph them (see p. 352), and joined the group for its Saturday meeting at the home of member Lucille F. Clark.

Christina E. Johnson, president of this group, was born in 1942 in Davenport, Iowa. Her family moved to California when she was two, and she lived there until migrating to Philadelphia in 1990. She knows of only one quilt in the family, which was made by her grandmother's sister, who also did embroidery. She began quilting in 1990, first on her own and then taking a beginning class. After attending the first conference of the National Association of African-American Quilters in Lancaster, Pennsylvania, in 1993, she founded the Quilters of the Round Table in order to promote African-American quilters and their quilting. To Mrs. Johnson, "Quilting is a passion and a means to learn and share the stories women have to tell the world about their joys and sorrows."

Cassandra Stancil Gunkel was born in 1954 in Portsmouth, Virginia. After school, jobs in the media took her from Virginia to Wisconsin, then to Texas, Ohio, and Indiana, and finally to Pennsylvania. Growing up in Virginia, she remembers many family members quilting; she has traced her quilting lineage back to her great-great-grandmother Clarkie Hiter Hughes (dates unknown), who was born in Shiloh, North Carolina, and was a seamstress, spinner, and quilter. She in turn passed along a repertoire of her sewing skills to two of her daughters: Nancy Annie Hughes Riddick (1869–1966) and Mary Elizabeth Hughes Smith (1873–1961), both of whom were also born in Shiloh and quilted. Two of her great-grandmother Nancy Riddick's daughters became quilters: Amy Riddick Butts (1904–94) and Nancy Riddick Wilson (1903–67), both of whom were born in Camden, North Carolina. Nancy Wilson then taught two of her daughters to sew: Shirley W. Stancil (b. 1926) and Vernice Bagby, both of whom were born in Norfolk, Virginia. Shirley Stancil was Mrs. Gunkel's mother. As Mrs. Gunkel says:

> I started quilting just before my baby was born in November 1993, because I needed crib covers. I learned from my great-aunt Ervin Butts Edney [dates unknown], whose mother was Amy Riddick Butts, and from studying my great-grandmother Nancy Annie Hughes Riddick's quilts. In fact, before I knew that my great-grandmother quilted, I dreamed she left me a quilt that was a map to her, and her family's history. I then discovered quilts in my old college steamer trunk, which an aunt identified for me. I was twelve when she died in 1966 and did not know she quilted at all. I have since discovered twenty more of her quilts and am now writing my [doctoral] dissertation on her.

In 1995, Mrs. Gunkel successfully defended her dissertation at the University of Pennsylvania. In her abstract, she describes her work with her great-grandmother's quilts as follows:

> Nancy Riddick's quilts are readable as historical texts that encode her experiences as a tenant farmer wife and her family's transition into middle-class life. Using theoretical perspectives from the anthropology of religion and womanist theology, Nancy Riddick's quilts are symbolically decoded with interpretations from her numerous belief communities. Drawing from studies of aesthetics, ethno-aesthetics, and structuralism, Nancy Riddick's quilts are structurally analyzed using quiltmaker categories, the improvisation process, and the quilter's home quilting environment. This analysis demonstrates the dynamic ways that African-American communities were stratified along belief and class lines from Reconstruction through the modern Civil Rights era.*

Asake-Denise Jones was born in 1957 and is part of a five-generation quilting chain. Her mother, Dorothy Cook Foye (born 1928 in Baltimore, Maryland), was a dressmaker. Both Dorothy's mother, Gertrude Davis Cook (1902–89), and her maternal grandmother, Effie Davis, who died at eighty-five—both of whom were born in Emporia, Virginia—were quilters. Mrs. Jones is passing the tradition on to her daughter Kwasida Jones.

---

* Cassandra A. Stancil, "Nancy Riddick's Quilts: A Model for Contextualizing African-American Material Culture Study," a dissertation in folklore and folklife, presented to the faculties of the University of Pennsylvania in partial fulfillment of the requirements for the degree of Doctor of Philosophy, 1995.

Quilters of the Round Table of the metropolitan Philadelphia area. *Back row (left to right):* Anita Parker, Geraldine Taylor, Emily I. Pryor, Sylvia H. Blackwell, Doris V. Wing, Delores Fields, Maxine Johnson, Marie A. George, Jacqueline I. Jenkins, and Cory W. Roberts. *Front row (left to right, staggered):* Lorraine A. Mahan, Cassandra S. Gunkel holding her daughter Naomi Ruth Gunkel, Asake-Denise Jones, Lucille F. Clark, Christina E. Johnson, Anita P. Jones, Barbara Imes-Jorden, and Kwasida Jones *(in front).*

DELAWARE COUNTY, PENNSYLVANIA, JUNE 1994 (FRAME 2, 2¼ CT)

Anita Peeples Jones was born in 1944 in Bryn Mawr, Pennsylvania. No one in her family quilted, but her mother was a seamstress, and "always had a needlework project—usually knitting or needlepoint. In 1968, I made my first quilt for my second son. I am self-taught, but have read lots of quilting books. In my collection is a Grandmother's Garden quilt that was made in the late 1800s in Philadelphia. To me quilting means the chance to express myself in an art that extends my sewing skills taught to me by my mother."

Lucille F. Clark, a native of Philadelphia, was born in 1928. No one in her family quilted, and as she says, "I basically taught myself. Later on I joined a quilt guild. I quilted because I had become overwhelmed with cross-stitch and needlepoint (no more wall space). You never run out of beds that need warmth. To me, quilting is a joy and a quiet pleasure."

Sylvia Harrod Blackwell was born in 1928 in Wendell, North Carolina, and came with her family to Philadelphia as an infant. No one in her family quilted, and she explains, "In the late 1980s, after retiring, I started to quilt, and I'm self-taught. I visited several quilt exhibitions in New York and became motivated. I had African fabric collected from making dolls, and I soon wanted to make a strip quilt incorporating African images and fabrics. I have committed myself to making a quilt for each grandchild. I have seven so far, and I have made four quilts. If health permits, I will complete my goal and do three more during the next few years. To me, quilting means relaxation and a form of legacy for my children and grandchildren."

Anita Parker was born in 1949 and is a native of Philadelphia. No one in her family quilted. As she tells it, "I saw a picture in a magazine of a miniature quilt. I tried to make it on my own, and later got several books from the library. Quilting gives me a sense of accomplishment and fulfillment that I never got from knitting, needlepoint, cross-stitch, or sewing. I have also met many wonderful friends through quilting."

Emily I. Pryor, a native of Philadelphia, said that no one in her family quilted. Now retired, she has been doing serious quilting with basic formal instruction since early 1993. However, she has been making baby quilts using a pattern for the past ten to fifteen years.

Cory W. Roberts was born in 1933 in New York City and migrated to Philadelphia in 1960. No one in her family quilted, and it was not until November 1993 when she retired that she started actively quilting.

Delores Fields was born in 1932 and is a native of Philadelphia. She saw her mother quilt while growing up, but did not actively quilt until September 1993. She says, "Quilting was an art which I wanted to learn, and I'm learning through the Quilters of the Round Table."

Barbara Imes-Jorden, a native of Philadelphia, was born in 1938. Growing up, she saw her mother, Anna Mae Coleman Imes (1916–84), and her mother's sister Grace Elizabeth Coleman Jackson (b. 1913) quilt, both of whom were from Philadelphia. She explains, "I started a beginners quilt course in September 1991, in the evening at a local high school. I always wanted to learn quilting, but always put it on hold until my later years. I was all alone. My dad passed away and I had been his caregiver. My husband was attending his Masonic meetings. I was on disability retirement and my sister was in night college courses, so finally the opportunity was here and the class was local—so I registered and never regretted it. Quilting means everything to me. I find that almost all areas of my being, my life, go on 'hold' until that part of my day with my quilting has been satisfied."

Jacqueline Imes Jenkins, Barbara's sister and also a Philadelphia native, was born in 1937. Unlike Barbara, she doesn't remember seeing anyone in her family quilt, and says, "I started quilting in 1992 because my sister invited me to join her in her summer quilting class. I knew how to sew because my mother was a seamstress and taught my sister and me to sew. I learned how to quilt from a young African-American woman, and learned all the intricate methods from my sister. To me, quilting is a wonderful cultural experience that has no constraints in time or cost. It is that resource which links me to my ancestors in a spiritual sort of way, and the work hours spent doing this marvelous task that has no boundaries helps to fill those unhappy and happy moments in my ancestors' lifetime which I know they lived."

TENNESSEE AND OREGON QUILTERS, JULY–AUGUST 1994

At the National Black Arts Festival (NBAF), in Atlanta, Georgia, during July and August, 1994, I had the opportunity to photograph Mary Mayfair Matthews, a Tennessee quilter, and Adriene Cruz, from Oregon.

MARY MAYFAIR MATTHEWS (TENNESSEE)

In 1992 when my Quincentenary quilt exhibition had opened at the National Civil Rights Museum in Memphis, Tennessee, a young woman named Rosemary Marr had asked me to look at some photographs of artwork by her mother, Mary Mayfair Matthews. These pictures stimulated my curiosity, and when I saw the actual work, I was even more impressed. This led to my curating, through The Group for Cultural Documentation, Ms. Matthews's debut exhibition, at the Georgia Council for the Arts' Carriage Works Gallery, as part of the 1994 NBAF. Several of Ms. Matthews's quilted wallhangings and improvisational quilts were included in the exhibit.

Mary Mayfair Matthews was born into a sharecropping family in Chulahoma, in north-central Mississippi, in 1938. Both her mother, Bessie Cox (1905–89), and her maternal grandmother, Anna Cox (1872–1975), were quilters, and she remembers quilting with her grandmother and other women in the community. She completed the

Mary Mayfair Matthews with her "little people" soft sculpture and paintings. Above her on the wall is one of her quilted wall hangings.

SHELBY COUNTY, TENNESSEE, MARCH 1994 (FRAME 17, 2¼ CT)

third grade before leaving school to join her family in the cotton fields. At twenty-eight, to escape a vicious cycle of poverty and abusive relationships, she took her four children and mother and moved to Memphis, Tennessee. There, while struggling to raise her children and working as a domestic, Ms. Matthews earned her GED. In the fall of 1991 following the violent death of her only son, Ms. Matthews began to concentrate time and attention on her art, building on the solace she had found over many years in sketching and drawing. Her grief from her son's death, added to that from her mother's two years earlier, rendered her unable to continue her regular employment. As an emotional and creative outlet, she turned to quilting and the making of soft sculpture. Rosemary, who had recently received her BFA degree, began taking her to art exhibits in Memphis and, noticing her excitement and interest, bought her a number of canvases and several tubes of acrylic paints. Now Ms. Matthews paints, quilts, or sculpts daily. She is essentially self-taught, an outsider in terms of formal training or in-depth exposure to recognized artistic traditions. Her works reflect her own upbringing and experience, as well as the dreams and loves of a life she never had.

ADRIENE CRUZ (OREGON)

Through Tamara Jeffries, who had become an arts administrator at
Hammonds House, a cultural arts center in Atlanta, I met a Portland,
Oregon, quilter named Adriene Cruz, whose work has been exhibited
nationally and internationally, and who was also being presented at the
1994 NBAF. Mrs. Cruz was born in 1953 in Harlem, New York. Although
no one in her family quilted, she has always worked with textiles.

> I used to do tapestry, crochet, wearable art, for close to eighteen
> years. And after I had children, it was difficult to crochet and I
> stopped, and after six years I was looking for something else to do.
> I had just started taking a quilting class in November of 1991, and
> EdJohnetta [Miller] [see pp. 283–84] wanted me to show a crochet
> piece, which I had to really push out because I wasn't crocheting.
> And she bullied me into doing it. The good thing was I went to
> Hartford and saw what was happening with contemporary African-
> American quilts. I think I had taken maybe two classes, and it was
> like a whole road opened up. Possibilities. The colors were there,
> the shapes, the form. I saw I could get into what I liked with cro-
> cheting, but it seemed more immediate. I didn't have to create the
> fabric; the fabric was there. It was just a matter of cutting it and
> placing another piece. So my first quilt was done in January of
> 1992.

I then asked her to talk about the quilt she was standing by when I took
her photograph:

> That's a good one. Valerie Maynard is a good friend of Gloria Smart,
> a woman whom I've always known. She's known me since I was an
> infant, and she's my mother's best friend. She is also a good friend
> of Valerie, who is a sculptor and artist from New York, who lives in
> Maine now. And she had shown Valerie pictures of my quilts, and
> Valerie called me up and said, "I want one, when can I get it?"
> About a month later, I met her in New York, and showed her the
> fabrics I had brought, and she loved all of them. And I paid atten-
> tion to what parts she liked in each of the fabrics and it was wide
> open. The only specification she had was that it was for a bed, so it's
> up hanging on the wall here, but it is for a bed.
>
> In addition to being usable, she wanted it stuffed with sage. She
> wanted sage for its healing properties. So there's sage in the little
> bags, and there's some stuffed in the side triangles as well. I went
> crazy with the sage after a while. Before I started cutting into the
> fabric, since she wanted sage, I visited my friend Roho who lives in
> Yakima, Washington, in kind of like a desert area. She has sage
> growing around her house. So I went there in September of 1992
> with the fabric and we put some sage in buckets of water, and we
> washed the fabric in sage and laid it out on the grass for the sun to
> dry it. It was wonderful. My children were there and my friend is in
> her seventies, and it was a three-generations kind of thing. It was

just a wonderful experience dealing with handling the fabric with the sage. I folded it up real careful, and it wasn't until February of 1993 that I even cut into this fabric. I think I was over-whelmed by just the whole idea that this thing had to be really grand and magnif-icent, and for two weeks in February I was totally into this cutting and piecing and laying it out, thinking about [Valerie's] work, some of the images I would see in her work and patterns that she would use. As for the center panel of the quilt, I remember thinking of it as a spine, or a love column, sending out good vibrations in all directions.

My last question was what quilting does for her:

It's a way. Quilting is a way for me to release a lot of emotion which I express through color. It's a medium I channel for other expressions. It's a language, the language that I'm using now in school.

Adriene Cruz.
PORTLAND, OREGON, AUGUST 1994 (FRAME 10, 2¼ CT)

And this project of yours, to me is a celebration of survival. The cel-ebration of survival, that we could go through so much over so many years, and this thing stays with us and continues to feed us and help us express ourselves. And we could trace a lot of it right back to Africa. The way different fabrics, different colors . . . just the way things are lined up or the way things are improvised, or what-ever, the connection is intact. It's still alive.

VERMONT, NOVEMBER 1994

CHARLOTTE

When I'm home in Washington, I regularly work out at a health spa. One day, I casually mentioned to a friend that I was on my way to Vermont. She said that she visited people there most summers, and because I hadn't located any African-American quilters in Vermont, I inquired if her friends were black (they were) and whether they quilted (they did). She checked with them and told me they were receptive to meeting with me. On my next trip to Vermont in connection with business for The Group for Cultural Documentation, I added a stop in Charlotte.

As I was nearing the town, I was surprised to see a sign on the highway that read, "Authentica," which was the name of the shop owned by the woman I was coming to visit. As I parked, the owner, Lydia Clemmons, greeted me. Mrs. Clemmons was born in 1923 in Ringgold,

Lydia M. Clemmons, art collector, with quilt made by June D. Thompson.
CHARLOTTE, VERMONT, NOVEMBER 1994
(FRAME 17, 2¼ CT)

Louisiana. When she was three weeks old, her parents moved to an oil boom town in Arkansas called Smackover. When she was twelve, her family migrated to a suburb of Chicago, Illinois. In 1963, she and her husband migrated to Vermont when he was hired as a pathologist at the University of Vermont, and they raised their five children there. Mrs. Clemmons' mother, Lucille Beck Monroe, also from Ringgold, did not quilt but was a seamstress and taught Lydia to sew. However, her maternal grandmother, Margery Beck, did quilt.

I was curious to know how it happened that this unique store full of artifacts and fabric from Africa wound up in rural Vermont. Mrs. Clemmons explained, "While on a trip to East Africa in 1984, I met a woman selling sisal bags, and that's how the business started. Now I go back to Africa at least once a year to replenish my stock. After going to fairs and craft shows here, I've also started collecting quilts, and have commissioned several from an African-American quilter which I plan to give to my children and friends." Two days later, just before I left Vermont, Mrs. Clemmons arranged for me to meet this quilter, June Thompson, who lives just north of Burlington.

BURLINGTON

June Thompson was born in 1929 in Brooklyn, New York, and raised in Englewood, New Jersey. Her mother, Myrtle Myers Prince (1908–89), who was born in Springfield, Massachusetts, taught her to sew at the age of twelve, and she treasures a quilt made by her mother in the 1940s. Her mother's mother, whom she called "Grandma [Louise] Parkus" (1884–1975) and who was born in Louisiana, did not quilt but was a seamstress. As Mrs. Thompson told me:

> My mother did block quilting out of odds and ends, of old blankets and leftover clothing and this was what I grew up with. I think that's why today I'm quilting, although mine are very different from hers. I began to quilt because I had a lot to say, and Faith Ringgold's story quilts inspired me to interpret some of my poems in quilt form.
>
> During my formative years [1934–47], I grew up during racially troubled times in New Jersey. There was much inequality

and discrimination in the schools and other areas. During my high school years, I took part in the first sit-in in our area at a racially discriminatory soda fountain. I was also part of a group of black high-school youngsters who refused to salute the flag because of lynchings, Jim Crow in the South, and bigotry in the North.

My college years [1947–51] and graduate school years [1951–53] were also eventful. I graduated from high school with honors but found it difficult to gain admittance at a Northern college. Finally the University of Rochester accepted me on the condition that my high-school friend, also black, come with me and share a room with me on campus. We had many interesting experiences as the first "Negroes" to live on campus. We both graduated Phi Beta Kappa. My roommate went back to South Carolina to find a teaching job, while I remained in Rochester, N.Y. I was not able to find a

June D. Thompson.
ESSEX JUNCTION, VERMONT, JUNE 1995 (FRAME 11, 2¼ CT)

teaching position at the high-school level there for seven years due to discrimination. During my teaching years [1958–89], thirteen of them in Rochester, I taught English and Latin at an inner-city high school and later taught Latin while foreign language department head at a well-to-do suburban junior-senior high school. The series of quilts on which I am now working reflect my feelings and experiences while teaching at these schools.

Now, during my years of reflection and retirement, as I look back on my life experiences as an African-American woman, I feel the urge to write. A book of poetry resulted. The series of theme quilts on which I am now working are based on five of these poems. My theme quilts are a combination of machine-appliqué, machine-embroidery, and machine-piecing. All are based on poems by me with the same names. The first is entitled *Balloon of Dreams*. It illustrates my feelings of absolute frustration while teaching at the inner-city school made up, in large part, of African Americans and Italians who fought constantly. A majority of my black students had simply given up. Prevailing racial attitudes killed their hopes and aspirations; they felt defeated, hated, of no value. They were intellectually destroyed.

Three of the others will be called *Black Girl, Busing,* and *Department Chairperson*. They all relate to my experiences as a teacher and administrator in educational settings where I was the only, or one of very few, African Americans.

Ruby Joyner.
PIMA COUNTY, ARIZONA,
NOVEMBER 1994
(FRAME 11, 2¼ CT)

Mrs. Thompson and her husband migrated to Vermont in 1970 with their two children when he was offered a professorship at the University of Vermont. One of the quilts she made for Mrs. Clemmons was called *Window on Vermont*; it depicts many of the things that she loves about the state, including covered bridges, farms, and sugar houses where maple syrup is made. Both of their husbands taught at the university, and they met in the early 1980s at an African-American faculty get-together.

ARIZONA, NOVEMBER 1994

TUCSON

While in Tucson on other business for The Group for Cultural Documentation, I was able to photograph additional quilters. Odiemae Lucas Elliott, a Women of Color Quilters' Network member, was born in 1937 in Holly Springs, Mississippi. She and her sister learned to quilt from their mother, Eddie Vienna Dean Lucas (1903–77), and Mrs. Elliott remembers that her mother's father, Rev. Elijah Dean, had three wives, all of whom were quilters. She also has vivid memories of Rev. Dean's mother, Paralee Dean (1835–1941), who was born a slave on a plantation near Senatobia, Mississippi. Mrs. Elliott remembers sitting at her great-grandmother's feet, and as she says:

> She'd tell me stories about how you could never question anything you were told to do. Contrary to [Alex Haley's] *Roots*, at least on her plantation, they were treated like animals. I mean at the slightest provocation you were beaten to death. I mean literally, publicly beaten to death, so that you would be an example for others. Paralee was too old to work in the fields, and when everyone else was gone I was left with her.
>
> All of the kids quilted. Mother had a frame and she used to put it up and we would just kind of collapse it at night, and then would bring it back the next day and just pick up where we left off. In the winter months when it was cold, and on the weekends and when we couldn't work in the fields, we did a lot of quilting. I left Mississippi when I was twenty and then joined the Women's Army Corps, and haven't lived in Mississippi since that time. I got married in Michigan in 1961, lived in Texas and Oregon, and came to Arizona in 1963.
>
> I didn't really become reacquainted with quilting until the 1980s. I sewed clothing to wear, and I think in the 1970s I became

sort of fascinated with wearable art—quilted vests and things like that. And I did a little of it. That got me interested in it, and then in the mid-1980s I thought about what would happen if I would just die. I have no daughters; I just have three sons, and the whole legacy would die and I would not have left my sons with anything. So I thought that I would just take a few classes and just quilt something to leave to my sons. Now that I'm retired, I'm making what I call "memory quilts" for my three boys. My son Sean Michael Elliott has been a star basketball player, in college at Arizona, and with the NBA San Antonio Spurs for the last six years, and he has given me my first grandchild, for whom I've made two baby quilts.

Left to right: Vera Lucas Pied and Odiemae Lucas Elliott, sisters from Holly Springs, Mississippi.
PIMA COUNTY, ARIZONA, NOVEMBER 1994
(FRAME 6, 2¼ CT)

Vera Lucas Avery Pied, Odiemae's sister, was born in 1940, also in Holly Springs, Mississippi. She too learned to quilt around the age of eleven from her mother. In 1959, she moved to Detroit, Michigan, where like Odiemae she joined the Women's Army Corps. She explains:

> I started quilting again in 1962 while in Texas on a military assignment with my spouse. I quilted out of loneliness from being away from my family. Some of the things I treasure most are quilts given to me by my mother and my husband's grandmother, and by my sister Odiemae. To me quilting is a continuation of cultural mores passed on by my mother. Quilting brings back warm memories of my mother, when my sister and I would help her quilt by the fireside on cold dark nights in Mississippi. My son Richard inherited my mother's Dutch Girl quilt and he uses it to carry in his truck in Colorado as a talisman against bad luck on his monthly trips to Cheyenne, Wyoming, in the dead of winter to attend his monthly Air National Guard drills.

I then visited quilter Ruby Joyner, who was born in 1931 in New York City. She migrated to Tucson in 1956 for the "good air," and is now extremely disappointed that the rapid population growth has greatly diminished its once excellent quality. No one in her family quilted. She said, "I started quilting in 1989, after taking a quilting class for beginners when my husband went on a business trip for three weeks. As a professional seamstress, I felt I could catch on fast. After that experience, I couldn't put it down and have been enjoying quilting ever since."

Onyx Quilting Club. *Left to right:* Betty Williams (vice president), Mae Bell Bledsoe (president), Noreen Drayton, Johnie Newis, and Edith Hagler.
PIMA COUNTY, ARIZONA, NOVEMBER 1994 (FRAME 5, 2¼ CT)

Later that afternoon, Odiemae invited members of the Onyx Quilting Club to her house for me to photograph. The group chose the name Onyx because it is a black gem, and all the Club's members are black.

Mae Bell Bledsoe was born in 1935 in Washington County, Arkansas, and her family migrated to Arizona in 1947. In November 1992, she founded the Onyx Quilting Club. Mrs. Bledsoe learned to quilt from her mother, Luvnia Weatherspoon (1902–82), and her maternal grandmother, Ninnie Gloston (1869–1951). From these two women, she also learned of Ninnie's mother, Rachel Bradshaw (1853–1920), who also quilted:

> This woman was a very good quilter, and she quilted all the time because her legs had been paralyzed. You see, she was twelve years old when word of freedom came at the end of the Civil War, but the people who owned the plantation she was on didn't pay any attention to freedom. And my great-grandmother [Rachel] tried to run away, and they still caught her and tried to beat her. The last time she tried to run, they beat her legs and feet so bad that she never could walk again. They tell me she used to get around on some kind of board. My grandmother and aunt used to talk about her all the time.

Left to right: Beatrice Davies and Edna A. McIver.
ALBUQUERQUE, NEW MEXICO, FEBRUARY 1995 (FRAME 15, 2¼ CT)

Minnie Noreen Drayton was born in 1928 in Detroit, Michigan. She said, "I grew up in a quilting family, watching my mother, grandmother, and their friends and neighbors. However, I didn't become interested until I came to Tucson in 1989 and met Mrs. Bledsoe. I joined the Onyx group in 1992, and a club member, Ms. Eva Windham, allowed me to come to her home for lessons. Tucson is now my winter home, but I still go back to Detroit every summer."

Edith Hagler was born in 1920 in Logan, West Virginia, and migrated to Tucson in 1964 from Whitman, West Virginia. Her mother quilted when she was young, and Mrs. Hagler says, "My mother helped me do my first quilting when I was six or seven years old. To me quilting makes me think of when I was a little girl working with my mother, and it brings back so many special thoughts and happiness."

Betty Brown Williams was born in 1918 in Heidelberg, Mississippi. While growing up, she saw her mother, Mariah Bingham Brown (1895–1973), and her maternal grandmother, Laura Carmichael Bingham

Left to right: Beatrice Davies, her daughter Andrea C. Davies, and her grandson Devonte
Kurt Watson. Mrs. Davies made this baby quilt for six-month-old Devonte.
ALBUQUERQUE, NEW MEXICO, FEBRUARY 1995 (FRAME 1, 2¼ CT)

(1868–1930), quilt. She was told that Laura's mother, Caroline
Carmichael (1833–73), also quilted. She said:

> When I was eleven years old, I made my first quilt. I will never
> forget it. They were very small scraps of material from leftovers
> from Mother's quilts. She showed me and my sister Laura Brown
> Jones [b. 1917], who was twelve years old, how to cut the one-
> inch blocks and make our quilts. My sister and I would say to
> each other, "We'll be forever making a quilt. She could have given
> us bigger pieces," but we did it. My mother helped us with the
> quilting.

Mrs. Williams moved to Chicago, Illinois, in 1952, and then settled in
Tucson in 1963. Today she loves making quilts inspired by the Bible,
several of which she calls *Good Friday, The Doves, Job's Tears,* and *The
Crown of Thorns.* She says, "I believe in God, I love God, and He is my
Keeper." Even though Mrs. Williams has tried in vain to teach her
daughters and granddaughters to quilt, they all want her quilts and love
them. They don't, however, want to take the time to make any

themselves. Mrs. Williams fears that this four-generation matrilineal quilting chain will end with her.

New Mexico, February 1995

Albuquerque

I added a stop in Albuquerque, New Mexico, during another trip for The Group for Cultural Documentation, to photograph additional quilters. My first stop was at the home of Beatrice Davies, who was working that day with a local artist, Edna McIver (see p. 363). Mrs. Davies was born around the mid-twenties in Des Moines, Iowa, and migrated to Albuquerque in 1968. She learned to quilt from her mother, Beatrice Celestine Hogsette Green (1895–1991), and her maternal grandmother, Mary Magdalene Dade Hogsette (1863–1943). They were both prolific quilters. Mrs. Davies's sister Evelyn Frazier (b. 1922) still has one of their grandmother's quilts, which was made at a church quilting bee. Mrs. Davies began by making baby quilts for each of her seven grandchildren. She treasures quilts made by her mother, especially one Fan quilt that they made together, and is sad that none of her four daughters seems to be interested in continuing the tradition.

Left to right: Ruby Dee Holloway and her daughter Carolyn Holloway. ALBUQUERQUE, NEW MEXICO, FEBRUARY 1995 (35 MM CT)

Edna McIver was born in 1939 in El Paso, Texas, and migrated to Albuquerque in 1971. No one on her mother's side quilted. She never knew her paternal grandmother, Jenny Engledow Nixon (1866–1934), but has a quilt of hers that she treasures. Mrs. Nixon was also a master seamstress and made most of the clothing for her family, as well as for other community members. Mrs. McIver explains, "Right after my husband and I got married, he was an intern at William Beaumont Army Hospital [in El Paso] and I was teaching at the time, and we didn't have two cents to rub together and I couldn't figure out what I would give him for Christmas. I thought, I know, I'll make a quilt, as something that would be very meaningful." At the time I met them, she and Mrs. Davies were quilting a wallhanging together.

The next quilter I visited was Ruby Dee Holloway, who was born in 1932 in Louisville, Mississippi, and initially moved to Albuquerque with her husband in 1957. His military service took them away, but they returned in 1973 after his retirement. Her mother, Ruby Viola Coleman Eiland (1901–85), made utilitarian throw-together quilts. As Mrs. Holloway said:

> Nobody really taught me. My mother always quilted and she would say to me, "Come and help me quilt." I would say, "I don't want to." She would say, "Go ahead then, you go ahead and do the cooking" or "you wash" or "you clean up." But I would always look at her. For some reason, I didn't want to do it, but I would look and I would say to myself, "How can anybody sit there and quilt all day and all night?" Well, here I am now quilting, and I love it.
>
> I have two girls and two boys, and each of them has a quilt. My oldest daughter, Ruby Lucille Holloway Montgomery, gave me my first grandbaby, Ruby Renelle, and I made her a quilt. So at one time there were four generations of Rubys. I have made quilts for my sisters, also. My brother got married, so I'm going to make him a quilt for a wedding present. My brother-in-law came out here to New Mexico to do some work around the house. He says, "I don't charge you anything, but why don't you make me a quilt." So I made him a quilt. My sister from Clarksdale, Mississippi, she retired from teaching school after thirty-eight years, and so I made her a quilt for a present. I have another sister who lives in Monroe, Louisiana, she's a schoolteacher, and I'm making her a quilt. I went to visit my sister in Chicago this past summer and she said to me, "When are you going to make me a quilt?" So I'm working on her quilt. I have a lot of irons in the fire. I have two sisters-in-law, and they're waiting for their quilts. I don't sell my quilts; I give them away.
>
> I worked very hard. I look back at that time—at the time I thought I was having a hard time but as I look at it now, it helped build my character, make me be more appreciative because I started to work as a maid when I was about seven or eight. And I worked for the same person, a lady named Mary Emma Strong. I worked just for one family, because at the time you couldn't work for anybody else. They had an understanding that if you were going to work, whether you wanted to work for them or not, you had to work for the same person. Nobody else would hire you and there was no other type of work.
>
> That's when my father made the decision. He said, "My five girls are not going to be maids all their lives, they're going to college." My mother was a school teacher. At that time she finished eighth grade and she took a test. They said. "If you pass this test, you can teach school." She passed the test. So when she married my dad, she said she got ready to go to work this day and he said, "Where you going?" She said, "I'm going to work." He said, "Oh no, there's one person working in this house, I'm going to do the work. You

Victoria D. White.
ALBUQUERQUE, NEW MEXICO, FEBRUARY 1995 (FRAME 2, 2¼ CT)

stay home." Of coures she didn't say anything, but she always told
us, "I want you to be a school teacher. If your husband says you
can't work, don't listen; you just work." So I'm from a family of
school teachers; even my brother was a school teacher. He teaches
school in Detroit, Michigan.

I went to college at Alcorn, which at the time was called Alcorn
Agricultural and Mechanical College. Now they changed the name
to Alcorn State University. I graduated in 1953; I went in 1950 and
graduated in three years. It was that I enjoyed college so because I
loved going to school and when the registrar called us in in our
junior year, they told me "You just need about three or four more

Joyce M. Williams.
BERKELEY, CALIFORNIA, JUNE
1995 (35 MM CT)

credits and you can graduate a year early." So I went to summer school.

But I was always at the college because I worked my way through. I stayed there year round and I would take some courses in the summertime and I had many jobs. I would get up at three o'clock to clean the dormitory up. Then I had to go and cook breakfast at the President's house because I majored in home economics and the President sent over to the classroom to get somebody to cook. I had so many jobs, because I worked all the way. I don't remember my mother giving me any money at all. I cooked in the President's home and I washed dishes in the mess hall, we called it, and I went to class. Then in the middle of the day I worked in the laundry. And I dried dishes and trays again in the mess hall and then went out for basketball practice.

And I kept my grades up. I really didn't have to study that much because when I look back at it, I thought it was hard to be having to work for some white lady. She taught me everthing, so I already knew it. She taught me how to cook. I had to do the cooking. And I washed and I took care of two children. And they would go off and I would care for the children. She had this big colonial house that had hardwood floors and I would wax those floors. At first she had a cook and a washperson and somebody to take care of the kids, somebody to take care of the grounds too. But I was so smart, she didn't tell me to do this, but it was exciting to me to see. I'd never seen such nice pretty things—I thought it was pretty—and I considered it being my doll house. I would just volunteer and wax the floors and she saw how well I could do that and she just got me to do it. And I'd be standing there watching her cook—well, she had somebody to cook for her—she'd be telling them how to cook and I'd be watching and I would just start doing it. So she stared teaching me how to cook. And to this day what I remember, and what I tell my husband, is how her husband said to me, "Ruby, cook me a lemon pie, cook me a chocolate pie." Any kind of pie he would name, I'd cook it. So apparently I memorized it because I don't remember reading any recipes of anything. But I know she taught me, was teaching me, all this, Mrs. Strong.

And I went to school every day. I had the type of parents who never kept us home. That was another thing. I would practice basketball after school, then this thing they call jogging now—at that time they called it trotting—I never walked. I always jogged. I had to get to another place. Then I would dash to her house; I didn't have time to do all this work because I had to go on home and work around the house also. So it would get dark and she would tell me to go home in her car. But I stayed at her house a little while longer because she was going to take me home. I could work fast. I mean I worked like a workhorse.

Quilting to me is a wonderful hobby. It relaxes me and you also are leaving something for posterity, because right now my children encourage me to make quilts. I think it's important to keep our heritage alive and pass it on to the next generation. And I try to encourage my daughter [Carolyn] who lives here to quilt.

The last New Mexico quilter I photographed was Victoria White (see p. 367), who was born in 1932 in Raleigh, North Carolina, and migrated to Rio Rancho in 1973. She learned to quilt and sew from her maternal grandmother, Sally Dunston (1863–1945), who was born in Wake Forest, North Carolina. As she told it:

> My grandmother was just amazing. You show her a picture of anything, she would sit down and cut out the pattern and she could make it. But she could not read and she could not write. But she could do anything you showed her to do. I just loved her and stayed around her all the time. We were inseparable, really. So everything she could do she taught me how to make it. I guess I started sewing when I was about three or four years old, and as long as I can remember I had a needle in my hand. She passed when I was thirteen.

Dorothy Moore Banks using her quilt to teach African-American history to elementary pupils in the Richmond, California, school district.

(PHOTO COURTESY OF THE BANKS FAMILY ARCHIVES. FEBRUARY 1991, FA-11)

> I first left North Carolina and went to New York to study fashion design. I went to Pratt Institute in Brooklyn. I stayed there and married and had children, and then my husband retired and we decided to move out here. And I've taught both of my daughters, Cornelia and Sandra, to quilt and they do a little bit of everything else. My son Michael, who is a landscape designer, also does beautiful handwork and drawings.

CALIFORNIA, 1995

BERKELEY

Joyce Mary Williams was born in New Orleans and migrated to Oakland, California, after graduating from Xavier University of Louisiana. Although no one in her family quilted, she learned to sew from her mother, Alberta Wilson (1907–80), who was also born in New Orleans, and her maternal grandmother, Elizabeth Jean Jacques Wilson (1864–1952), who was born on the island nation of

Jacquelyn Hughes Mooney and her granddaughter, Mary Eleanor Mooney-Walker. The quilt is a depiction of "Second Lining," a traditional New Orleans funeral procession.

SAN DIEGO, CALIFORNIA, DECEMBER 1995 (PHOTOGRAPH COURTESY OF CHARLES LUNDY)

Dominica. She says that her mother "loved all kinds of handwork: tatting, crocheting, knitting, and embroidering." Her grandmother also helped make costumes for Mardi Gras. Mrs. Williams started to quilt in Berkeley in the 1970s, after hearing about the resurgence of quilting that started with Jonathan Holstein's landmark exhibit (see p. 127). She studied with Lucille Hilty, who is a Mennonite quilter from Ohio. Mrs. Williams is the only African-American member of the multiethnic East Bay Heritage Quilters. When I asked what quilting meant to her, Mrs. Williams replied:

> I'll tell you, I've never had so much fun. I've done all the handwork that my mother was willing to teach me and had the patience to teach me, but I've had a lot of fun with quilting. When my mother was critically ill in 1980, I was making a quilt for a raffle for the San Francisco Bach Choral Group—I sang with that group for about twenty-five years—and I had the quilt in the frame in the living room because I often had to stay up late to be sure she got her final dose of medicine before I would lie down and go to bed. I'd stay at the quilt frame and quilt for hours, and I didn't seem to need to have any more sleep than what I got. I'd get maybefour hours in a night. I'd put the radio on low and I'd sit there and tell myself, I'm going to do that much, and then I'd look at the clock and if I finished early I'd just do a little more. It really helped me work out a very difficult time in my life because she had pancreatic cancer and that's a very painful kind of cancer. It helped me work through that time very easily.

> I've really enjoyed quilting. And I've enjoyed meeting all the people, all the quilters. I just wish I had the time to go out to a lot of other things besides my small quilting groups. I belong to two small groups of quilters who work together, and I'm the only African American in both groups. I wish I could meet more African-American quilters, especially some of the older women who have quilted all their lives.

BENICIA

Dorothy Moore Banks (see p. 369) was born in Bakersfield, California, in 1927, and migrated to Benicia in 1984. She learned to quilt from her paternal grandmother, Luvenia Moore (1881-1966) who was born in Whitepost, Virginia. As Mrs. Banks says:

> As far back as my memory serves me, I can see her quilting. She quilted from necessity, because we couldn't afford to buy blankets. I participated in quilting, but not by choice. When we came home from school, we were directed to cut quilt pieces for my grandmother to use the next day. Each year, as soon as school was out for the summer, we removed these quilts from our beds to wash them. This was done outside, in a #3 galvanized tub. We heated water, put the quilts in, stomped them with our bare feet, wrung them out the best we could, and then hung them on the fence to dry.
>
> One special memory has to do with my aunt, Mary Daniels, of Bakersfield, who taught a quilting class at the local community college. She needed one more student to meet her enrollment quota—it took her two weeks to convince me to join her class! The method she taught was "lap quilting." I enjoy it very much because I can take my work with me, and I'm not limited to the old way of quilting, using frames and "horses."

Mrs. Banks' work is represented in many private collections, and has been exhibited throughout California.

SAN DIEGO

Jacquelyn Hughes Mooney was born in 1950 in New Orleans, Louisiana. Her mother, Elenaor Hughes Mooney (b. 1916) of New Orleans, is a seamstress, and while she has pieced tops, she has never finished a quilt. Jacquelyn migrated to California in 1965 and currently lives in San Diego. In 1992 she began teaching herself to quilt and has become prolific, both as a quilter and as a textile artist. She has made quilts for her three children and five granchildren, and her work is highly sought after. As a member of African-American Women on Tour, a national

Gustina M. Atlas.
CLAIBORNE COUNTY, MISSISSIPPI, DECEMBER 1994 (FRAME 7, 2¼ CT)

Gwendolyn Magee.
HINDS COUNTY, MISSISSIPPI,
SEPTEMBER 1995 (FRAME
[15-16], 2¼ CT)

program encouraging empowerment through workshops and conferences, she continues to receive commissions for her quilts and related art. Her work is now in many private collections, including those of writers Alice Walker, Sonia Sanchez, Terry McMillan, and Bebe Moore Campbell; and of actresses Ruby Dee, Phyllis Yvonne Stickney, and Margaret Avery. Jacquelyn has begun to teach her four-year-old granddaughter, Mary Eleanor Mooney-Walker, to quilt.

MISSISSIPPI, DECEMBER 1994 AND SEPTEMBER 1995

In December 1994, while in Port Gibson, I photographed quilter Gustina M. Atlas (see p. 371).

JACKSON

In the late summer of 1995, Victoria Faoro, executive director of the Museum of the American Quilter's Society, told me about an African-American quilter from Jackson, Mississippi, Gwendolyn A. Magee, whose quilt had just been selected for exhibition at the museum in the traditional piecing/amateur category. I then called Mrs. Magee and she agreed to participate in the project. Mrs. Magee was born in 1943 and raised in High Point, North Carolina. As she tells it:

> I never saw anyone quilting while I was growing up. However, my mother's [Annie Lee Jones] passion was arts and crafts, and she had a full-size workshop built in our backyard . . . and I grew up amidst doll making, doll collecting, leather working, jewelry making, crocheting, knitting, weaving, ceramics, and just about any craft you can name, except quilting. I started quilting in 1989 because Kamili, my oldest daughter, was graduating from high school and I wanted to make a quilt for her to take to college. I didn't know anyone in Jackson [Mississippi] who quilted, nor did I know about any quilting groups. As an adoptee, I have no real sense of personal heritage that connects me with a past. For all intents and purposes, my past started and ended with my adoption and I've always felt a drive or need to connect, somehow, with the future. Quilting is one of the avenues through which, for me, this is possible. Quilting to me is a tangible, palpable expression of my love for the family and friends for whom my quilts are made, and

The African-American Quilters of Baltimore, at the Waverly Branch, Enoch Pratt Library. *Back row (left to right):* Regina M. Stein, Kathleen Patterson, Monalisa De Gross, Ethel H. Cotton, Ernestine Johnson, and Wanda D. Thomas. *Middle row (left to right):* Bernice Clark, Shelley C. Moody, Clarissa G. Price, Phyllis White, and Carole Y. Lyles. *Front row (left to right):* Margaret Johnson, Anne M. Warner, Barbara G. Pietila, and Evelyn C. Strothers.

BALTIMORE COUNTY, MARYLAND, JANUARY 1996
(FRAME 12-13, 2¼ CT)

Allison and Shirley Blakely.
MONTGOMERY COUNTY, MARYLAND, JUNE 1995 (35 MM CT)

it also engenders considerable feelings of pride to know that I am able to create work that others, particularly those close to me, appreciate and value. My daughters expressed to me throughout their college years that their quilts essentially became their security blankets; that no matter what else was going on in their lives, they could wrap themselves up in their quilts to invoke a feeling of home, and know that they were loved. I could not ask for more.

Through college and work experiences, Mrs. Magee lived in several states before settling in Jackson in 1972.

MARYLAND, JUNE 1995 AND JANUARY 1996

SILVER SPRING

Shirley Blakely, whom I photographed in June 1995, was born in 1944 in Graceville, Florida. She migrated to the Washington, D.C. area in 1971. Although she did not quilt as a young child, she watched her mother, Maudie Victoria Reynolds Taylor (b. 1926), who was from Chambers County, Alabama, who did piecing by herself and then quilted with a group. She also saw her stepgrandmother Lucinda Reynolds (1901–94) quilt. Mrs. Blakely learned to sew from her mother, however, and says, "I really enjoy it, and sewing is part of my life.

Actually my very first quilt was when you brought me the design and material for your original quilt called *The Maroons* in 1992, and I've done a couple of quilts since then."

Shirley explained to me the two special family quilts in the photograph with her. "The Pineapple quilt was made by members of my husband, Allison's, former church in Portland, Oregon, as a wedding gift for us. And the other is a Heritage quilt that Allison's paternal grandmother, Cora Blakely [1902–65], who was born in Mt. Hebron, Alabama, made for him. She made a different Heritage quilt for each of her grandchildren. His mother, Alice Blakely [1922–83], also from Mt. Hebron, was also very active in a sewing circle in Portland, Oregon."

BALTIMORE

It seemed appropriate that the final documentation for this survey be done where it all began, in Baltimore. On January 6, 1996, through their founder, Barbara Pietila, I arranged to photograph the African-American Quilters of Baltimore (AAQB) (see p. 373), of which I am a member. AAQB's mission is to preserve the art of quilting in the African-American community, and they've taken as their motto, "Each one teach one." Of the current nineteen members, eighteen are women, seventeen of whom are African Americans.

CONCLUSION

Now that we've completed this journey together, I'd like to share some "back home" thoughts with you about what I've experienced, about what unifies this world of quilting by African Americans, and about how its documentation might be carried forward. First, as I reflect on the journey, I marvel at what a special gift I've been given in the nurturing and enrichment provided me through the remarkable openness and candor with which so many of the quilters and preservers shared so much of themselves. I also know there is much more out there, and that, for sure, I haven't "completed" this work. Rather, after more than twenty years, I've picked an arbitrary stopping point, even though there are still a few entire states and many communities with African Americans whose quilts and stories remain undocumented and untold—sources as rich, powerful, and surprising as those already tapped. This journey thus ends for me not with completeness, yet with the satisfaction of having developed an extensive body of work that I hope will serve as a guide for others.

What Unifies the World of Quilting by African Americans?

I hope the book communicates the startling range of what I heard and saw about how the quilters learned their craft, why they quilt, what they create, and their consciousness about what they're doing. We met quilters who grew up in quilting traditions and carry those forward, essentially unchanged from their own early experiences. We met others who, though they grew up in the tradition, are incorporating distinctive innovations in designs and materials. We also met individuals with limited or no early exposure who took up quilting as adults, learning in both formal and informal settings. We also met some who have transformed quilting into textile art more suggestive of painting, meant for walls and not beds, and who may be totally unfamiliar with traditional quilting techniques. We met men as well as women—and while there are certainly fewer male quilters, their numbers and contributions are significant, and overall, the range of their work seems as broad as the women's. People said their quilts were made to keep warm, record history, commemorate struggle and triumph, give to loved ones, heal and hurt, generate income.

It is important that we don't let this diversity prevent us from recognizing that there is a distinct "world of quilting by African Americans," even if its precise borders are elusive. Based on my study, I am confident that this world exists and that its elements form a unified whole that can be differentiated from other, broader contexts to which it relates—although, of course, all these dynamics are mutually illuminating. Frankly, I can't prove some of the assertions I make about this world—certainly not with the clarity and authority common to much traditional scholarship—but I know and feel their truth as the quilters know and feel the truths of how their quilts relate to their lives. Basically, I see what defines this world in terms of two dimensions: first, what I call "the continuity of black expressive culture"; and second, how quilting manifests and clarifies the broader complexity, struggle, and triumph of African-American life.

Let me start with "the continuity of black expressive culture." To me, this concept is complex and multidimensional. First, "continuity" involves the transmission of both aesthetics and techniques, although the transmission is rarely straightforward. In quilting, this continuity is easiest to see when the quilts include patterns and techniques that appear to have clear African echoes. However, it also is reflected in quilts by African Americans with patterns and techniques that are far more likely to remind us of work derived from a European heritage. And, it is further complicated by the significant number of quilters who seem to move effortlessly from quilting that reminds us of one of these traditions, to quilting reminiscent of the other or of strange and wonderful combinations.

The continuity is also there in the work of African Americans who adapt quilting to the broader world of fabric artistry and who may see themselves more as "artists" than as "quilters."

So what is at the core of the continuity? I believe it to be the meaning of the quilts and the experience of the quilters. That experience, while always individual, and always artistically new for the quilter, also always involves more than the creation of that particular quilt. It involves the quilter's broader context—an African-American life experience—and establishes communion with other quilters, as well as with deeper personal, familial, and cultural significances that, as we've seen throughout the book, virtually always accompany quilting. It is this communion that gives common meaning to the world of quilting by African Americans, and it is this that is the source of its cultural continuity.

I believe this to be true whether the quilters are "folk" or "artists": what we are studying is how things actually work and how they are experienced in particular African-American cultural settings— whether that of the sharecropper in Mississippi who quilts with little contact beyond her immediate community, or the New York artist who quilts for gallery exhibits. Sometimes it's hard to appreciate that this has always been so, that there is a cultural continuity linking these very different settings over time as well as across space, despite dynamic and changing cultural specifics, influences, and responses. Today, through books or workshops, quilters may become aware of the broader currents of what's going on in quilting; their grandmothers may have done the same by seeing local newspapers, and even if they couldn't read, they may have copied or been influenced by the quilt patterns that appeared in them weekly. While the details of both the changes and the continuity may be different, the process is the same. It's wrong for us to assume that communities and their craftspeople were totally isolated, or that they had no access to what was going on in the broader quilting or cultural contexts, or that we are able to assess expressive continuity simply by seeking linear connections and surface similarities—rather, the continuity of African-American expressive culture is as complex as the rest of our lives and history.

I see the second dimension of what I mean by the "world of quilting by African Americans" as its wholeness—its ability to illuminate our more general understanding of African-American life. Although this may be true to varying degrees of other folkcraft areas, no others seem to have as universal a presence as quilting, which has survived—both geographically and historically— our migrations from South to North and from field to factory. Quilting seems to have virtually universal distribution, with its practitioners crossing all social and economic lines. Its roots, like the roots of our lives, were in Africa. To those roots were grafted new physical requirements for survival, new raw materials and new settings in which to use them, new limitations on privacy and interaction—and all these demanded new responses. Further, the almost universally shared experience of Africans' "Middle Passage" to slavery was soon replaced by a more divergent set of experiences, each significantly different from the others—Southern and Northern, plantation and urban, freed and escaped, isolated and assimilated, benevolent and sadistic.

Each unique combination of these variants brought its own dynamics and changes to African-American life and culture, and as we explore the variety of artifacts and stories within the world of quilting, we learn more about all this, because it is all reflected accurately by what we see. Similarly, when we find ourselves at a loss to understand some particular aspect of the quilting world, what we know of African-American life in general will often provide clues to the otherwise elusive meaning of what we've found. So along this dimension too, what we see is that understanding the world of quilting by African Americans, while no less complex, is as rich and rewarding as coming to grips with the broader African-American experience.

BEING A MAN IN A WOMAN'S WORLD

The world of quilting by African Americans is primarily a woman's world. Most of the quilters are women, and traditionally quilting provided opportunity for gathering by themselves, talking freely in the company of women—either because what they were discussing was women's business, was seen as inappropriate for men's ears, or might cause the women embarrassment in men's presence. In fact, I believe that a contributing factor to the resurgence of interest in quilting over the past decades has been its feminist resonance through its clear affirmation of women's skills, independence, strength, interconnectedness, and survival. In light of the above, I think it's important to share my perceptions about how my gender affected my fieldwork over these years. On the one hand—perhaps because of my continuous and serious interest going back to my earliest childhood memories—I never questioned the integrity of my involvement in this world, nor thought my focus on it anything but appropriate. At the same time, I certainly was aware of the issues likely to be raised about my own ability as a man to understand this world fully. Overall, I believe that my work has not suffered, and that whatever I have missed because of my gender has not compromised what is here. The key that unlocks the treasures of this world is a focus on the quilters and preservers, and on how their quilts relate to their lives. This focus has provided me with what I believe to be unprecedented access, along with direct and honest communion. At the same time, I'm sure that some stories were not shared with me, and that some of what I was told was in code that might have been clearer to a female researcher—and I celebrate the additional insights that I know women will bring to this work.

I also think that as a man, I provided some distinct contributions. As we've seen, men represent a small but significant part of the quilting community. Some of these men are older, now retired, and relish the communion with their wives that quilting provides; others grew up in quilting households and have quilted throughout their lives, either unaware of or undisturbed by being a sole male presence; others are textile artists attracted to quilting's potential. I also met boys and young men whose interest in quilting grew from time they spent with their mothers or grandmothers, just as had mine and that of others in earlier generations. Often these men and boys were somewhat shy about their quilting and concerned about whether others might disapprove of how they

spent their time, whether quilting was a fitting interest for men. I believe that both they, and often the women around them, were encouraged by my personal involvement with quilting, as well as by my interest in and valuing of their work.

WHAT LIES AHEAD

As suggested earlier, it is clear that we have just begun to scratch the surface of what there is to document and learn from the world of quilting by African Americans. First, there are entire states with quilters and preservers still undocumented, numerous communities remaining in those states where some work has been done, and individuals not yet identified even in those communities already "fully" covered. Then, of course, there are changes over time as practitioners grow and move forward, new practitioners become involved, and the broader context evolves—all calling for a corresponding continuity of documentation, capturing these moments in history.

So there is much to do, a need and many wonderful opportunities throughout the country to carry the work forward. The results will be most illuminating and valuable if the work is approached from a stance that respects, values, and honors the quilters and preservers and involves them as more than just the objects of study. With this approach will come deeper understanding, and we will be able to transmit and maintain what we learn, and strengthen who we are—as artists and as African Americans.

A corollary of this appeal for expanded documentation is the impact I hope it will have on academic research and scholarship related to the world of quilting by African Americans. It should contribute to a more complex and inclusive scholarly view of this world, with increased clarity as to how this quilting relates to each and every aspect of the broader quilting context, along with increased valuing of its unique characteristics. And if that is what happens, then as our overall understanding of quilting moves forward, quilting by African Americans will finally play its appropriate role.

Another result might be that in the broader study of quilting, increased attention will be paid to quilters' lives and the contexts in which they do their magnificent work. For sure, the illumination this provides to understanding quilting by African Americans can be brought to our understanding of quilting by others. Finally, I would hope that this approach to studying cultural tradition, continuity, and evolution would be more widely applied to other fields of inquiry, to yield similarly valuable results.

The world of quilting by African Americans provides us a profound example of how from scraps barely enough for survival, we created beauty, and then engaged the knowledge and aesthetic we found around us, sharing what we knew and incorporating what we learned—simultaneously becoming part of the mainstream, and yet continuing our distinct expressive culture. Our quilting is our history, and as a quilter said to me, "it comes from our hearts and souls."

Girtia Lukes (see p. 219).
(35 MM CT)

GALLERY OF
QUILTED
PHOTOGRAPHS

The "quilted photographs" on these pages and on the back of the book illustrate my most recent approach to integrating these two art forms. As part of the preparation for the national tour of *A Communion of the Spirits* (see p. xii), I commissioned, from various practitioners, quilted borders to use in mounting some of the photographs for the exhibition. In each of those included here (all of which appear elsewhere in the book without the borders; see page references), the border was quilted by the quilter in the photograph. For others in the exhibit, I asked a quilter for a border to use with work done and preserved by a different artist. As these "quilted photographs" reveal, the line between quilting and its related art forms is a thin one, and across it, often are joined important threads of African-American life and expressive culture.

Nell Smith (see p. 226).
(35 MM CT)

Sherry Whetstone-McCall (see p. 232).
(35 MM CT)

Jim S. Smoote II (see p. 246).
(35 MM CT)

Damian P. Mazloomi and his
mother, Dr. Carolyn Mazloomi (see
p. 270).
(FRAME 2, 2¼ CT)

Claire E. Carter (see p.
276).
(35 MM CT)

Francelise Dawkins (see p. 287).
(35 MM CT)

Mary Randall Scott, Esq. (see p. 288).
(35 MM CT)

Marlene O'Bryant-Seabrook (see
pp. 340 and 341).
(35 MM CT)

Gwendolyn Magee (see p. 372).
(35 MM CT)

A BIBLIOGRAPHY OF INFLUENCES IN THE DEVELOPMENT OF
A Communion of the Spirits

In addition to books and exhibits related to the world of African-American quilting, either directly or as general background, the bibliography contains materials that I consider to have had strong influence over the years in shaping my understanding of the broader contextual issues.

Bell-Scott, Patricia, Beverly Guy-Sheftall, Jacqueline Jones Royster, Janet Sims-Wood, Miriam DeCosta-Willis, and Lucie Fultz, eds. *Double Stitch: Black Women Write about Mothers and Daughters.* Boston: Beacon Press, 1991.

Benberry, Cuesta. *Always There: The African-American Presence in American Quilts.* Catalogue printed in conjunction with the exhibition at the Museum of History and Science, Louisville, Kentucky, February 7–March 31, 1992.

Benberry, Cuesta Ray, and Carol Pinney Crabb,. *A Patchwork of Pieces: An Anthology of Early Quilt Stories, 1845–1940.* Paducah, Kentucky: American Quilter's Society, 1993.

Boas, Franz. *Anthropology and Modern Life.* Reprint, New York: Dover Press, 1986.

Brackman, Barbara. *Encyclopedia of Pieced Quilt Patterns.* Paducah, Kentucky: American Quilter's Society, 1993.

Callahan, Nancy. *The Freedom Quilting Bee.* Tuscaloosa, Alabama: University of Alabama Press, 1987.

Flournoy, Valerie. *The Patchwork Quilt.* New York: Dial Books for Young Readers, 1985.

Freeman, Roland L. *Something to Keep You Warm.* Mississippi State Historical Museum, a division of the Department of Archives and History, June 14–August 9, 1981. This exhibit first opened in 1978 at the Mississippi State Historical Museum without a catalogue and was redone in 1981 with a catalogue.

_____ *Some Things of Value: Images of African and African-American Folklife* (an exhibition), August 2–September 20, 1992, The Apex Museum, Atlanta, Georgia.

_____ *Southern Roads/City Pavements.* New York: International Center of Photography, 1981.

_____ *Stand by Me: African-American Expressive Culture in Philadelphia.* Washington, D.C.: Smithsonian Institution, 1990.

_____ "African-American Expressive Culture in Philadelphia," *National Geographic* magazine. August 1990, Vol. 178 No. 2., pp. 66–91.

_____ *The Arabbers of Baltimore.* Centreville, Maryland: Cornell Maritime Press, 1989.

_____ *Expressions of the Soul: Three Perspectives on Baltimore's African-American Folklife.* Baltimore, Maryland: The Eubie Black National Museum and Cultural Center, 1992.

_____ *Margaret Walker's "For My People": A Tribute by Roland L. Freeman.* Jackson and London: University Press of Mississippi, 1992.

_____ "Blanket Statements," *The Philadelphia Inquirer* magazine. February 16, 1992, pp. 18–23 and cover photograph.

_____ *More Than Just Something to Keep You Warm: A Quincentenary Exhibit.* Philadelphia, PA: Springside School, 1992.

_____ "More Than Just Something to Keep You Warm," *American Quilter* magazine. Winter 1992, Vol. VIII No. 4, pp. 14–19.

_____ "Folkroots: Images of Mississippi Black Folklife (1974-1976)," *Southern Exposure* magazine. Summer and Fall 1977, pp. 29–35.

Freeman, Roland L. and Rosemary L. Bray, "Keepsakes," *Essence* magazine. November 1978, pp. 106–114.

Fry, Gladys-Marie. *Made by Men, African-American Traditional Quilts* (exhibition and exhibit brochure). College Park: University of Maryland, 1996.

_____ *Stitched from the Soul: Slave Quilts from the Ante-bellum South.* New York: Museum of American

Folk Art and Dutton Studio Books, 1990. (Also an exhibition of the same name.)

_____ "Harriet Powers: Portrait of a Black Quilter," in *Missing Pieces: Georgia Folk Art 1770–1976* (Anna Wadsworth, ed.). Atlanta, Georgia: Georgia Council for the Arts and Humanities, 1976.

_____ "Two Narrative Quilts" in *The World and I* magazine, February 1988, pp. 522–31.

German, Sandra. "Women of Color Quilters Network," a research paper presented to the American Quilt Society Study Group in Portland, Maine and subsequently published in their newsletter, *Uncoverings*, 1993.

Gilcher, William. *Anything for Wisement: A Film on Southern Cultural History.* College Park, Maryland: The Visual Press, University of Maryland at College Park, 1992.

Glassie, Henry. "Folk Art." In Richard M. Dorson, ed. *Folklore and Folklife: An Introduction*, pp. 253–280. Chicago: University of Chicago Press, 1972.

Grudin, Eva Ungar. *Stitching Memories: African-American Story Quilts*, Williamstown, Massachusetts: Williams College Museum of Art, 1990.

Hall, Carrie and Rose G. Kretsinger. *The Romance of the Patchwork Quilt in America.* Caldwell, Idaho: Caxton Printers, Ltd., 1935.

Hammond, Joyce D. *Tifaifai and Quilts of Polynesia.* Honolulu, Hawaii: The University of Hawaii Press, 1986.

Herskovits, Melville J. *Cultural Anthropology.* New York: Alfred A. Knopf, 1955.

_____ *Dahomey: An Ancient West African Kingdom.* 2 vols. New York. J.J. Augustin, 1938.

_____ *The Myth of the Negro Past.* 1941; reprinted., Boston: Beacon Press, 1958.

Holloway, Joseph E. (ed.). *Africanisms in American Culture.* Bloomington and Indianapolis: Indiana University Press, 1990.

Horton, Laurel and Lynn Robertson Myers. *Social Fabric: South Carolina's Traditional Quilts.* Columbus, South Carolina. McKissick Museum, The University of South Carolina, 1985.

Hurston, Zora Neale. *Tell My Horse.* (Reprinted) Berkeley: Turtle Island, 1981.

_____ *Mules and Men.* (Reprinted) Bloomington and London: Indiana University Press, 1978.

Kent, Kate p. "Appliqué." In Linn Shapiro, ed., *Black People and Their Culture: Selected Writings from the African Diaspora*, pp. 58–62. Washington, D.C.: Smithsonian Institution, 1976.

Konscius, Jura. "Museum Quilts for the Home," Home Front, *The Washington Post*, December 20, 1991.

Lamb, Venice. *West African Weaving.* London: Duckworth, 1975.

Lamb, Venice, and Alastair Lamb,. *West African Narrow Strip-Weaving.* Washington: Textile Museum, 1975.

Leon, Eli. *Who'd A Thought It: Improvisation in African-American Quiltmaking*, with an introduction by Robert Farris Thompson. Published in conjunction with an exhibition at the San Francisco Craft and Folk Art Museum, December 31, 1987–February 28, 1988.

Livingston, Jane and John Beardsley. *Black Folk Art in America 1930–1980.* Washington, D.C.: Corcoran Gallery of Art, 1982.

Made by Hand, Mississippi Folk Art. Jackson, Mississippi: Mississippi State Historical Museum, 1980.

Mazrui, Ali A. *The Africans: A Triple Heritage.* Boston: Little, Brown and Company, 1986.

Metcalf, Eugene and Michael Hall. *The Ties That Bind: Folk Art in Contemporary American Culture.* Cincinnati, Ohio: The Contemporary Arts Center, 1986.

Morris, Patricia. Interview with quilter Malissa Banks in *I Ain't Lyin'.* Mississippi Cultural Crossroads: Spring 1981, Vol. I, pp. 13–18.

Oshins, Lisa Turner. *Quilt Collections: A Directory for the United States and Canada.* Washington, D.C.: Acropolis Books Ltd., 1987.

Picton, John and John Mack. *African Textiles.* New York: Harper and Row, 1989.

Pilgrim, Paul D. and Gerald E. Roy. *Gatherings: America's Quilt Heritage.* Paducah, Kentucky: American Quilter's Society, 1995.

Price, Richard, ed. *Maroon Societies: Rebel Slave Communities in the Americas.* Baltimore: The Johns Hopkins University Press, 1979.

Price, Richard and Sally Price. *Afro-American Arts of the Suriname Rain Forest.* Los Angeles: The University of California Press and the Museum of Cultural History, 1980.

Quilters' Newsletter magazine. Entry by Carolyn Mazloomi. August 1985.

Ramsey, Bets, editor. *Quilt Close-Up: Five Southern Views.* The Hunter Museum of Art, Chattanooga, Tennessee, 1983.

Ramsey, Bets and Waldvogel, Merikay. *The Quilts of Tennessee*. Nashville, Tennessee: Rutledge Hill Press, 1986.

Ringgold, Faith. *Tar Beach*. New York: Crown Publishers, Inc., 1991.

Roche, Emma Langdon. *Historic Sketches of the South*. New York: The Knickerbocker Press, 1914.

Rogers, Patricia Dane. "The Quilt that Struck a Nerve," Washington Home, *The Washington Post*, March 19, 1992.

Sieber, Roy. *African Textiles and Decorative Arts* (exhibition catalog). New York: The Museum of Modern Art, 1972.

Sims, Lowery S., and Adrian Piper. *Next Generation: Southern Black Aesthetic*. Chapel Hill, North Carolina: University of North Carolina Press, 1990.

Smithsonian Institution, Center for Folklife Programs and Cultural Studies. *1992 Festival of American Folklife Program*, "Maroons."

Springhillian, The (newspaper). Article on Africatown. Mobile, Alabama, December 18, 1936.

Still, William. *The Underground Railroad*. (Reprinted) New York: Arno Press, 1968.

Thompson, Robert Farris. *African Art in Motion*, published in conjunction with an exhibition at the National Gallery of Art, Washington, D.C., Frederick S. Wight Art Gallery, University of California, Los Angeles, Spring/Summer 1974.

_____ *Flash of the Spirit: African and Afro-American Art and Philosophy*, see Rhythmic Textiles, pages 207–23. New York: Random House, 1983.

_____ "The Flash of the Spirit: Haiti's Africanising Vodon Art," in *Haitian Art*, by Ute Stebich. Brooklyn, New York. The Brooklyn Museum, 1978.

_____ *Four Moments of the Sun: Koingo Art in Two Worlds* (with Pierre Cornet). Washington, D.C.: The National Gallery of Art, 1981.

Vlach, John Michael. *The Afro-American Tradition in Decorative Arts*, Cleveland, Ohio: The Cleveland Museum of Art, 1978.

Wahlman, Maude Southwell. *Signs and Symbols: African Images in African-American Quilts*. New York: Museum of American Folk Art, 1993.

Waldvogel, Merikay. *Soft Covers for Hard Times: Quiltmaking and the Great Depression*. Nashville, Tennessee: Rutledge Hill Press, 1990.

Wardlaw, Alvia J. *The Art of John Biggers: View from the Upper Room*. Houston, Texas: Harry N. Abrams, Inc., in Association with The Museum of Fine Arts, 1995.

Woodson, Carter G. *The Mis-Education of the Negro*. Washington, D.C.: The Associated Publishers, Inc., 1933.

Wright, Richard. *Native Son*. Harper & Brothers, 1940.

Zegart, Shelly and Jonathan Holstein. *Expanding Quilt Scholarship: The lectures, conferences and other presentations of Louisville Celebrates the American Quilt*. Louisville, Kentucky: The Kentucky Quilt Project, Inc., 1994.

INDEX